monkey meets world

by John Kovaleski

**Andrews McMeel
Publishing**

Kansas City

Bo Nanas is distributed internationally by the Washington Post Writers Group.

Bo Nanas copyright © 2005 by John Kovaleski. All rights reserved. Printed in the United States of America. No part of this book may be used or reproduced in any manner whatsoever without written permission except in the case of reprints in the context of reviews. For information, write Andrews McMeel Publishing, an Andrews McMeel Universal company, 4520 Main Street, Kansas City, Missouri 64111.

05 06 07 08 09 VON 10 9 8 7 6 5 4 3 2 1

ISBN-13: 978-0-7407-5446-3
ISBN-10: 0-7407-5446-7

Library of Congress Control Number: 2005925660

www.andrewsmcmeel.com

The strips in this collection originally appeared in newspapers from May 2003 to February 2004.

For Jack and Elaine,
my parents

For Lori, Jay, and Mike,
my siblings

And for Jocelyn,
the love of my life

FOREWORD
by Dan Piraro

Being such a huge and important figure in the world of newspaper cartoons, I will rarely stoop to a task that does not involve the feeding of my voracious ego or bank account. But this is one of those rare occasions.

Bo Nanas is a relatively new comic feature with two things going for it that I find particularly endearing: The main character's nose is bigger than mine, and its creator, John Kovaleski, has less hair than I do. These two factors, combined with the wit and creativity with which *Bo Nan* (as we in the industry call it) is crafted make it irresistible.

I had known John Kovaleski for a few years before he launched *Bo Nanas,* and I began reading it because I wanted to see him fail. I find that demeaning my colleagues is an excellent way to feel better about myself. To my great disappointment, however, I liked the first week of strips I read. So I wrote it off to beginner's luck. The next week was good, too, but I figured I was still experiencing some afterglow from the first. As the weeks and months went by and the feature not only maintained its quality but steadily improved, I began to face a harsh reality—I may have to concede that what I'd said to our colleagues at the hotel bar during the last cartoonists' convention about John's chances of success with *Bo Nanas* may have been wrong.

John has a winning combination in *Bo Na* (as we in the industry call it): an easy wit and wisdom that amuses and delights, and a memorable cast of characters. For example, the relationship between Bo and his landlady, Mrs. Yannes, is profound. Tension mounts daily between these two passionate, bi-polar characters while we, as invisible onlookers, wonder when/if Bo will finally ask her why she is dressed like a clown. Personally, I cannot wait for the day that she finally takes the curlers out of her hair. Will Bo then suddenly see her as a "woman"?

Having a monkey as an independent character living side-by-side with humans gives John numerous opportunities to comment on the contradictions of human behavior as they relate to the natural world. Bo lives among us but frequently points out how our arrogance as a species affects our fellow animals. A series of cartoons in which Bo is mistakenly confined in a pet store cage, then buys his own freedom and that of all the other "pets," points out that what we see as the routine treatment of animals is often painful exploitation. In another series, Bo makes a human feel guilty for chaining up his dog.

Most of the time, John's writing is less editorial and he often veers headlong into some very surreal territory. A terrible day capped off with a toothbrush that bursts into flames is among my personal favorites. Many times, I've had similar problems with household objects and would have given my kingdom for a talking monkey to help out.

And that's the point in a nutshell behind *BN* (as we in the industry call it): We could all benefit from spending time with a talking monkey.

Since John has only a year of cartoons in the proverbial bag, I look forward to finding out where he will take us in the future. Will he rest on his laurels and regurgitate the same dozen jokes decade after decade as I have, or will he step up to the plate and use this cute little critter to keep human society from self-absorbed catastrophe and worldwide destruction?

I've got all my hopes and dreams pinned on this little ink monkey. I encourage you to do the same.

Bo Nanas

by John Kovaleski

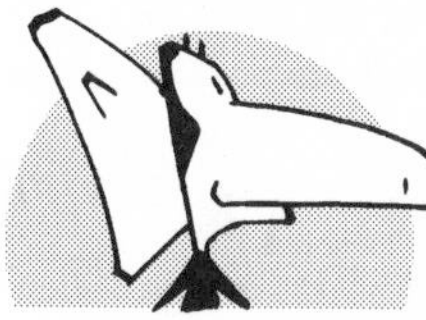

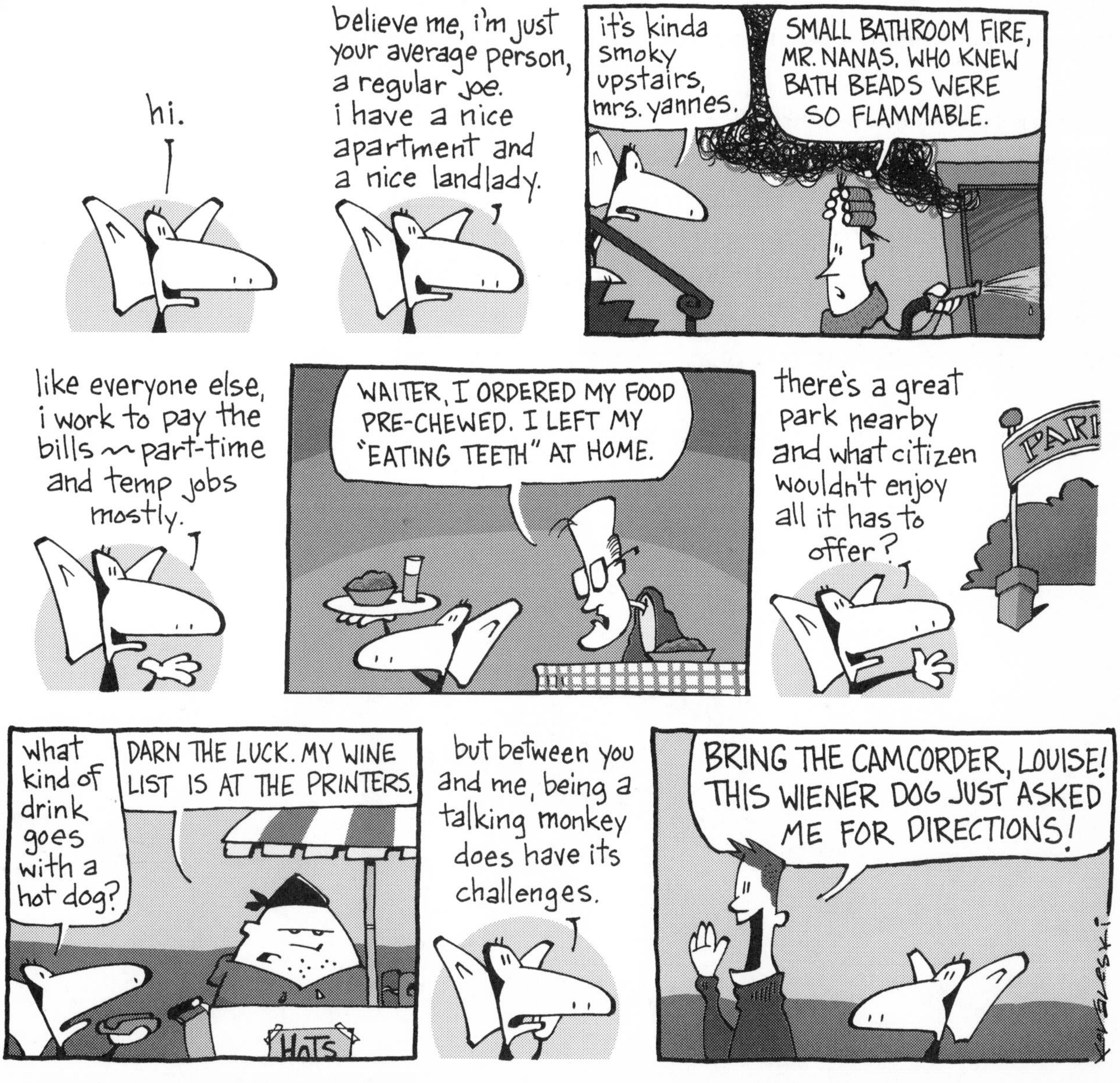
hi.
believe me, i'm just your average person, a regular joe. i have a nice apartment and a nice landlady.
it's kinda smoky upstairs, mrs. yannes.
SMALL BATHROOM FIRE, MR. NANAS. WHO KNEW BATH BEADS WERE SO FLAMMABLE.
like everyone else, i work to pay the bills ~ part-time and temp jobs mostly.
WAITER, I ORDERED MY FOOD PRE-CHEWED. I LEFT MY "EATING TEETH" AT HOME.
there's a great park nearby and what citizen wouldn't enjoy all it has to offer?
PARK
what kind of drink goes with a hot dog?
DARN THE LUCK. MY WINE LIST IS AT THE PRINTERS.
HOTS
but between you and me, being a talking monkey does have its challenges.
BRING THE CAMCORDER, LOUISE! THIS WIENER DOG JUST ASKED ME FOR DIRECTIONS!
KOVALESKI

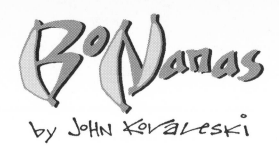

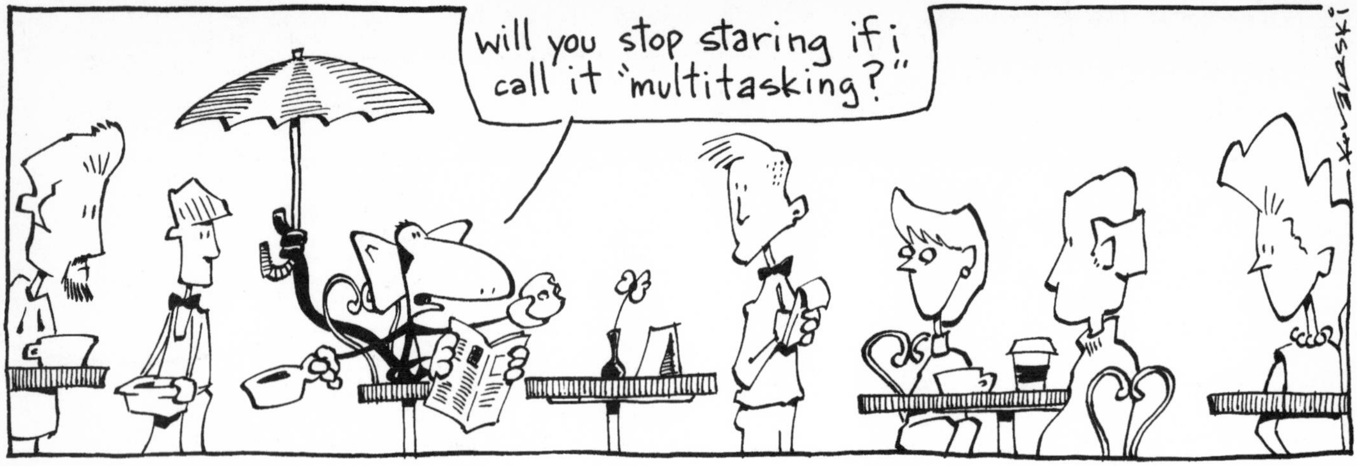
will you stop staring if i call it "multitasking?"
kovaleski

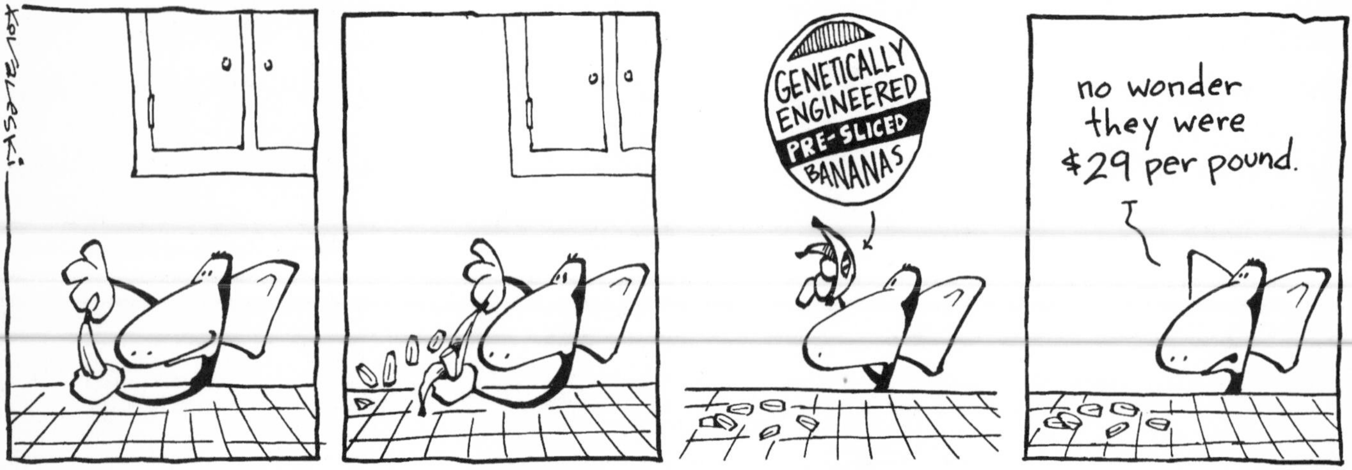
kovaleski
GENETICALLY ENGINEERED PRE-SLICED BANANAS
no wonder they were $29 per pound.

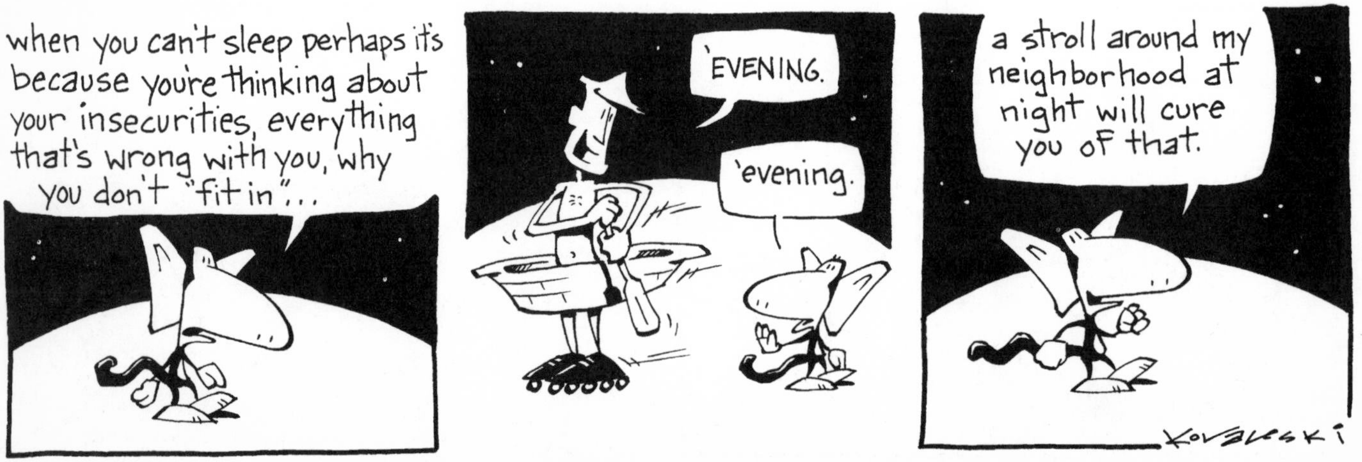
when you can't sleep perhaps it's because you're thinking about your insecurities, everything that's wrong with you, why you don't "fit in"...
'EVENING.
'evening.
a stroll around my neighborhood at night will cure you of that.
kovaleski

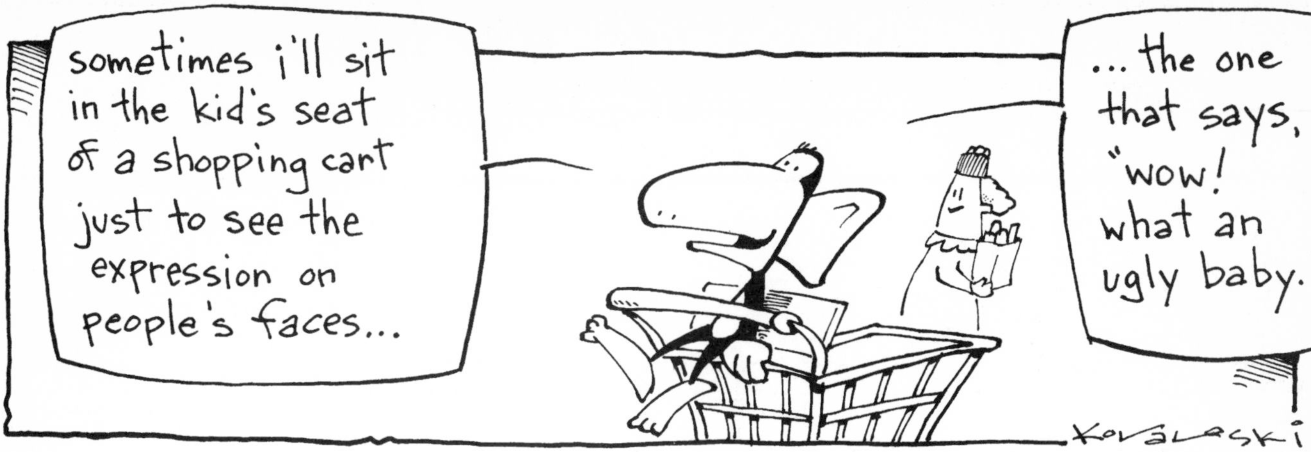
sometimes i'll sit in the kid's seat of a shopping cart just to see the expression on people's faces...
... the one that says, "wow! what an ugly baby."
KOVALESKI

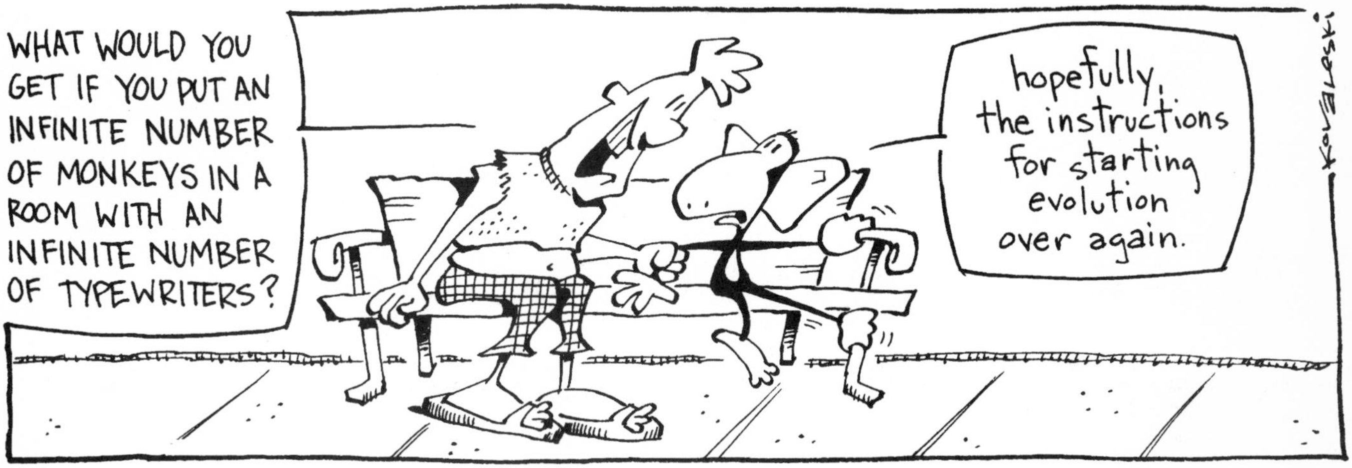
WHAT WOULD YOU GET IF YOU PUT AN INFINITE NUMBER OF MONKEYS IN A ROOM WITH AN INFINITE NUMBER OF TYPEWRITERS?
hopefully, the instructions for starting evolution over again.
KOVALESKI

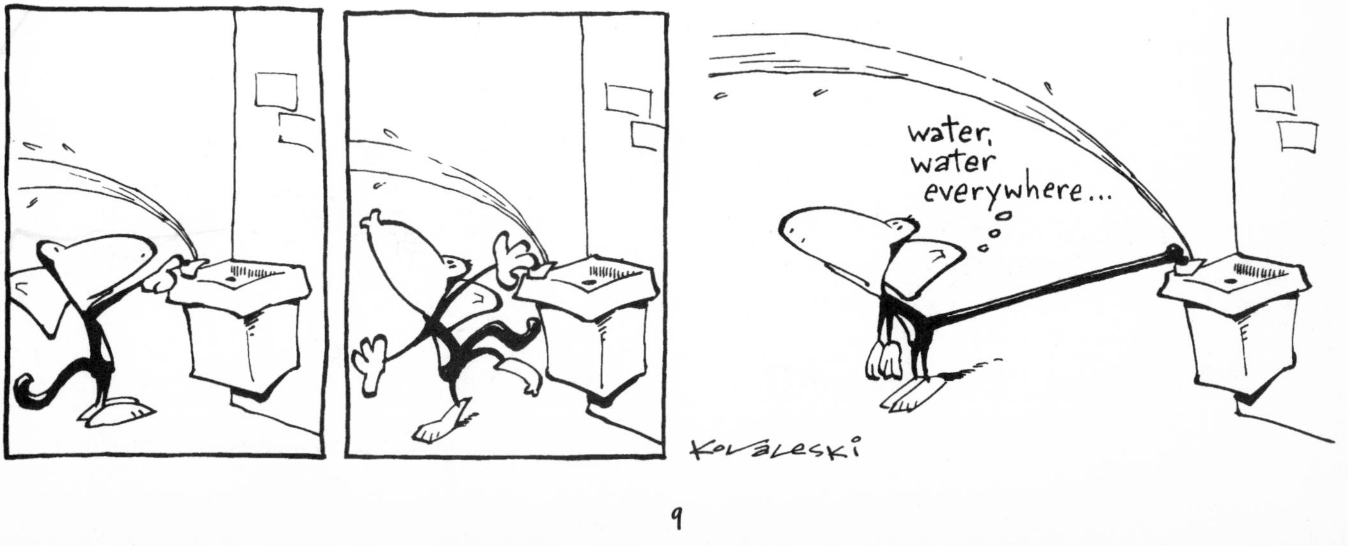
water, water everywhere...
KOVALESKI

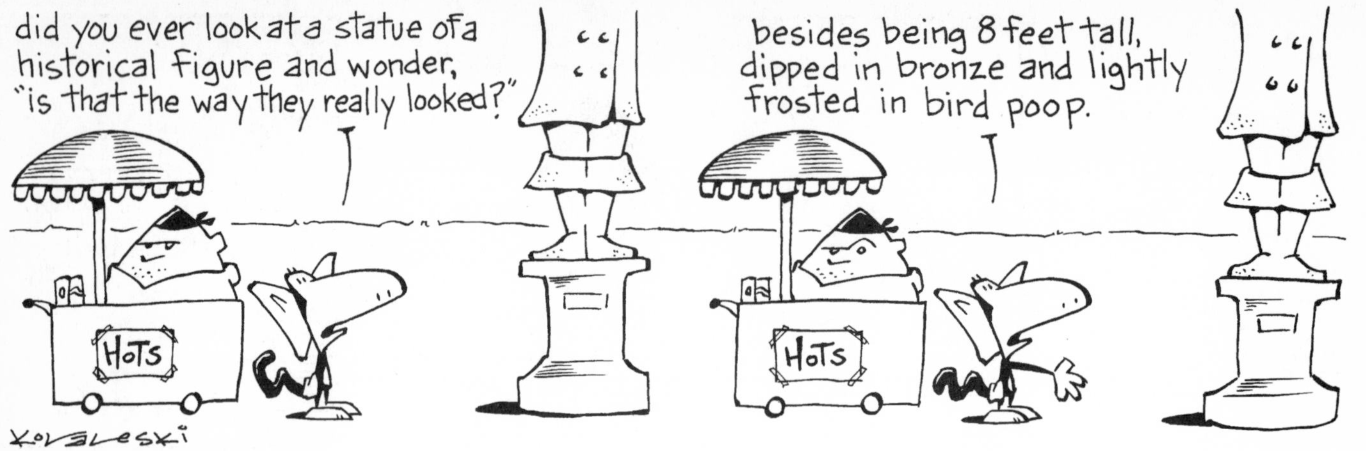
did you ever look at a statue of a historical figure and wonder, "is that the way they really looked?"
besides being 8 feet tall, dipped in bronze and lightly frosted in bird poop.
HOTS
HOTS
KOVALESKI

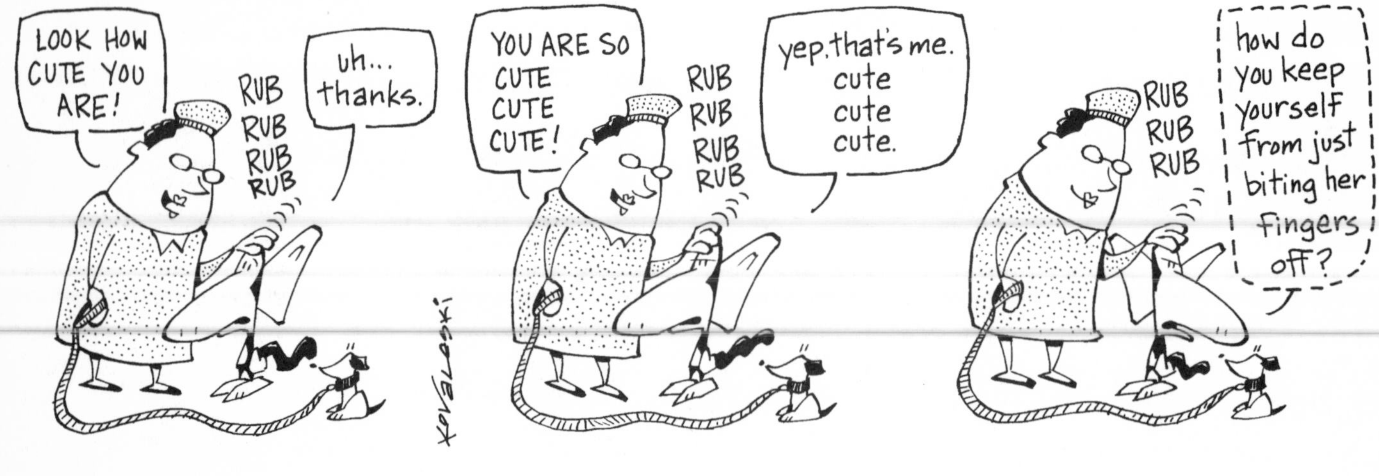
LOOK HOW CUTE YOU ARE!
RUB RUB RUB RUB
uh... thanks.
YOU ARE SO CUTE CUTE CUTE!
RUB RUB RUB RUB
yep, that's me. cute cute cute.
RUB RUB RUB
how do you keep yourself from just biting her fingers off?
KOVALESKI

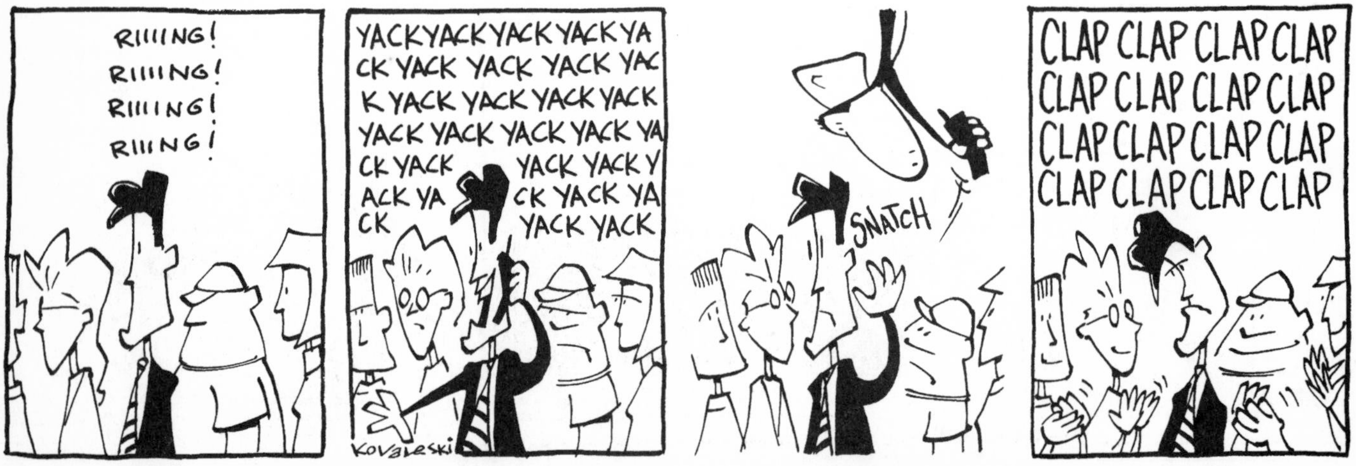
RIIIING! RIIIING! RIIIING! RIIING!
YACK YACK YACK YACK YACK YACK YACK YACK YACK YACK YACK YACK YACK YACK YACK YACK YACK YACK YACK YACK YACK YACK YACK YACK YACK YACK YACK
SNATCH
CLAP CLAP CLAP CLAP CLAP CLAP CLAP CLAP CLAP CLAP CLAP CLAP CLAP CLAP CLAP CLAP
KOVALESKI

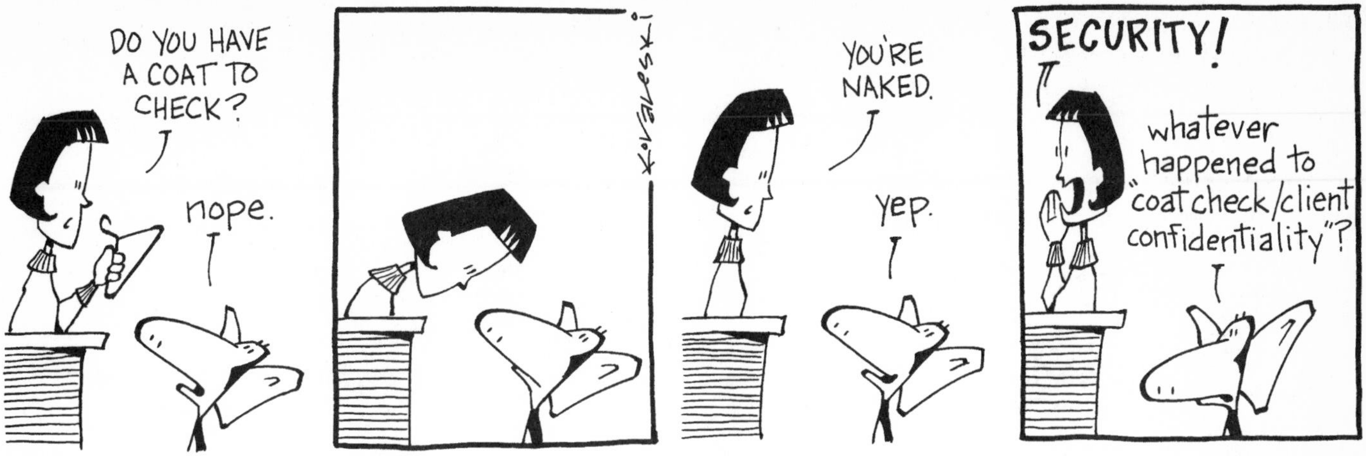
DO YOU HAVE A COAT TO CHECK?
nope.
KOVALESKI
YOU'RE NAKED.
yep.
SECURITY!
whatever happened to "coat check/client confidentiality"?

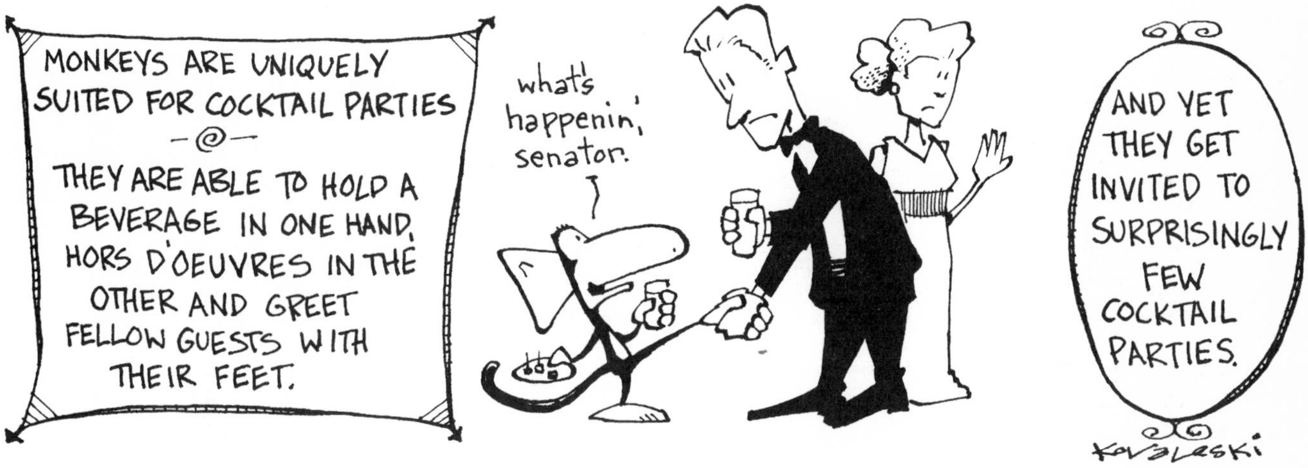
MONKEYS ARE UNIQUELY SUITED FOR COCKTAIL PARTIES
THEY ARE ABLE TO HOLD A BEVERAGE IN ONE HAND, HORS D'OEUVRES IN THE OTHER AND GREET FELLOW GUESTS WITH THEIR FEET.
what's happenin', senator.
AND YET THEY GET INVITED TO SURPRISINGLY FEW COCKTAIL PARTIES.
KOVALESKI

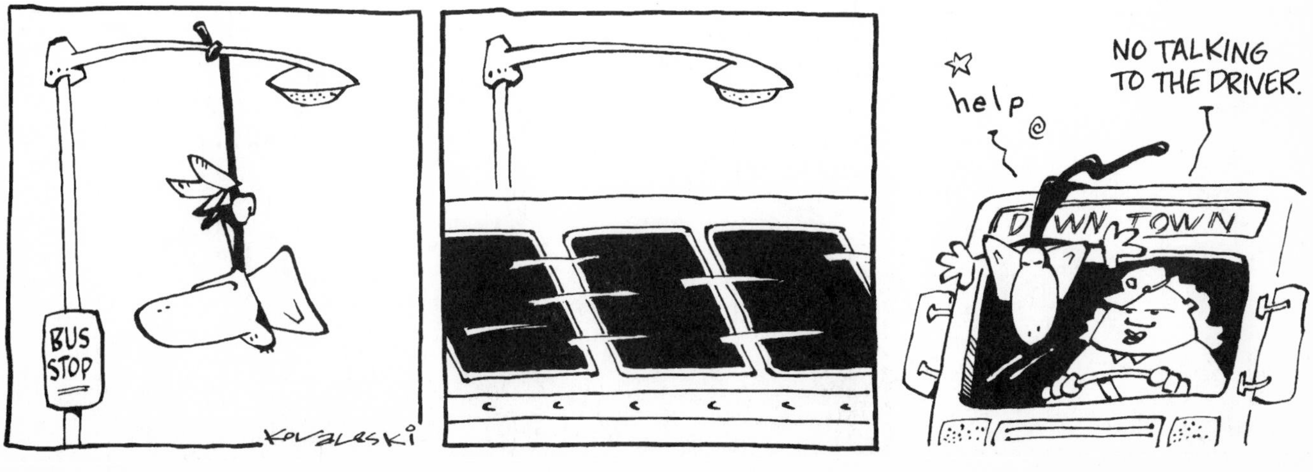
BUS STOP
KOVALESKI
help
NO TALKING TO THE DRIVER.
DOWNTOWN

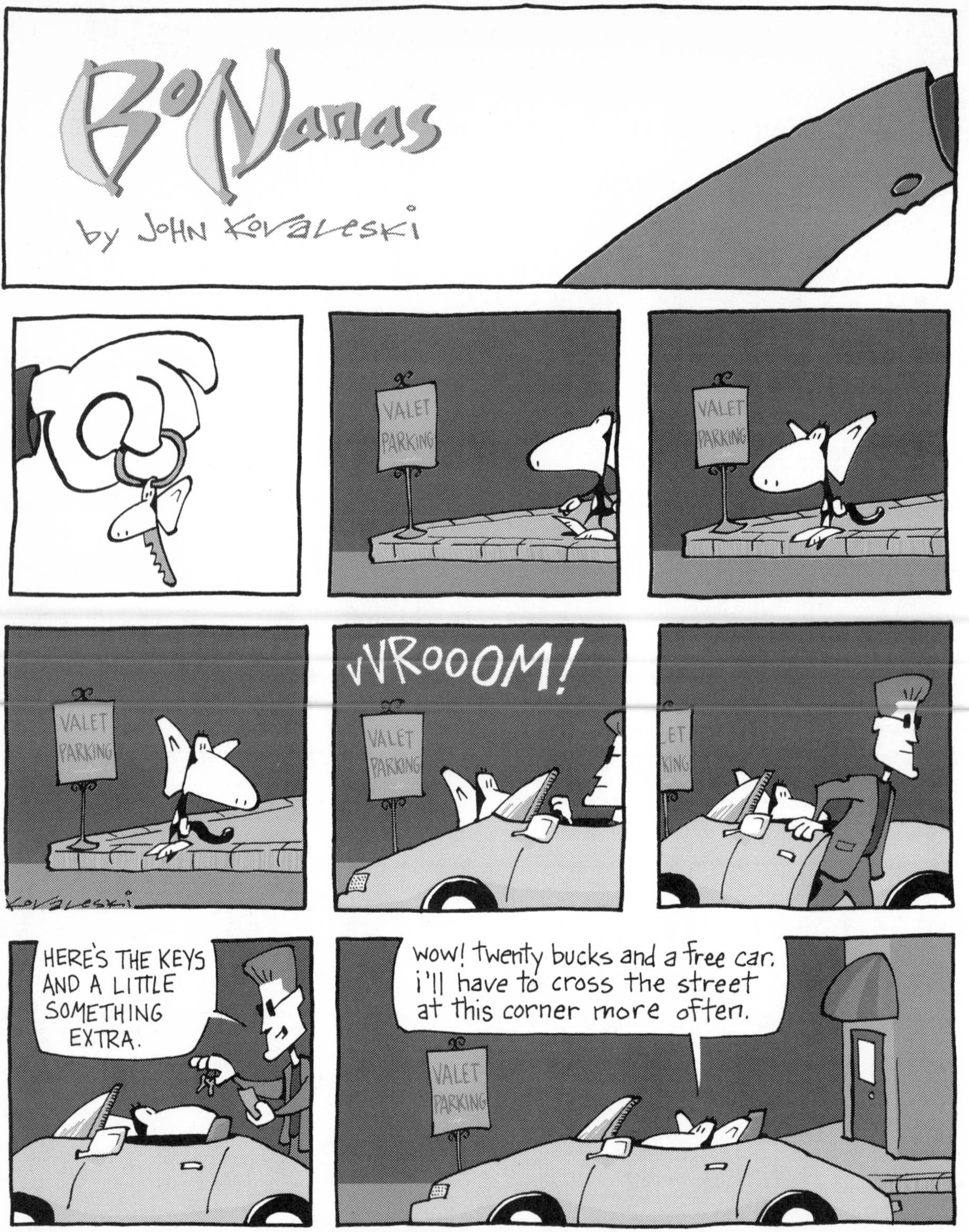
BoNanas
by JOHN KOVALESKI
VALET PARKING
VALET PARKING
VALET PARKING
KOVALESKI
vVROOOM!
VALET PARKING
ET KING
HERE'S THE KEYS AND A LITTLE SOMETHING EXTRA.
wow! twenty bucks and a free car. i'll have to cross the street at this corner more often.
VALET PARKING

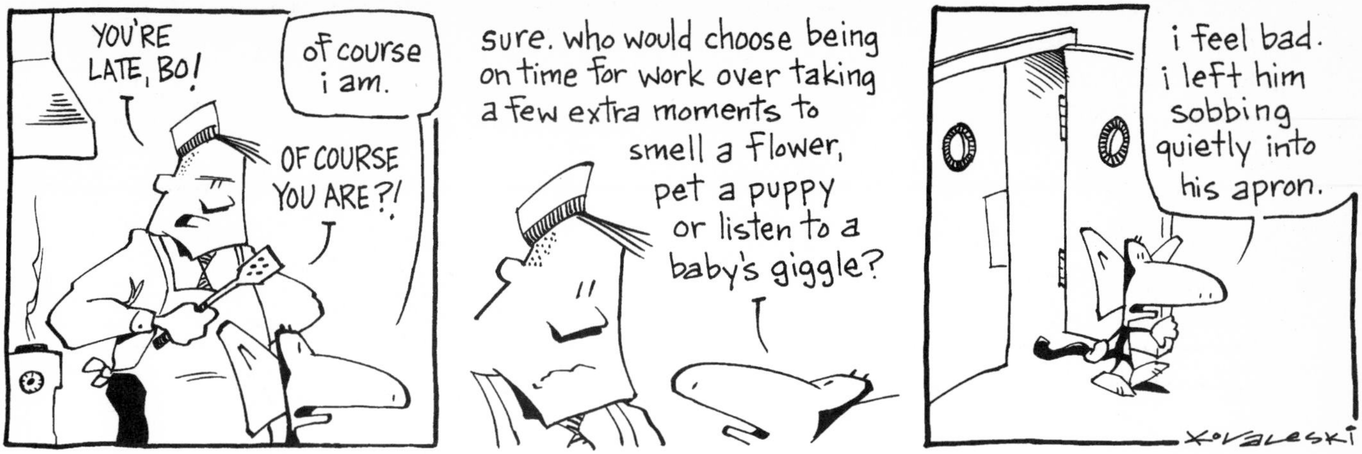
YOU'RE LATE, BO!
of course i am.
OF COURSE YOU ARE?!
sure. who would choose being on time for work over taking a few extra moments to smell a flower, pet a puppy or listen to a baby's giggle?
i feel bad. i left him sobbing quietly into his apron.
kovaleski

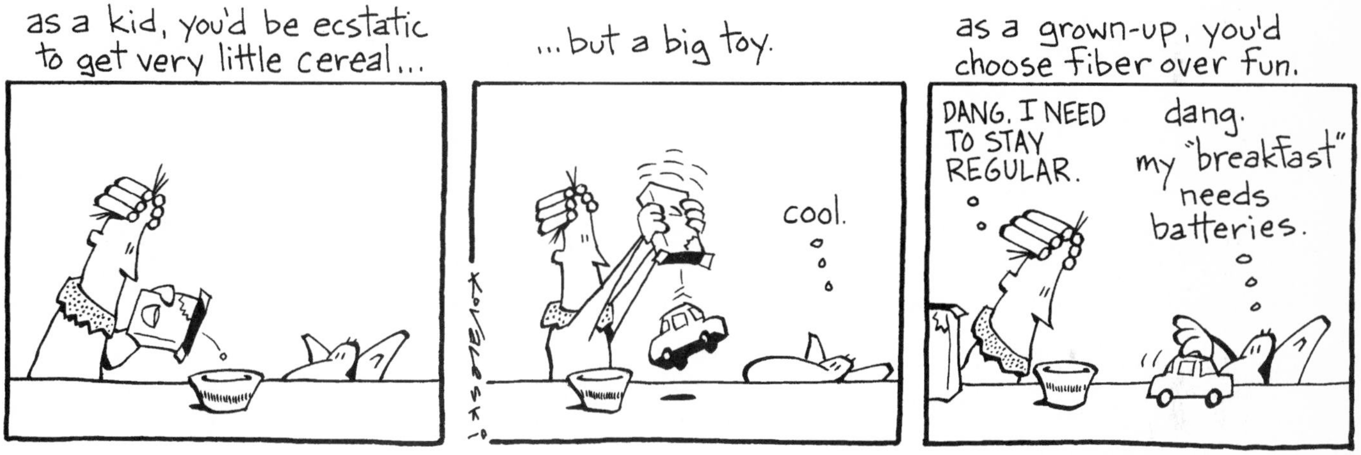
as a kid, you'd be ecstatic to get very little cereal...
...but a big toy.
cool.
kovaleski
as a grown-up, you'd choose fiber over fun.
DANG. I NEED TO STAY REGULAR.
dang. my "breakfast" needs batteries.

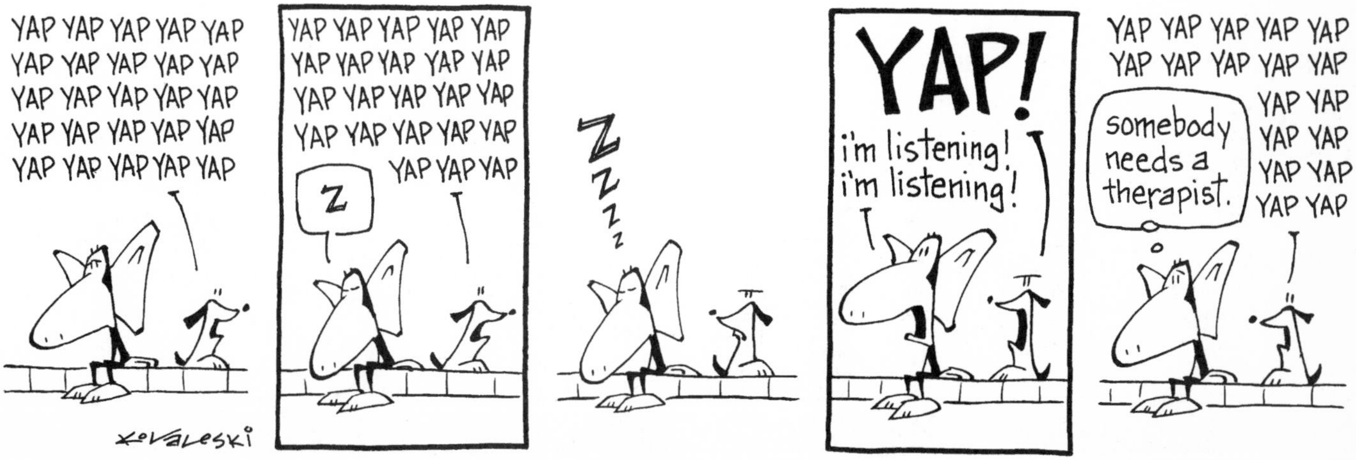
YAP YAP YAP YAP YAP YAP YAP YAP YAP YAP YAP YAP YAP YAP YAP YAP YAP YAP YAP YAP YAP YAP YAP YAP YAP
kovaleski
YAP YAP YAP YAP YAP YAP YAP YAP YAP YAP YAP YAP YAP YAP YAP YAP YAP YAP YAP YAP YAP YAP YAP
Z
ZZZZ
YAP!
i'm listening! i'm listening!
YAP YAP YAP YAP YAP YAP YAP YAP YAP YAP YAP YAP YAP YAP YAP YAP YAP YAP
somebody needs a therapist.

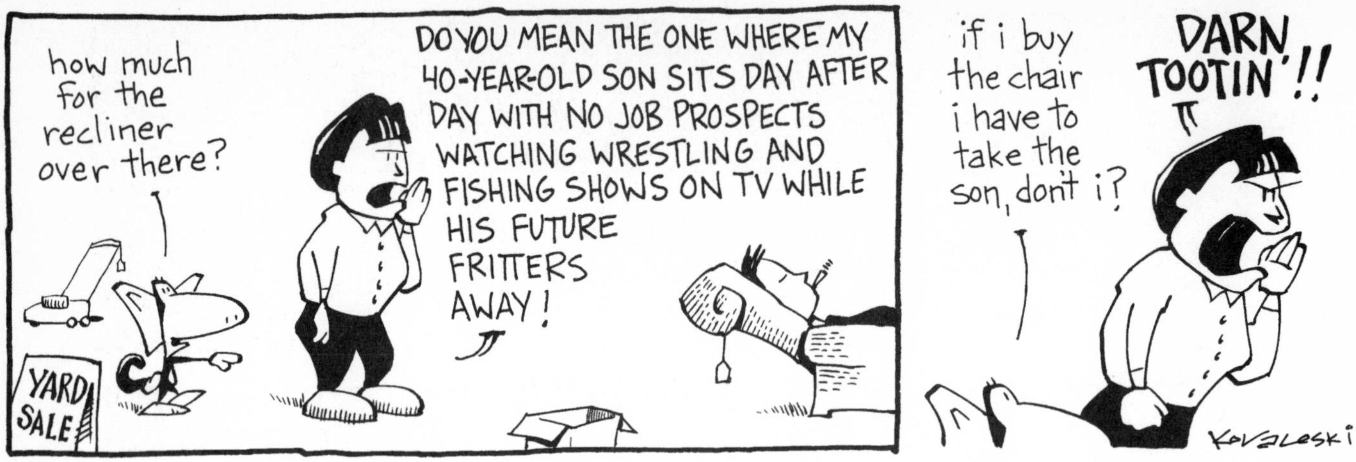
how much for the recliner over there?
DO YOU MEAN THE ONE WHERE MY 40-YEAR-OLD SON SITS DAY AFTER DAY WITH NO JOB PROSPECTS WATCHING WRESTLING AND FISHING SHOWS ON TV WHILE HIS FUTURE FRITTERS AWAY!
YARD SALE
if i buy the chair i have to take the son, don't i?
DARN TOOTIN'!!
KOVALESKI

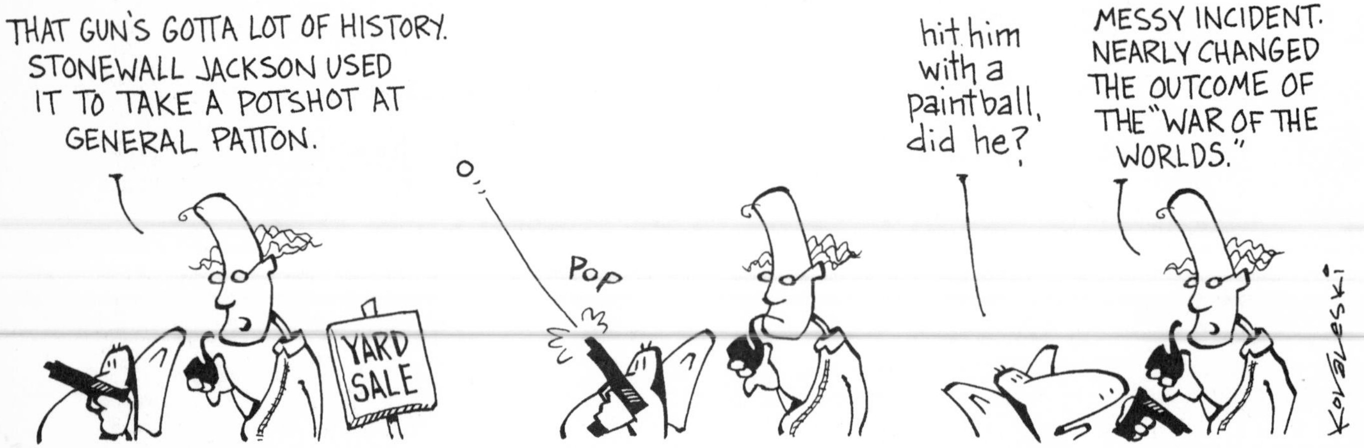
THAT GUN'S GOTTA LOT OF HISTORY. STONEWALL JACKSON USED IT TO TAKE A POTSHOT AT GENERAL PATTON.
YARD SALE
POP
hit him with a paintball, did he?
MESSY INCIDENT. NEARLY CHANGED THE OUTCOME OF THE "WAR OF THE WORLDS."
KOVALESKI

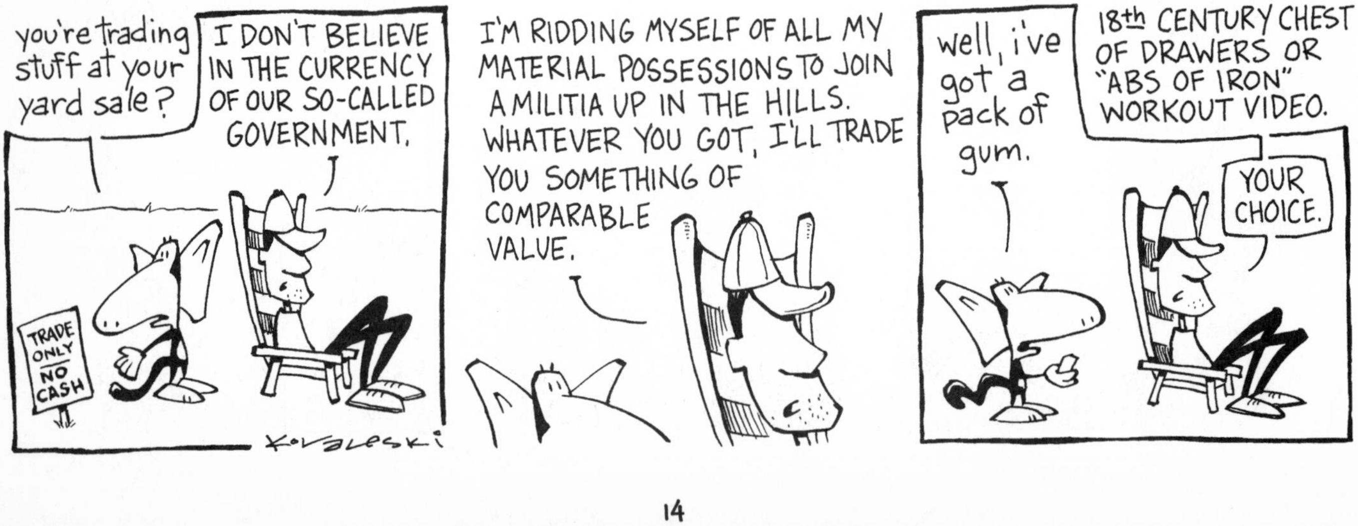
you're trading stuff at your yard sale?
I DON'T BELIEVE IN THE CURRENCY OF OUR SO-CALLED GOVERNMENT.
TRADE ONLY NO CASH
KOVALESKI
I'M RIDDING MYSELF OF ALL MY MATERIAL POSSESSIONS TO JOIN A MILITIA UP IN THE HILLS. WHATEVER YOU GOT, I'LL TRADE YOU SOMETHING OF COMPARABLE VALUE.
well, i've got a pack of gum.
18th CENTURY CHEST OF DRAWERS OR "ABS OF IRON" WORKOUT VIDEO.
YOUR CHOICE.

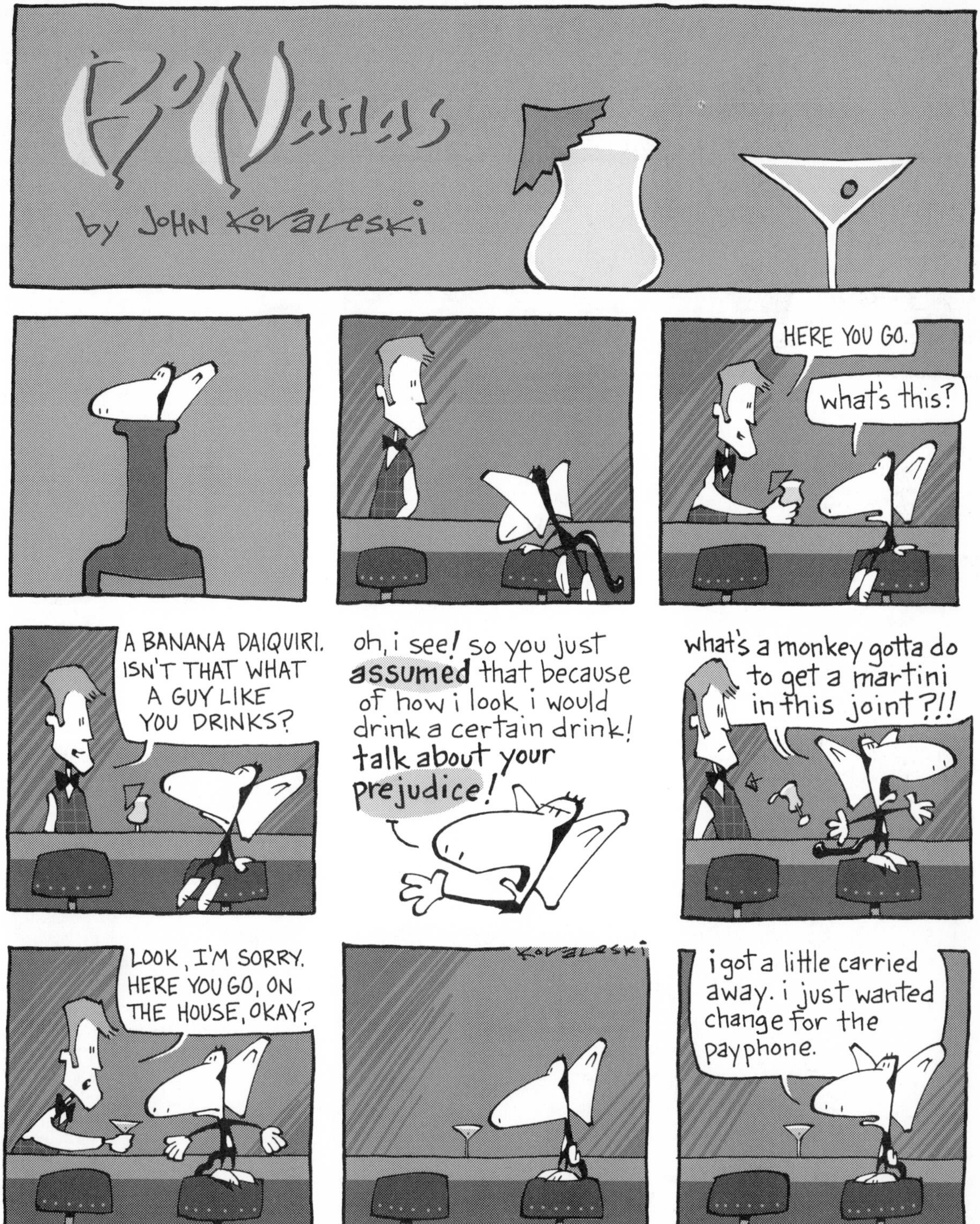
by JOHN KOVALESKI
HERE YOU GO.
what's this?
A BANANA DAIQUIRI. ISN'T THAT WHAT A GUY LIKE YOU DRINKS?
oh, i see! so you just assumed that because of how i look i would drink a certain drink! talk about your prejudice!
what's a monkey gotta do to get a martini in this joint?!!
LOOK, I'M SORRY. HERE YOU GO, ON THE HOUSE, OKAY?
KOVALESKI
i got a little carried away. i just wanted change for the payphone.

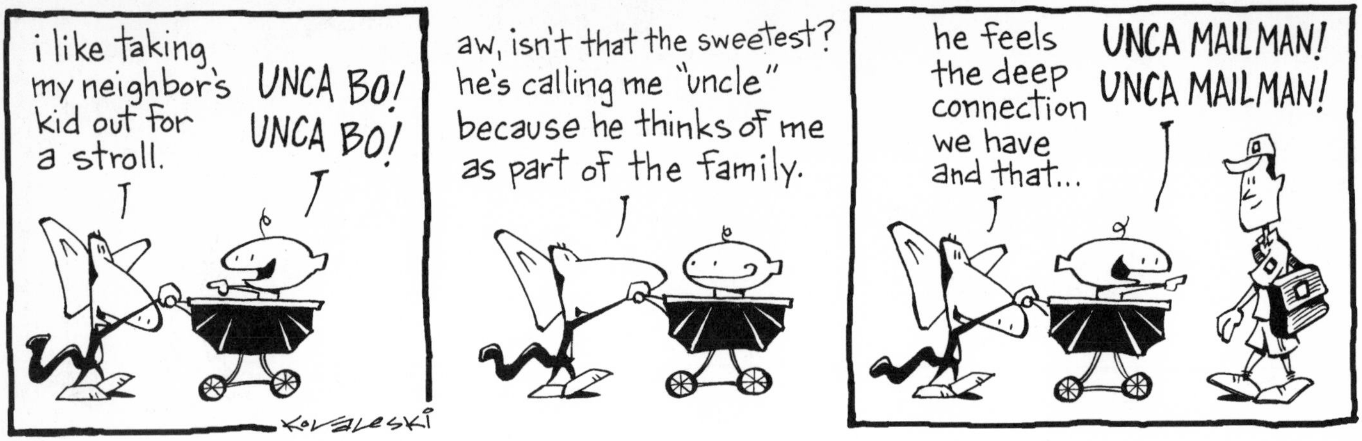
i like taking my neighbor's kid out for a stroll.
UNCA BO! UNCA BO!
KOVALESKI
aw, isn't that the sweetest? he's calling me "uncle" because he thinks of me as part of the family.
he feels the deep connection we have and that...
UNCA MAILMAN! UNCA MAILMAN!

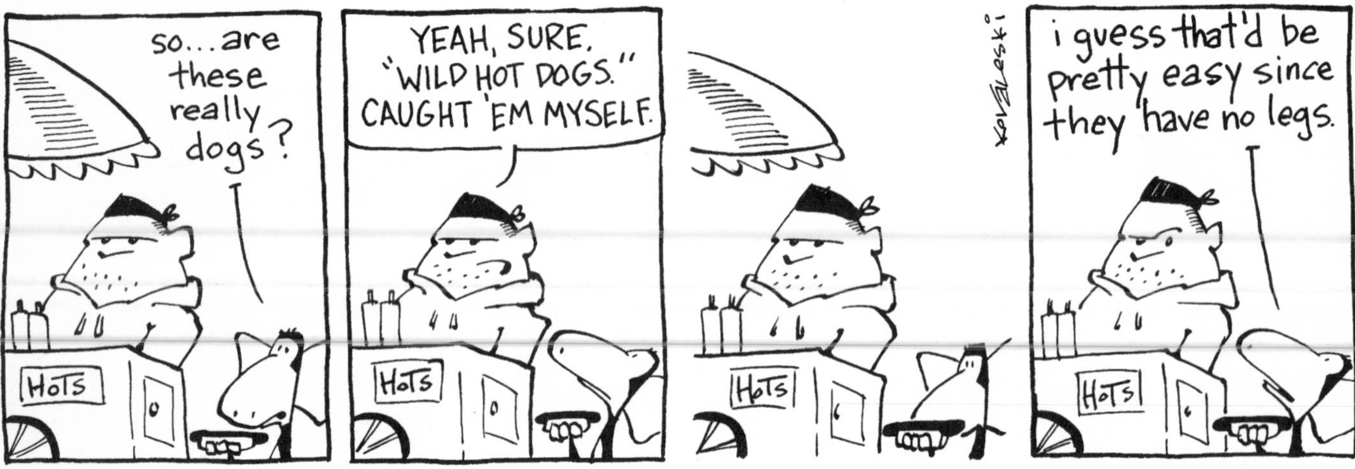
so... are these really dogs?
YEAH, SURE. "WILD HOT DOGS." CAUGHT 'EM MYSELF.
HOTS
KOVALESKI
i guess that'd be pretty easy since they have no legs.

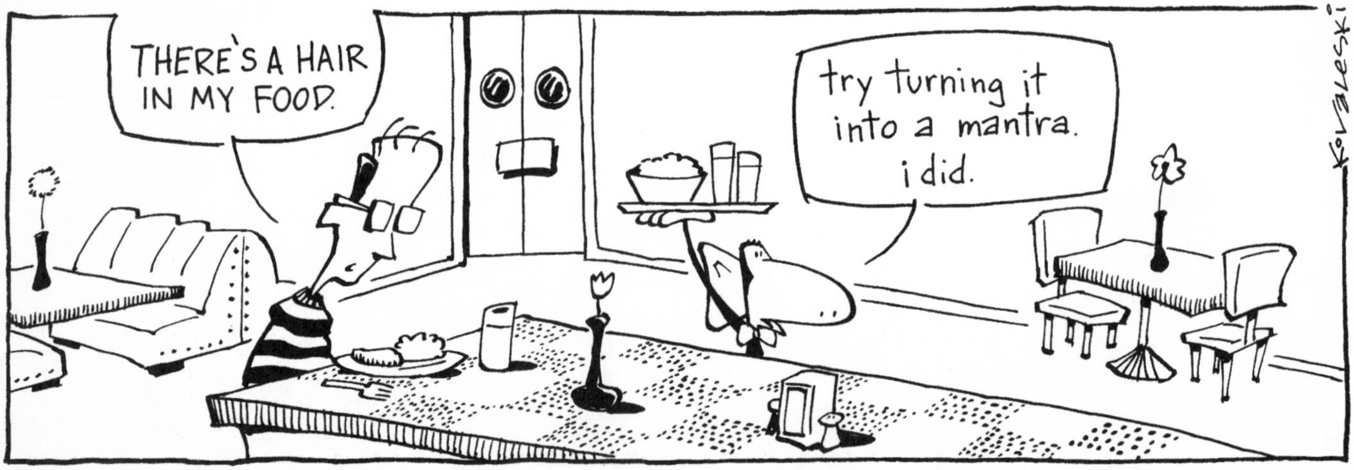
THERE'S A HAIR IN MY FOOD.
try turning it into a mantra. i did.
KOVALESKI

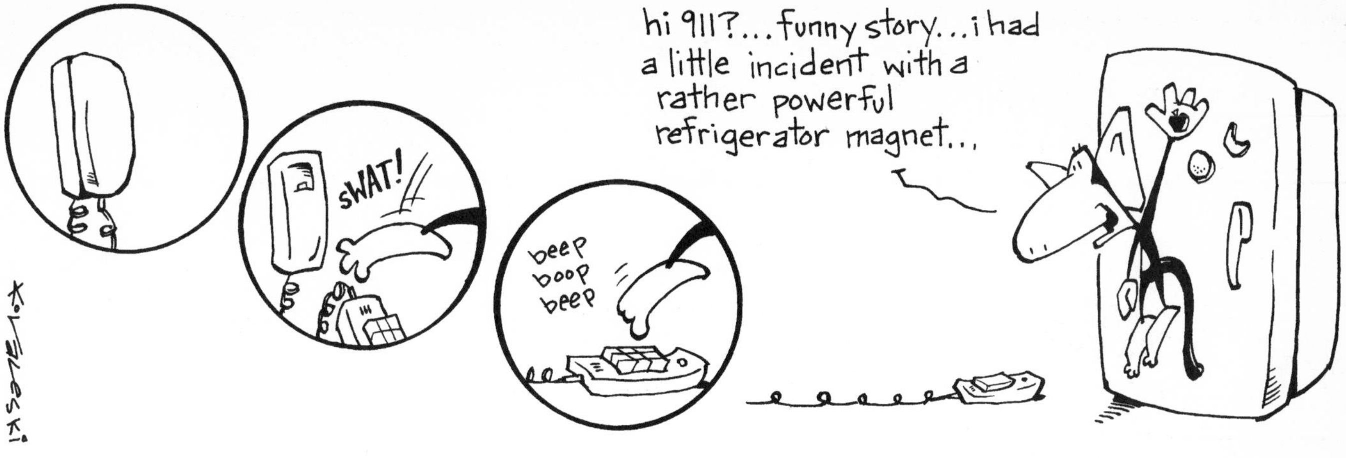
SWAT!
beep
boop
beep
hi 911?... funny story... i had a little incident with a rather powerful refrigerator magnet...
Kovaleski

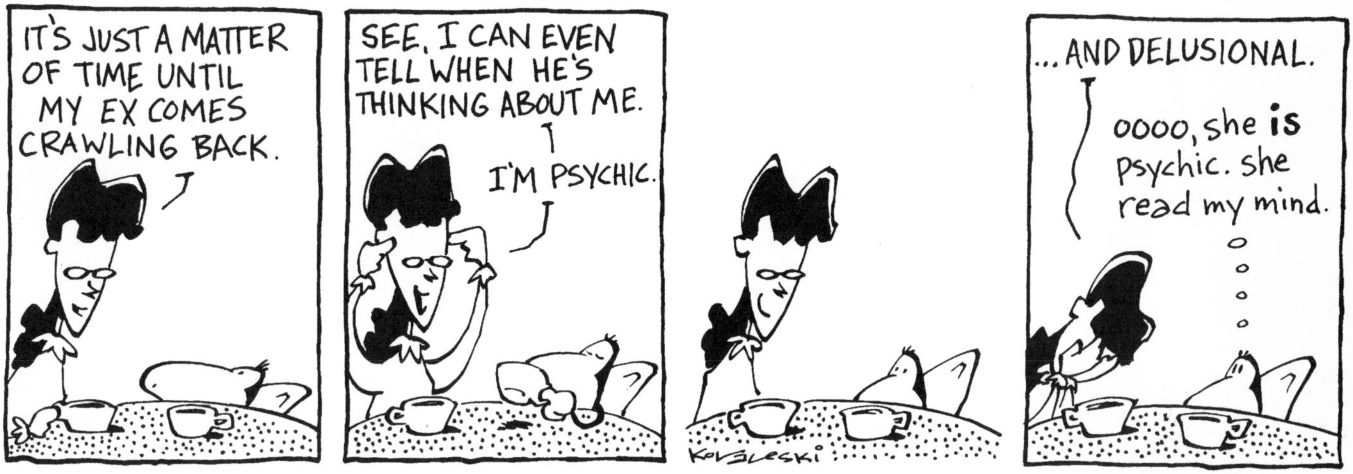
IT'S JUST A MATTER OF TIME UNTIL MY EX COMES CRAWLING BACK.
SEE, I CAN EVEN TELL WHEN HE'S THINKING ABOUT ME.
I'M PSYCHIC.
...AND DELUSIONAL.
oooo, she **is** psychic. she read my mind.
Kovaleski

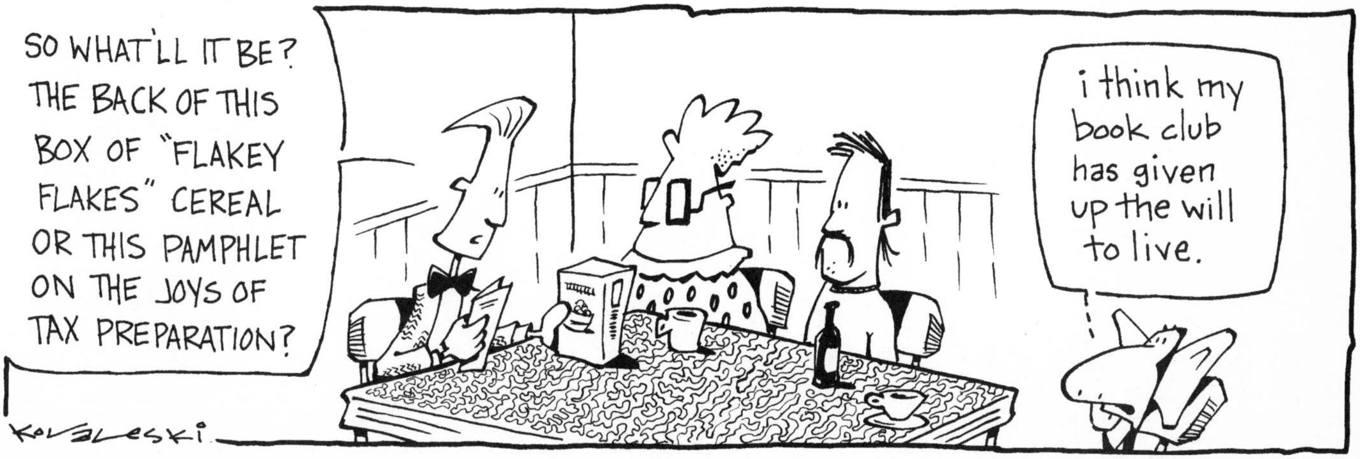
SO WHAT'LL IT BE? THE BACK OF THIS BOX OF "FLAKEY FLAKES" CEREAL OR THIS PAMPHLET ON THE JOYS OF TAX PREPARATION?
i think my book club has given up the will to live.
Kovaleski

Bo Nanas

by John Kovaleski

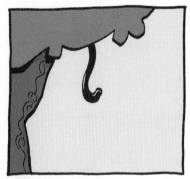

if you look hard enough you can find a spot in a park where no one has ever been before.

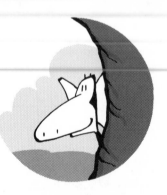

an unspoiled niche for you and you alone.

ahhh...

MY PRIVATE PLACE DISCOVERED 7/19

DREAM ON, "COLUMBUS," I FOUND THIS PLACE MONTHS BEFORE YOU SO BEAT IT!

TAKE A HIKE, "SECRET GARDENERS." I'VE BEEN HERE SINCE THE EARLY '70s

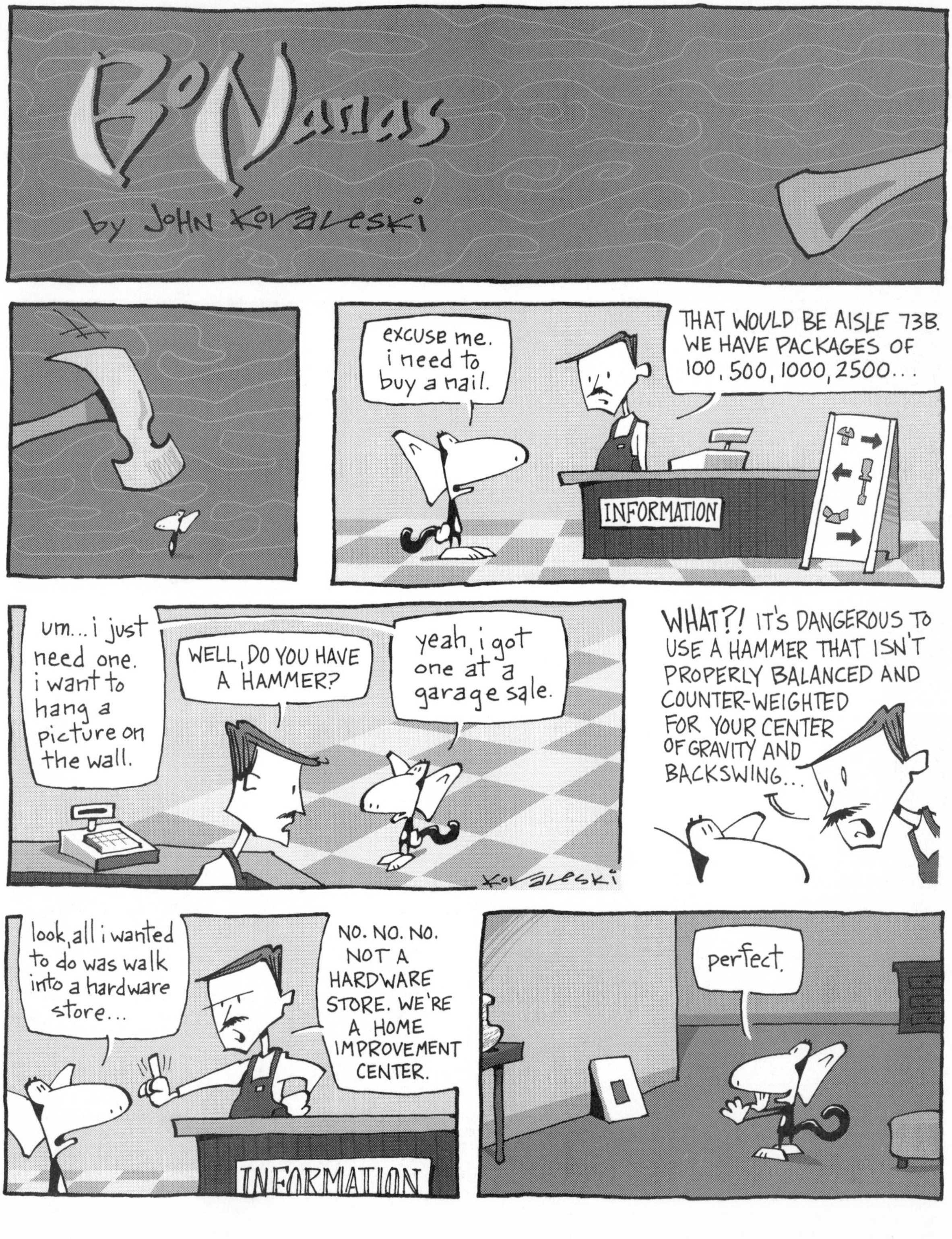
BoNanas
by John Kovaleski
excuse me. i need to buy a nail.
THAT WOULD BE AISLE 73B. WE HAVE PACKAGES OF 100, 500, 1000, 2500...
INFORMATION
um... i just need one. i want to hang a picture on the wall.
WELL, DO YOU HAVE A HAMMER?
yeah, i got one at a garage sale.
KOVALESKI
WHAT?! IT'S DANGEROUS TO USE A HAMMER THAT ISN'T PROPERLY BALANCED AND COUNTER-WEIGHTED FOR YOUR CENTER OF GRAVITY AND BACKSWING...
look, all i wanted to do was walk into a hardware store...
NO. NO. NO. NOT A HARDWARE STORE. WE'RE A HOME IMPROVEMENT CENTER.
INFORMATION
perfect.

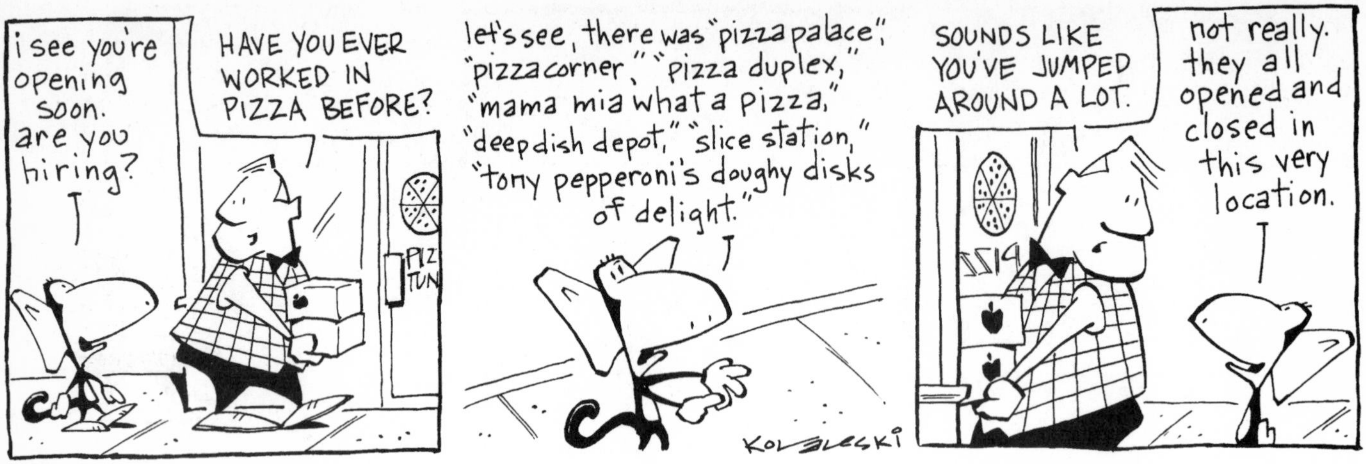
i see you're opening soon. are you hiring?
HAVE YOU EVER WORKED IN PIZZA BEFORE?
PIZ TUN
let's see, there was "pizza palace", "pizza corner," "pizza duplex," "mama mia what a pizza," "deepdish depot," "slice station," "tony pepperoni's doughy disks of delight."
SOUNDS LIKE YOU'VE JUMPED AROUND A LOT.
not really. they all opened and closed in this very location.
KOVALESKI

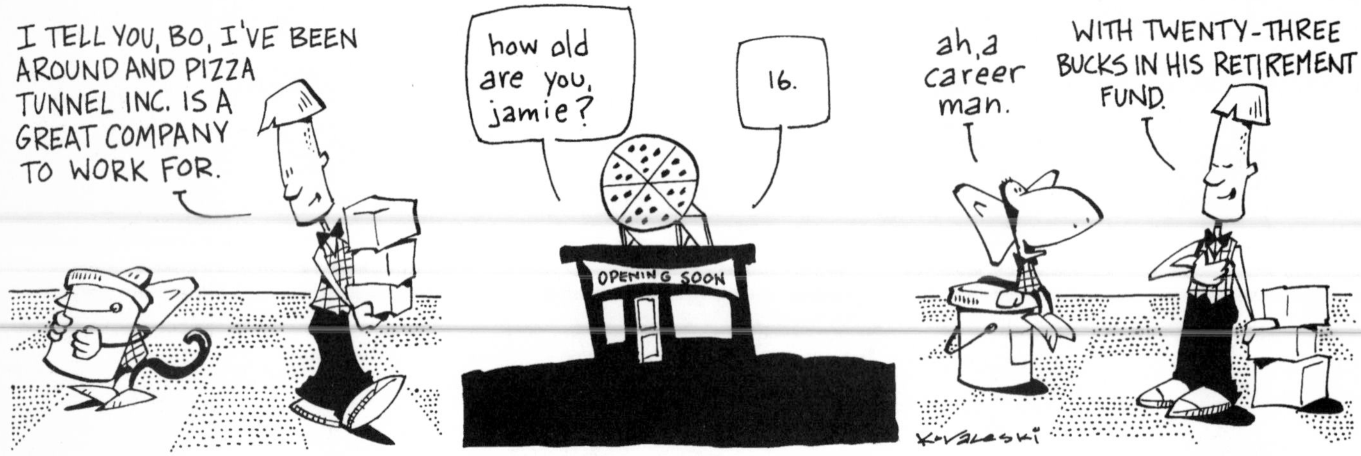
I TELL YOU, BO, I'VE BEEN AROUND AND PIZZA TUNNEL INC. IS A GREAT COMPANY TO WORK FOR.
how old are you, jamie?
16.
OPENING SOON
ah, a career man.
WITH TWENTY-THREE BUCKS IN HIS RETIREMENT FUND.
KOVALESKI

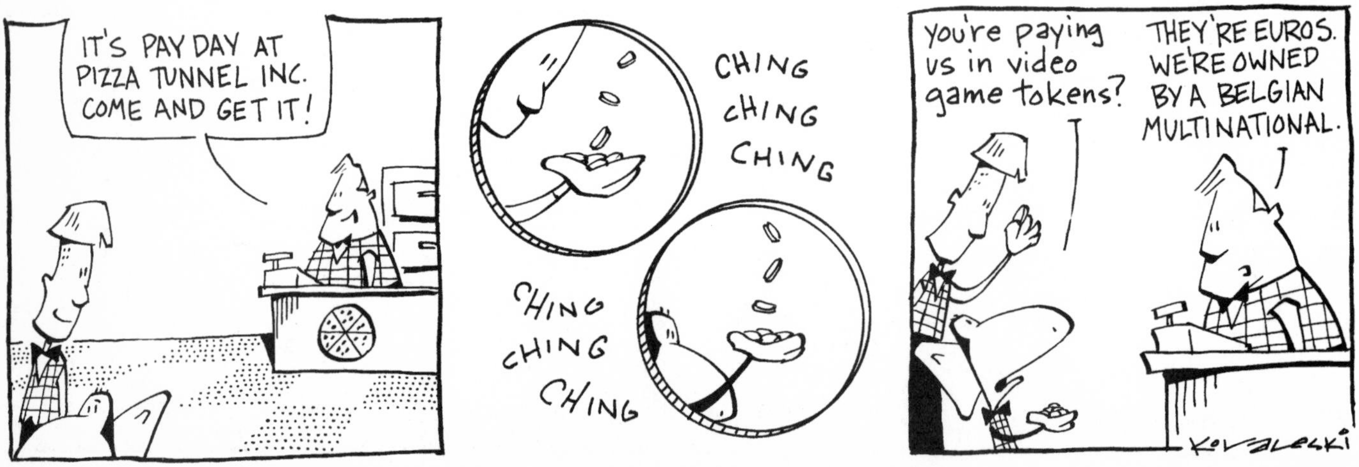
IT'S PAY DAY AT PIZZA TUNNEL INC. COME AND GET IT!
CHING CHING CHING
CHING CHING CHING
you're paying us in video game tokens?
THEY'RE EUROS. WE'RE OWNED BY A BELGIAN MULTINATIONAL.
KOVALESKI

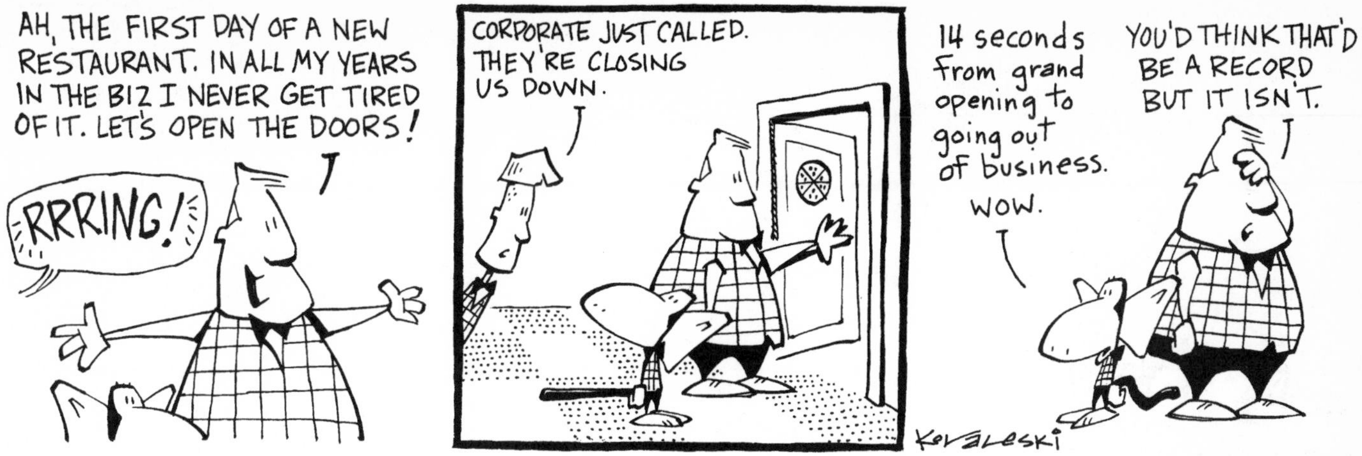
AH, THE FIRST DAY OF A NEW RESTAURANT. IN ALL MY YEARS IN THE BIZ I NEVER GET TIRED OF IT. LET'S OPEN THE DOORS!
RRRING!
CORPORATE JUST CALLED. THEY'RE CLOSING US DOWN.
14 seconds from grand opening to going out of business.
WOW.
YOU'D THINK THAT'D BE A RECORD BUT IT ISN'T.
KOVALESKI

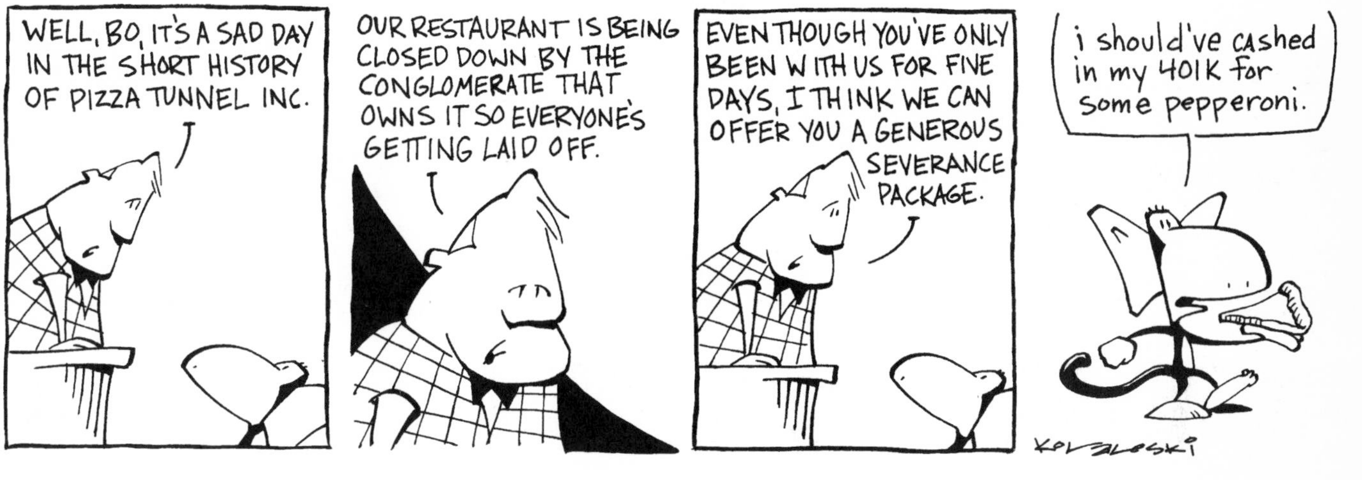
WELL, BO, IT'S A SAD DAY IN THE SHORT HISTORY OF PIZZA TUNNEL INC.
OUR RESTAURANT IS BEING CLOSED DOWN BY THE CONGLOMERATE THAT OWNS IT SO EVERYONE'S GETTING LAID OFF.
EVEN THOUGH YOU'VE ONLY BEEN WITH US FOR FIVE DAYS, I THINK WE CAN OFFER YOU A GENEROUS SEVERANCE PACKAGE.
i should've cashed in my 401K for some pepperoni.
KOVALESKI

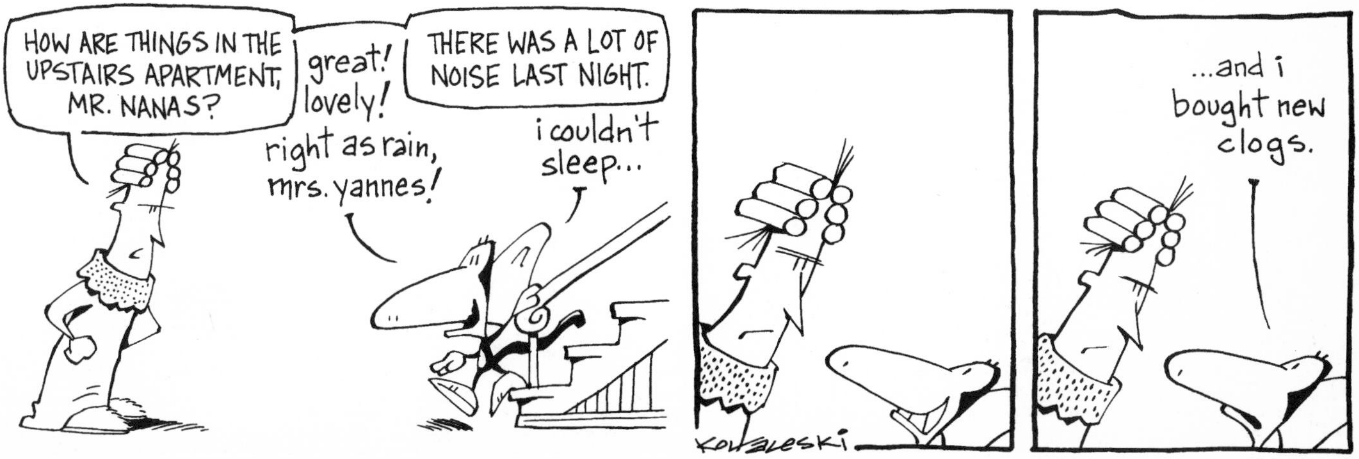
HOW ARE THINGS IN THE UPSTAIRS APARTMENT, MR. NANAS?
great! lovely! right as rain, mrs. yannes!
THERE WAS A LOT OF NOISE LAST NIGHT.
i couldn't sleep...
...and i bought new clogs.
KOVALESKI

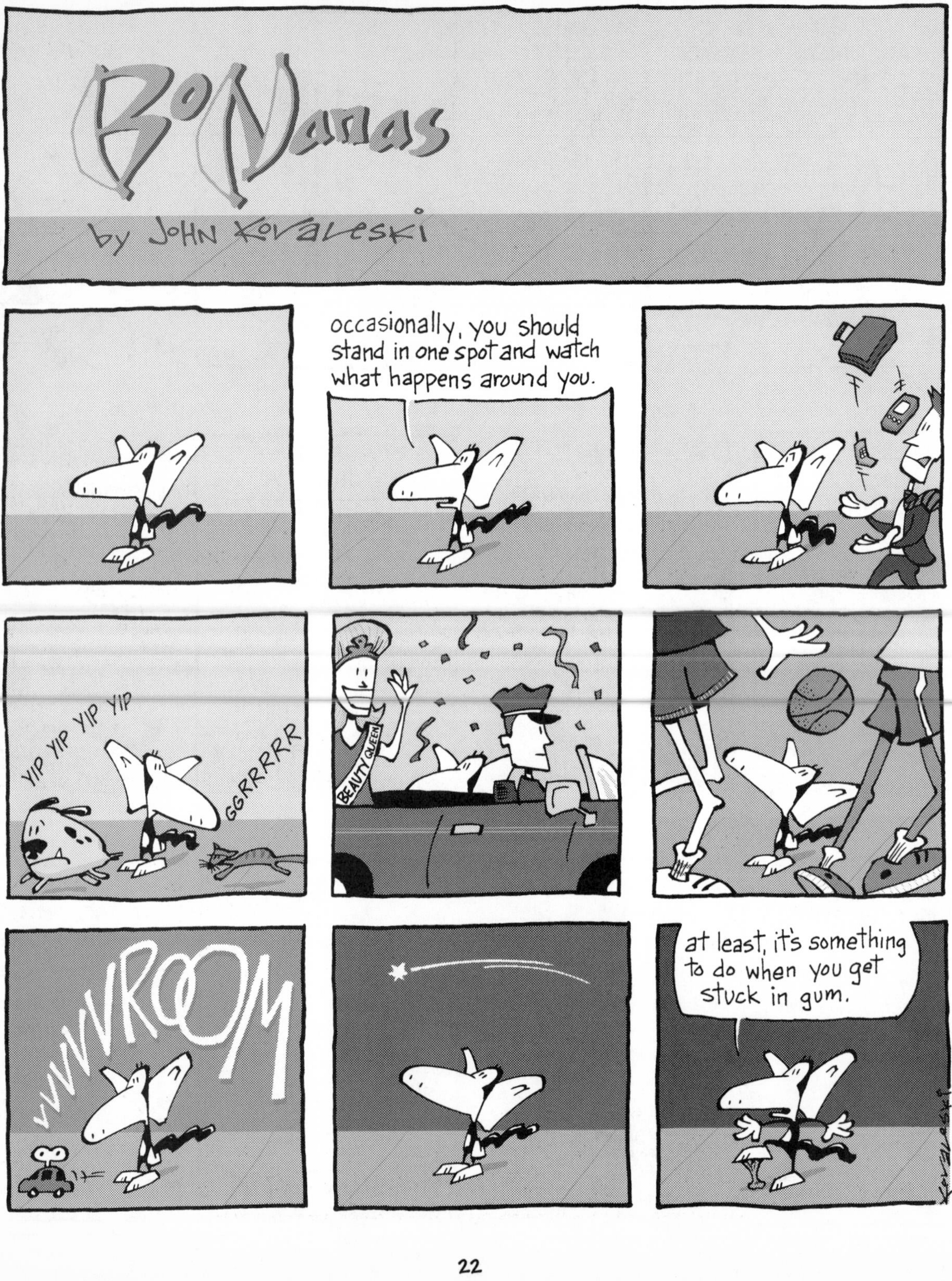
Bo Nanas
by John Kovaleski
occasionally, you should stand in one spot and watch what happens around you.
YIP YIP YIP YIP
GGRRRRR
BEAUTY QUEEN
VVVVVROOM
at least, it's something to do when you get stuck in gum.
Kovaleski

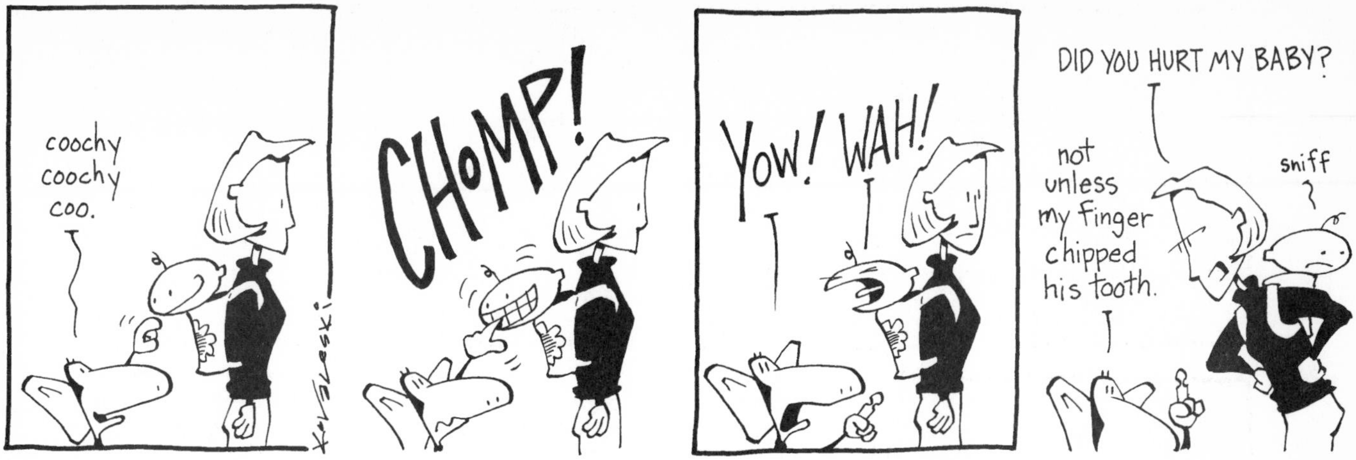
coochy coochy coo.
KOVALESKI
CHOMP!
YOW! WAH!
DID YOU HURT MY BABY?
not unless my finger chipped his tooth.
sniff

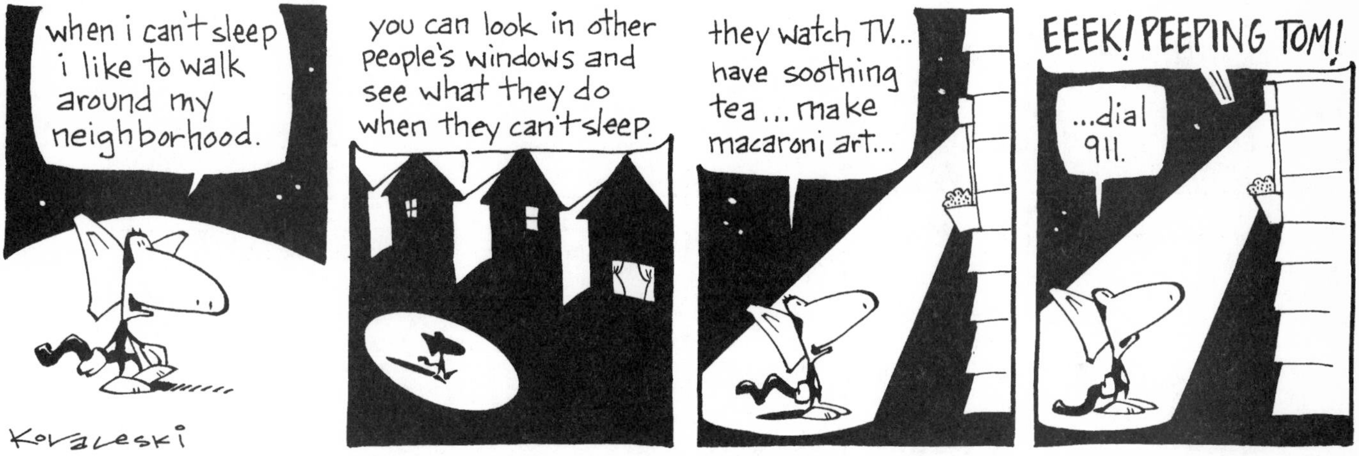
when i can't sleep i like to walk around my neighborhood.
KOVALESKI
you can look in other people's windows and see what they do when they can't sleep.
they watch TV... have soothing tea... make macaroni art...
EEEK! PEEPING TOM!
...dial 911.

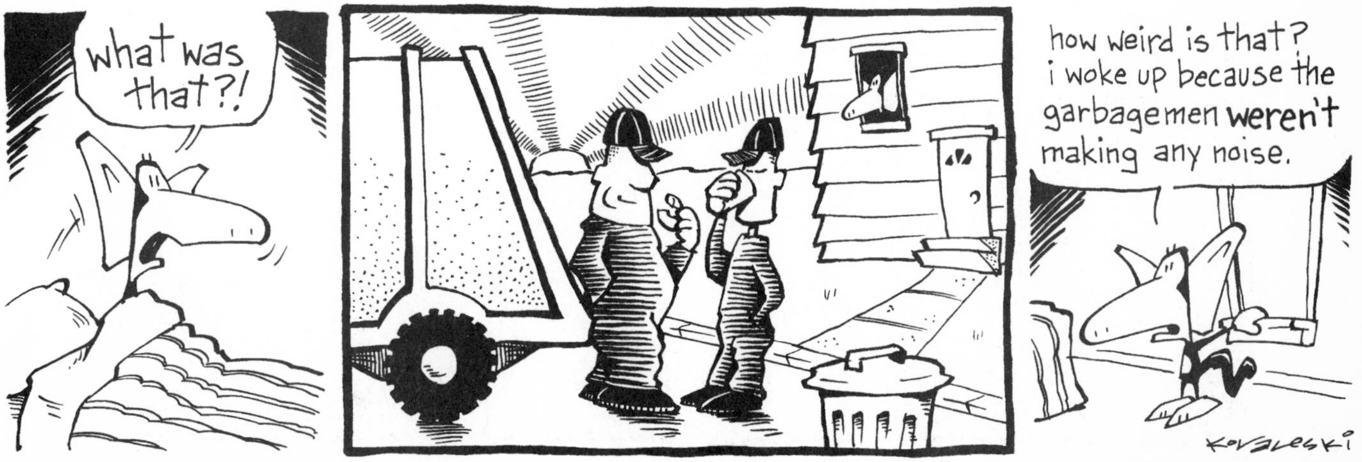
what was that?!
how weird is that? i woke up because the garbagemen **weren't** making any noise.
KOVALESKI

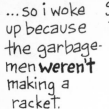
...so i woke up because the garbagemen **weren't** making a racket.

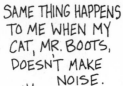
SAME THING HAPPENS TO ME WHEN MY CAT, MR. BOOTS, DOESN'T MAKE NOISE.

mr. boots died in '73. he's now stuffed and on display in your living room.

I KNOW THAT. HE USUALLY FALLS OFF THE MANTEL AROUND 4:00 AM.

I LIKE YOU, BO, BUT... but what? did i do something wrong?

YOU WERE PAWING THROUGH MY HAIR.

oh.

so it was too early in the relationship for grooming then?

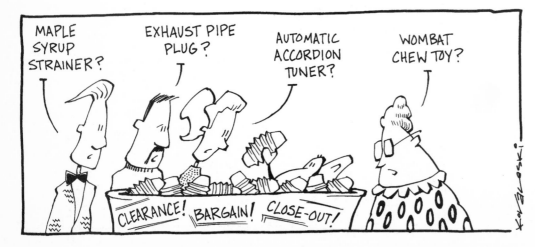
MAPLE SYRUP STRAINER?

EXHAUST PIPE PLUG?

AUTOMATIC ACCORDION TUNER?

WOMBAT CHEW TOY?

CLEARANCE! BARGAIN! CLOSE-OUT!

if something is cheap enough, buy it and figure out what it is later.

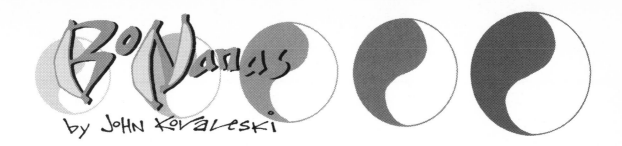

Bo Nanas

by John Kovaleski

what's going on?

IT IS NOT FOR ME TO SAY, FRIEND.

pardon?

I AM FROM **ZNN** — THE "ZEN NEWS NETWORK."

WE FEEL THAT "NEWS" HAPPENS ALL AROUND US AND WHO ARE WE TO PASS JUDGMENT ON WHAT IS WORTHY TO SHOW ON TV?

SO WE SET UP A CAMERA AND LET EVENTS UNFOLD.

WHETHER IT'S A CAR CRASH OR CLOUDS MOVING ACROSS THE SKY, WE SHOOT WHATEVER IS HAPPENING AND SHOW IT LIVE, 24 HOURS A DAY, ON CABLE.

AS YOU CAN IMAGINE YOU'LL FIND US BETWEEN "THE CHEESE CHANNEL" AND "THE LINOLEUM NETWORK."

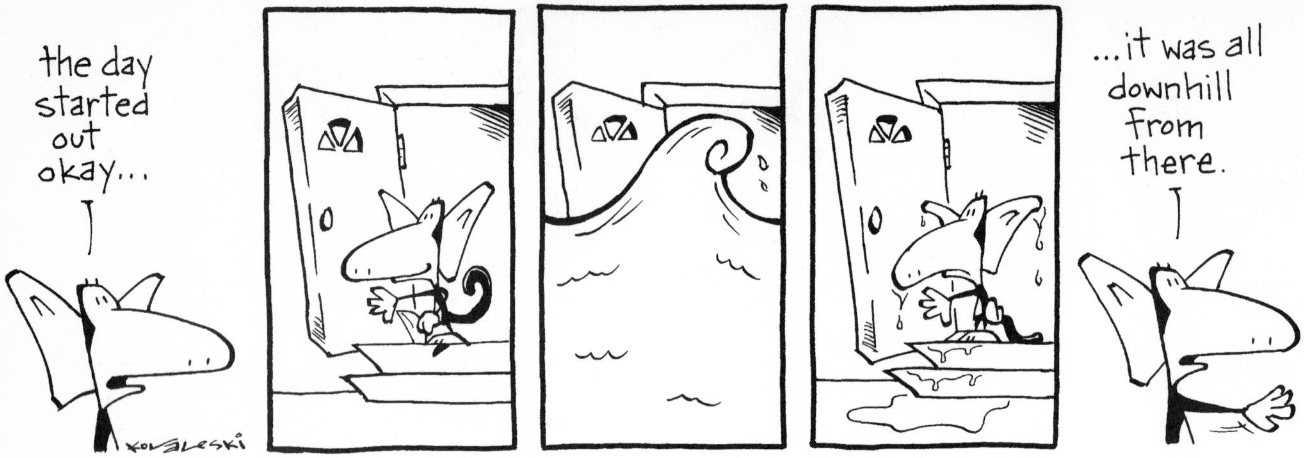
the day started out okay...
...it was all downhill from there.
KOVALESKI

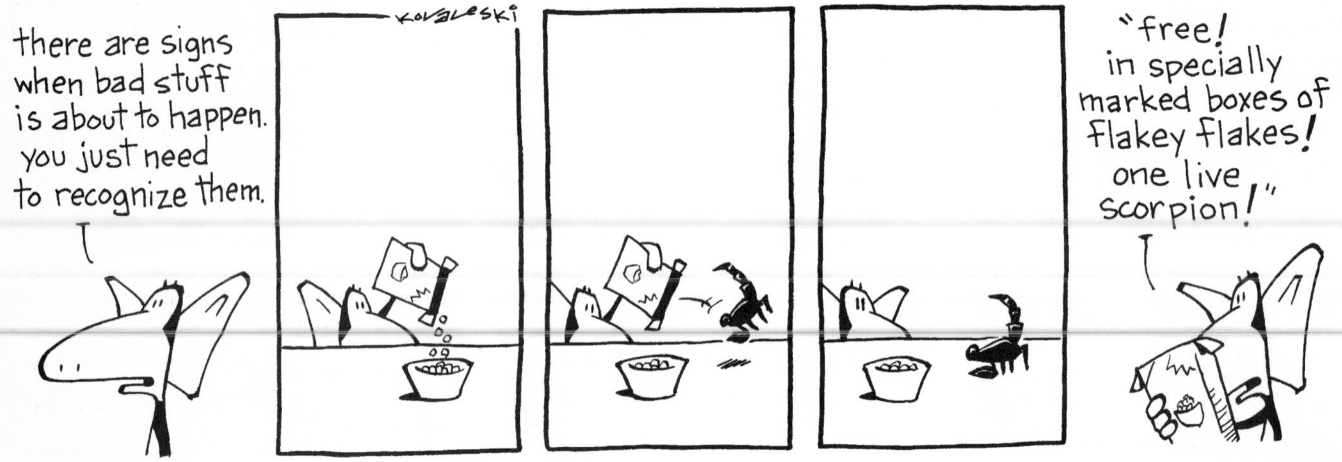
there are signs when bad stuff is about to happen. you just need to recognize them.
"free! in specially marked boxes of flakey flakes! one live scorpion!"
KOVALESKI

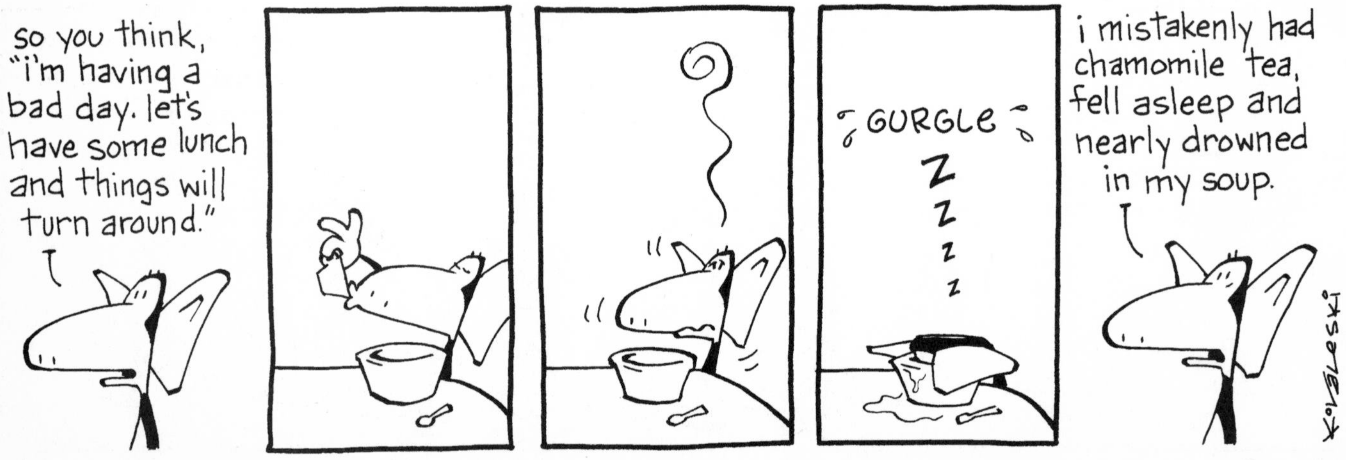
so you think, "i'm having a bad day. let's have some lunch and things will turn around."
GURGLE
Z Z Z Z
i mistakenly had chamomile tea, fell asleep and nearly drowned in my soup.
KOVALESKI

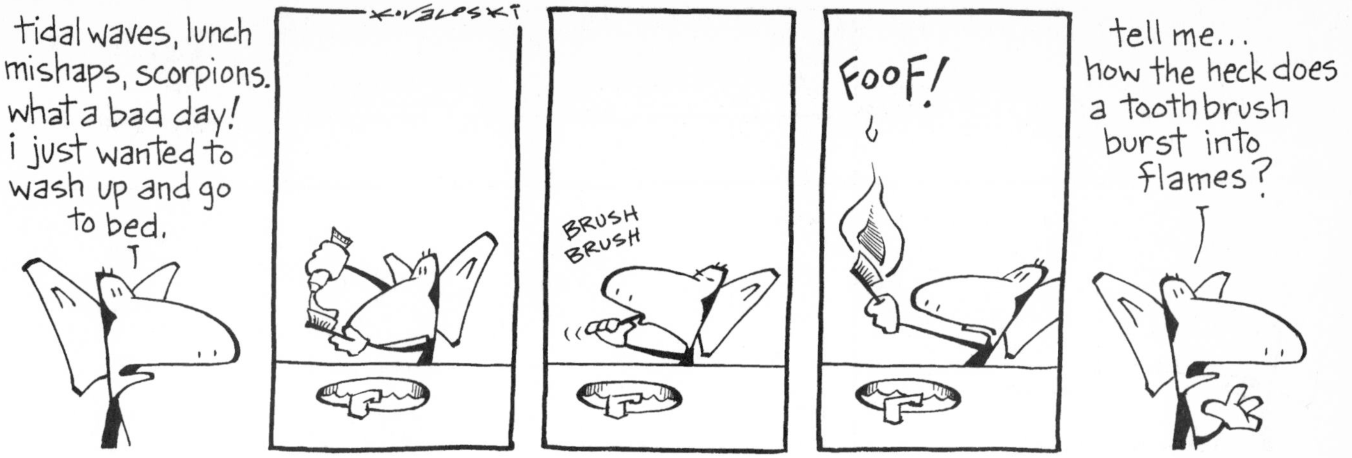

tidal waves, lunch mishaps, scorpions. what a bad day! i just wanted to wash up and go to bed.
KOVALESKI
BRUSH BRUSH
FOOF!
tell me... how the heck does a tooth brush burst into flames?

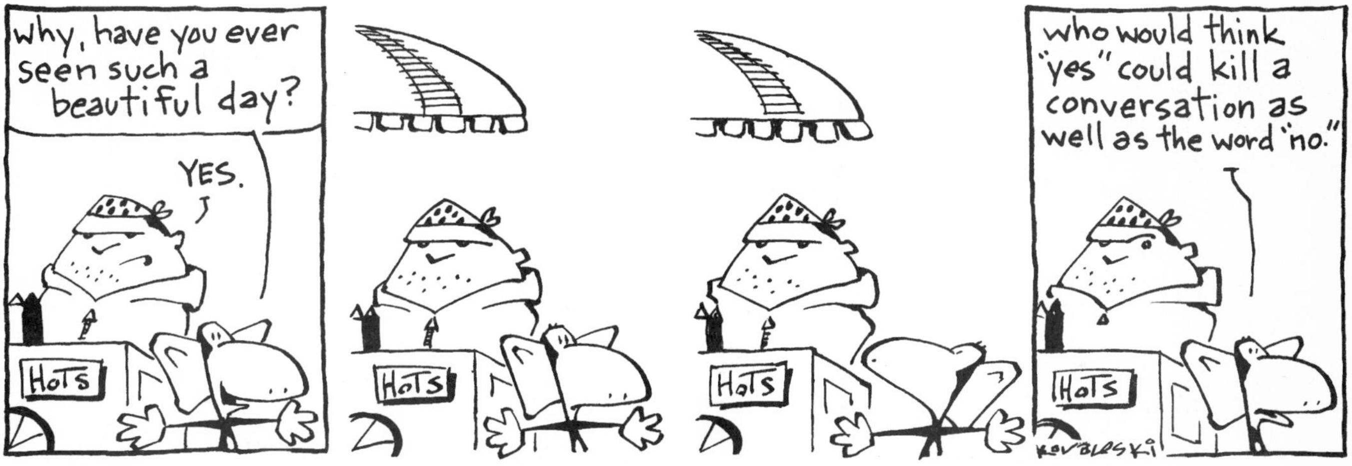

why, have you ever seen such a beautiful day?
YES.
HOTS
who would think "yes" could kill a conversation as well as the word "no."
KOVALESKI

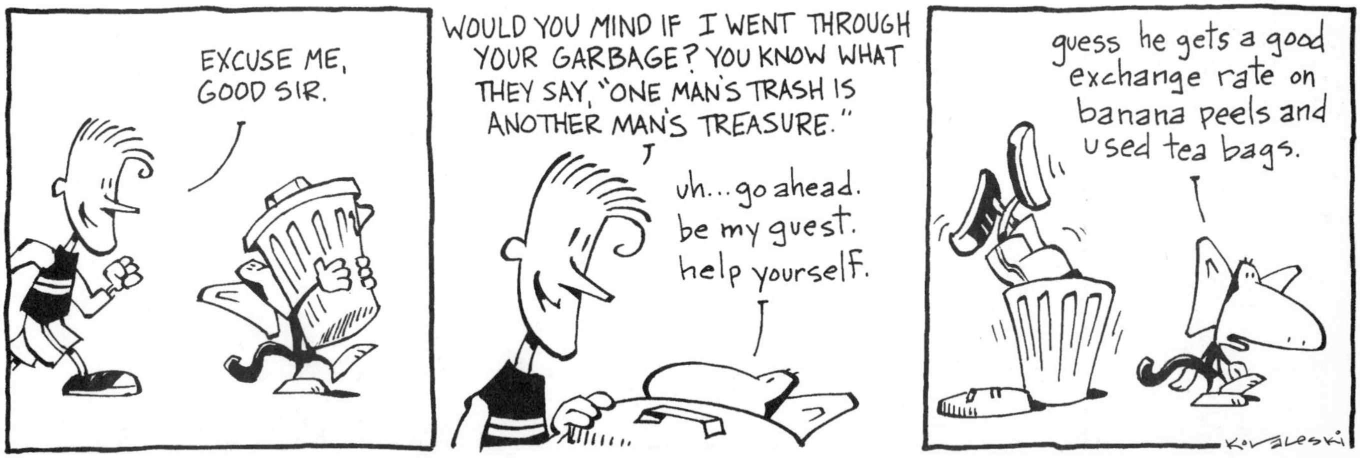

EXCUSE ME, GOOD SIR.
WOULD YOU MIND IF I WENT THROUGH YOUR GARBAGE? YOU KNOW WHAT THEY SAY, "ONE MAN'S TRASH IS ANOTHER MAN'S TREASURE."
uh... go ahead. be my guest. help yourself.
guess he gets a good exchange rate on banana peels and used tea bags.
KOVALESKI

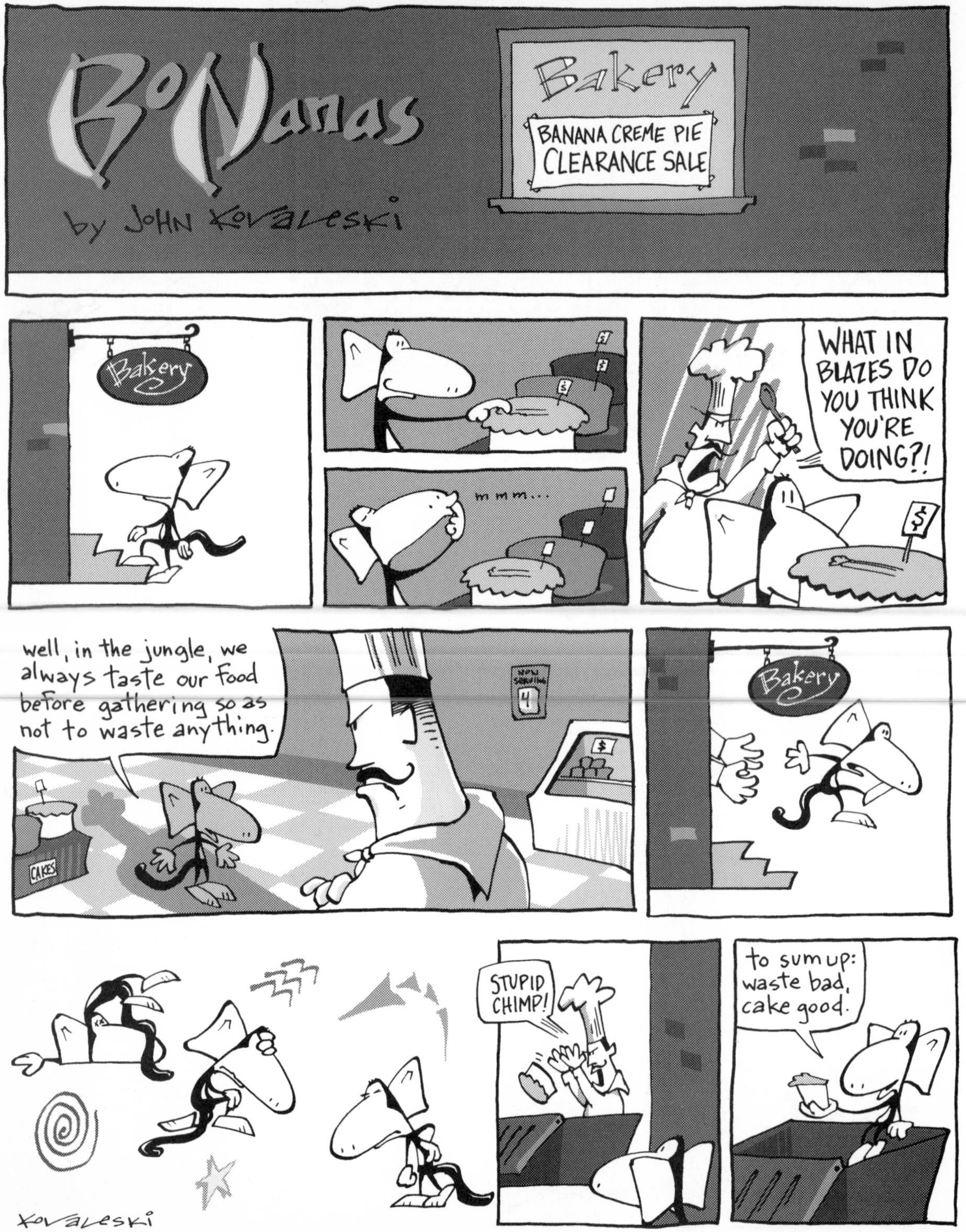
BoNanas
by John Kovaleski
Bakery
BANANA CREME PIE CLEARANCE SALE
Bakery
mmm...
WHAT IN BLAZES DO YOU THINK YOU'RE DOING?!
well, in the jungle, we always taste our food before gathering so as not to waste anything.
NOW SERVING 4
CAKES
Bakery
STUPID CHIMP!
to sum up: waste bad, cake good.
Kovaleski

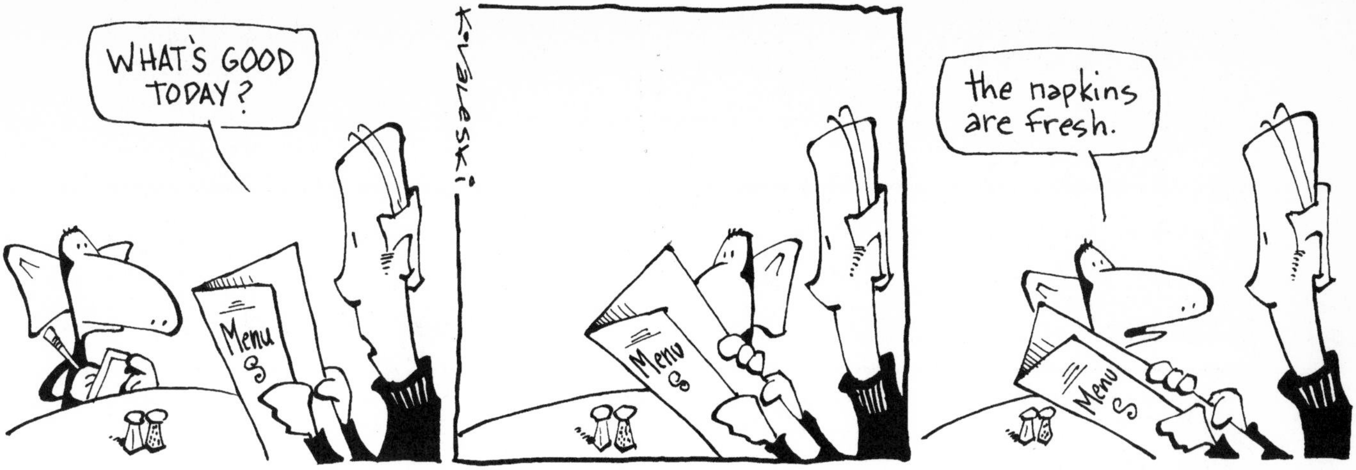
WHAT'S GOOD TODAY?
kovaleski
the napkins are fresh.
Menu

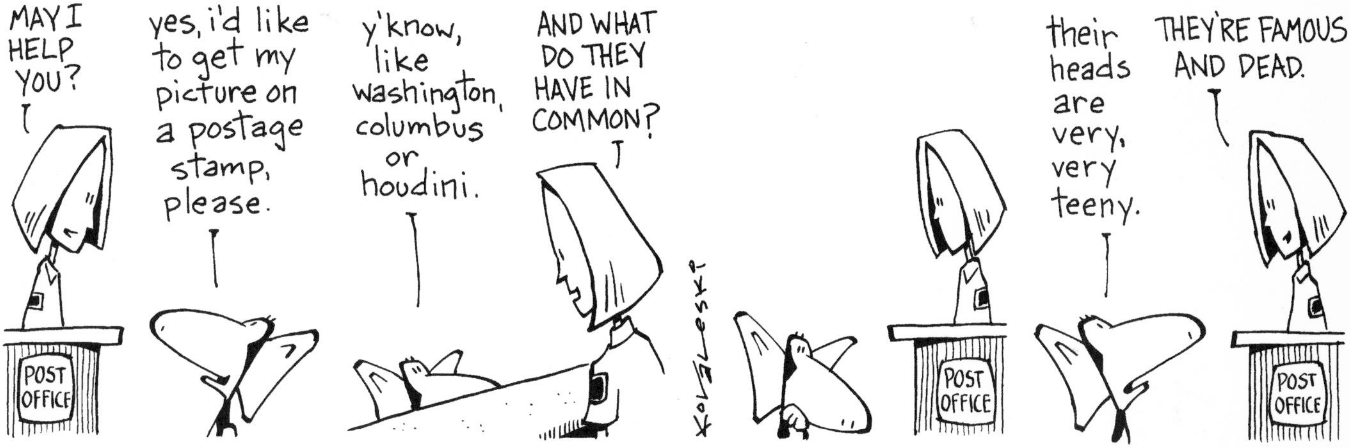
MAY I HELP YOU?
POST OFFICE
yes, i'd like to get my picture on a postage stamp, please.
y'know, like washington, columbus or houdini.
AND WHAT DO THEY HAVE IN COMMON?
kovaleski
their heads are very, very teeny.
THEY'RE FAMOUS AND DEAD.

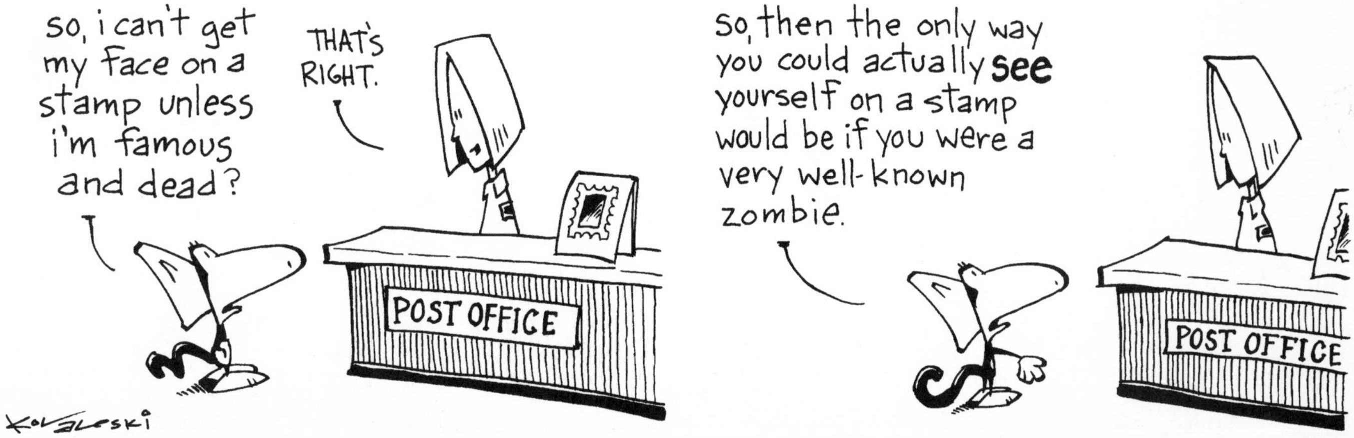
so, i can't get my face on a stamp unless i'm famous and dead?
THAT'S RIGHT.
POST OFFICE
kovaleski
so, then the only way you could actually **see** yourself on a stamp would be if you were a very well-known zombie.
POST OFFICE

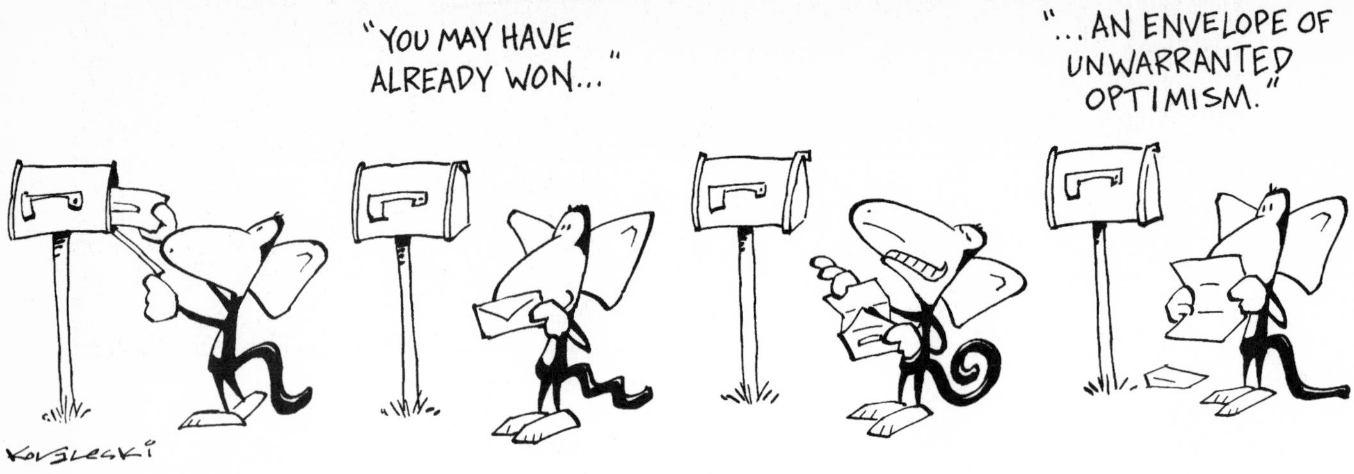
"YOU MAY HAVE ALREADY WON..."
"...AN ENVELOPE OF UNWARRANTED OPTIMISM."
KOVALESKI

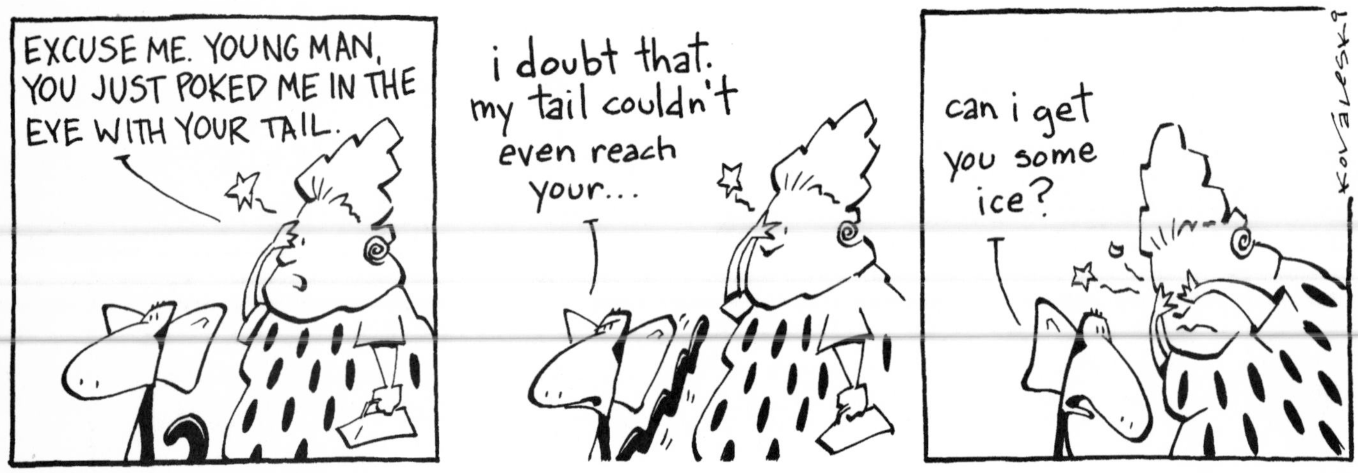
EXCUSE ME. YOUNG MAN, YOU JUST POKED ME IN THE EYE WITH YOUR TAIL.
i doubt that. my tail couldn't even reach your...
can i get you some ice?
KOVALESKI

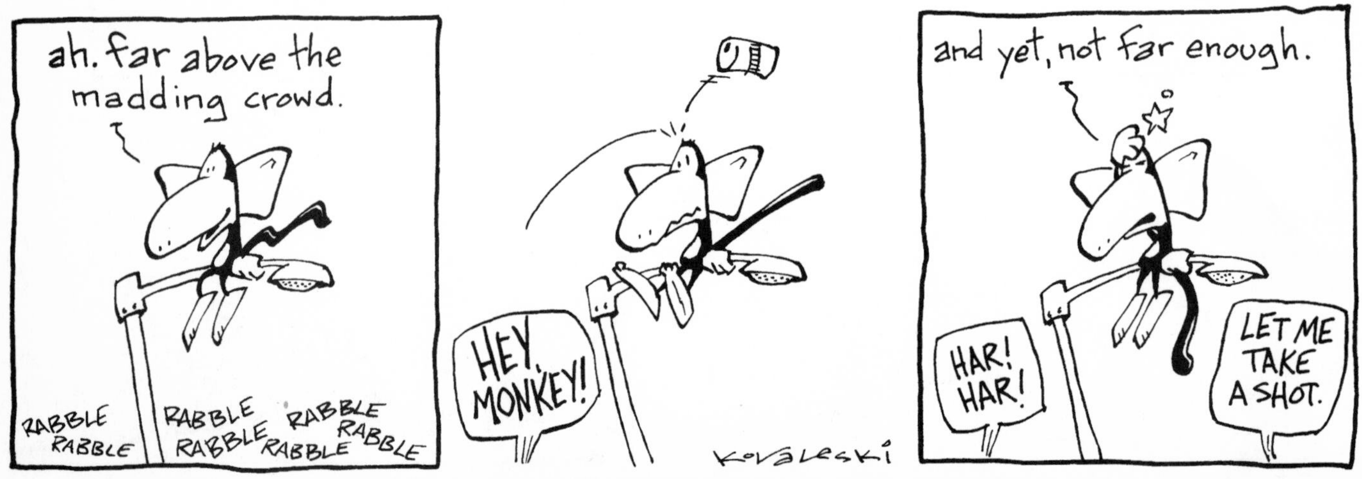
ah. far above the madding crowd.
RABBLE RABBLE RABBLE RABBLE RABBLE RABBLE RABBLE RABBLE
HEY, MONKEY!
and yet, not far enough.
HAR! HAR!
LET ME TAKE A SHOT.
KOVALESKI

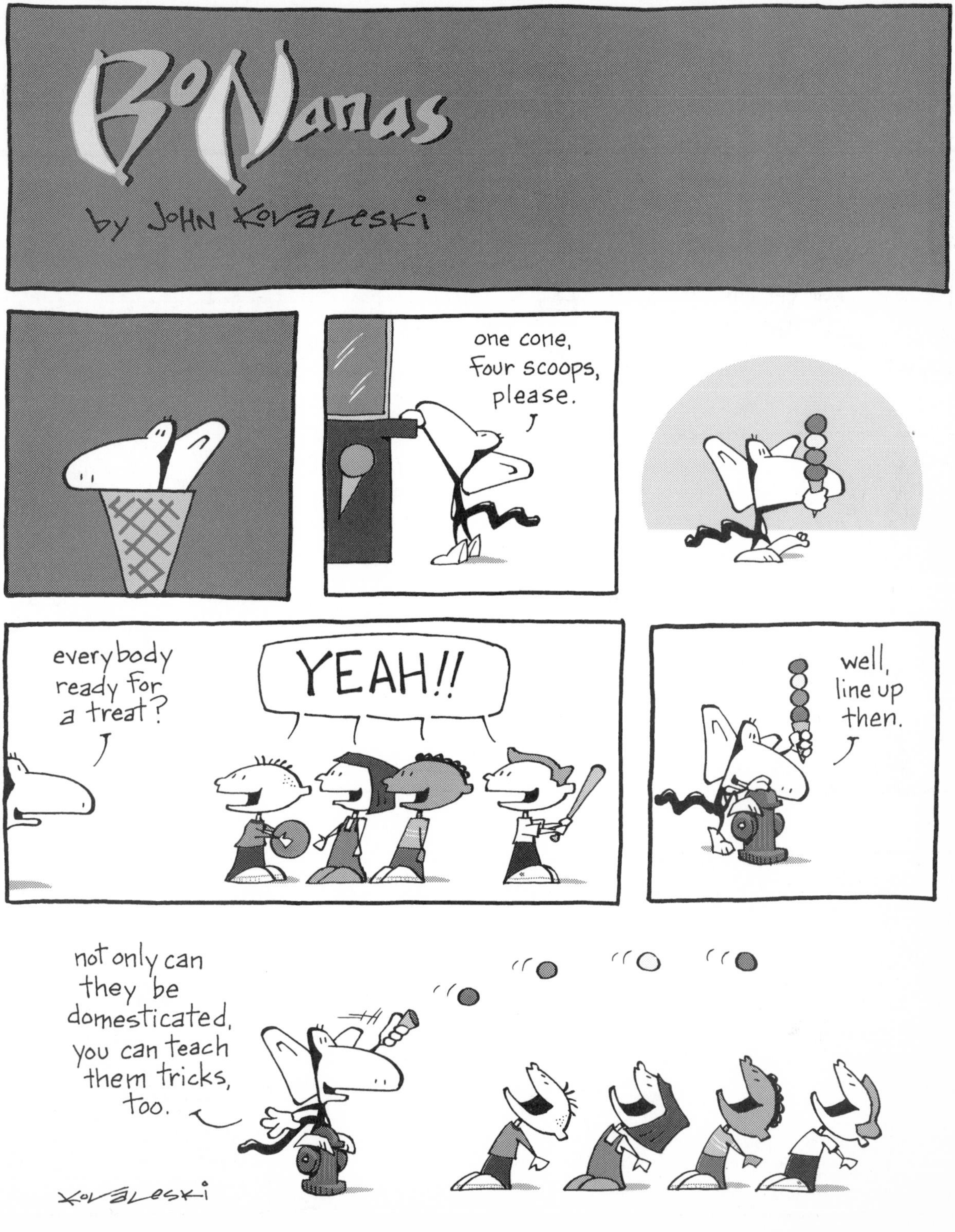
BoNanas
by JOHN KOVALESKI
one cone, four scoops, please.
everybody ready for a treat?
YEAH!!
well, line up then.
not only can they be domesticated, you can teach them tricks, too.
KOVALESKI

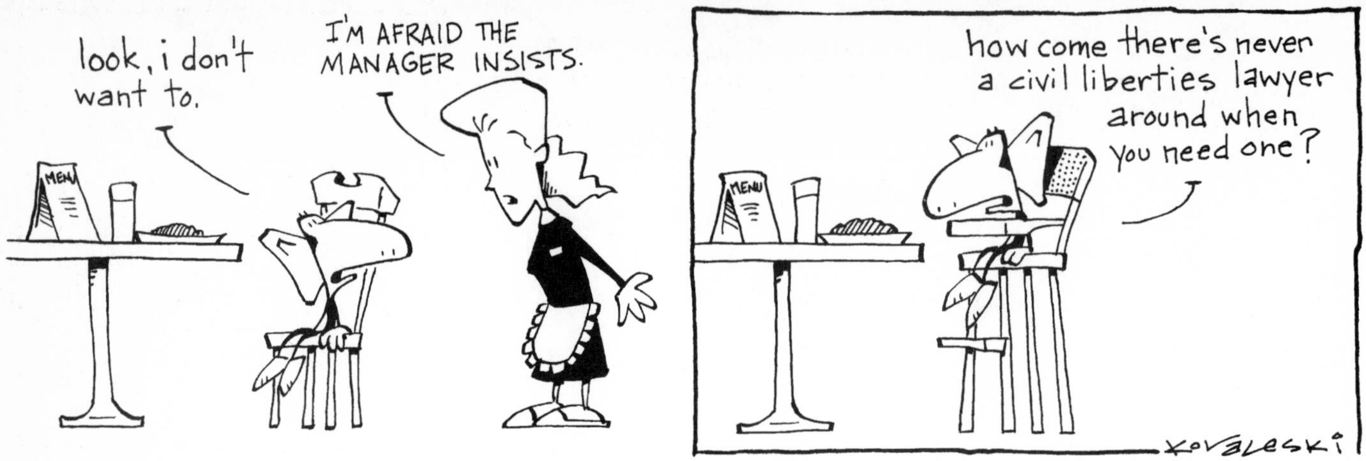
look, i don't want to.
I'M AFRAID THE MANAGER INSISTS.
how come there's never a civil liberties lawyer around when you need one?
KOVALESKI

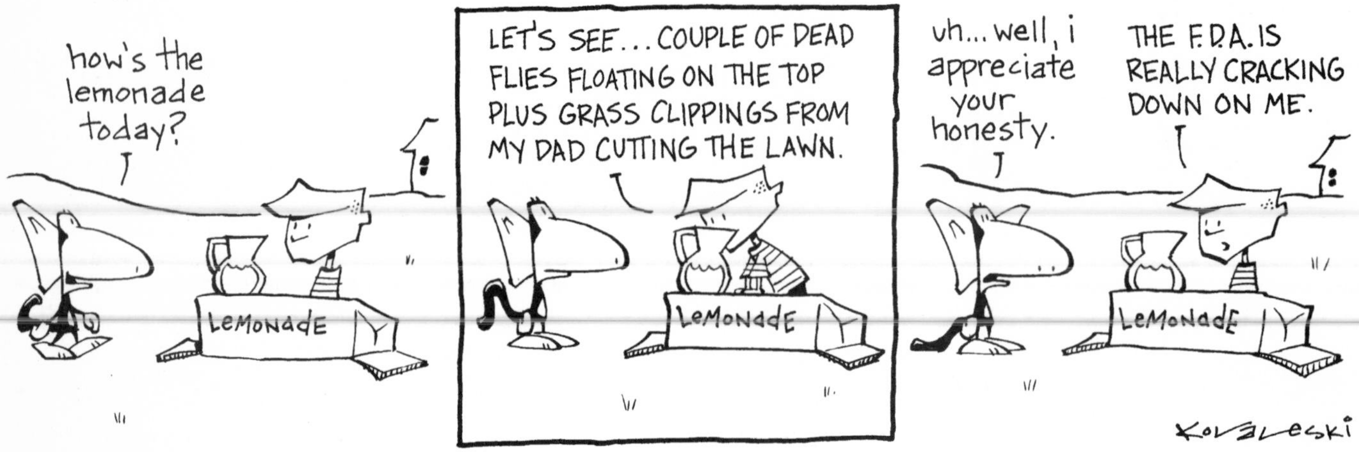
how's the lemonade today?
LET'S SEE... COUPLE OF DEAD FLIES FLOATING ON THE TOP PLUS GRASS CLIPPINGS FROM MY DAD CUTTING THE LAWN.
uh... well, i appreciate your honesty.
THE F.D.A. IS REALLY CRACKING DOWN ON ME.
LEMONADE
KOVALESKI

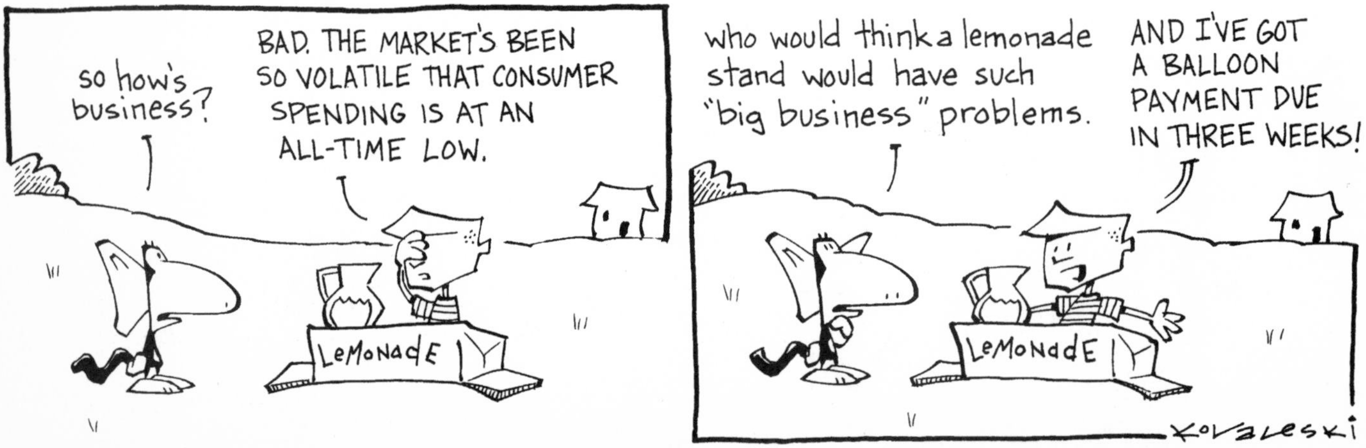
so how's business?
BAD. THE MARKET'S BEEN SO VOLATILE THAT CONSUMER SPENDING IS AT AN ALL-TIME LOW.
who would think a lemonade stand would have such "big business" problems.
AND I'VE GOT A BALLOON PAYMENT DUE IN THREE WEEKS!
LEMONADE
KOVALESKI

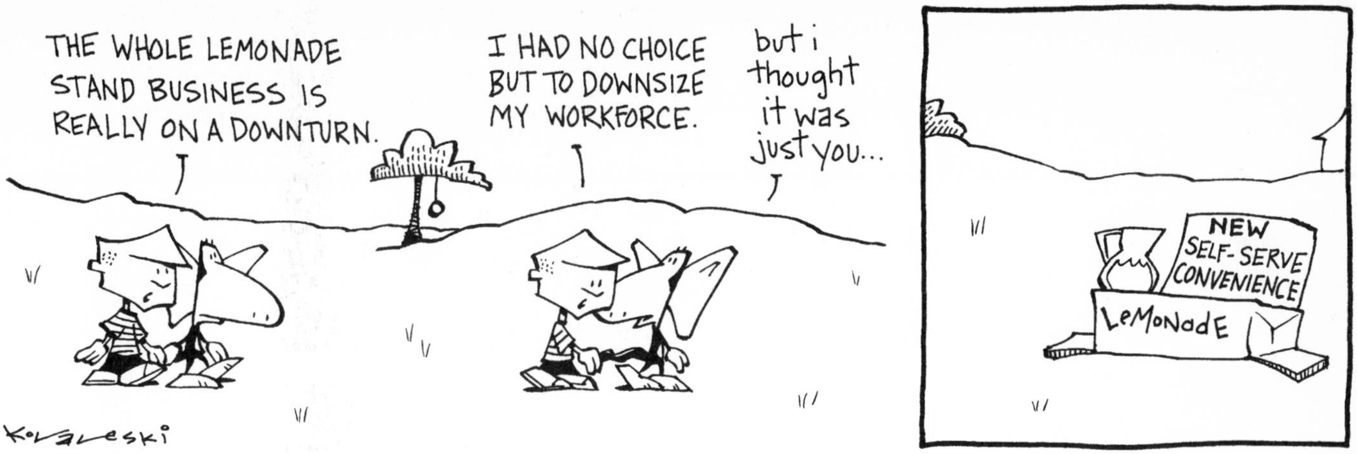
THE WHOLE LEMONADE STAND BUSINESS IS REALLY ON A DOWNTURN.
I HAD NO CHOICE BUT TO DOWNSIZE MY WORKFORCE.
but i thought it was just you...
NEW SELF-SERVE CONVENIENCE
LeMoNadE
KOVALESKI

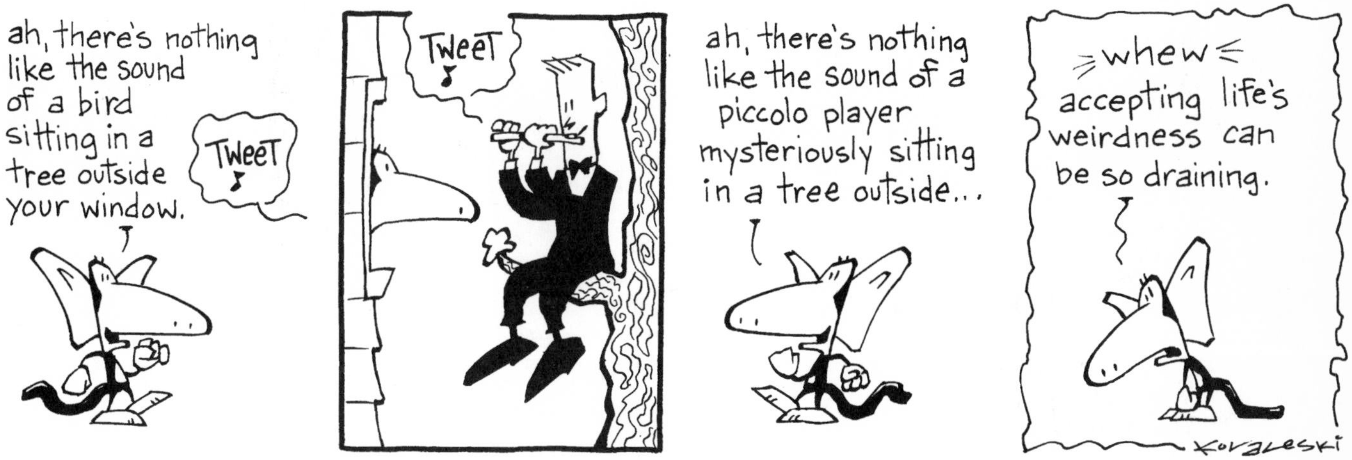
ah, there's nothing like the sound of a bird sitting in a tree outside your window.
TWEET
TWEET
ah, there's nothing like the sound of a piccolo player mysteriously sitting in a tree outside...
whew
accepting life's weirdness can be so draining.
KOVALESKI

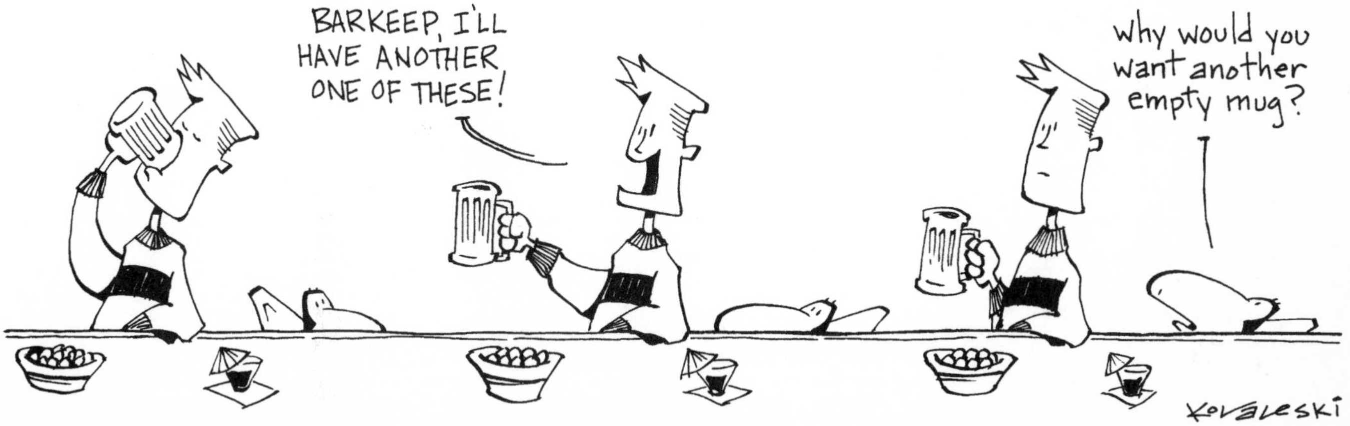
BARKEEP, I'LL HAVE ANOTHER ONE OF THESE!
Why would you want another empty mug?
KOVALESKI

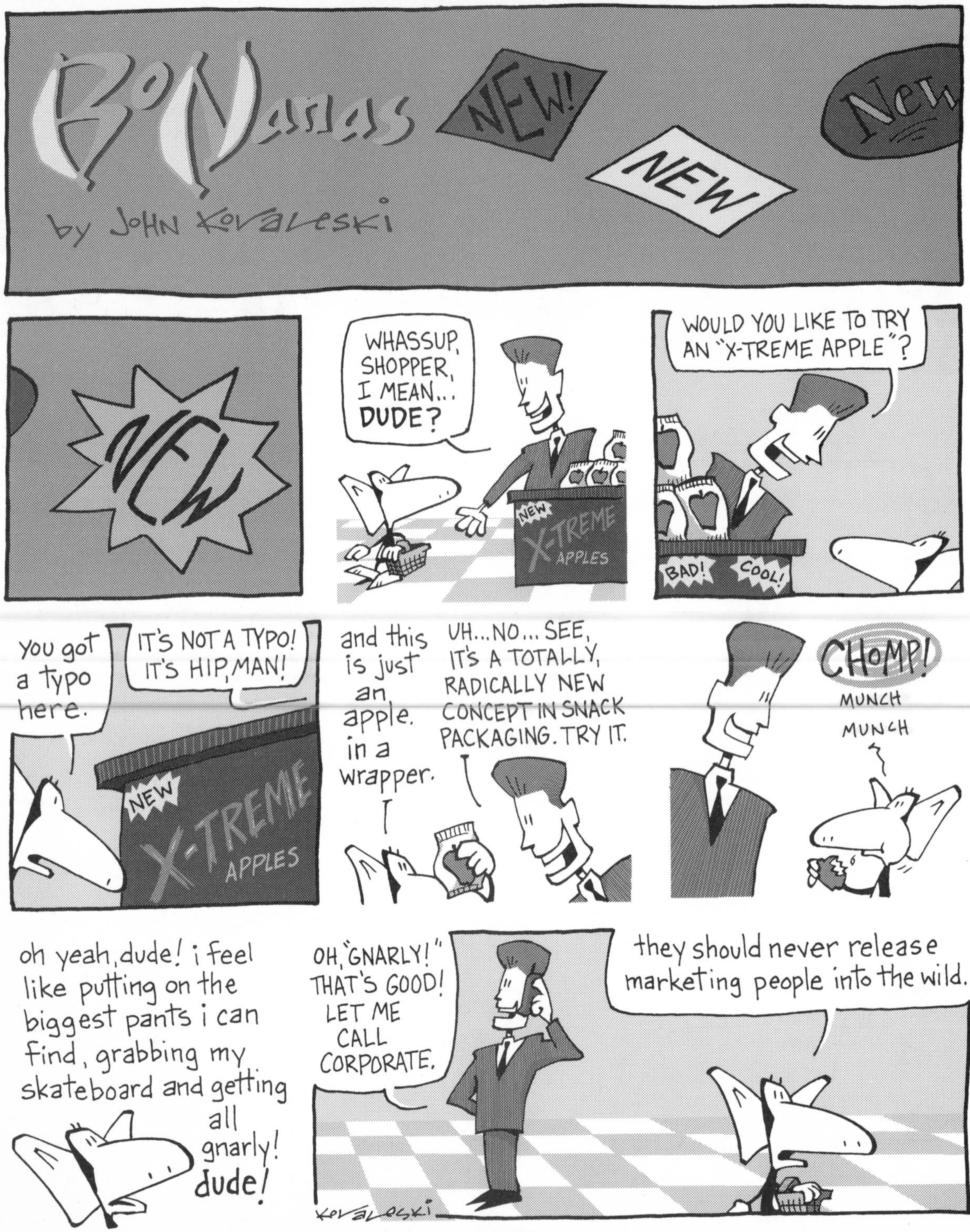

Bo Nanas
NEW!
New
NEW
by JOHN KOVALESKI
NEW
WHASSUP, SHOPPER, I MEAN... DUDE?
NEW X-TREME APPLES
WOULD YOU LIKE TO TRY AN "X-TREME APPLE"?
BAD!
COOL!
You got a typo here.
IT'S NOT A TYPO! IT'S HIP, MAN!
NEW X-TREME APPLES
and this is just an apple. in a wrapper.
UH... NO... SEE, IT'S A TOTALLY, RADICALLY NEW CONCEPT IN SNACK PACKAGING. TRY IT.
CHOMP!
MUNCH
MUNCH
oh yeah, dude! i feel like putting on the biggest pants i can find, grabbing my skateboard and getting all gnarly! dude!
OH, "GNARLY!" THAT'S GOOD! LET ME CALL CORPORATE.
they should never release marketing people into the wild.
KOVALESKI

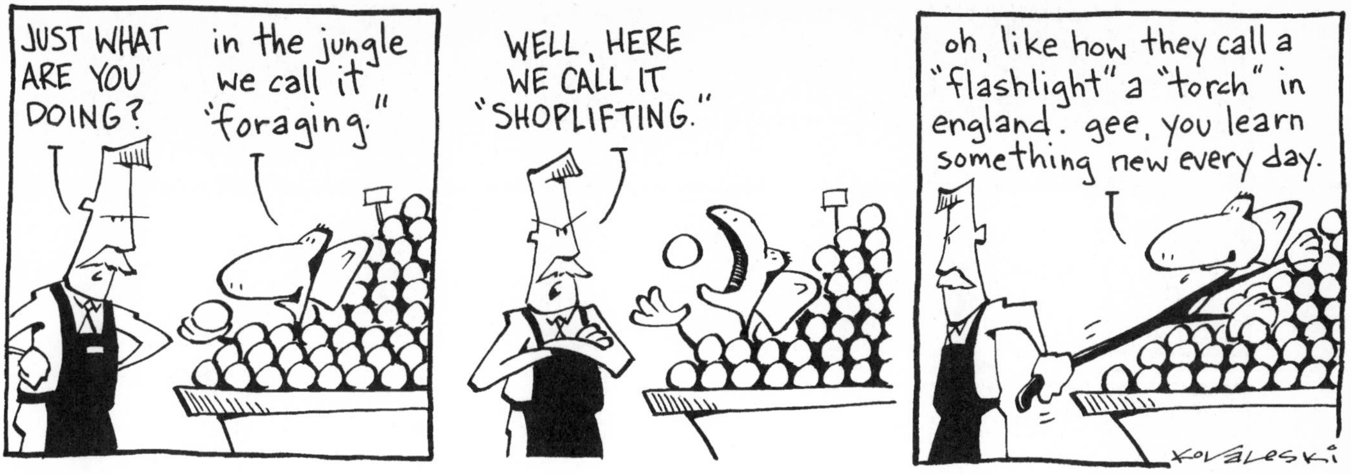
JUST WHAT ARE YOU DOING?
in the jungle we call it "foraging."
WELL, HERE WE CALL IT "SHOPLIFTING."
oh, like how they call a "flashlight" a "torch" in england. gee, you learn something new every day.
KOVALESKI

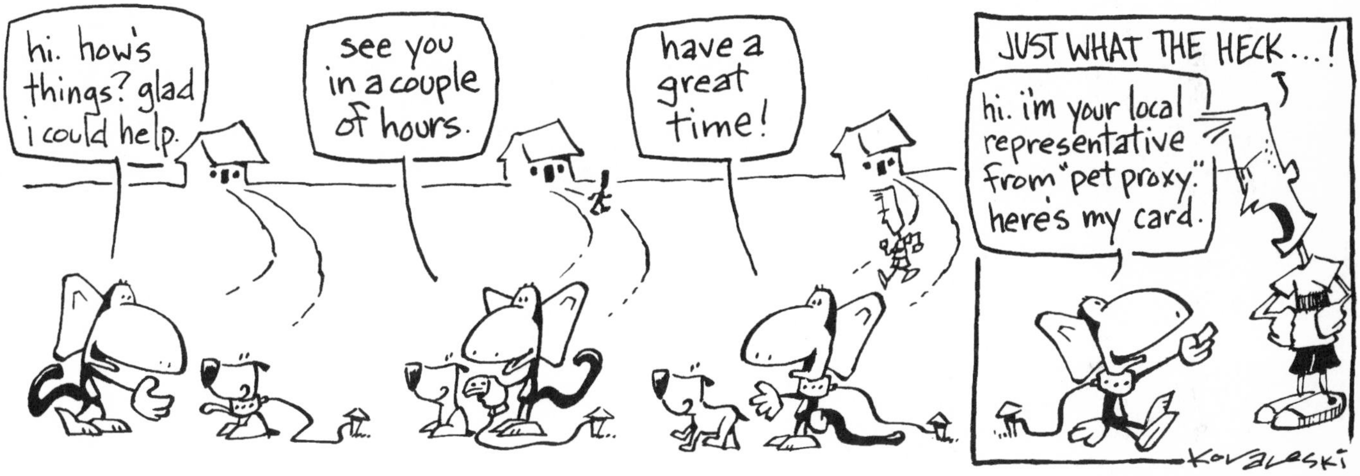
hi. how's things? glad i could help.
see you in a couple of hours.
have a great time!
JUST WHAT THE HECK...!
hi. i'm your local representative from "pet proxy." here's my card.
KOVALESKI

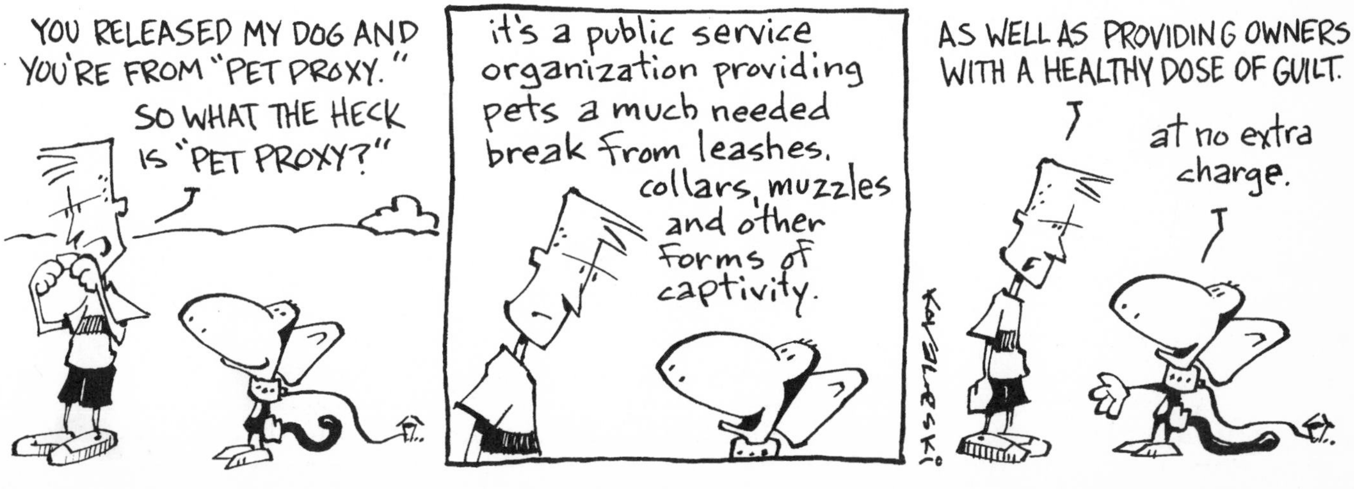
YOU RELEASED MY DOG AND YOU'RE FROM "PET PROXY."
SO WHAT THE HECK IS "PET PROXY?"
it's a public service organization providing pets a much needed break from leashes.
collars, muzzles and other forms of captivity.
KOVALESKI
AS WELL AS PROVIDING OWNERS WITH A HEALTHY DOSE OF GUILT.
at no extra charge.

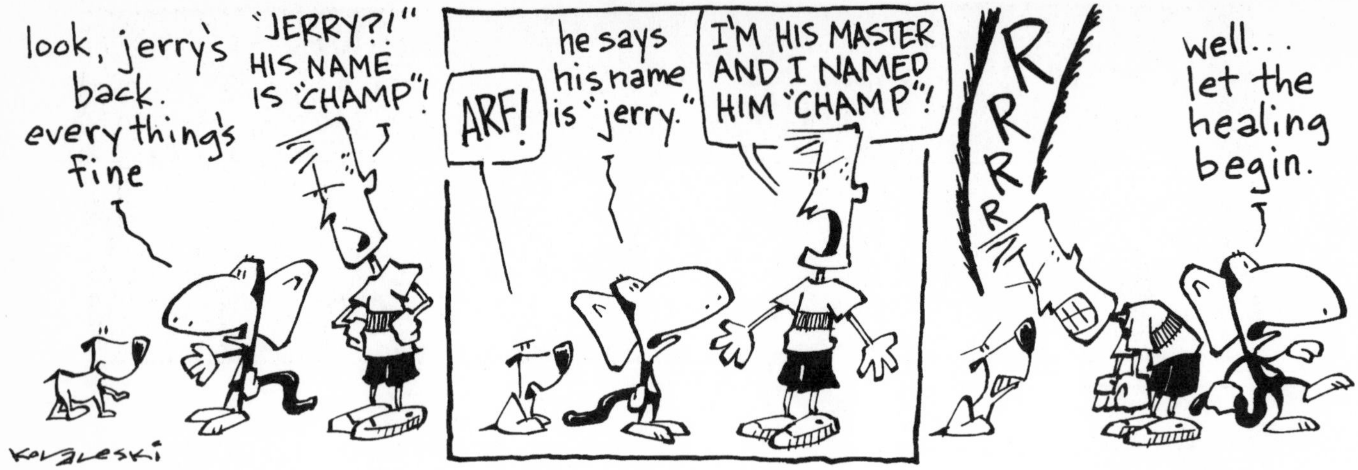
look, jerry's back. every thing's fine
"JERRY?!" HIS NAME IS "CHAMP"!
ARF!
he says his name is "jerry."
I'M HIS MASTER AND I NAMED HIM "CHAMP"!
RRRR
well... let the healing begin.
KOVALESKI

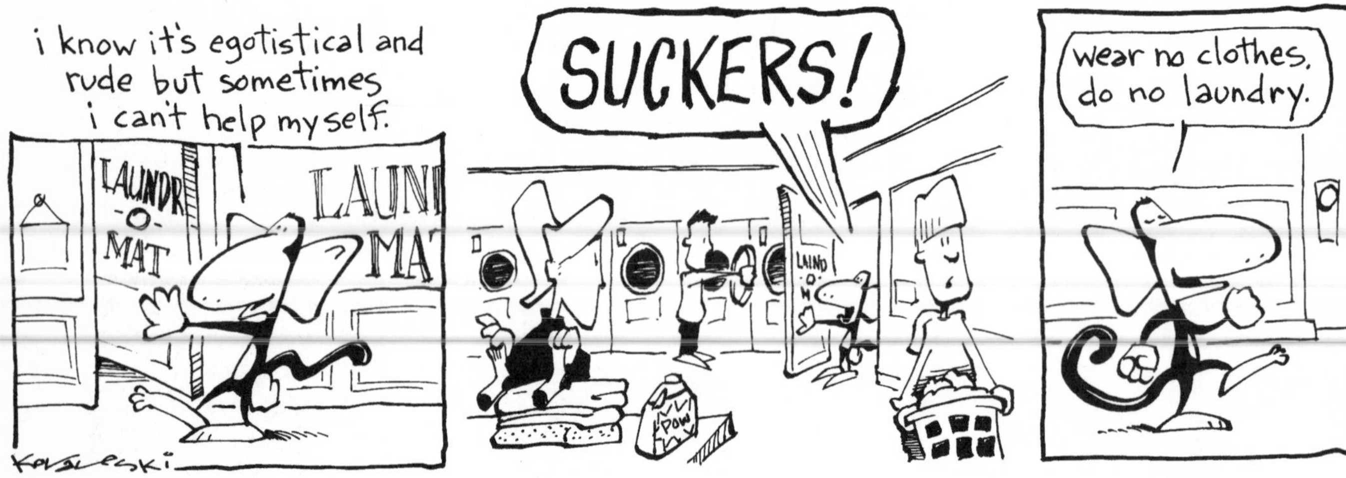
i know it's egotistical and rude but sometimes i can't help myself.
LAUNDR-O-MAT
LAUN MAT
SUCKERS!
POW
wear no clothes, do no laundry.
KOVALESKI

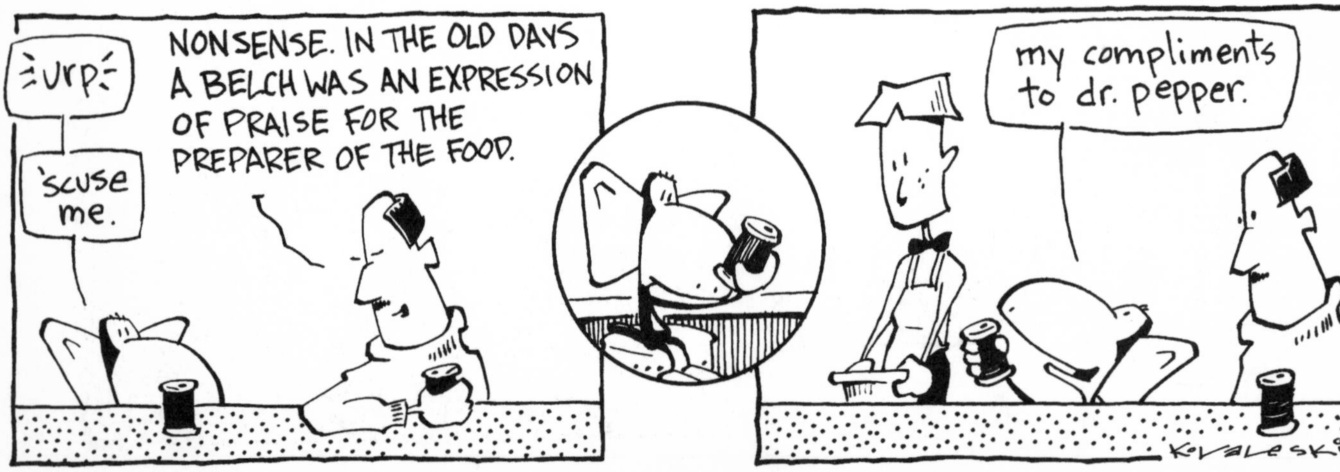
urp
'scuse me.
NONSENSE. IN THE OLD DAYS A BELCH WAS AN EXPRESSION OF PRAISE FOR THE PREPARER OF THE FOOD.
my compliments to dr. pepper.
KOVALESKI

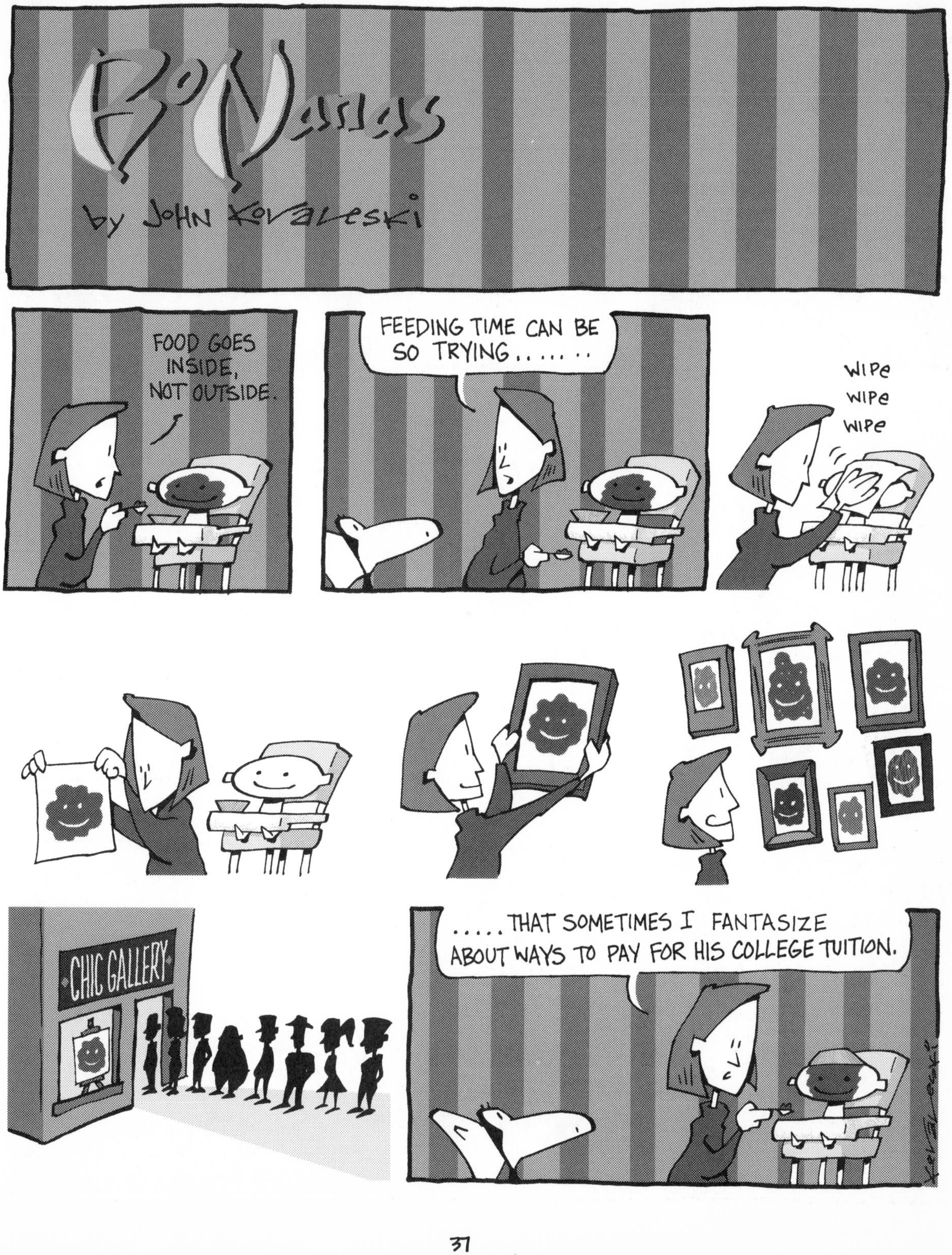

BoNeheads
by John Kovaleski
FOOD GOES INSIDE, NOT OUTSIDE.
FEEDING TIME CAN BE SO TRYING......
WIPE WIPE WIPE
CHIC GALLERY
.....THAT SOMETIMES I FANTASIZE ABOUT WAYS TO PAY FOR HIS COLLEGE TUITION.
KOVALESKI

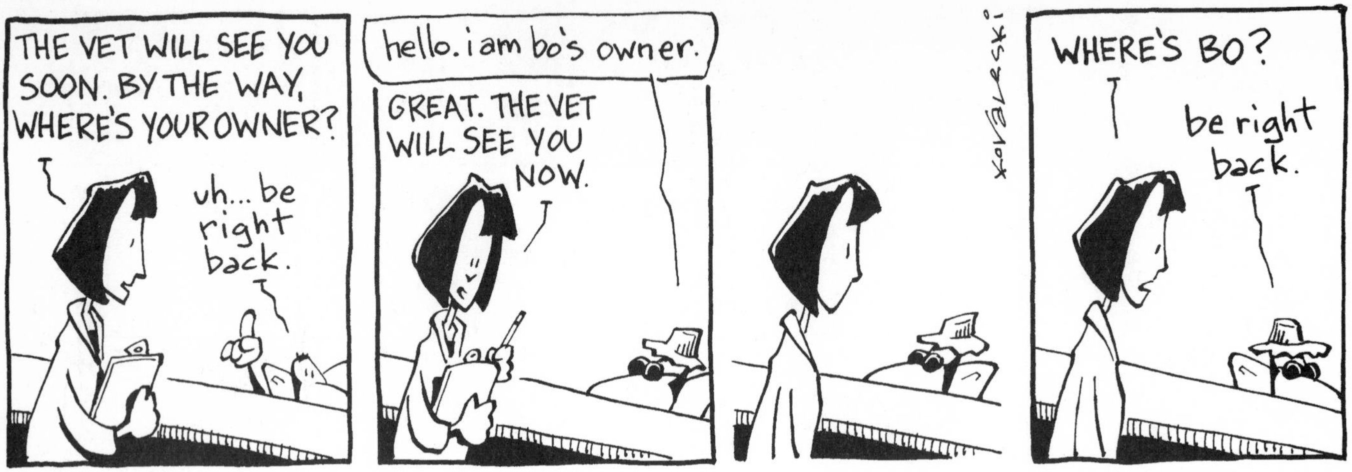
THE VET WILL SEE YOU SOON. BY THE WAY, WHERE'S YOUR OWNER?
uh... be right back.
hello. i am bo's owner.
GREAT. THE VET WILL SEE YOU NOW.
KOVALESKI
WHERE'S BO?
be right back.

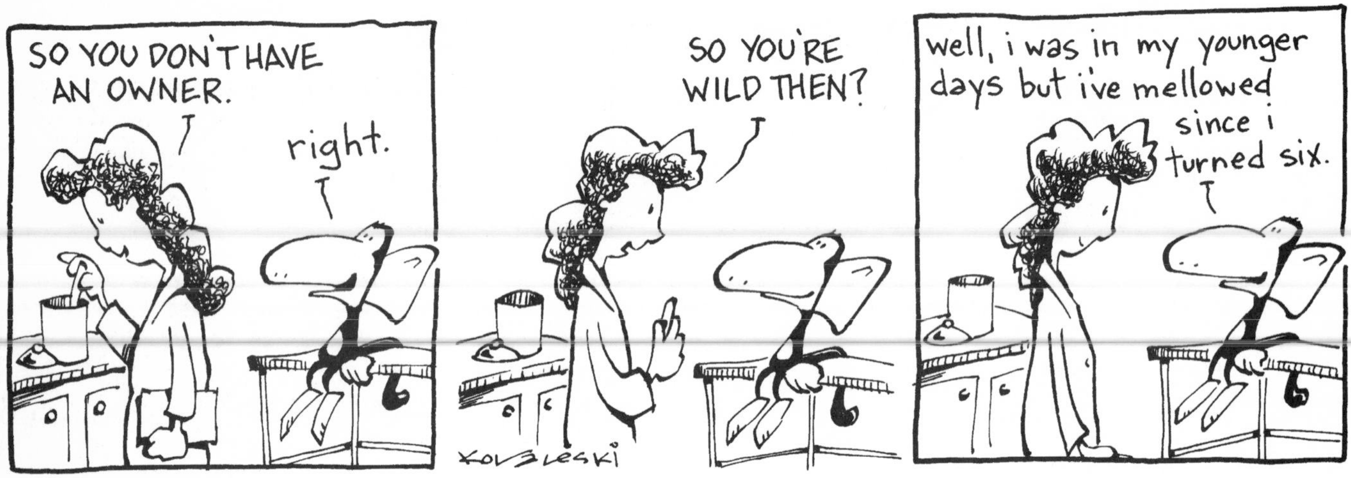
SO YOU DON'T HAVE AN OWNER.
right.
SO YOU'RE WILD THEN?
KOVALESKI
well, i was in my younger days but i've mellowed since i turned six.

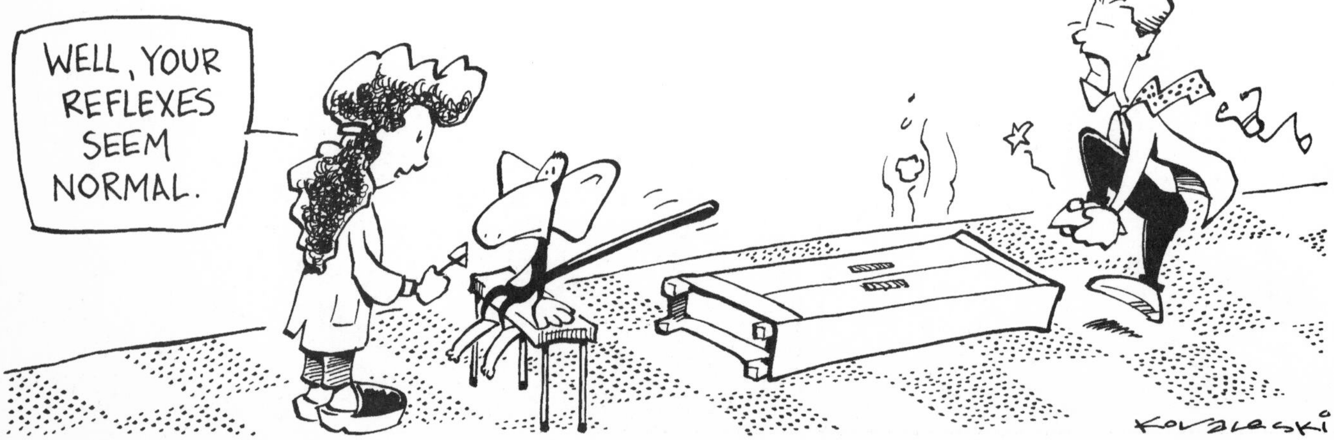
WELL, YOUR REFLEXES SEEM NORMAL.
KOVALESKI

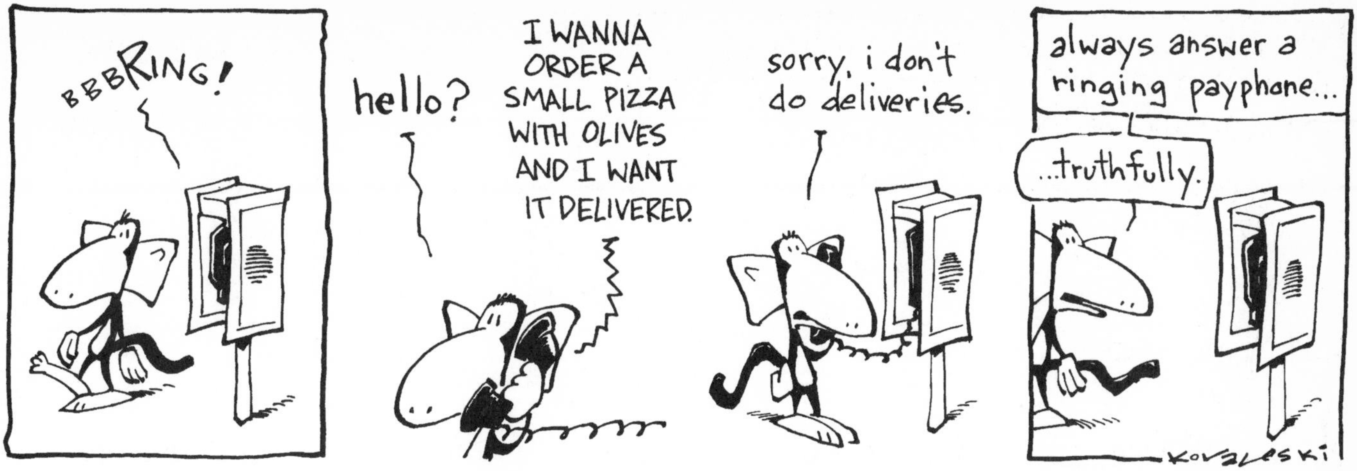
BBBRING!
hello?
I WANNA ORDER A SMALL PIZZA WITH OLIVES AND I WANT IT DELIVERED.
sorry, i don't do deliveries.
always answer a ringing payphone...
...truthfully.
KOVALESKI

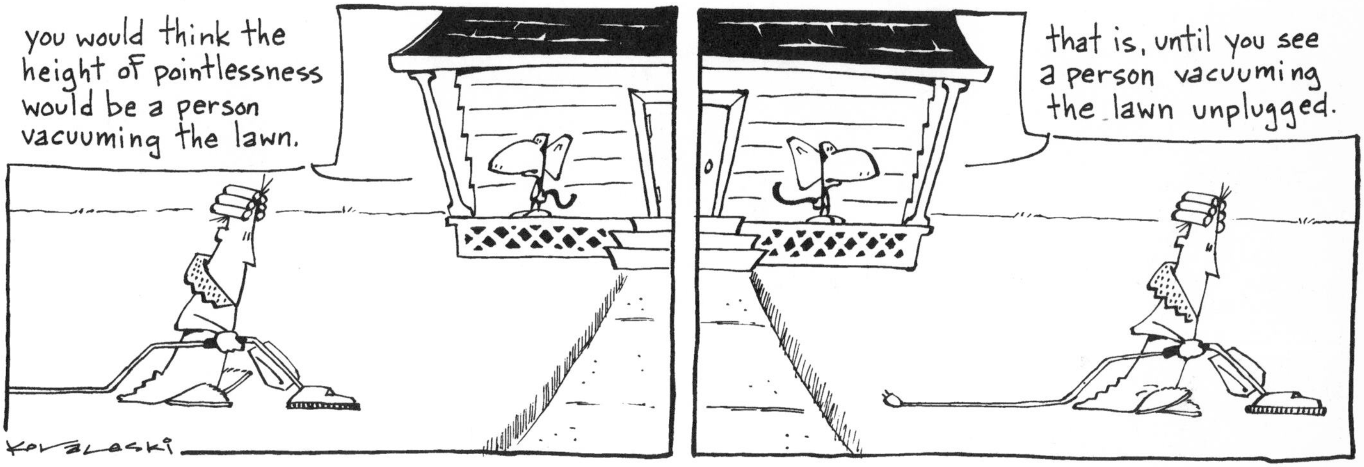
you would think the height of pointlessness would be a person vacuuming the lawn.
that is, until you see a person vacuuming the lawn unplugged.
KOVALESKI

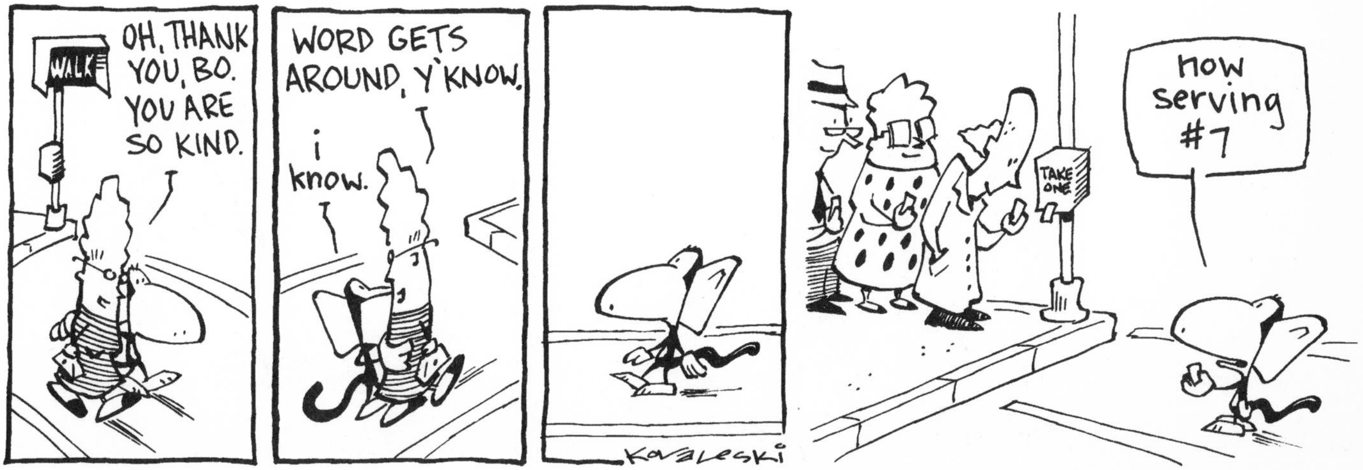
WALK
OH, THANK YOU, BO. YOU ARE SO KIND.
WORD GETS AROUND, Y'KNOW.
i know.
TAKE ONE
now serving #7
KOVALESKI

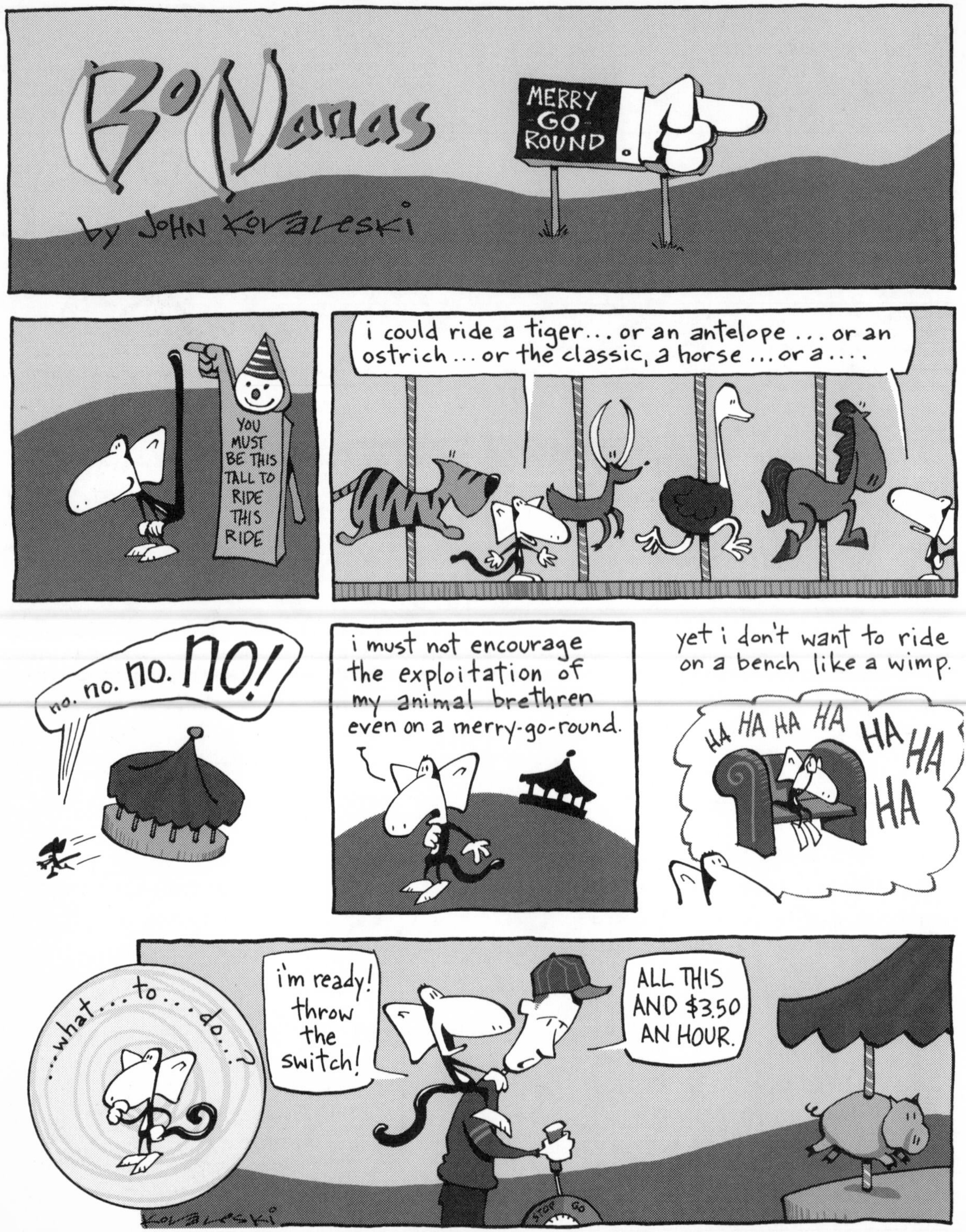
BoNanas
by JOHN KOVALESKI
MERRY GO ROUND
YOU MUST BE THIS TALL TO RIDE THIS RIDE
i could ride a tiger... or an antelope ... or an ostrich... or the classic, a horse ... or a....
no. no. no. NO!
i must not encourage the exploitation of my animal brethren even on a merry-go-round.
yet i don't want to ride on a bench like a wimp.
HA HA HA HA HA HA HA
...what...to...do...?
i'm ready! throw the switch!
ALL THIS AND $3.50 AN HOUR.
STOP GO
KOVALESKI

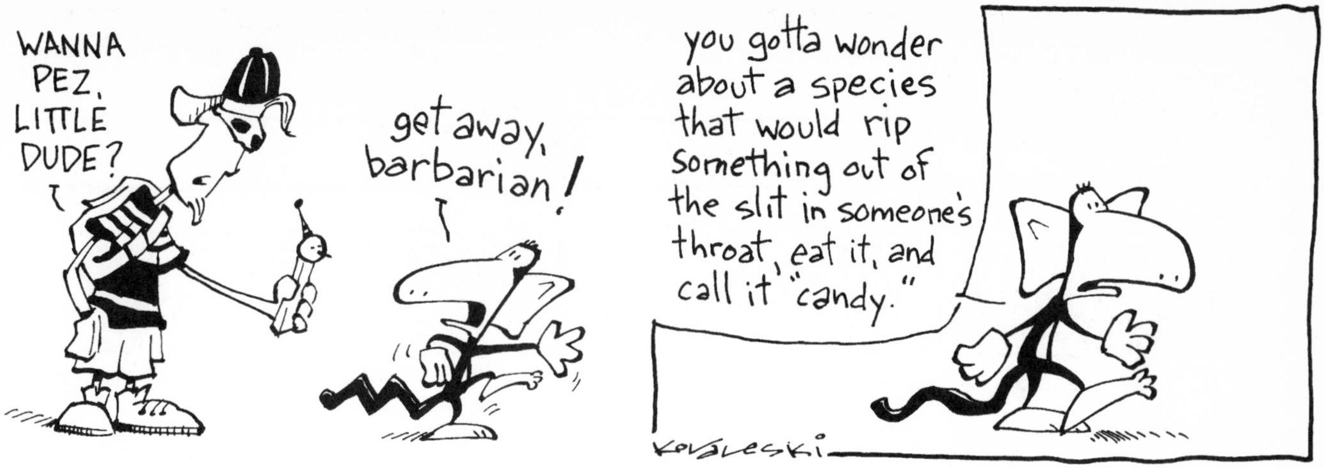
WANNA PEZ, LITTLE DUDE?
get away, barbarian!
you gotta wonder about a species that would rip something out of the slit in someone's throat, eat it, and call it "candy."
KOVALESKI

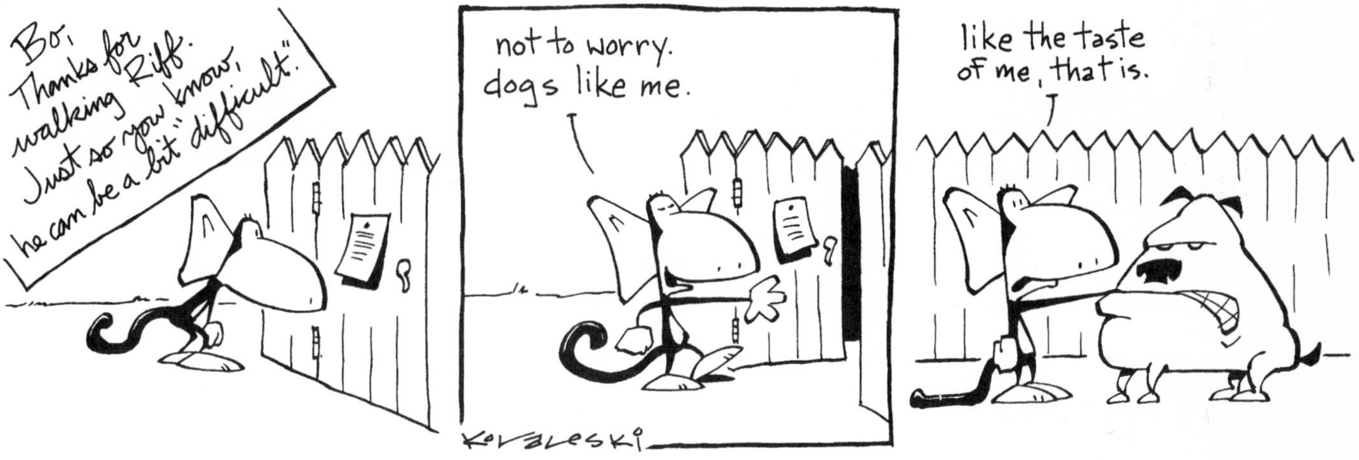
Bo, Thanks for walking Riff. Just so you know, he can be a bit "difficult."
not to worry. dogs like me.
KOVALESKI
like the taste of me, that is.

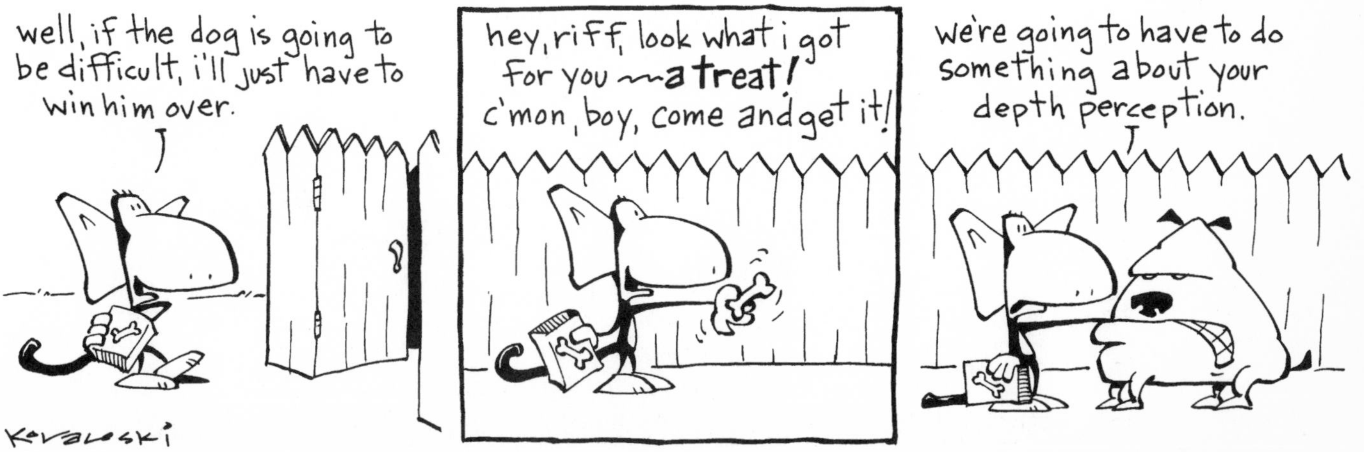
well, if the dog is going to be difficult, i'll just have to win him over.
KOVALESKI
hey, riff, look what i got for you ~ a treat! c'mon, boy, come and get it!
we're going to have to do something about your depth perception.

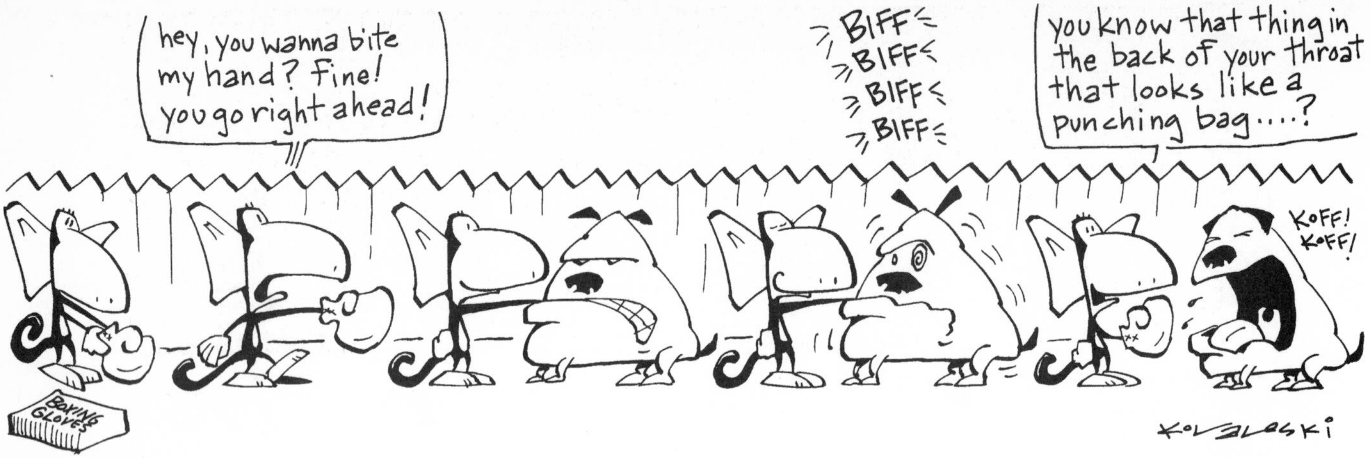

hey, you wanna bite my hand? fine! you go right ahead!
BOXING GLOVES
BIFF BIFF BIFF BIFF
you know that thing in the back of your throat that looks like a punching bag....?
KOFF! KOFF!
KOVALESKI

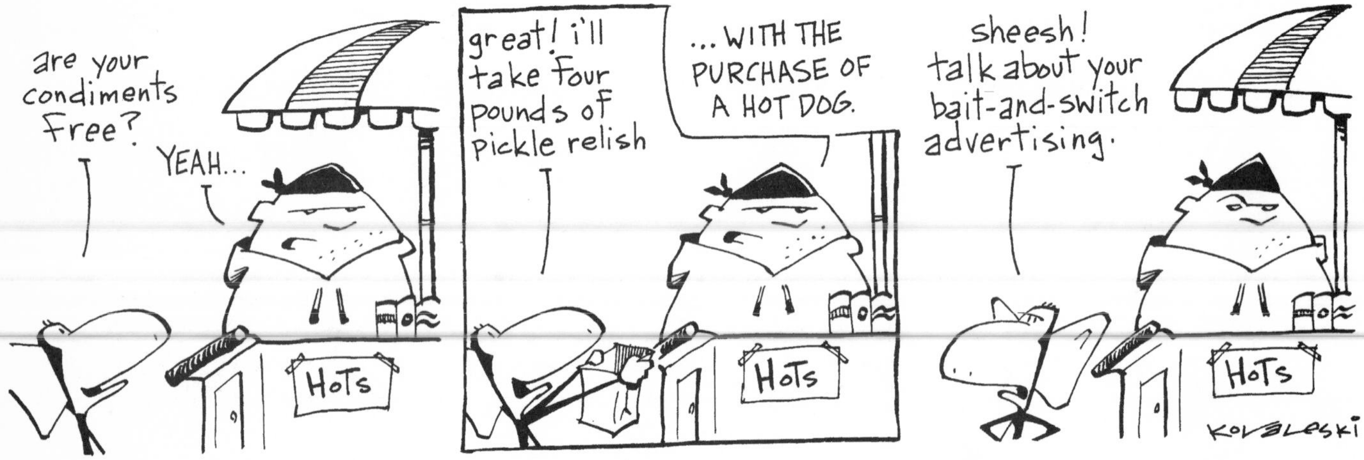

are your condiments free?
YEAH...
HOTS
great! i'll take four pounds of pickle relish
...WITH THE PURCHASE OF A HOT DOG.
HOTS
sheesh! talk about your bait-and-switch advertising.
HOTS
KOVALESKI

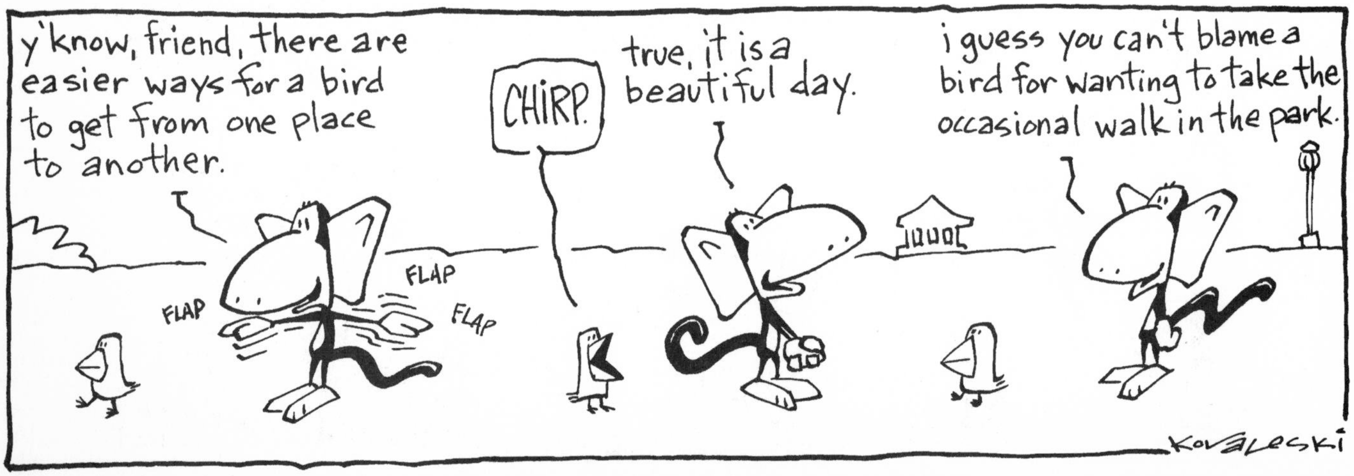

y'know, friend, there are easier ways for a bird to get from one place to another.
FLAP
FLAP
FLAP
CHIRP.
true, it is a beautiful day.
i guess you can't blame a bird for wanting to take the occasional walk in the park.
KOVALESKI

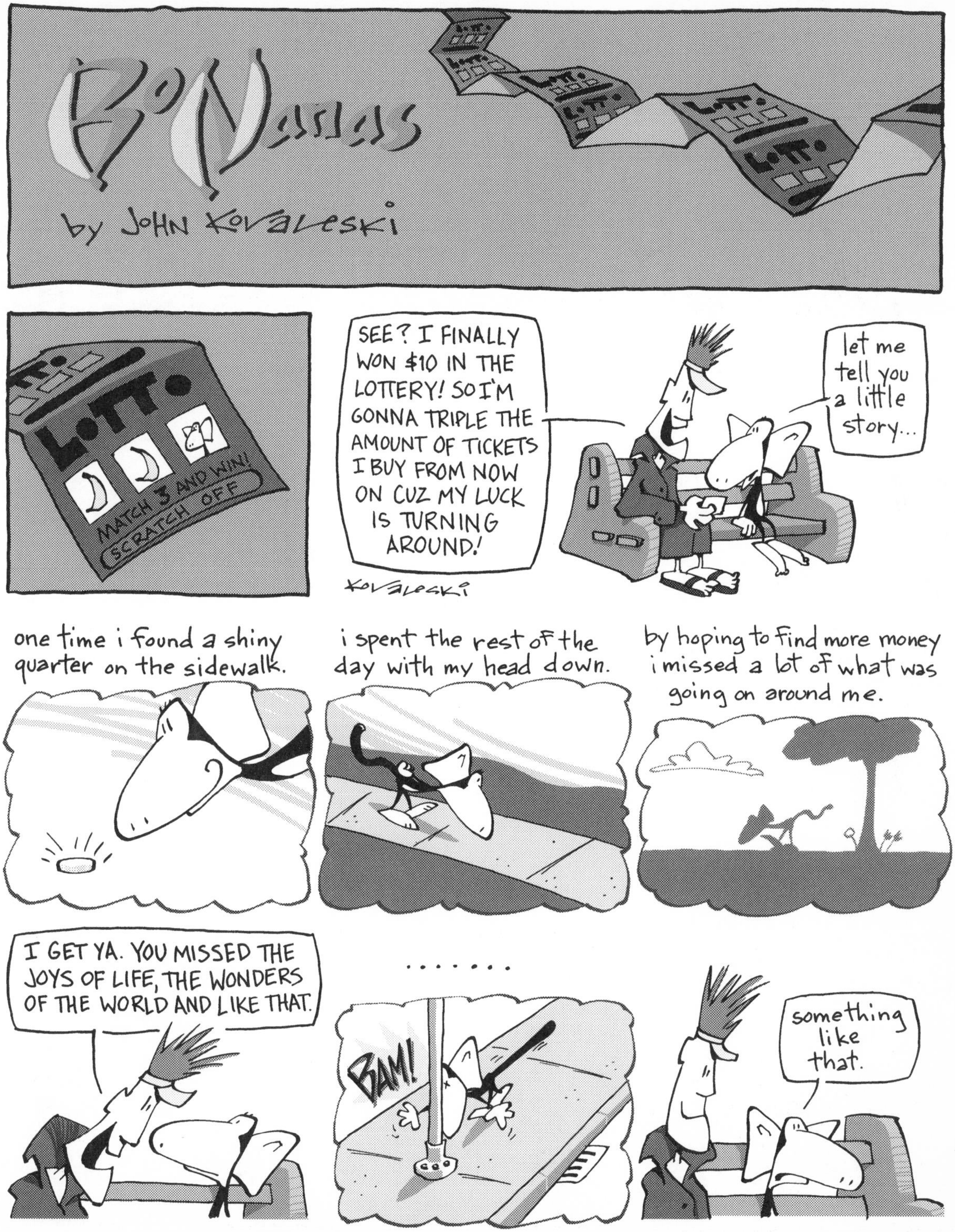
BoNdgggs
by John Kovaleski
LOTTO
MATCH 3 AND WIN!
SCRATCH OFF
SEE? I FINALLY WON $10 IN THE LOTTERY! SO I'M GONNA TRIPLE THE AMOUNT OF TICKETS I BUY FROM NOW ON CUZ MY LUCK IS TURNING AROUND!
let me tell you a little story...
KOVALESKI
one time i found a shiny quarter on the sidewalk.
i spent the rest of the day with my head down.
by hoping to find more money i missed a lot of what was going on around me.
I GET YA. YOU MISSED THE JOYS OF LIFE, THE WONDERS OF THE WORLD AND LIKE THAT.
....
BAM!
something like that.

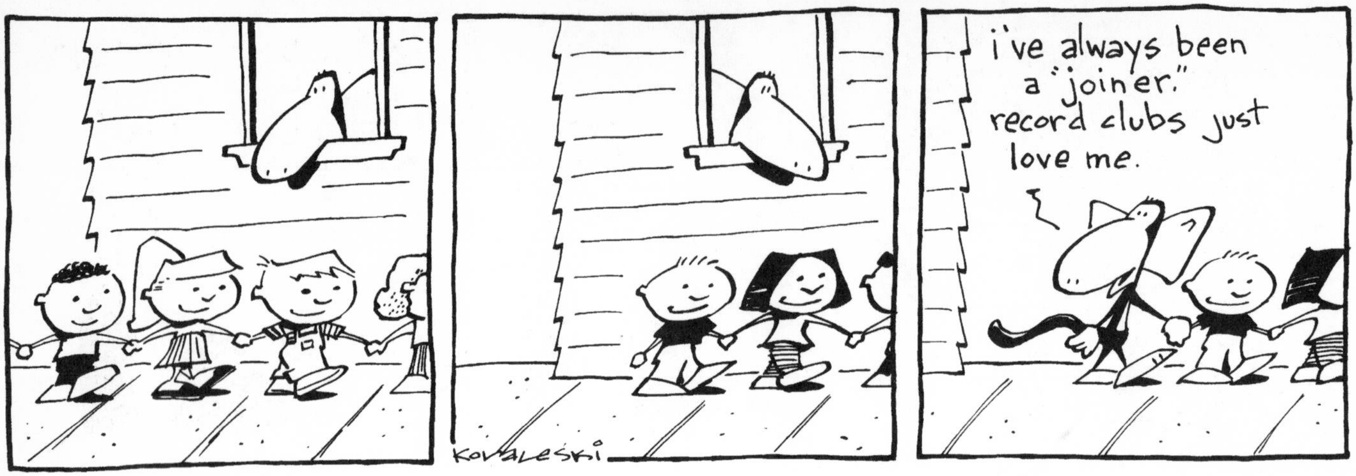
kovaleski
i've always been a "joiner." record clubs just love me.

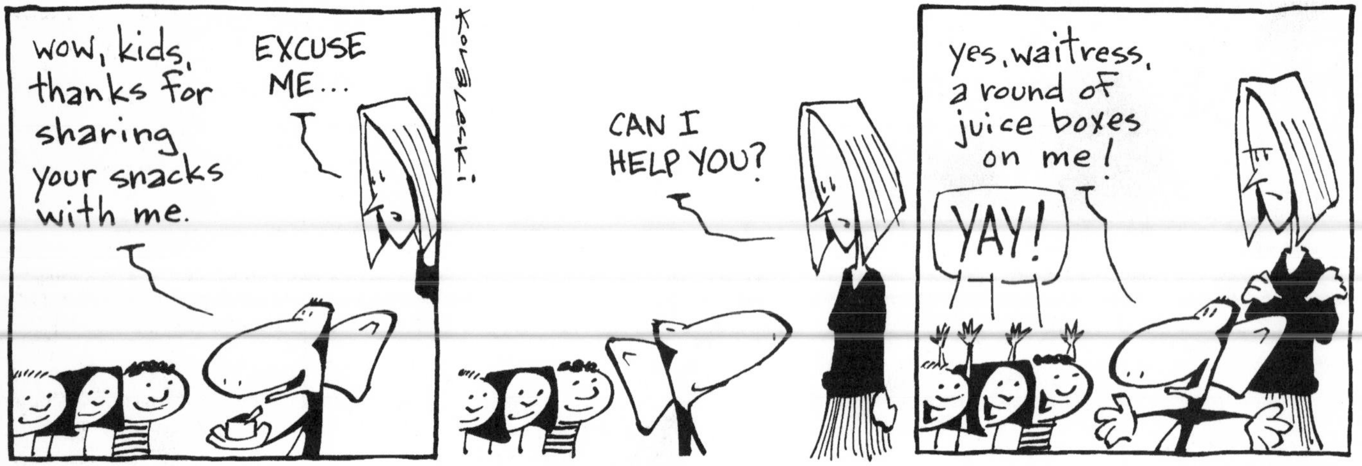
wow, kids, thanks for sharing your snacks with me.
EXCUSE ME...
kovaleski
CAN I HELP YOU?
yes, waitress, a round of juice boxes on me!
YAY!

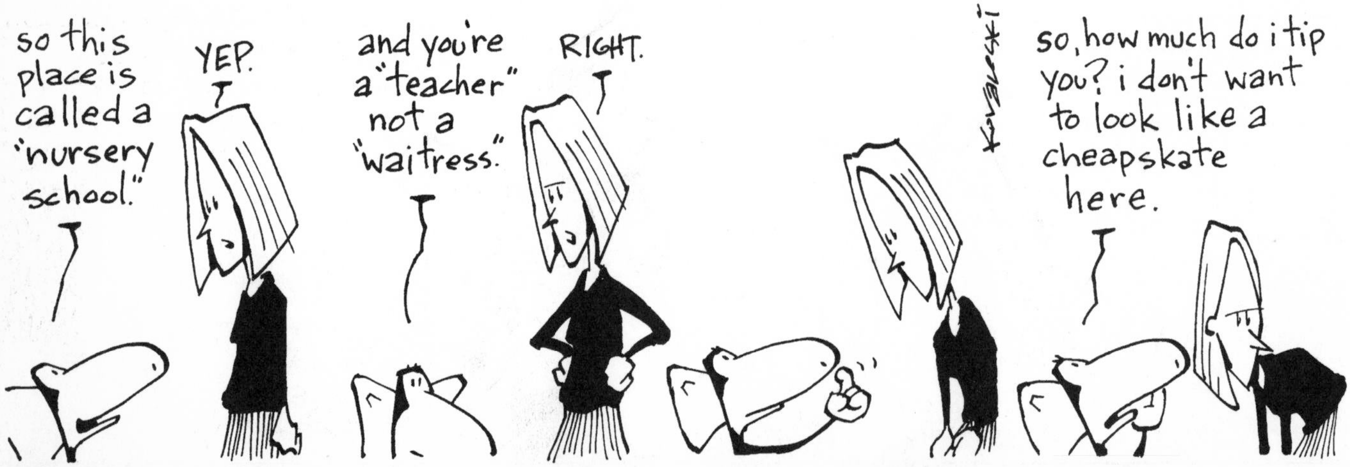
so this place is called a "nursery school."
YEP.
and you're a "teacher" not a "waitress."
RIGHT.
kovaleski
so, how much do i tip you? i don't want to look like a cheapskate here.

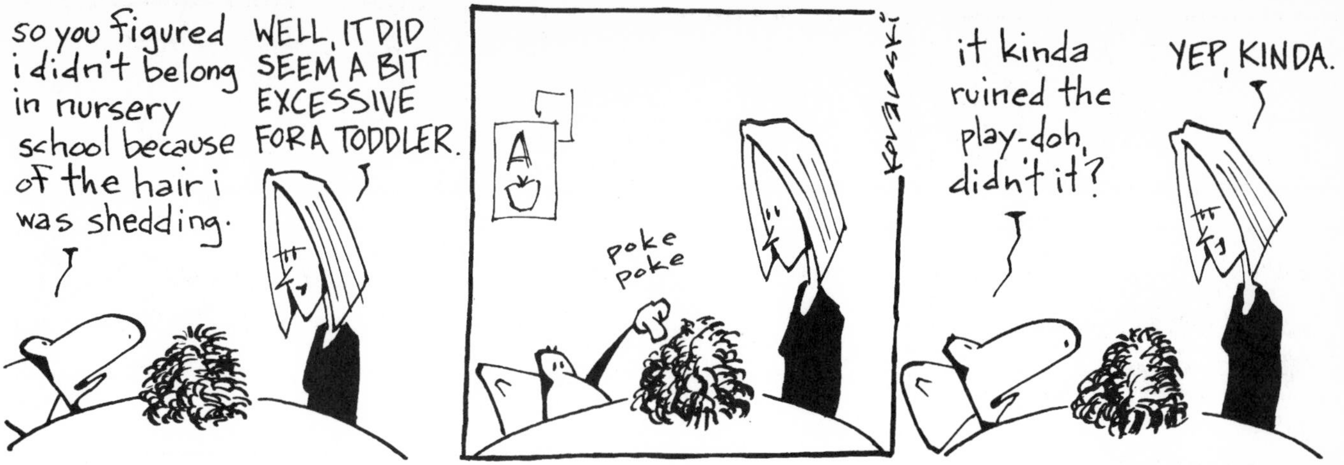
so you figured i didn't belong in nursery school because of the hair i was shedding.
WELL, IT DID SEEM A BIT EXCESSIVE FOR A TODDLER.
poke poke
KOVALESKI
it kinda ruined the play-doh, didn't it?
YEP, KINDA.

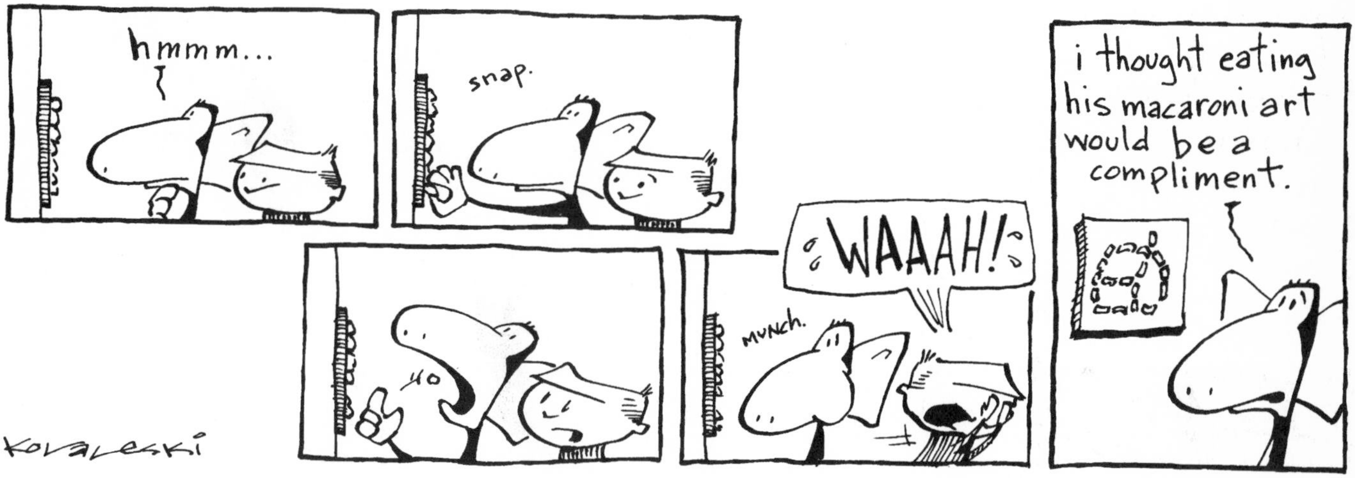
hmmm...
snap.
MUNCH.
WAAAH!
i thought eating his macaroni art would be a compliment.
KOVALESKI

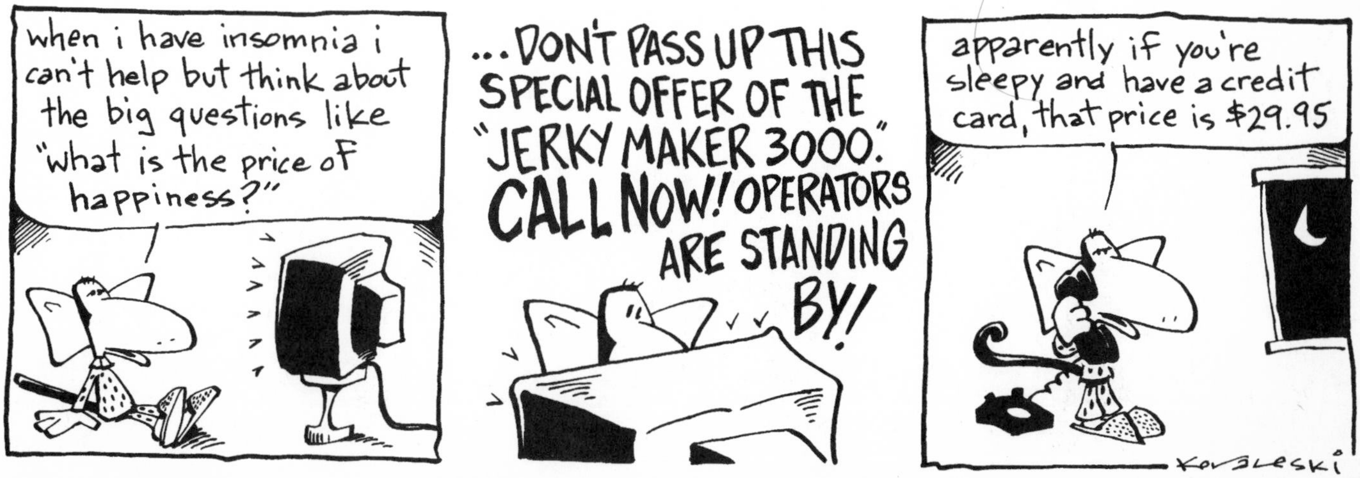
when i have insomnia i can't help but think about the big questions like "what is the price of happiness?"
...DON'T PASS UP THIS SPECIAL OFFER OF THE "JERKY MAKER 3000." CALL NOW! OPERATORS ARE STANDING BY!
apparently if you're sleepy and have a credit card, that price is $29.95
KOVALESKI

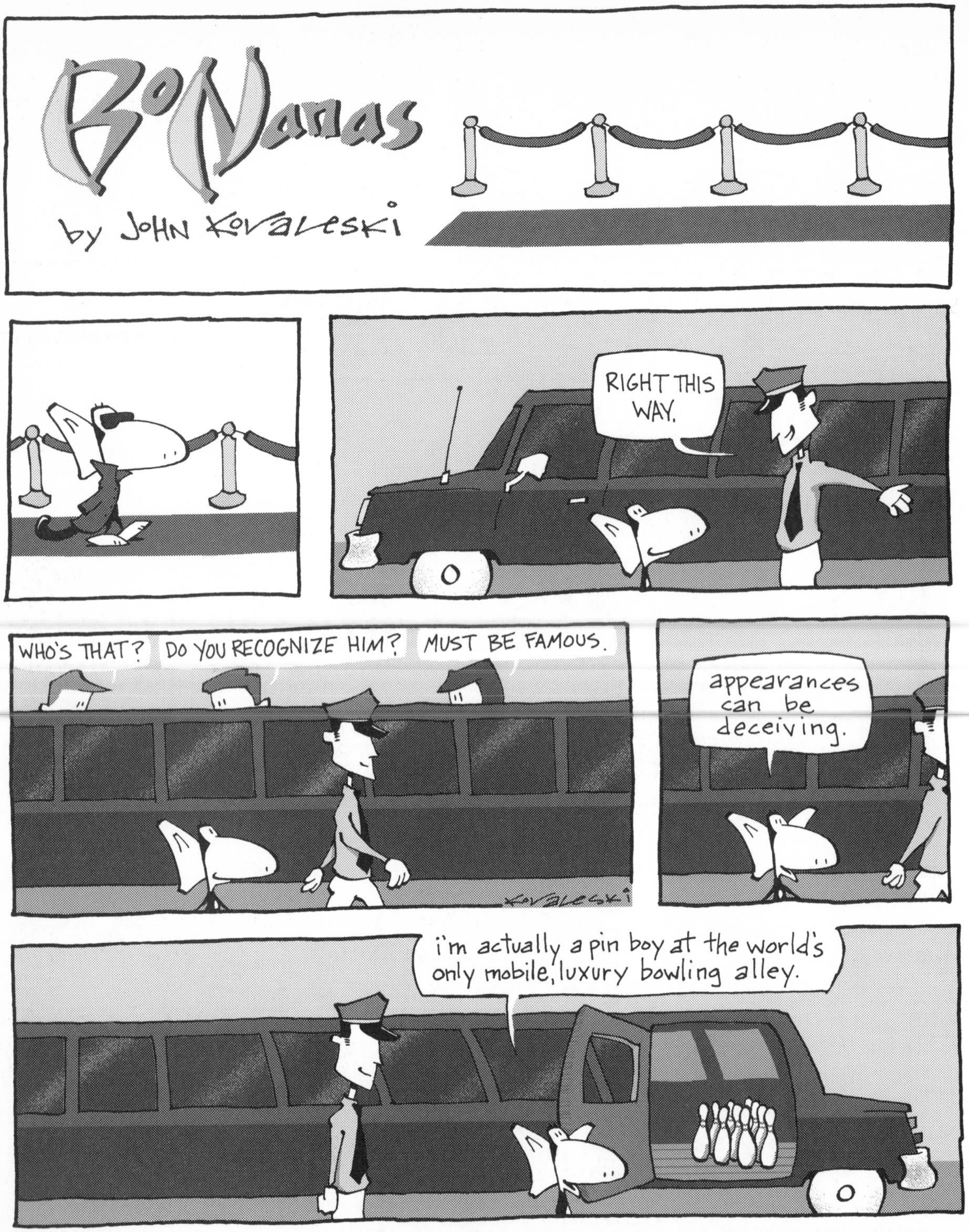
BoNanas
by JOHN KOVALESKI
RIGHT THIS WAY.
WHO'S THAT?
DO YOU RECOGNIZE HIM?
MUST BE FAMOUS.
KOVALESKI
appearances can be deceiving.
i'm actually a pin boy at the world's only mobile, luxury bowling alley.

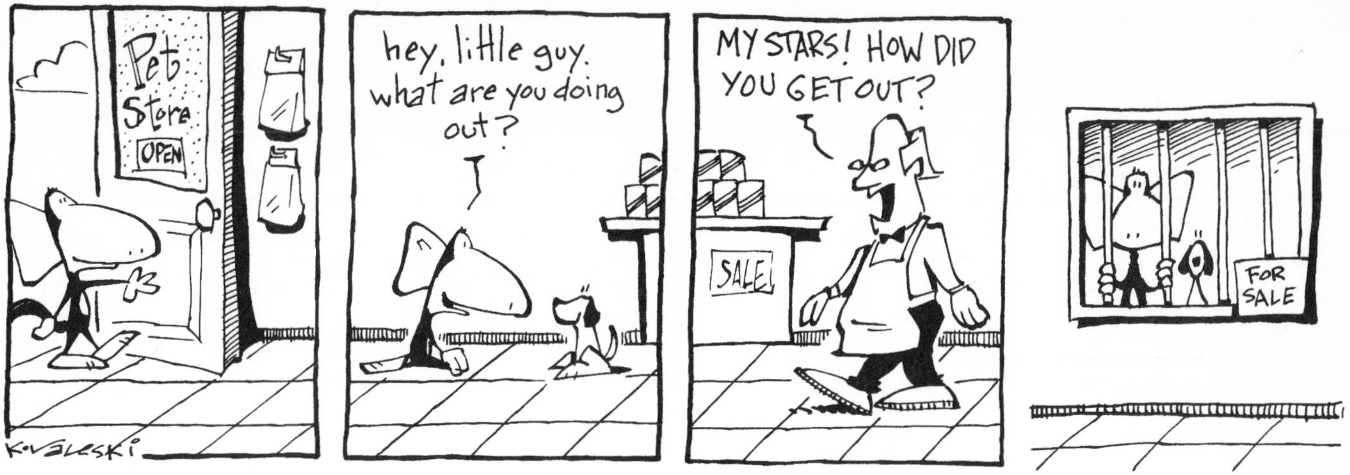
Pet Store
OPEN
kovaleski
hey, little guy. what are you doing out?
SALE
MY STARS! HOW DID YOU GET OUT?
FOR SALE

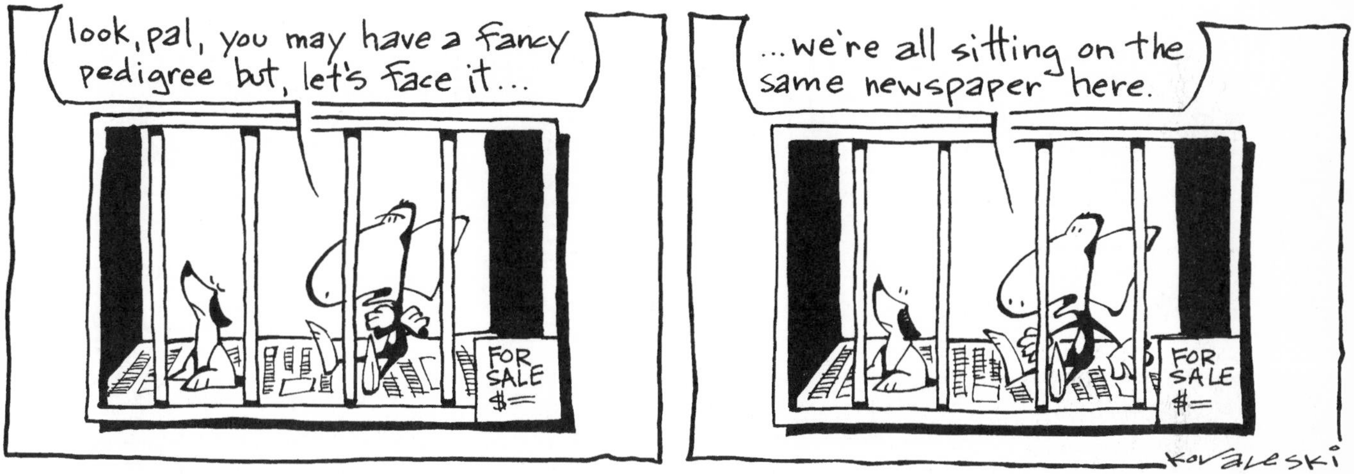
look, pal, you may have a fancy pedigree but, let's face it...
FOR SALE $
...we're all sitting on the same newspaper here.
FOR SALE $
kovaleski

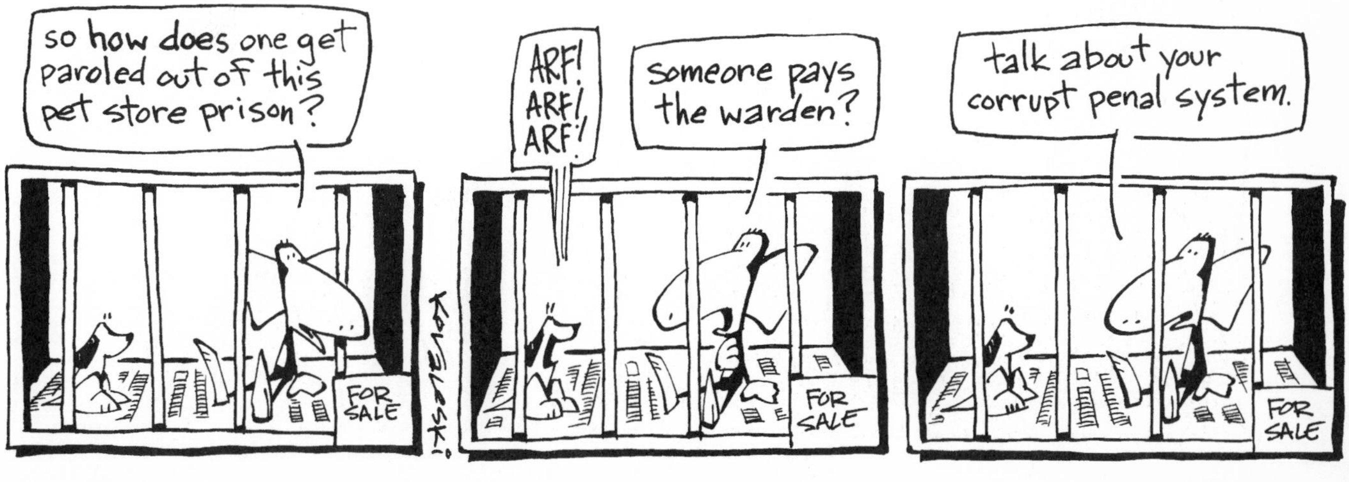
so how does one get paroled out of this pet store prison?
FOR SALE
kovaleski
ARF! ARF! ARF!
Someone pays the warden?
FOR SALE
talk about your corrupt penal system.
FOR SALE

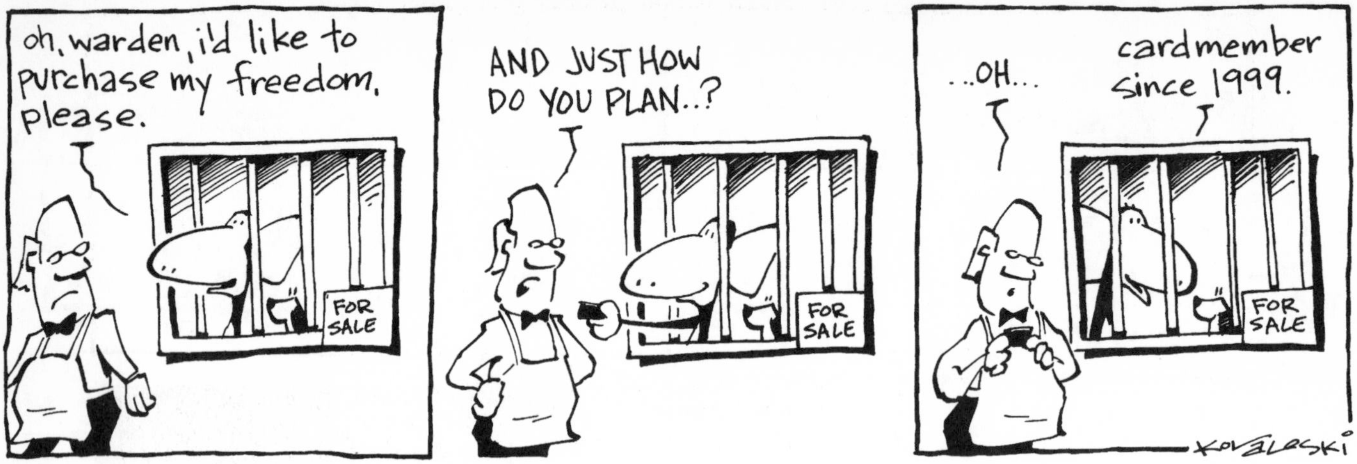
oh, warden, i'd like to purchase my freedom, please.
AND JUST HOW DO YOU PLAN..?
...OH...
cardmember since 1999.
FOR SALE
FOR SALE
FOR SALE
KOVALESKI

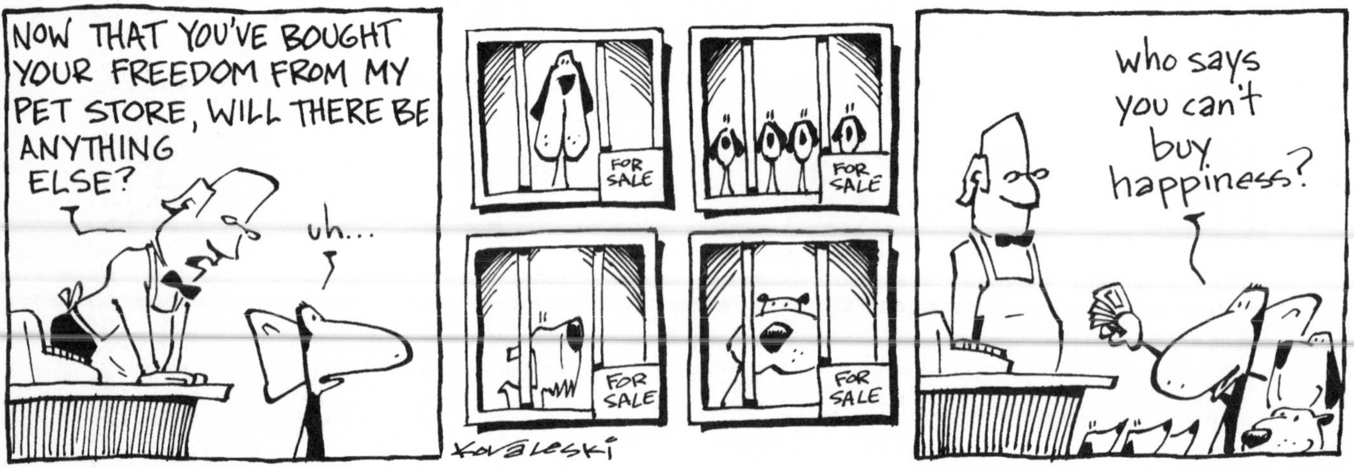
NOW THAT YOU'VE BOUGHT YOUR FREEDOM FROM MY PET STORE, WILL THERE BE ANYTHING ELSE?
uh...
FOR SALE
FOR SALE
FOR SALE
FOR SALE
KOVALESKI
who says you can't buy happiness?

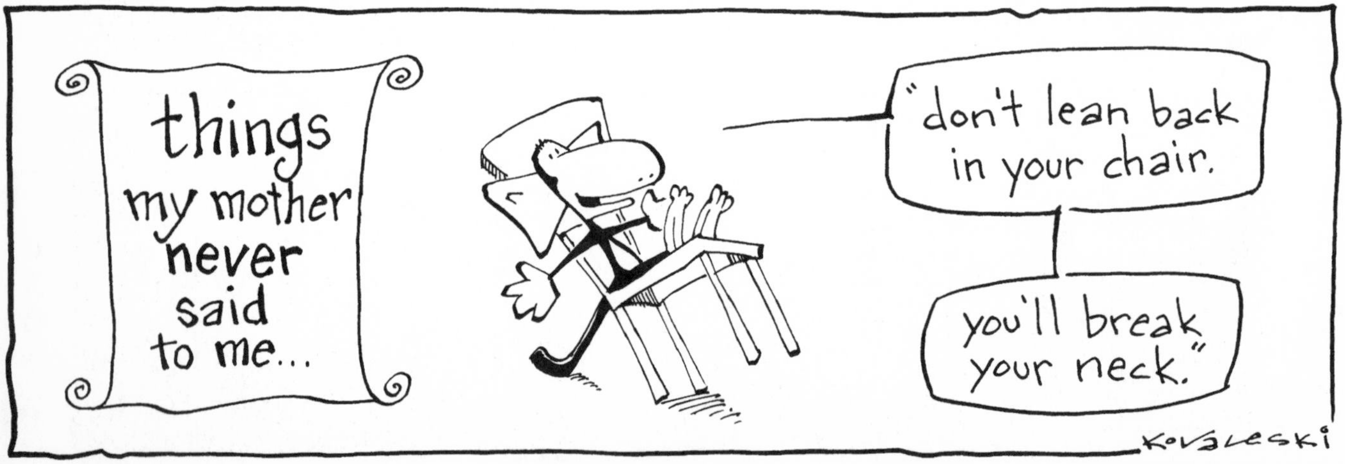
things my mother never said to me...
"don't lean back in your chair.
you'll break your neck."
KOVALESKI

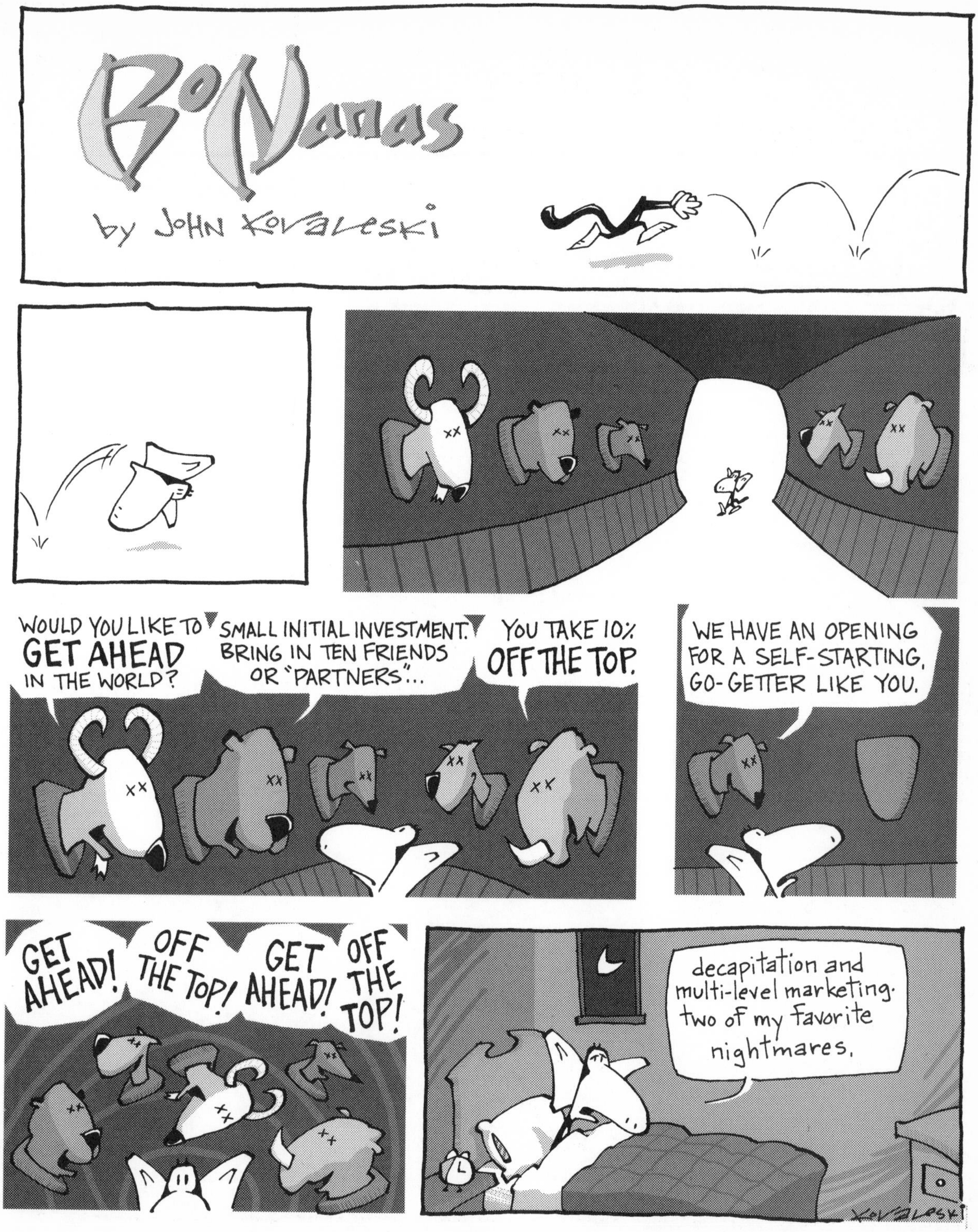
BoNanas
by John Kovaleski
WOULD YOU LIKE TO GET AHEAD IN THE WORLD?
SMALL INITIAL INVESTMENT. BRING IN TEN FRIENDS OR "PARTNERS"...
YOU TAKE 10% OFF THE TOP.
WE HAVE AN OPENING FOR A SELF-STARTING, GO-GETTER LIKE YOU.
GET AHEAD!
OFF THE TOP!
GET AHEAD!
OFF THE TOP!
decapitation and multi-level marketing. two of my favorite nightmares.
KOVALESKI

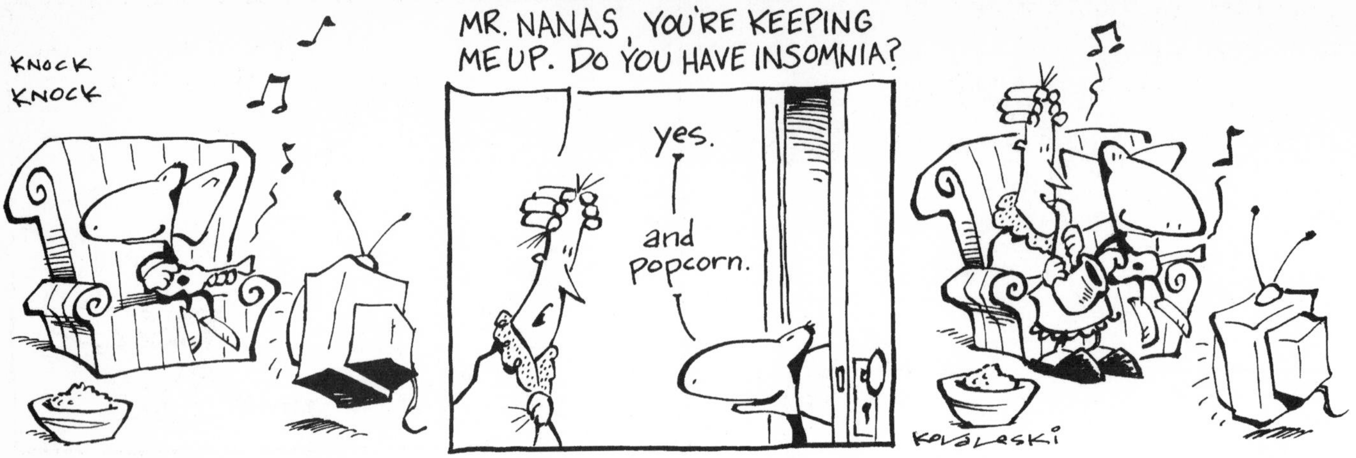
KNOCK
KNOCK
MR. NANAS, YOU'RE KEEPING ME UP. DO YOU HAVE INSOMNIA?
yes.
and popcorn.
KOVALESKI

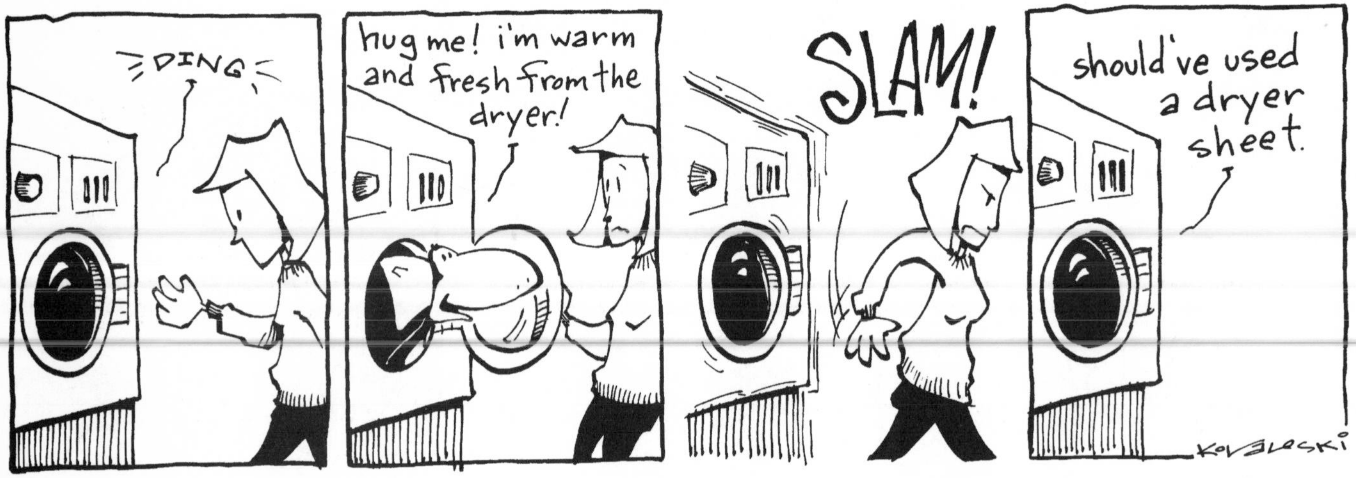
DING
hug me! i'm warm and fresh from the dryer!
SLAM!
should've used a dryer sheet.
KOVALESKI

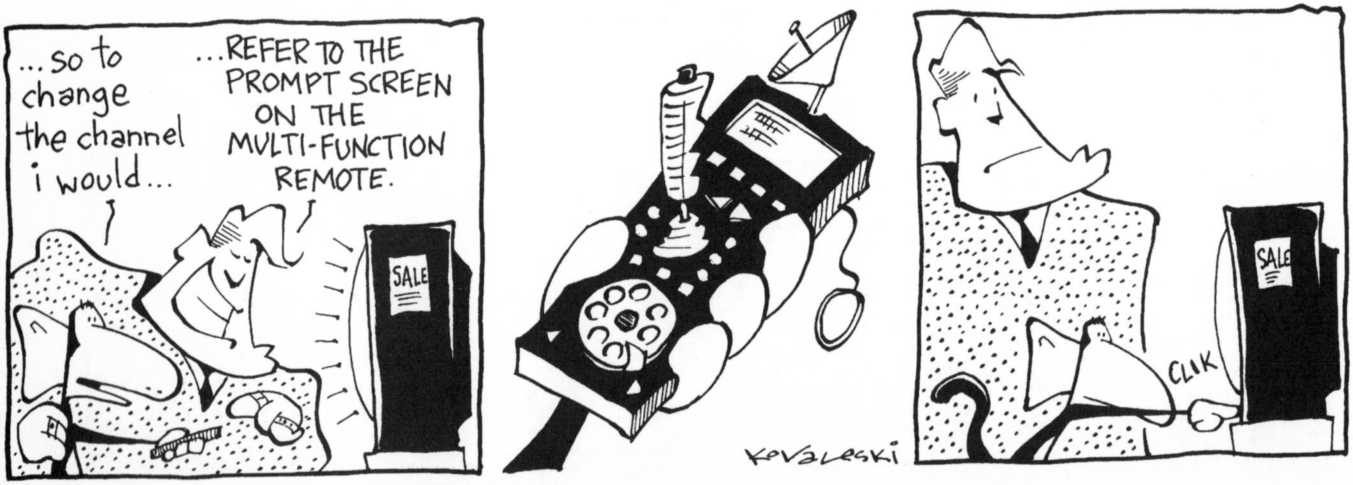
...so to change the channel i would...
...REFER TO THE PROMPT SCREEN ON THE MULTI-FUNCTION REMOTE.
SALE
KOVALESKI
SALE
CLIK

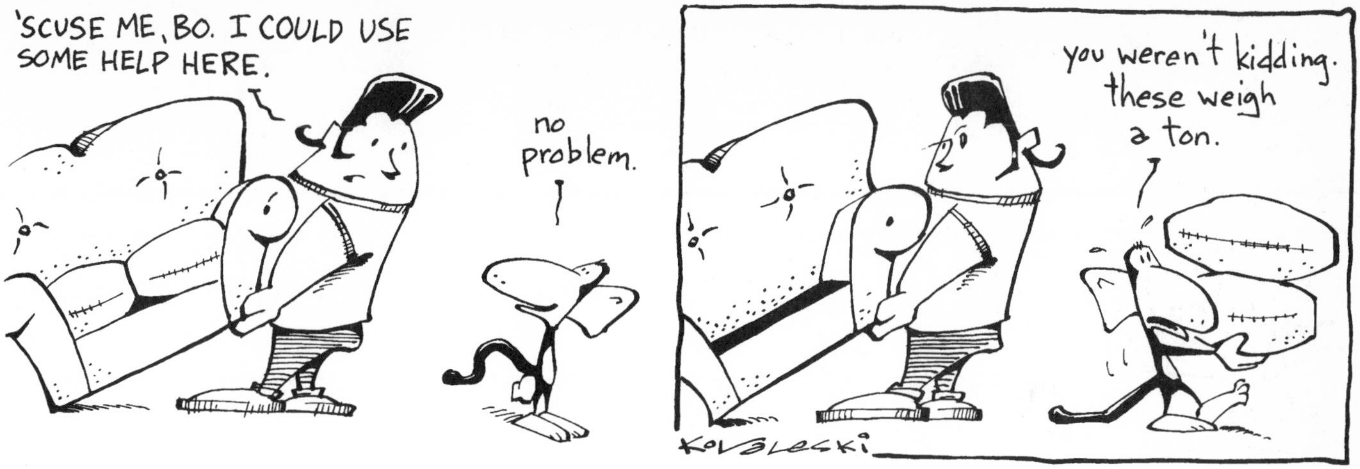
'SCUSE ME, BO. I COULD USE SOME HELP HERE.
no problem.
you weren't kidding. these weigh a ton.
KOVALESKI

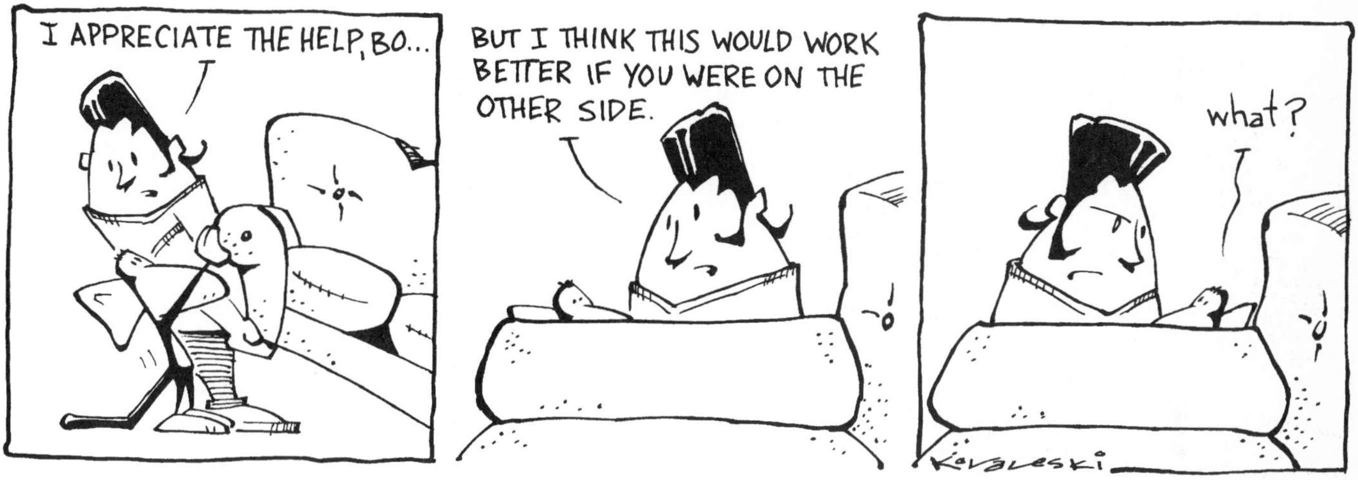
I APPRECIATE THE HELP, BO...
BUT I THINK THIS WOULD WORK BETTER IF YOU WERE ON THE OTHER SIDE.
what?
KOVALESKI

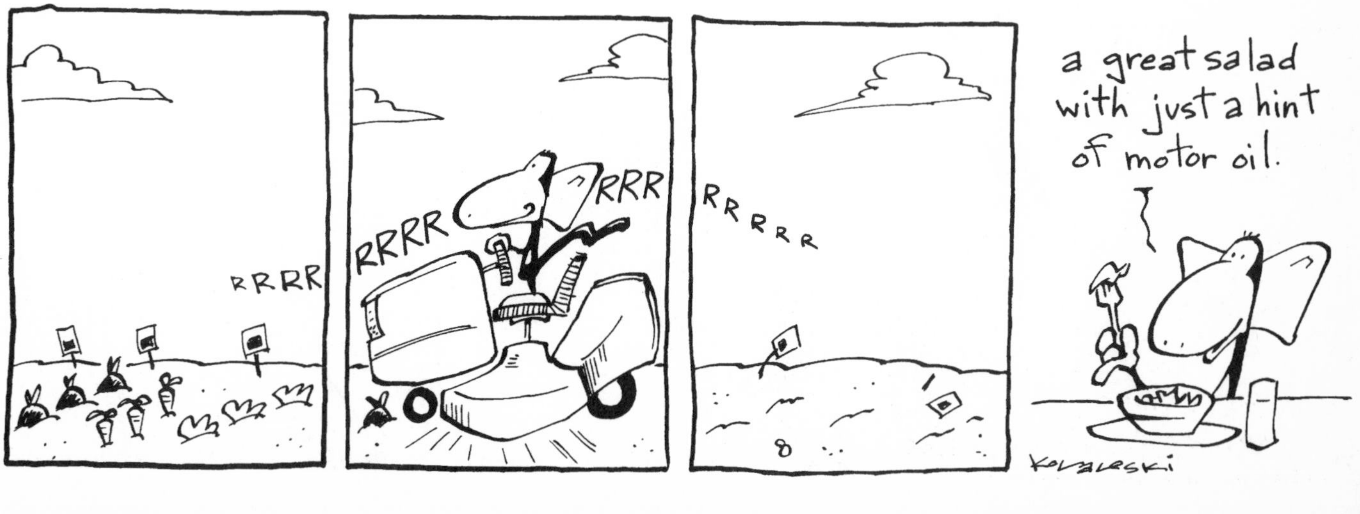
RRRR
RRRR
RRR
RRRRR
a great salad with just a hint of motor oil.
KOVALESKI

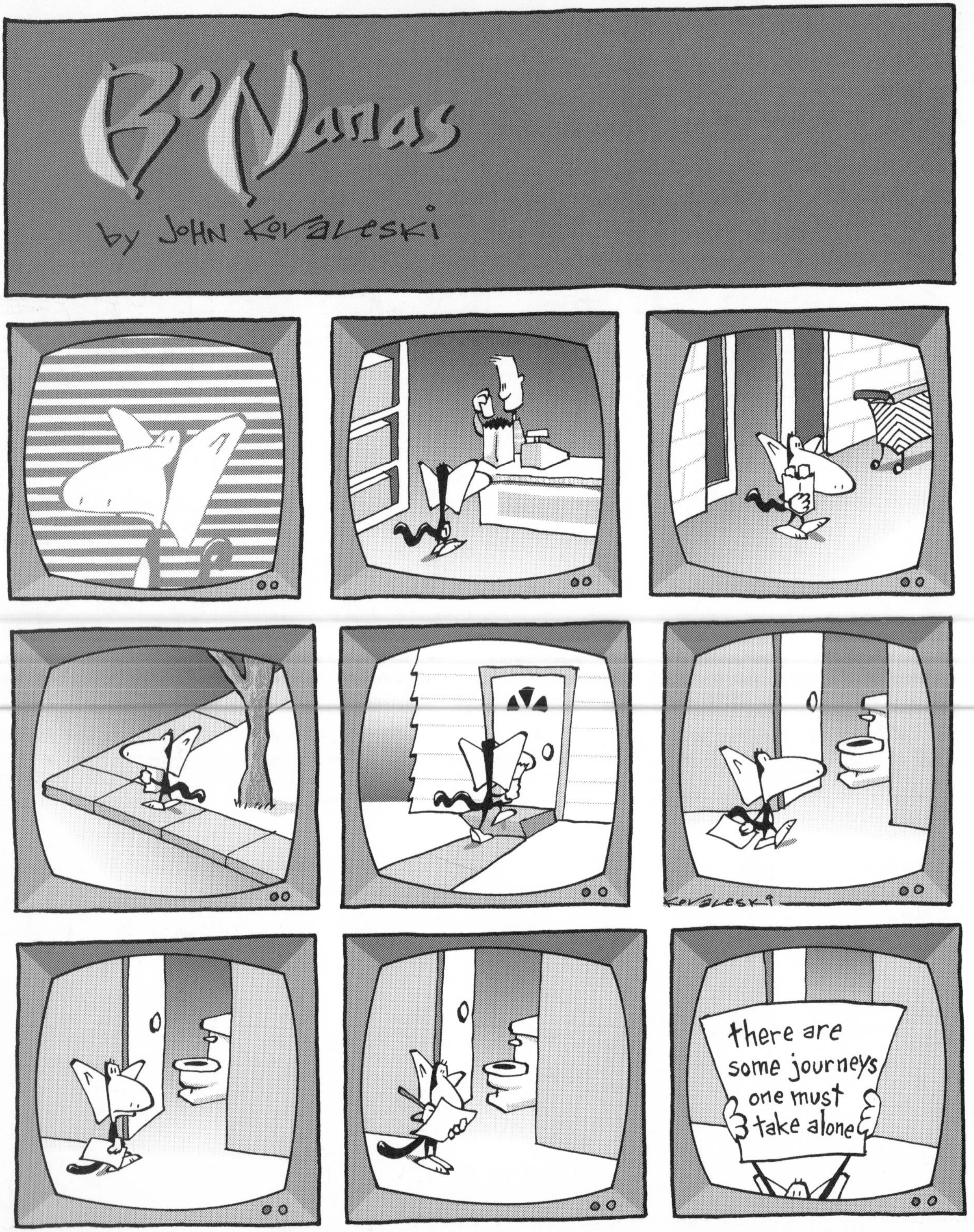
BoNanas
by JOHN KOVALESKI
KOVALESKI
there are some journeys one must take alone

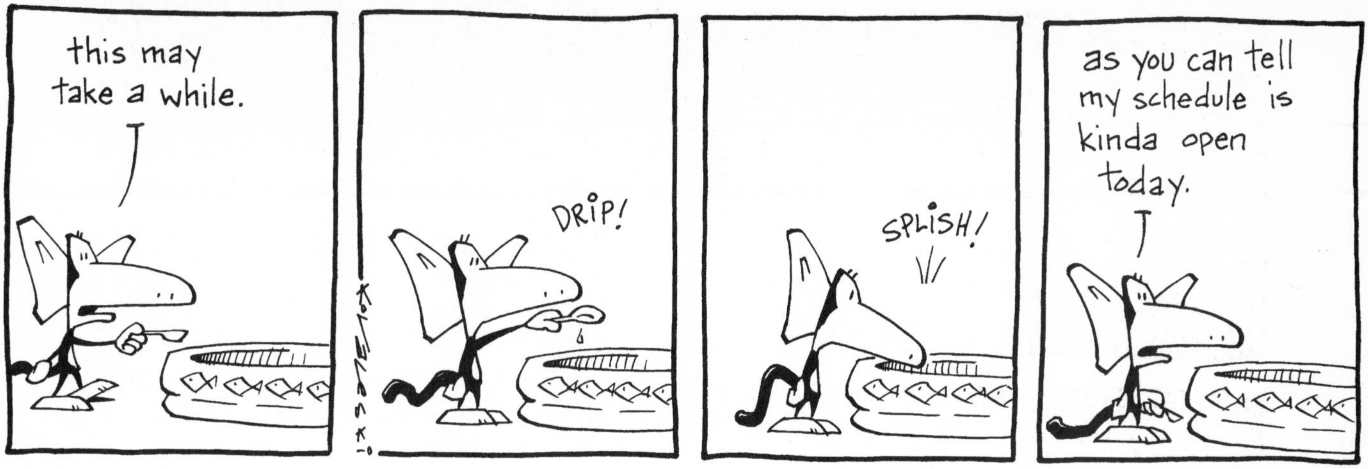
this may take a while.
DRIP!
SPLISH!
as you can tell my schedule is kinda open today.

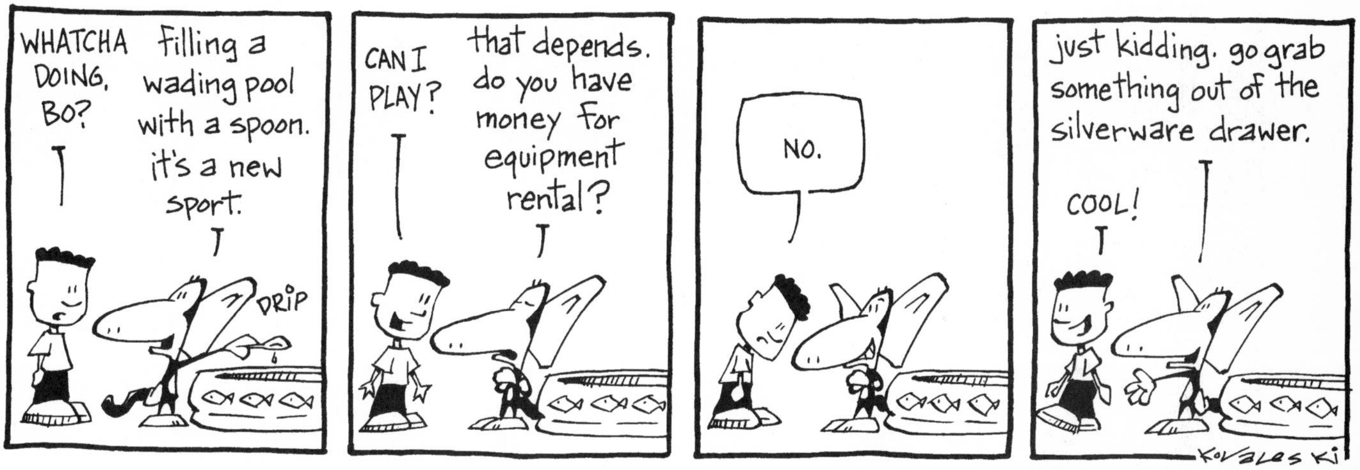
WHATCHA DOING, BO?
filling a wading pool with a spoon. it's a new sport.
DRIP
CAN I PLAY?
that depends. do you have money for equipment rental?
NO.
just kidding. go grab something out of the silverware drawer.
COOL!
KOVALESKI

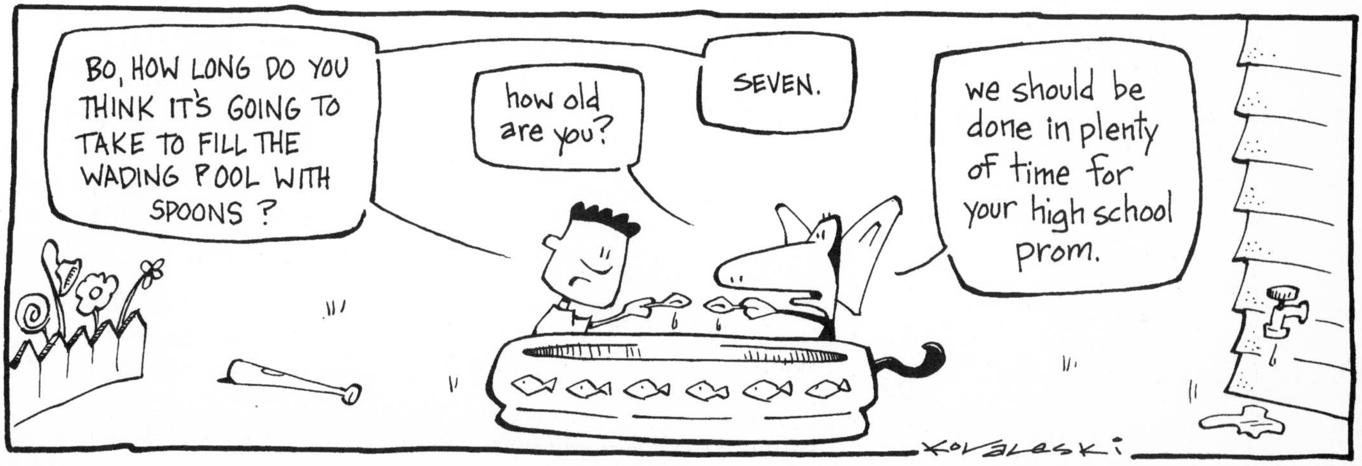
BO, HOW LONG DO YOU THINK IT'S GOING TO TAKE TO FILL THE WADING POOL WITH SPOONS?
how old are you?
SEVEN.
we should be done in plenty of time for your high school prom.
KOVALESKI

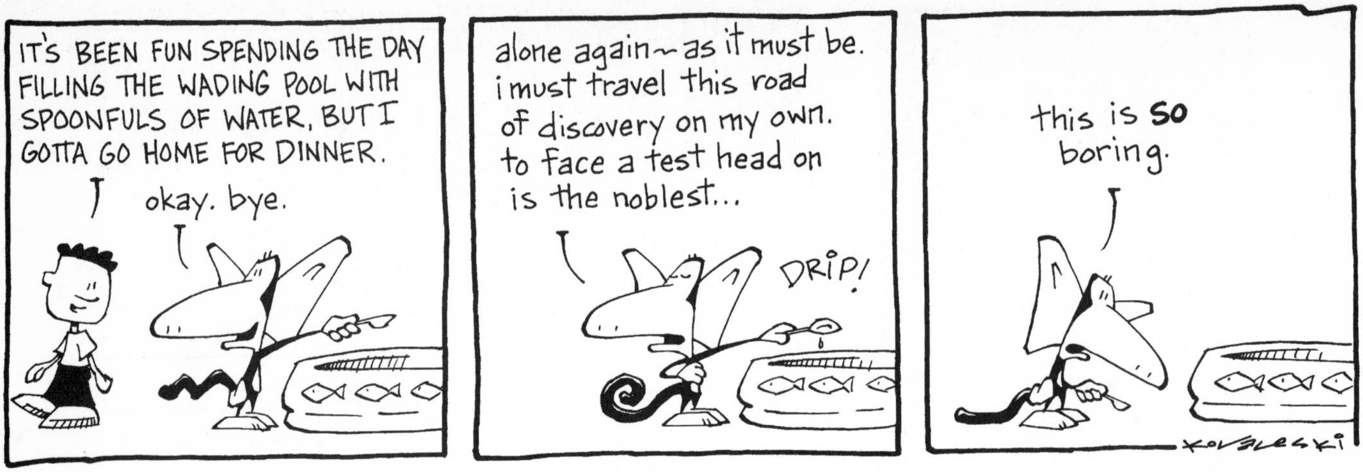
IT'S BEEN FUN SPENDING THE DAY FILLING THE WADING POOL WITH SPOONFULS OF WATER, BUT I GOTTA GO HOME FOR DINNER.
okay. bye.
alone again~as it must be. i must travel this road of discovery on my own. to face a test head on is the noblest...
DRIP!
this is **SO** boring.
KOVALESKI

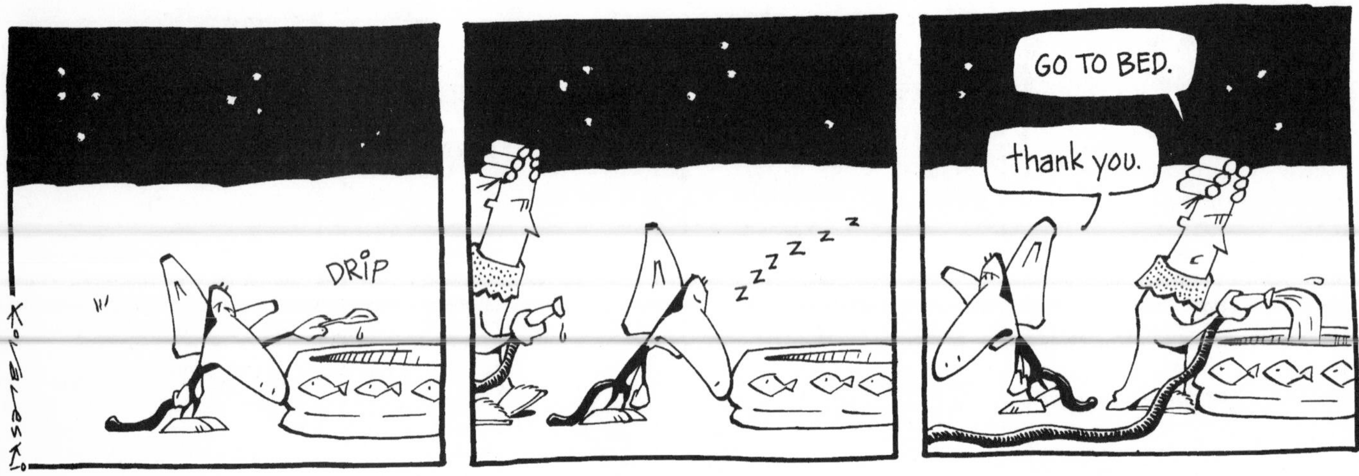
DRIP
KOVALESKI
ZZZZZZ
GO TO BED.
thank you.

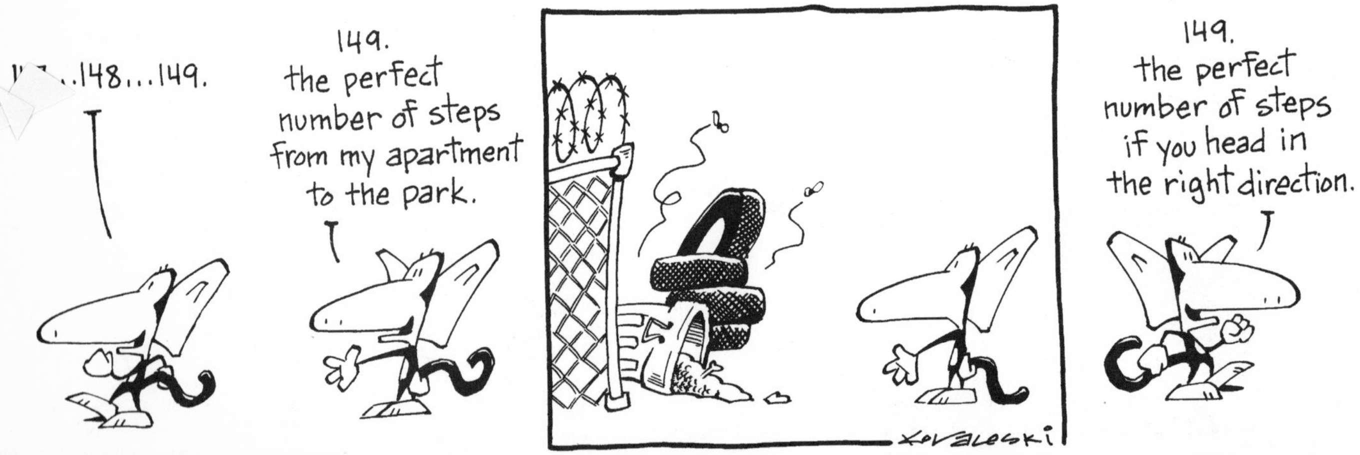
..148...149.
149. the perfect number of steps from my apartment to the park.
KOVALESKI
149. the perfect number of steps if you head in the right direction.

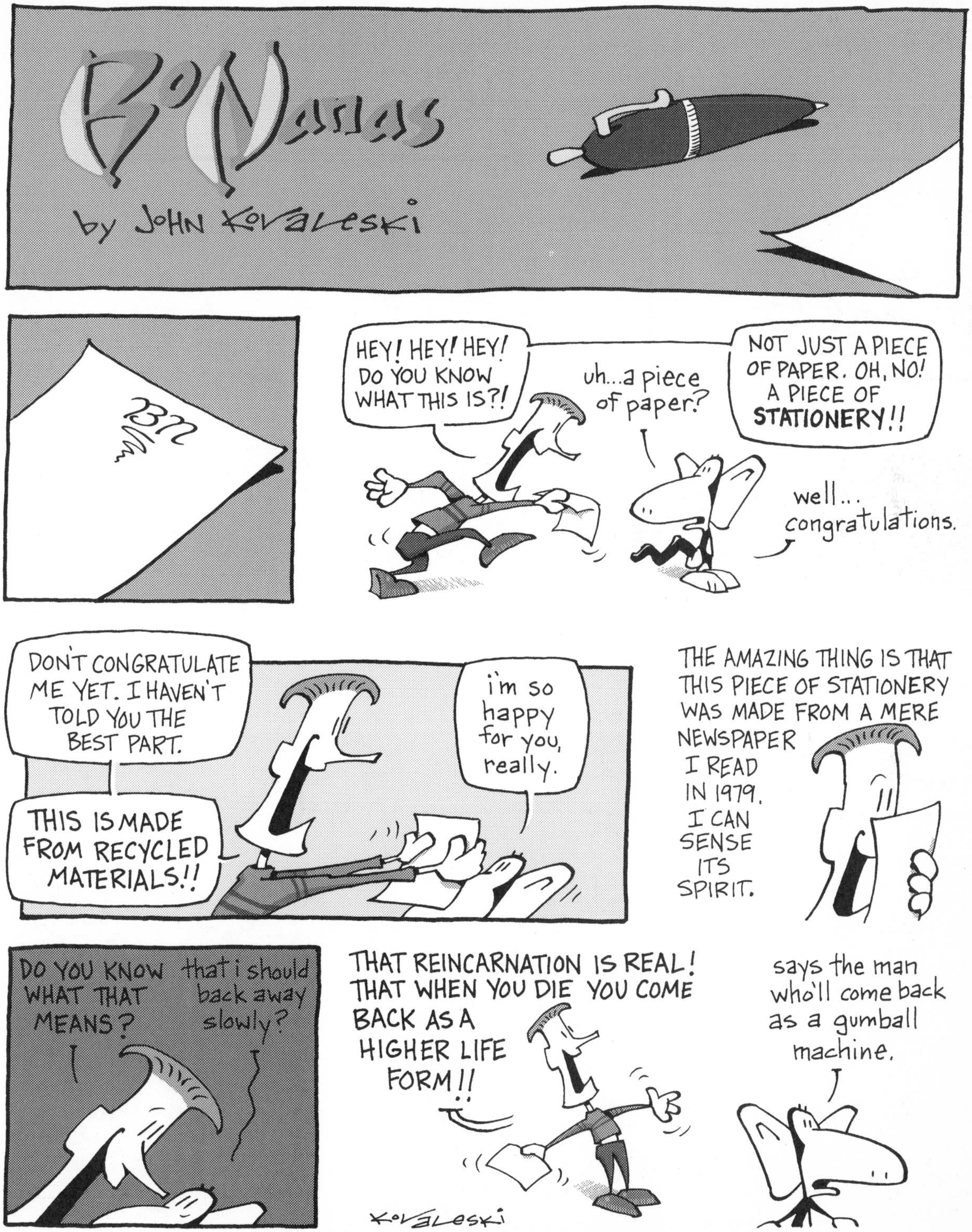
BoNaRa?
by JOHN KOVALESKI
HEY! HEY! HEY! DO YOU KNOW WHAT THIS IS?!
uh...a piece of paper?
NOT JUST A PIECE OF PAPER. OH, NO! A PIECE OF STATIONERY!!
well... congratulations.
DON'T CONGRATULATE ME YET. I HAVEN'T TOLD YOU THE BEST PART.
THIS IS MADE FROM RECYCLED MATERIALS!!
i'm so happy for you, really.
THE AMAZING THING IS THAT THIS PIECE OF STATIONERY WAS MADE FROM A MERE NEWSPAPER I READ IN 1979. I CAN SENSE ITS SPIRIT.
DO YOU KNOW WHAT THAT MEANS?
that i should back away slowly?
THAT REINCARNATION IS REAL! THAT WHEN YOU DIE YOU COME BACK AS A HIGHER LIFE FORM!!
says the man who'll come back as a gumball machine.
KOVALESKI

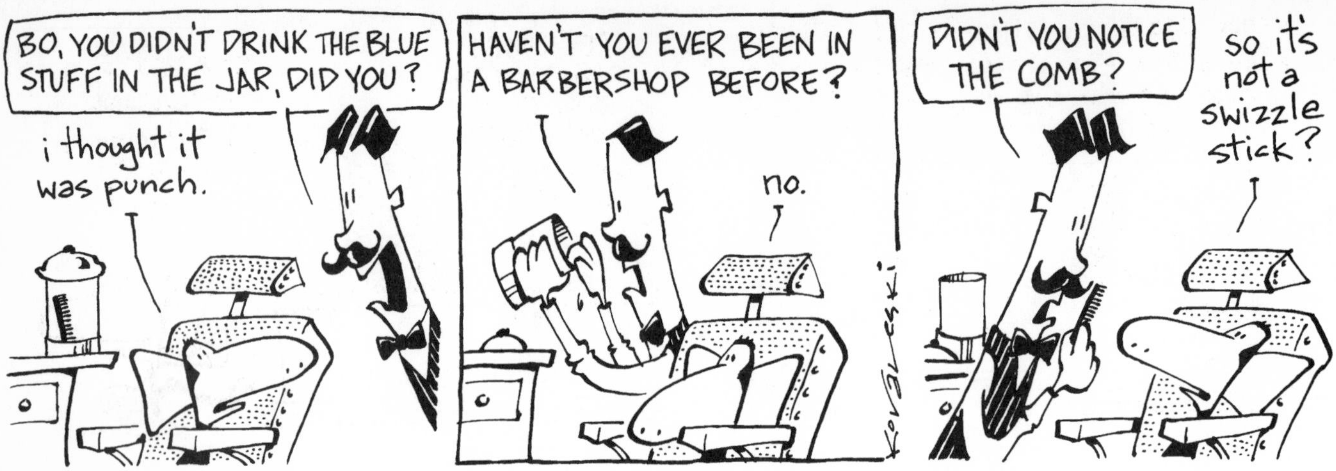
BO, YOU DIDN'T DRINK THE BLUE STUFF IN THE JAR, DID YOU?
i thought it was punch.
HAVEN'T YOU EVER BEEN IN A BARBERSHOP BEFORE?
no.
DIDN'T YOU NOTICE THE COMB?
so it's not a swizzle stick?
KOVALESKI

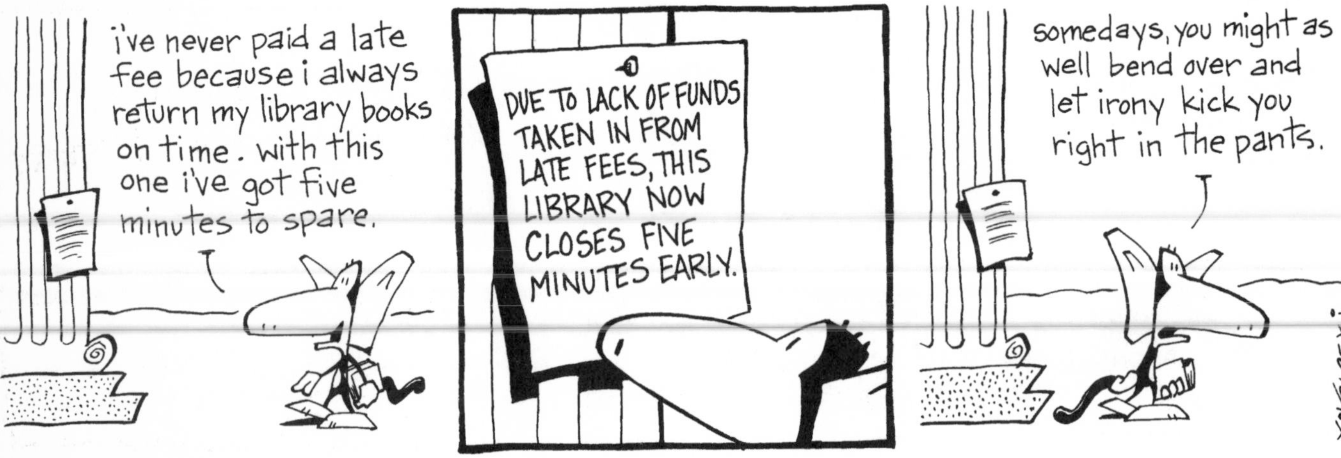
i've never paid a late fee because i always return my library books on time. with this one i've got five minutes to spare.
DUE TO LACK OF FUNDS TAKEN IN FROM LATE FEES, THIS LIBRARY NOW CLOSES FIVE MINUTES EARLY.
somedays, you might as well bend over and let irony kick you right in the pants.
KOVALESKI

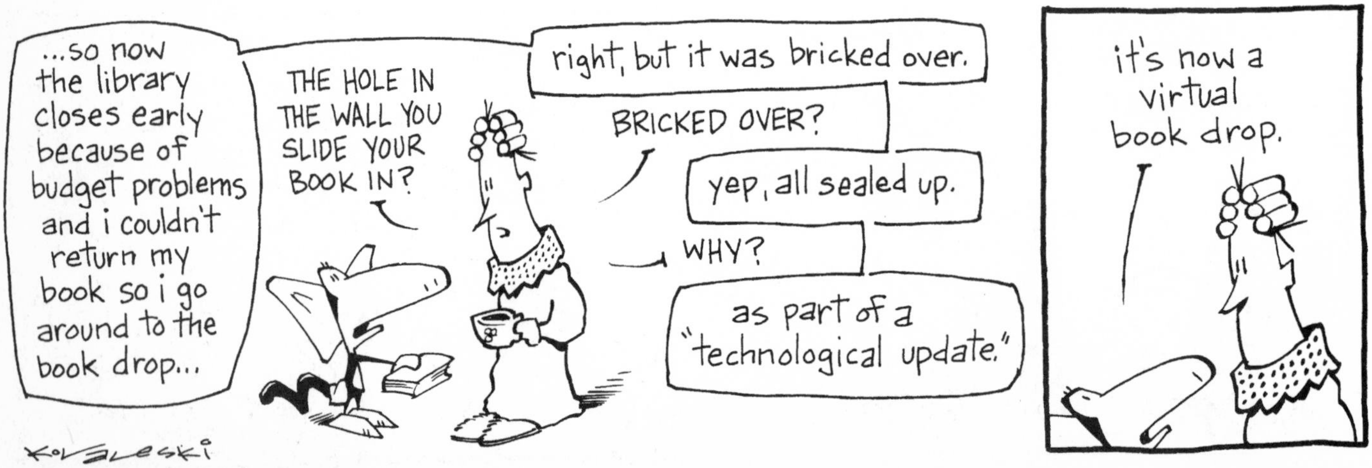
...so now the library closes early because of budget problems and i couldn't return my book so i go around to the book drop...
THE HOLE IN THE WALL YOU SLIDE YOUR BOOK IN?
right, but it was bricked over.
BRICKED OVER?
yep, all sealed up.
WHY?
as part of a "technological update."
it's now a virtual book drop.
KOVALESKI

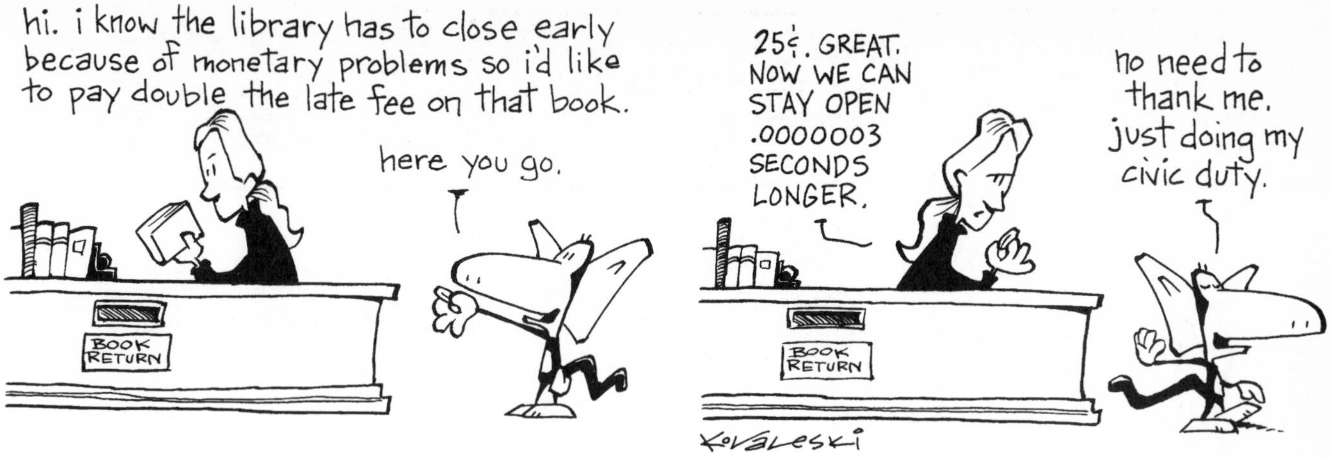
hi. i know the library has to close early because of monetary problems so i'd like to pay double the late fee on that book.
here you go.
BOOK RETURN
25¢. GREAT. NOW WE CAN STAY OPEN .0000003 SECONDS LONGER.
no need to thank me. just doing my civic duty.
BOOK RETURN
KOVALESKI

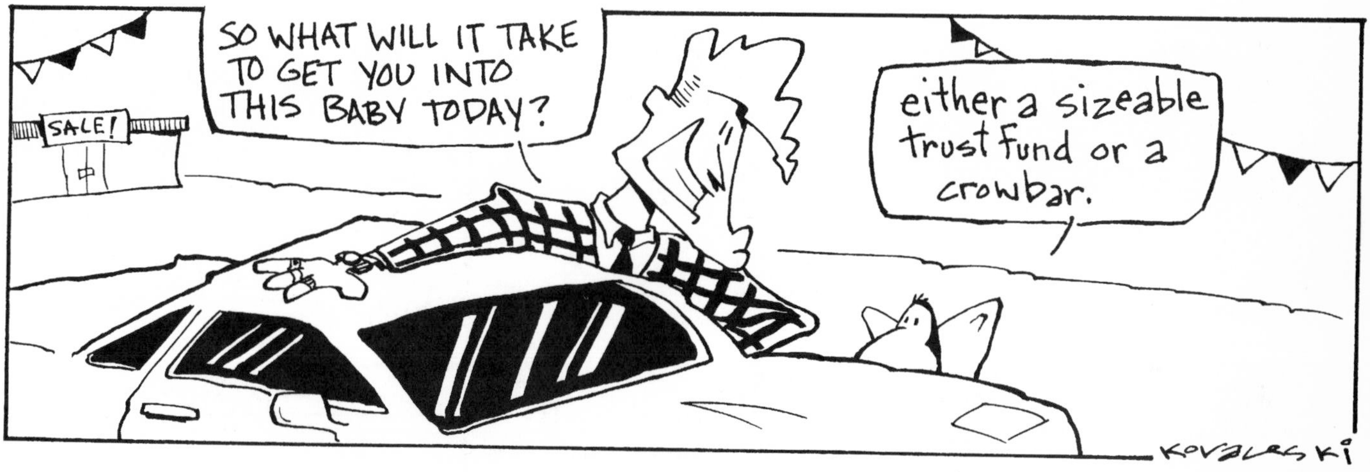
SALE!
SO WHAT WILL IT TAKE TO GET YOU INTO THIS BABY TODAY?
either a sizeable trust fund or a crowbar.
KOVALESKI

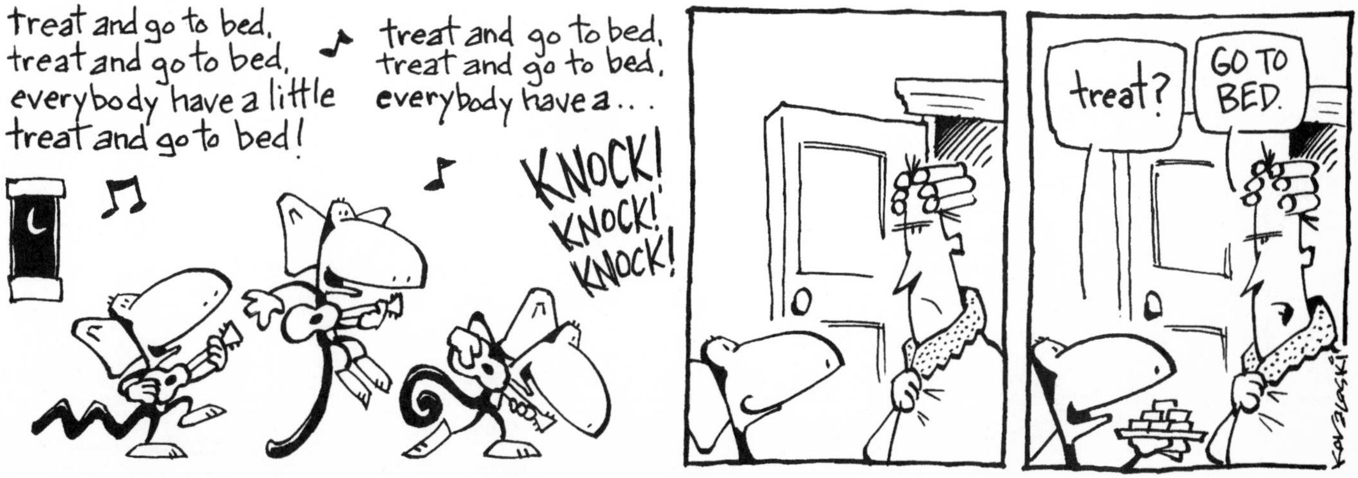
treat and go to bed, treat and go to bed, everybody have a little treat and go to bed!
treat and go to bed, treat and go to bed, everybody have a . . .
KNOCK! KNOCK! KNOCK!
treat?
GO TO BED.
KOVALESKI

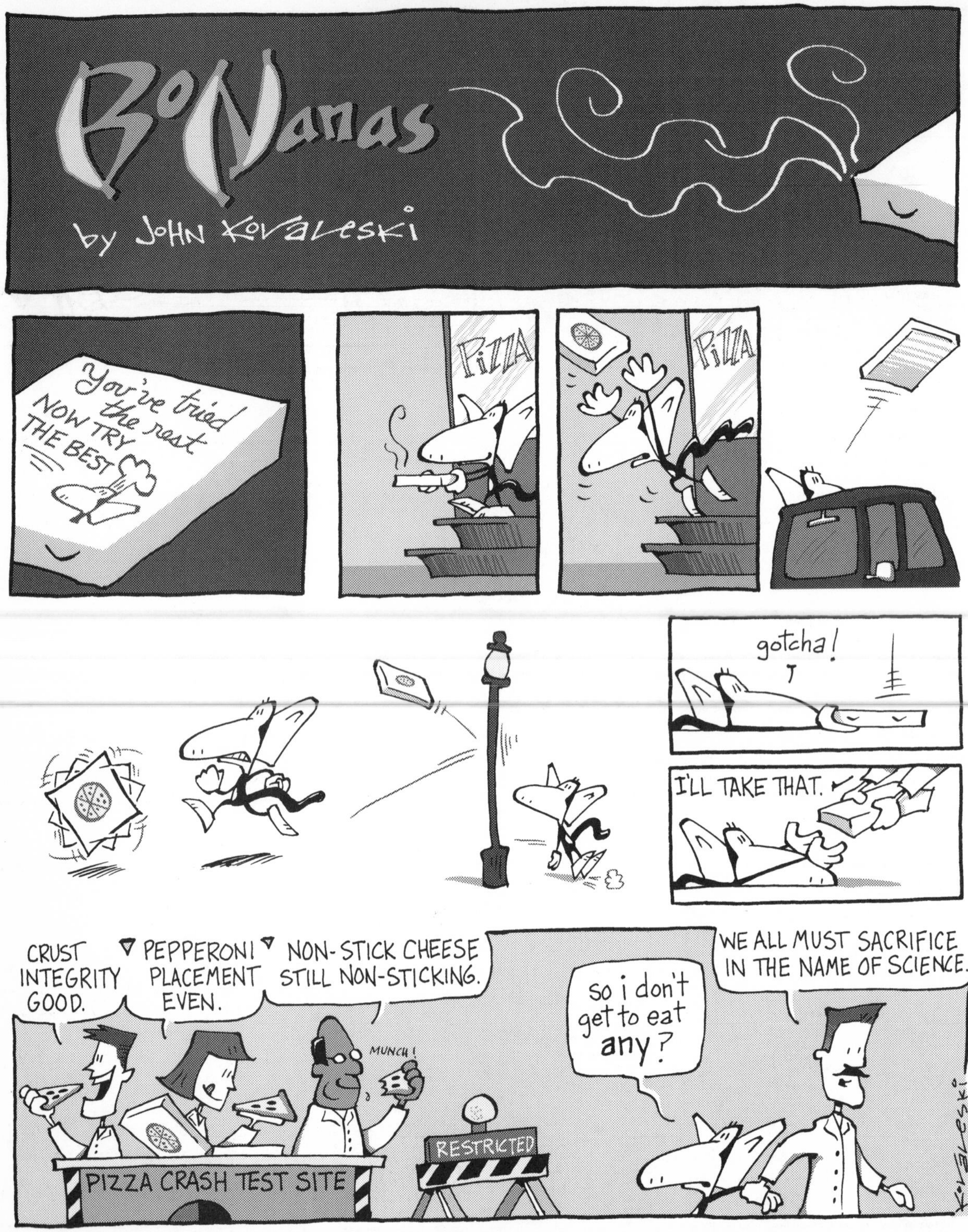

BoNanas
by JOHN KOVALESKI
You've tried the rest! NOW TRY THE BEST
PIZZA
PIZZA
gotcha!
I'LL TAKE THAT.
CRUST INTEGRITY GOOD.
PEPPERONI PLACEMENT EVEN.
NON-STICK CHEESE STILL NON-STICKING.
MUNCH!
so i don't get to eat any?
WE ALL MUST SACRIFICE IN THE NAME OF SCIENCE.
RESTRICTED
PIZZA CRASH TEST SITE
KOVALESKI

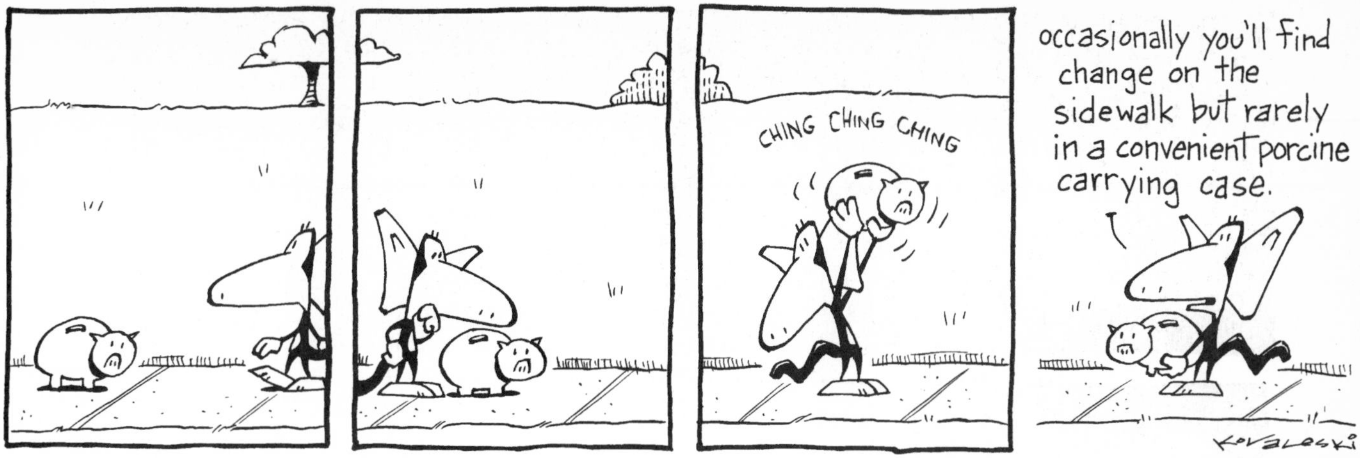
CHING CHING CHING
occasionally you'll find change on the sidewalk but rarely in a convenient porcine carrying case.
KOVALESKI

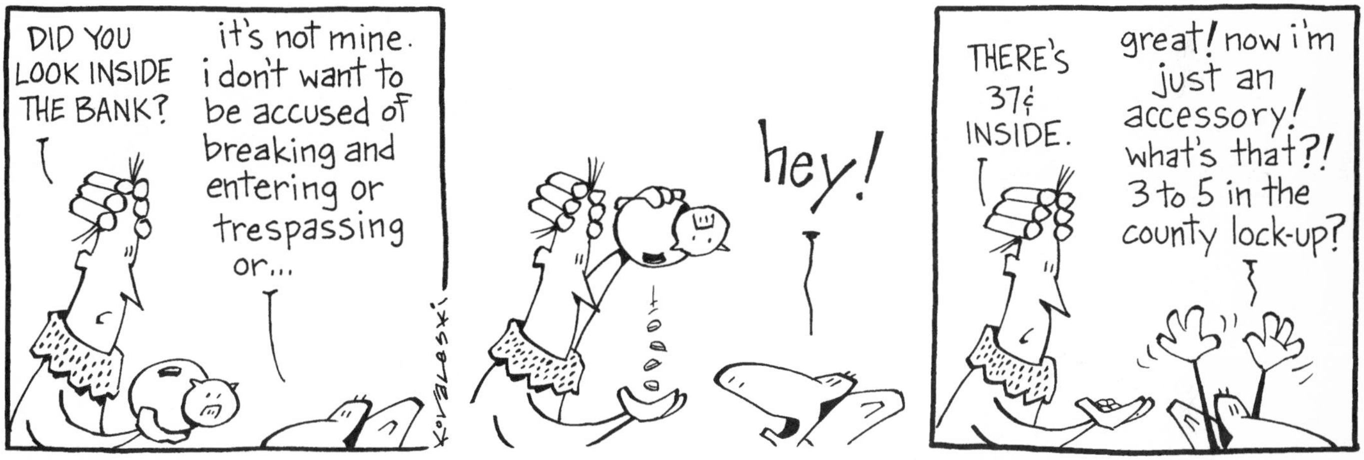
DID YOU LOOK INSIDE THE BANK?
it's not mine. i don't want to be accused of breaking and entering or trespassing or...
KOVALESKI
hey!
THERE'S 37¢ INSIDE.
great! now i'm just an accessory! what's that?! 3 to 5 in the county lock-up?

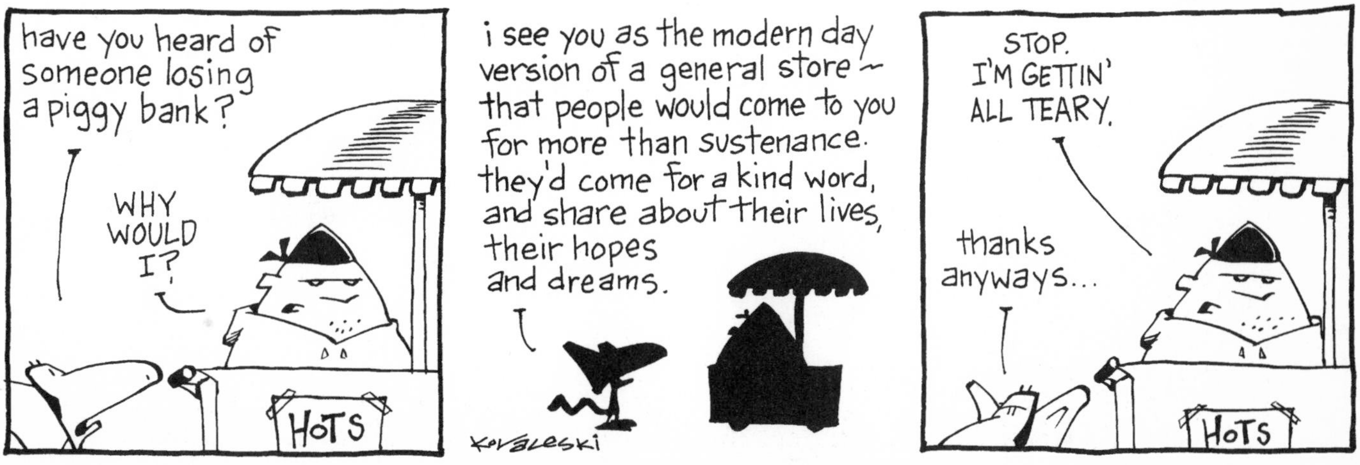
have you heard of someone losing a piggy bank?
WHY WOULD I?
HOTS
i see you as the modern day version of a general store ~ that people would come to you for more than sustenance. they'd come for a kind word, and share about their lives, their hopes and dreams.
KOVALESKI
STOP. I'M GETTIN' ALL TEARY.
thanks anyways...
HOTS

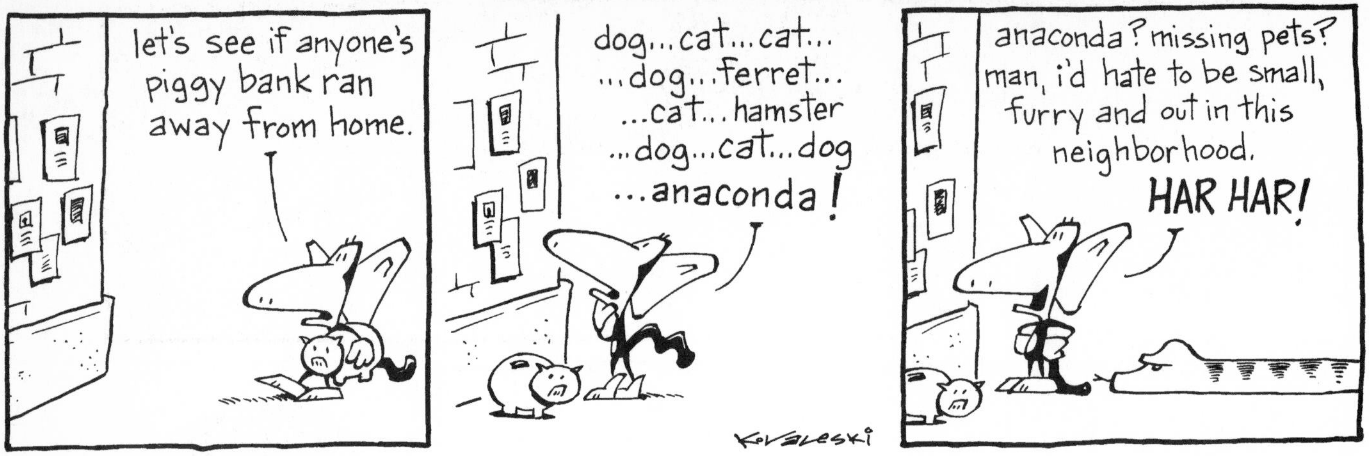
let's see if anyone's piggy bank ran away from home.
dog...cat...cat... ...dog...ferret... ...cat...hamster ...dog...cat...dog ...anaconda!
KOVALESKI
anaconda? missing pets? man, i'd hate to be small, furry and out in this neighborhood.
HAR HAR!

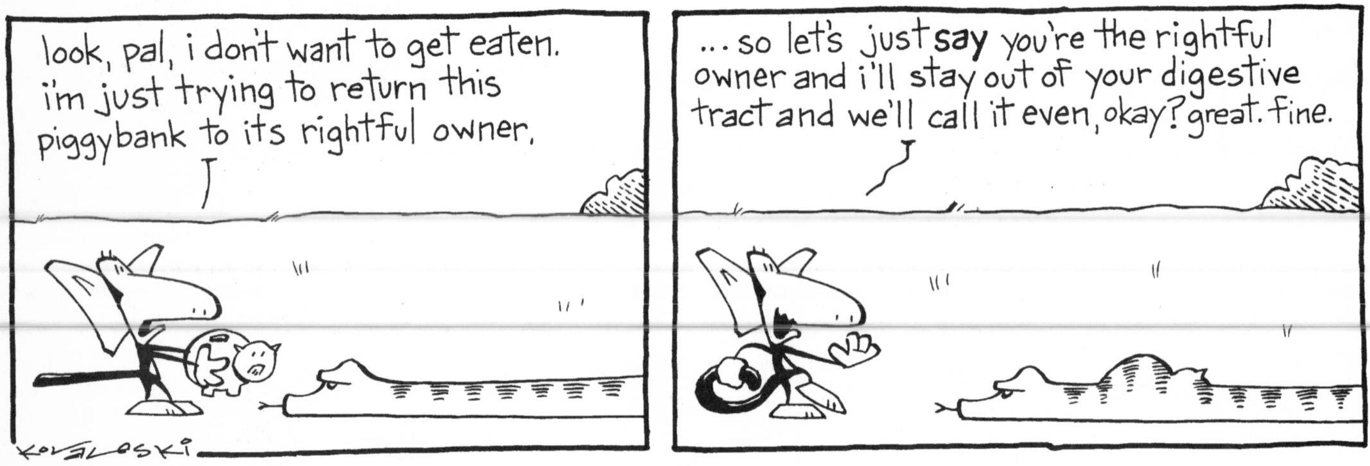
look, pal, i don't want to get eaten. i'm just trying to return this piggybank to its rightful owner,
KOVALESKI
...so let's just **say** you're the rightful owner and i'll stay out of your digestive tract and we'll call it even, okay? great. fine.

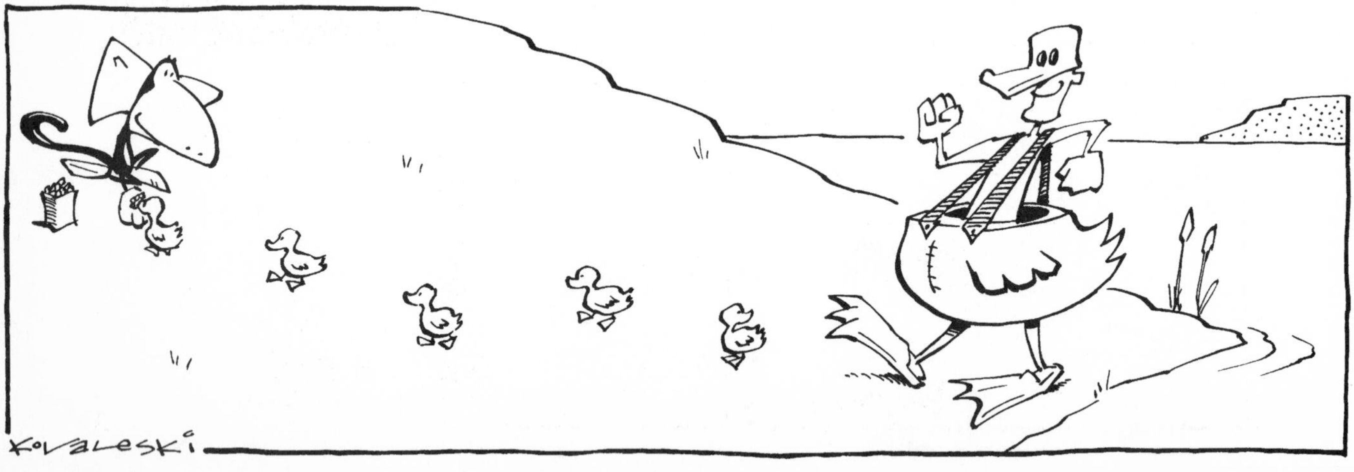
KOVALESKI

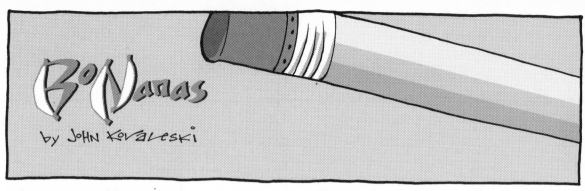

Bo'Nanas by John Kovaleski

hi.

HI.

so, whatcha doing?

WALKING.

i mean, whatcha doing with the giant pencil?

CARRYING IT.

no, i mean, why?

IF I DIDN'T CARRY IT, IT WOULD GET ALL DIRTY ON THE GROUND.

no, i mean what's the purpose of it?

TO GET PEOPLE TO ASK INCREASINGLY FRUSTRATING QUESTIONS AS I GIVE THEM ELUSIVE ANSWERS.

she should have said so in the first place.

Kovaleski

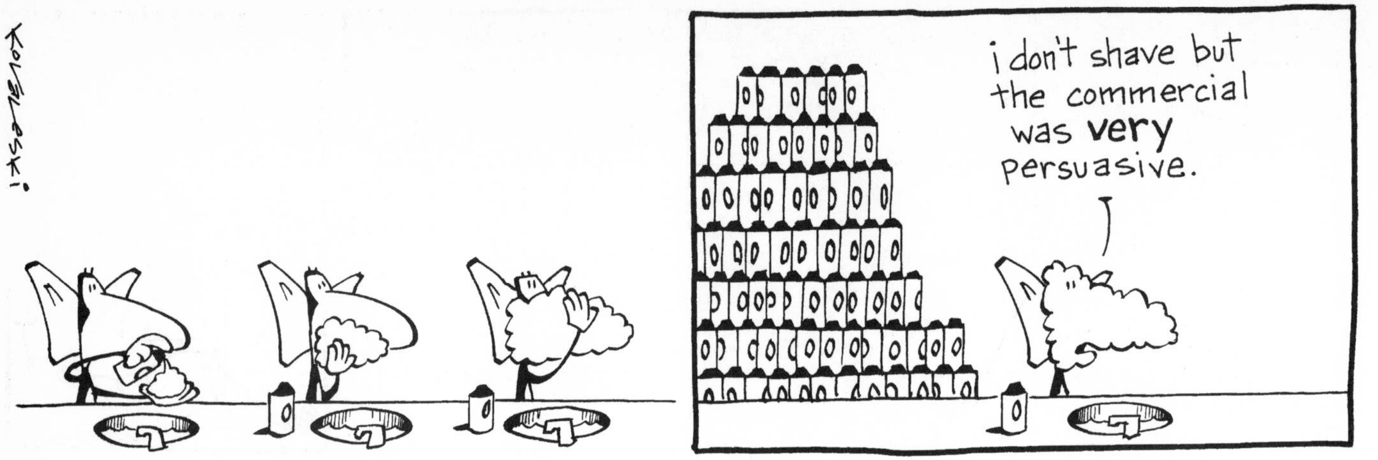
KOVALESKI!
i don't shave but the commercial was **very** persuasive.

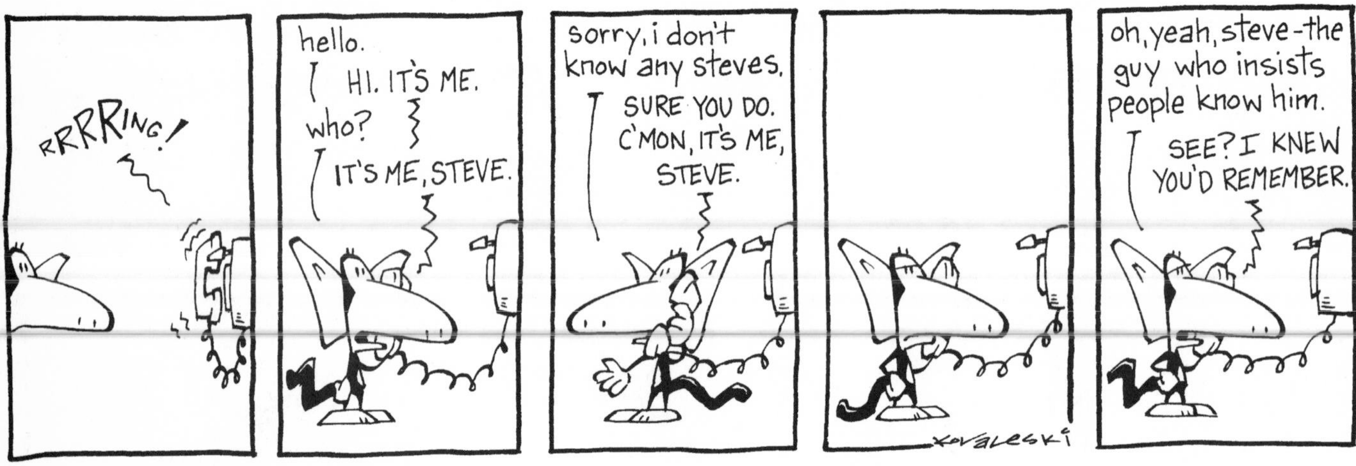
RRRRING!
hello.
HI. IT'S ME.
who?
IT'S ME, STEVE.
sorry, i don't know any steves.
SURE YOU DO. C'MON, IT'S ME, STEVE.
KOVALESKI
oh, yeah, steve - the guy who insists people know him.
SEE? I KNEW YOU'D REMEMBER.

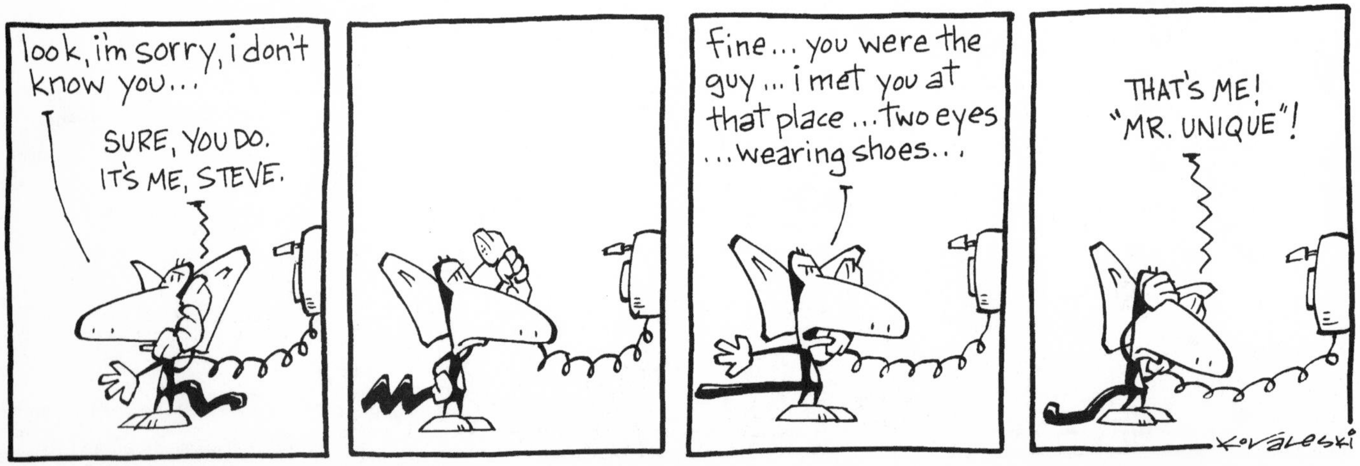
look, i'm sorry, i don't know you...
SURE, YOU DO. IT'S ME, STEVE.
fine... you were the guy... i met you at that place... two eyes ...wearing shoes...
THAT'S ME! "MR. UNIQUE"!
KOVALESKI

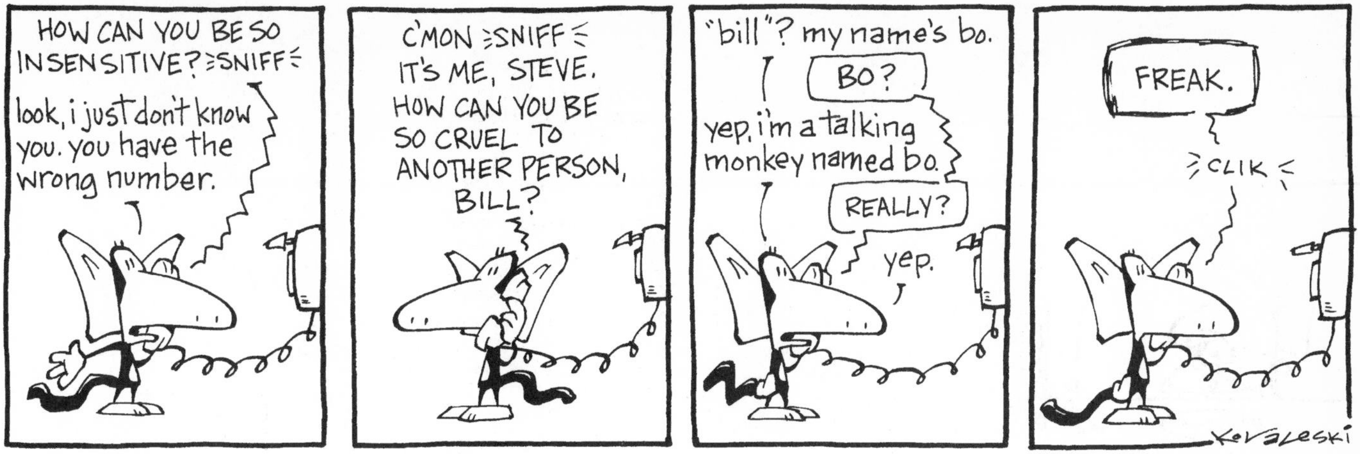
HOW CAN YOU BE SO INSENSITIVE? ≥SNIFF≤
look, i just don't know you. you have the wrong number.
C'MON ≥SNIFF≤ IT'S ME, STEVE. HOW CAN YOU BE SO CRUEL TO ANOTHER PERSON, BILL?
"bill"? my name's bo.
BO?
yep, i'm a talking monkey named bo.
REALLY?
yep.
FREAK.
≥CLIK≤
KOVALESKI

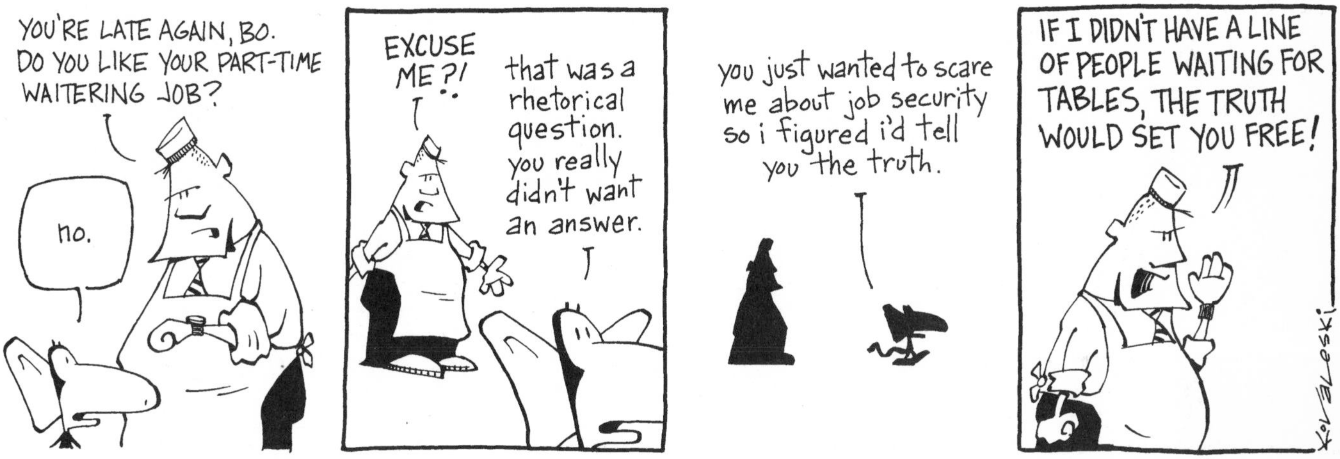
YOU'RE LATE AGAIN, BO. DO YOU LIKE YOUR PART-TIME WAITERING JOB?
no.
EXCUSE ME?!
that was a rhetorical question. you really didn't want an answer.
you just wanted to scare me about job security so i figured i'd tell you the truth.
IF I DIDN'T HAVE A LINE OF PEOPLE WAITING FOR TABLES, THE TRUTH WOULD SET YOU FREE!
KOVALESKI

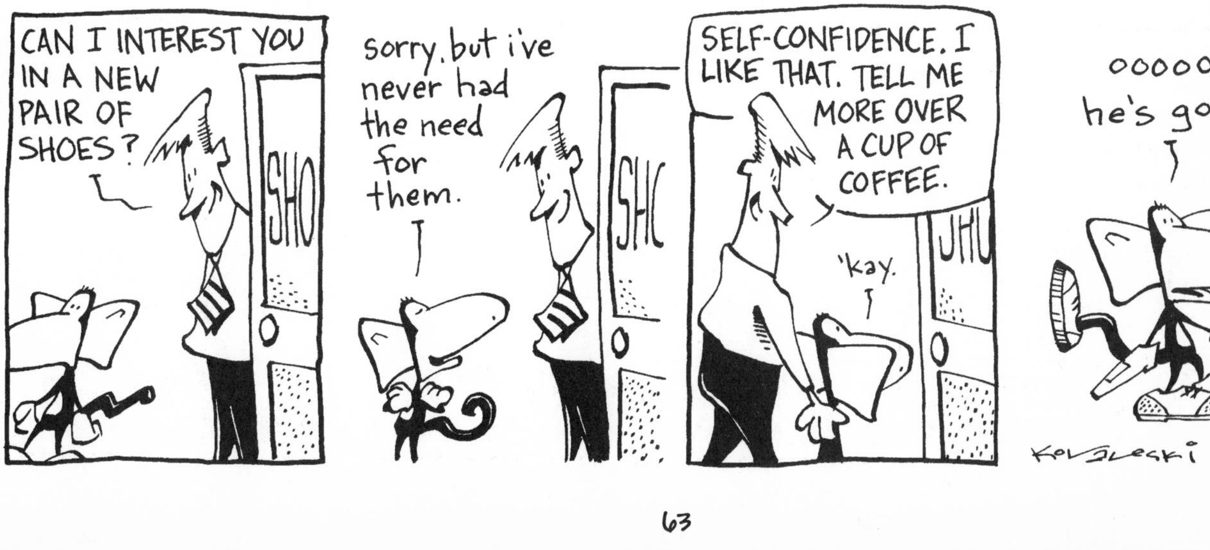
CAN I INTEREST YOU IN A NEW PAIR OF SHOES?
SHO
sorry, but i've never had the need for them.
SHC
SELF-CONFIDENCE. I LIKE THAT. TELL ME MORE OVER A CUP OF COFFEE.
'kay.
ooooo, he's good.
KOVALESKI

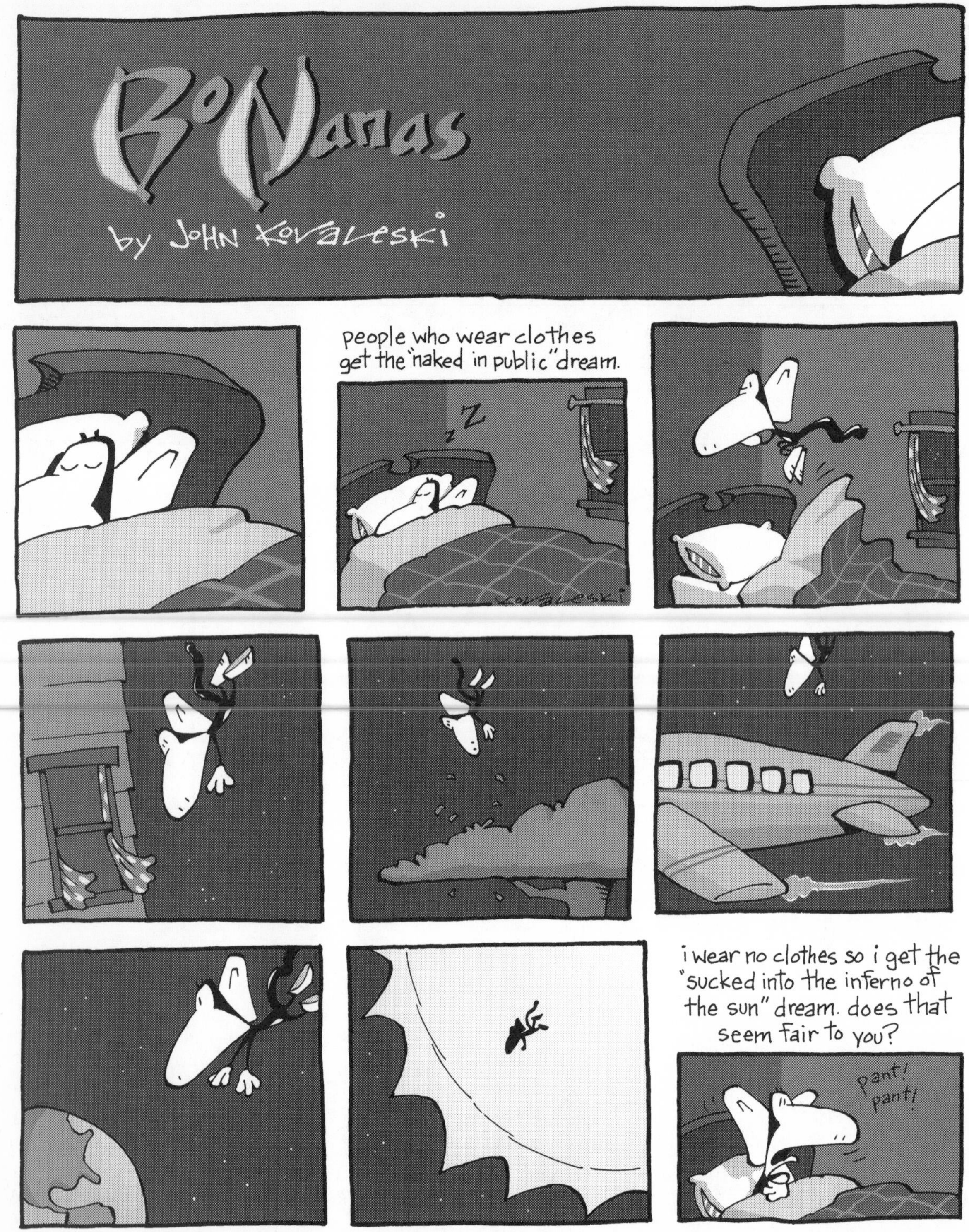
BoNanas
by JOHN KOVALESKI
people who wear clothes get the "naked in public" dream.
z
Z
KOVALESKI
i wear no clothes so i get the "sucked into the inferno of the sun" dream. does that seem fair to you?
pant!
pant!

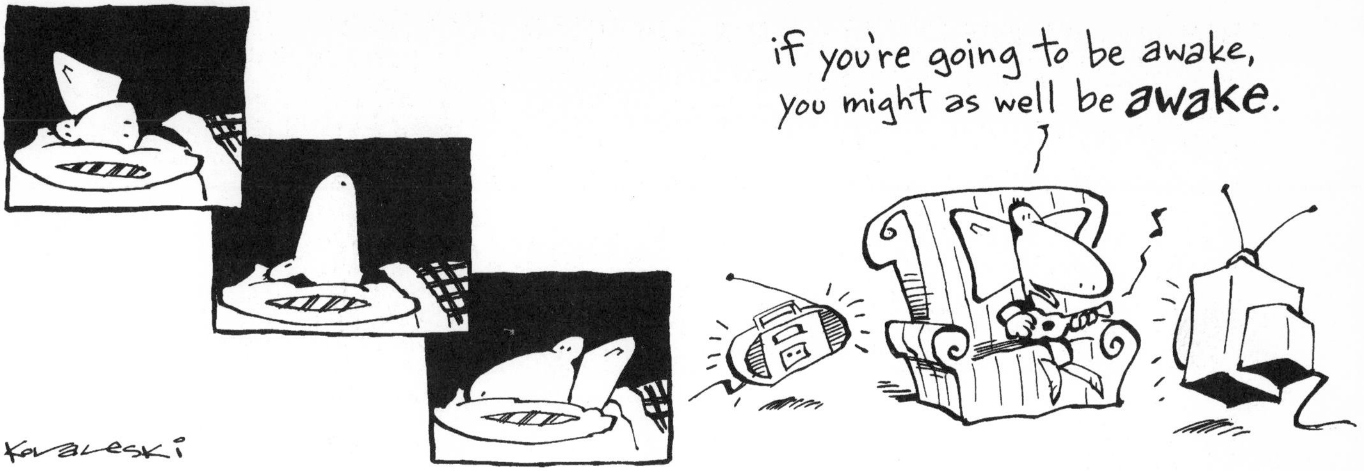
if you're going to be awake,
you might as well be **awake**.
KOVALESKI

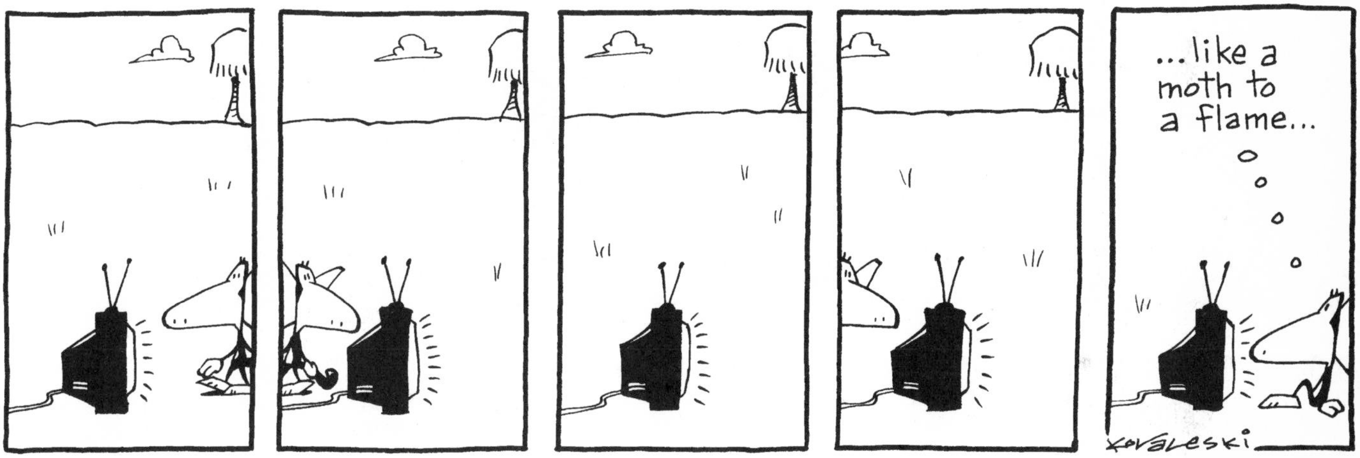
...like a
moth to
a flame...
KOVALESKI

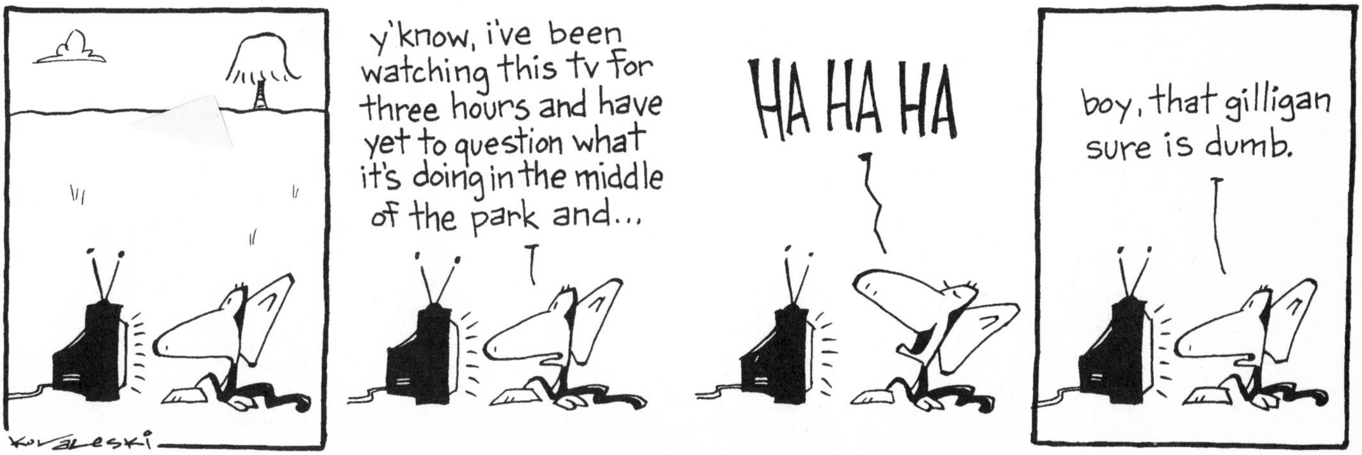
y'know, i've been
watching this tv for
three hours and have
yet to question what
it's doing in the middle
of the park and...
HA HA HA
boy, that gilligan
sure is dumb.
KOVALESKI

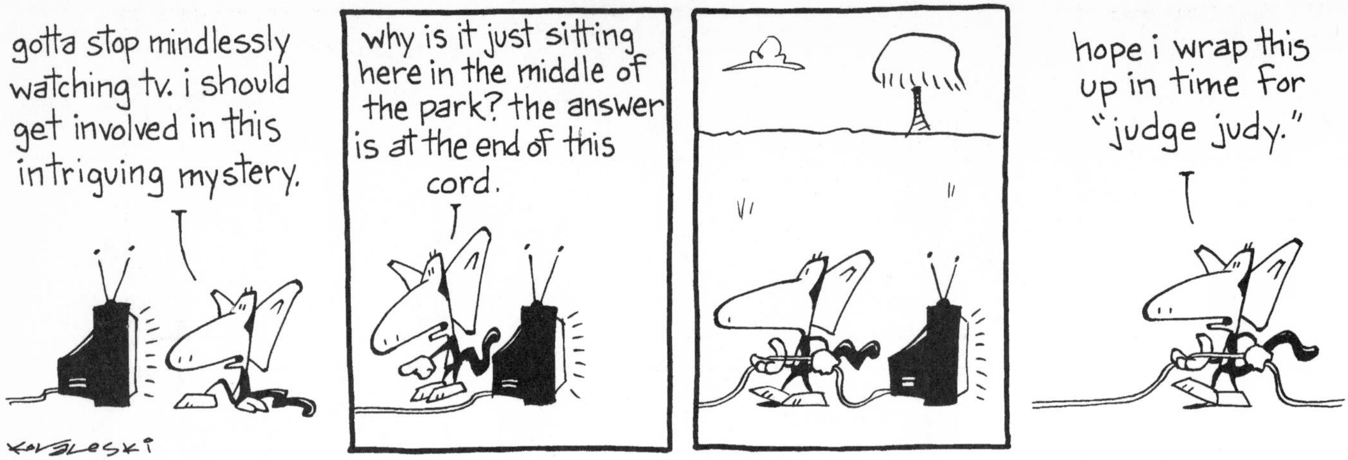
gotta stop mindlessly watching tv. i should get involved in this intriguing mystery.
kovaleski
why is it just sitting here in the middle of the park? the answer is at the end of this cord.
hope i wrap this up in time for "judge judy."

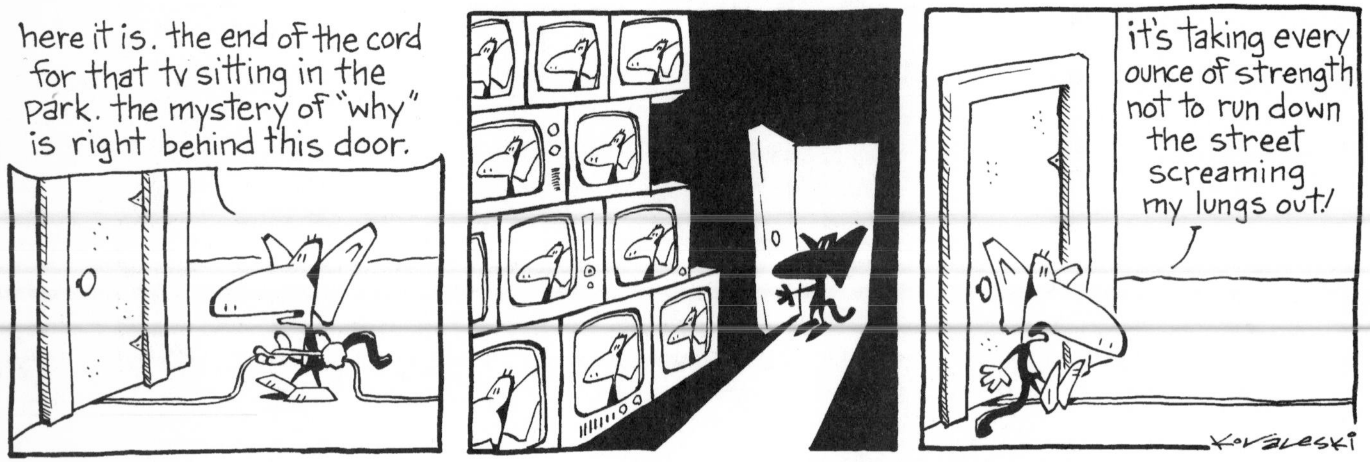
here it is. the end of the cord for that tv sitting in the park. the mystery of "why" is right behind this door.
it's taking every ounce of strength not to run down the street screaming my lungs out!
kovaleski

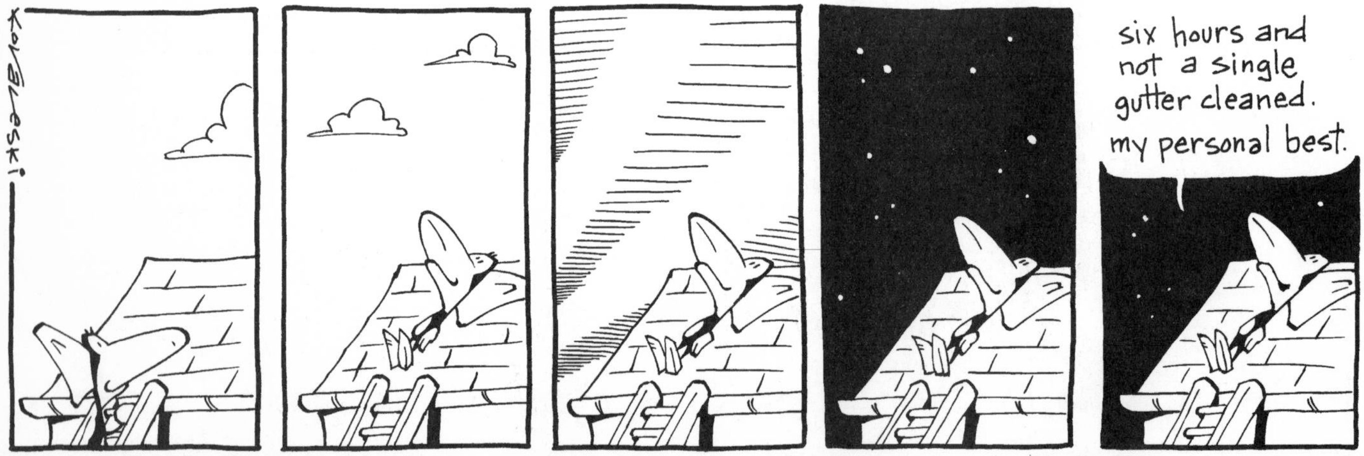
kovaleski
six hours and not a single gutter cleaned. my personal best.

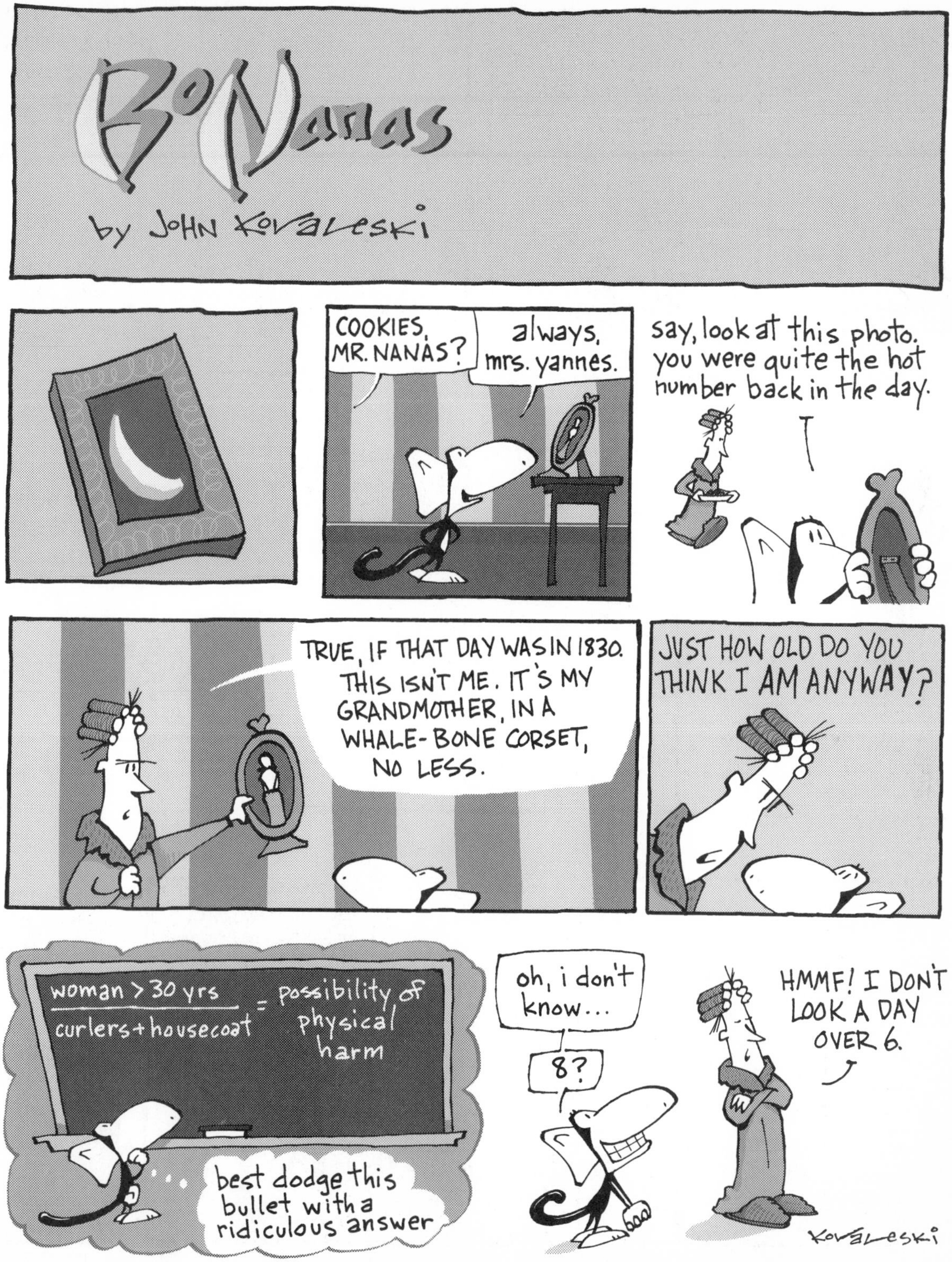
BoNanas
by JOHN KOVALESKI
COOKIES, MR. NANAS?
always, mrs. yannes.
say, look at this photo. you were quite the hot number back in the day.
TRUE, IF THAT DAY WAS IN 1830. THIS ISN'T ME. IT'S MY GRANDMOTHER, IN A WHALE-BONE CORSET, NO LESS.
JUST HOW OLD DO YOU THINK I AM ANYWAY?
woman > 30 yrs / curlers + housecoat = possibility of physical harm
best dodge this bullet with a ridiculous answer
oh, i don't know...
8?
HMMF! I DON'T LOOK A DAY OVER 6.
KOVALESKI

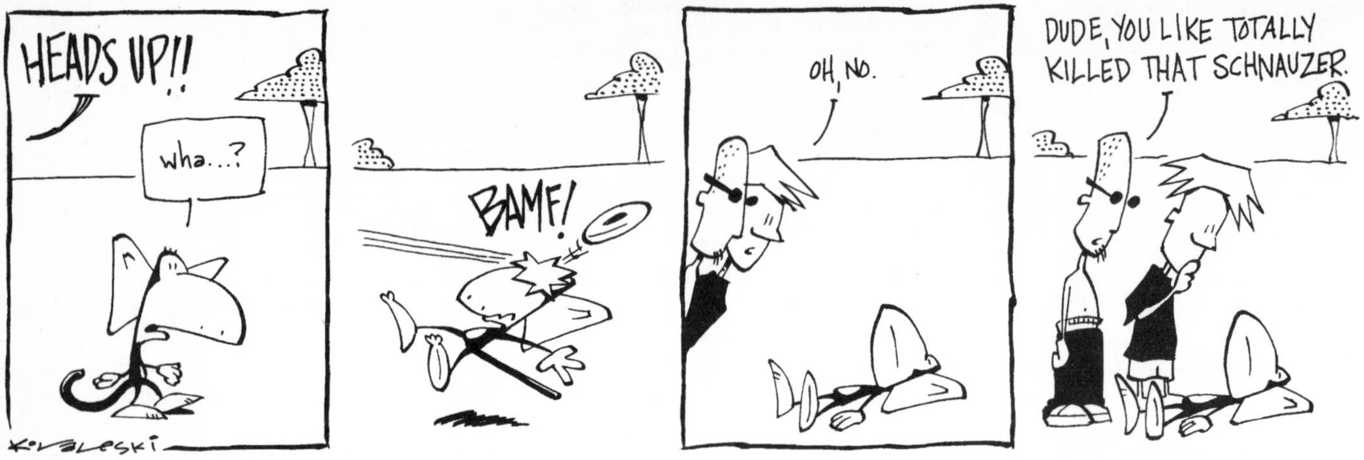
HEADS UP!!
wha...?
BAMF!
OH, NO.
DUDE, YOU LIKE TOTALLY KILLED THAT SCHNAUZER.
KOVALESKI

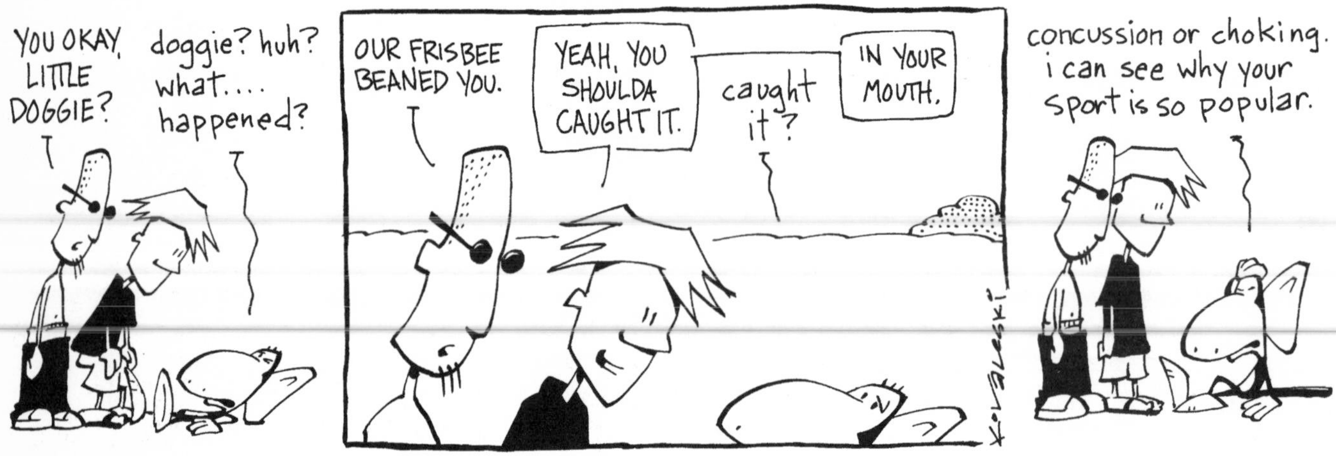
YOU OKAY, LITTLE DOGGIE?
doggie? huh? what.... happened?
OUR FRISBEE BEANED YOU.
YEAH, YOU SHOULDA CAUGHT IT.
caught it?
IN YOUR MOUTH.
concussion or choking. i can see why your sport is so popular.
KOVALESKI

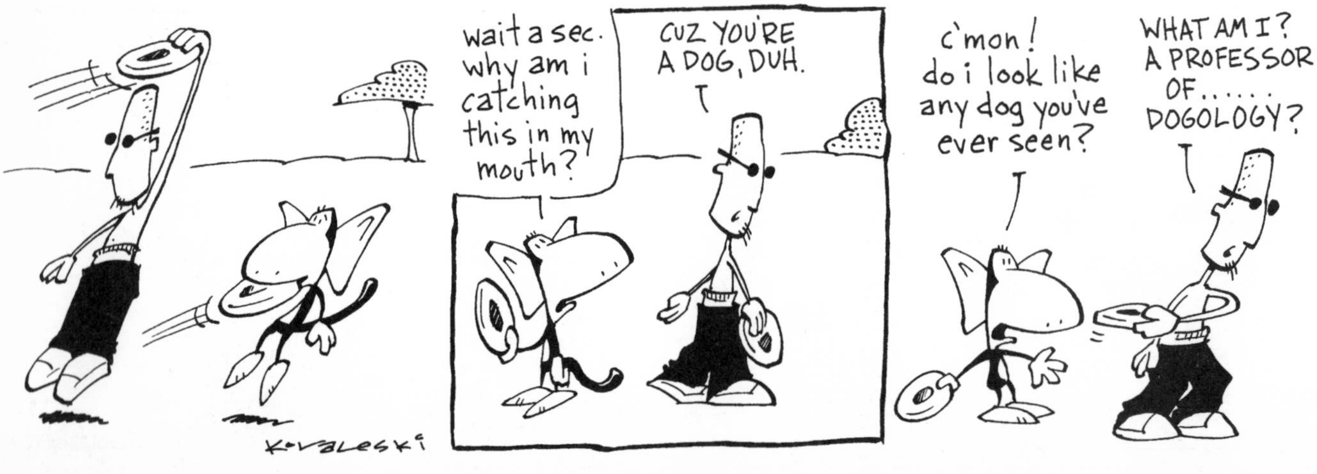
wait a sec. why am i catching this in my mouth?
CUZ YOU'RE A DOG, DUH.
c'mon! do i look like any dog you've ever seen?
WHAT AM I? A PROFESSOR OF...... DOGOLOGY?
KOVALESKI

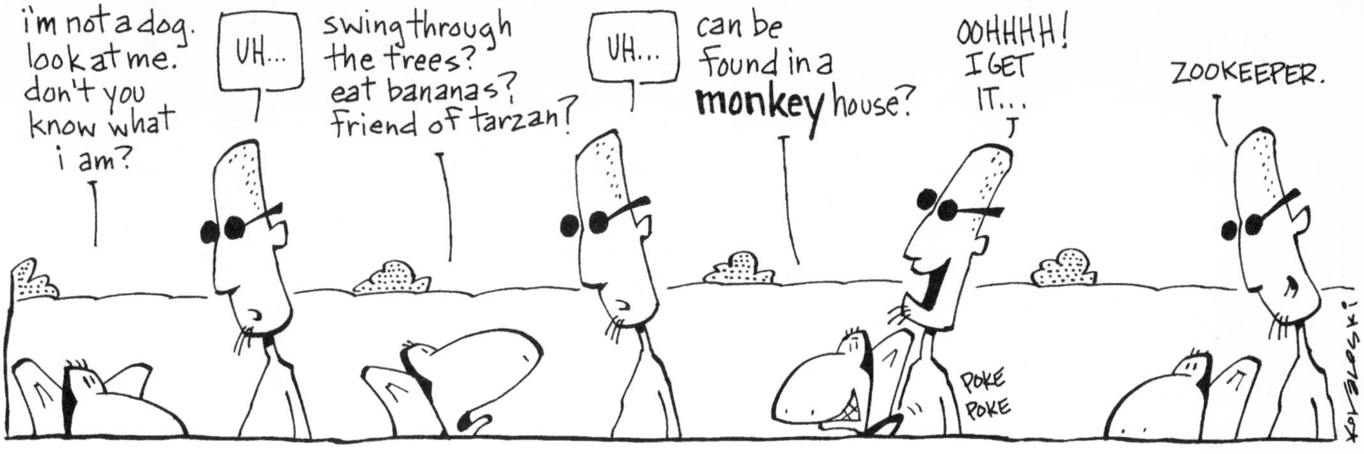
i'm not a dog. look at me. don't you know what i am?
UH...
swing through the trees? eat bananas? friend of tarzan?
UH...
can be found in a **monkey** house?
OOHHHH! I GET IT...
POKE POKE
ZOOKEEPER.
KOVALESKI

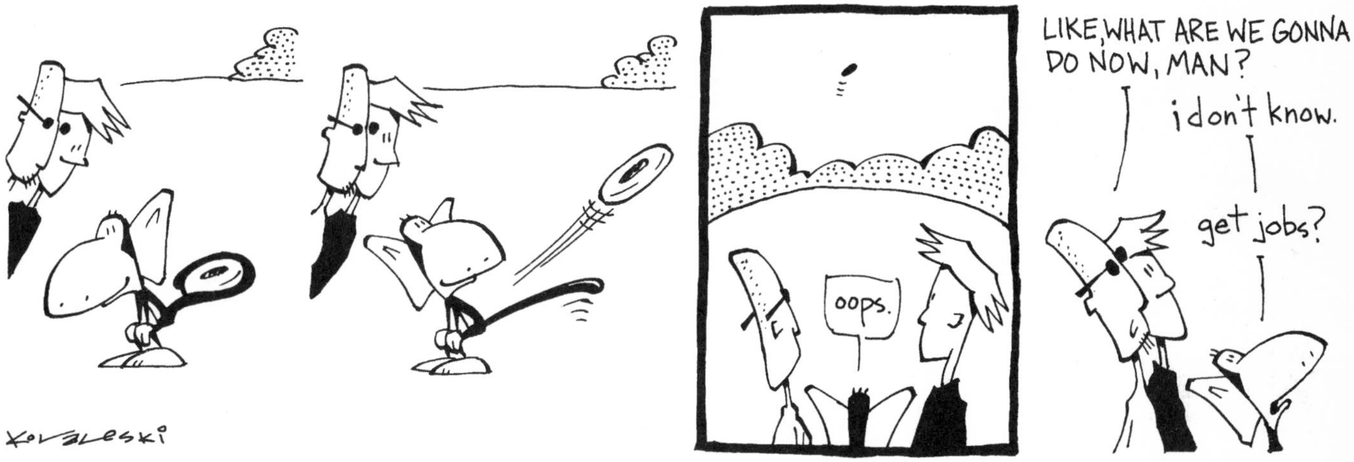
KOVALESKI
oops.
LIKE, WHAT ARE WE GONNA DO NOW, MAN?
i don't know.
get jobs?

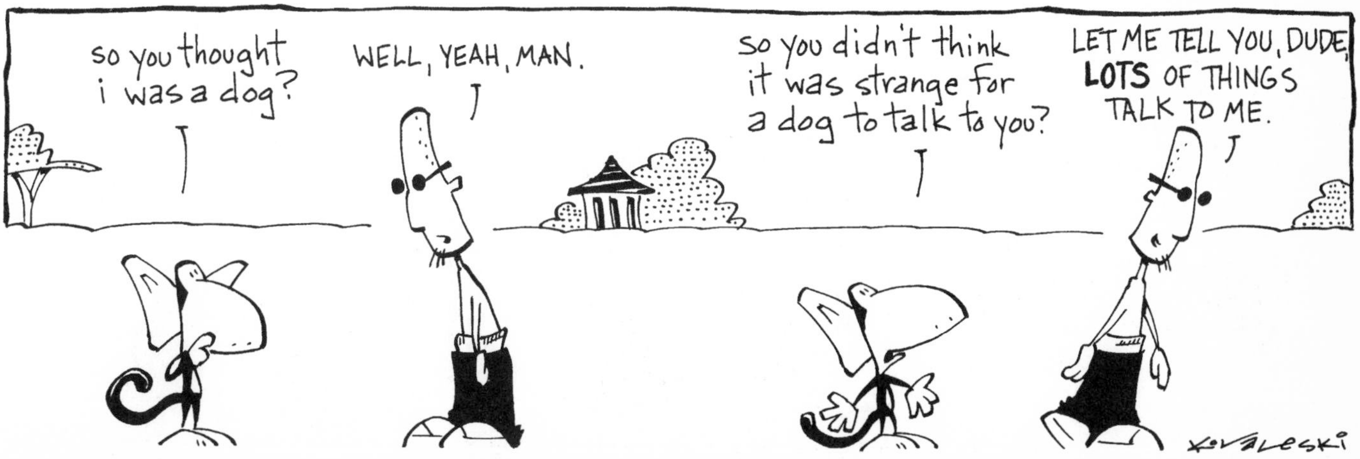
so you thought i was a dog?
WELL, YEAH, MAN.
so you didn't think it was strange for a dog to talk to you?
LET ME TELL YOU, DUDE, **LOTS** OF THINGS TALK TO ME.
KOVALESKI

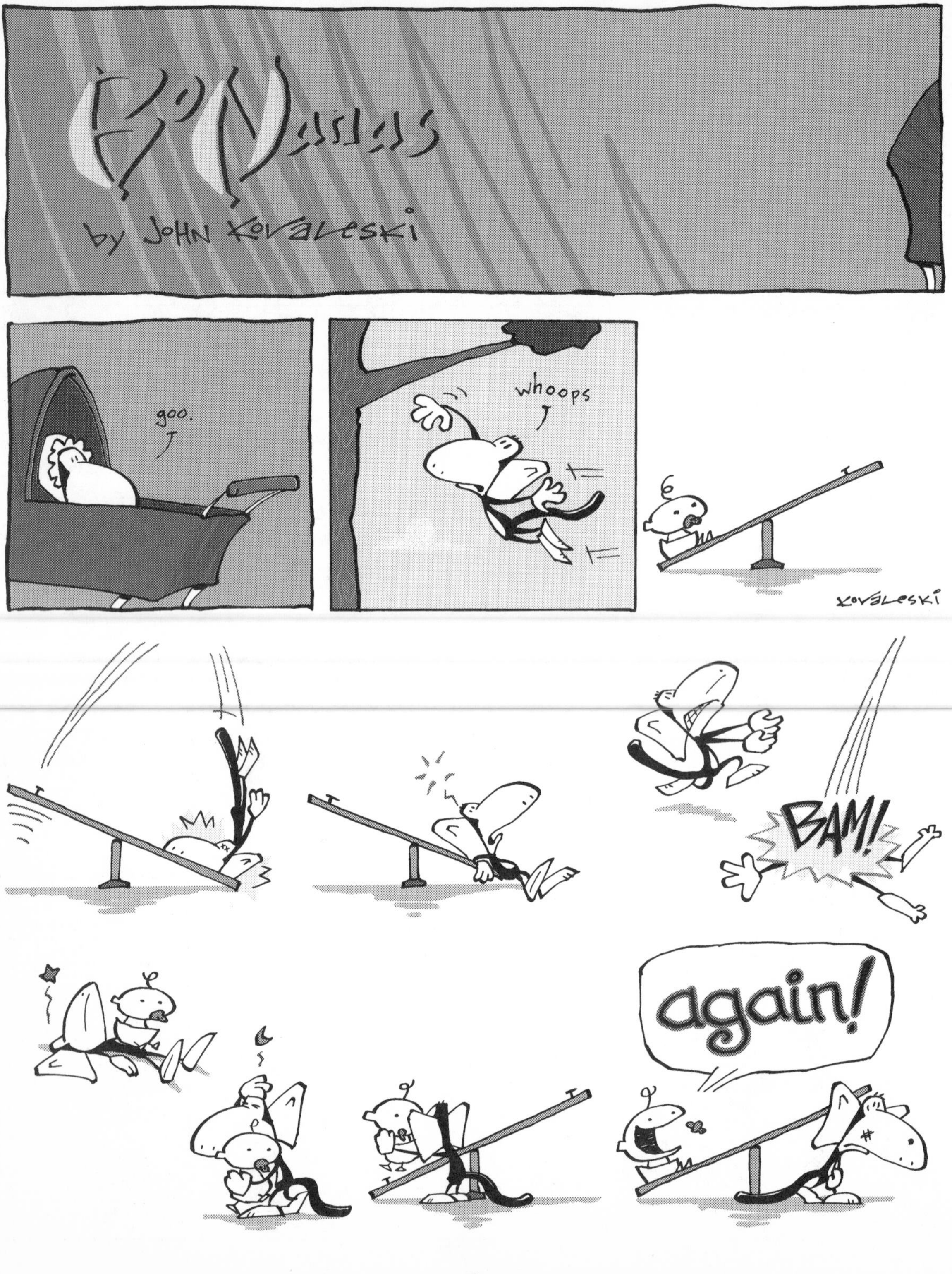
Bo Nanas
by John Kovaleski
goo.
whoops
Kovaleski
BAM!
again!

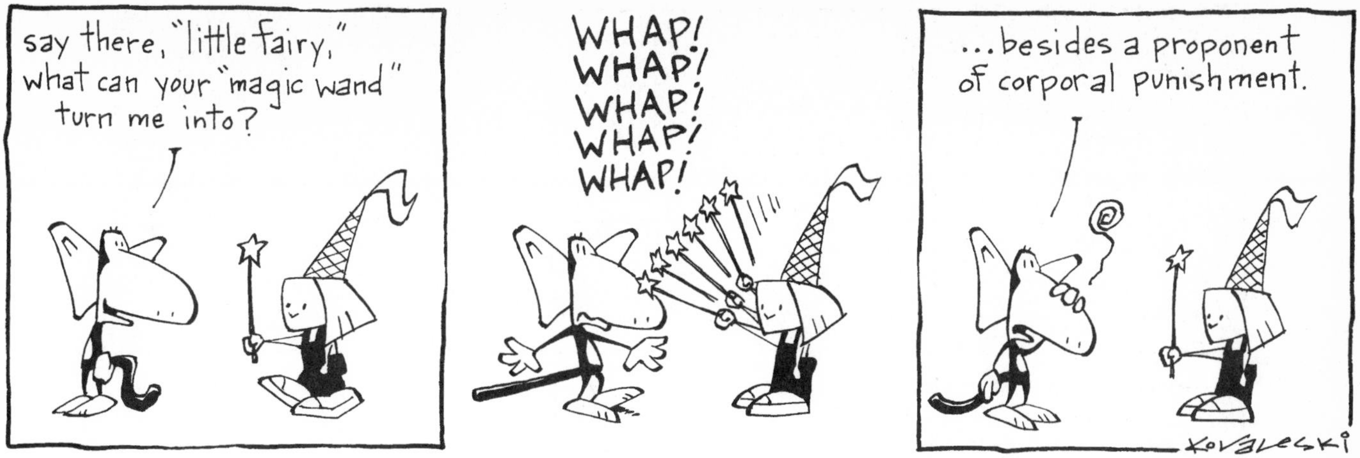
say there, "little fairy," what can your "magic wand" turn me into?
WHAP! WHAP! WHAP! WHAP! WHAP!
...besides a proponent of corporal punishment.
KOVALESKI

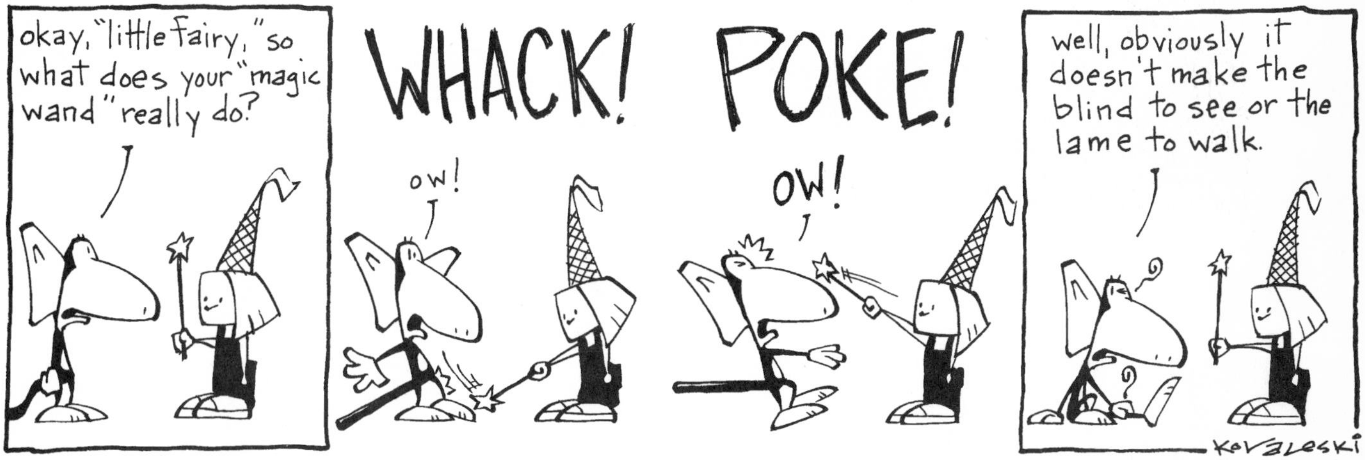
okay, "little fairy," so what does your "magic wand" really do?
WHACK!
OW!
POKE!
OW!
well, obviously it doesn't make the blind to see or the lame to walk.
KOVALESKI

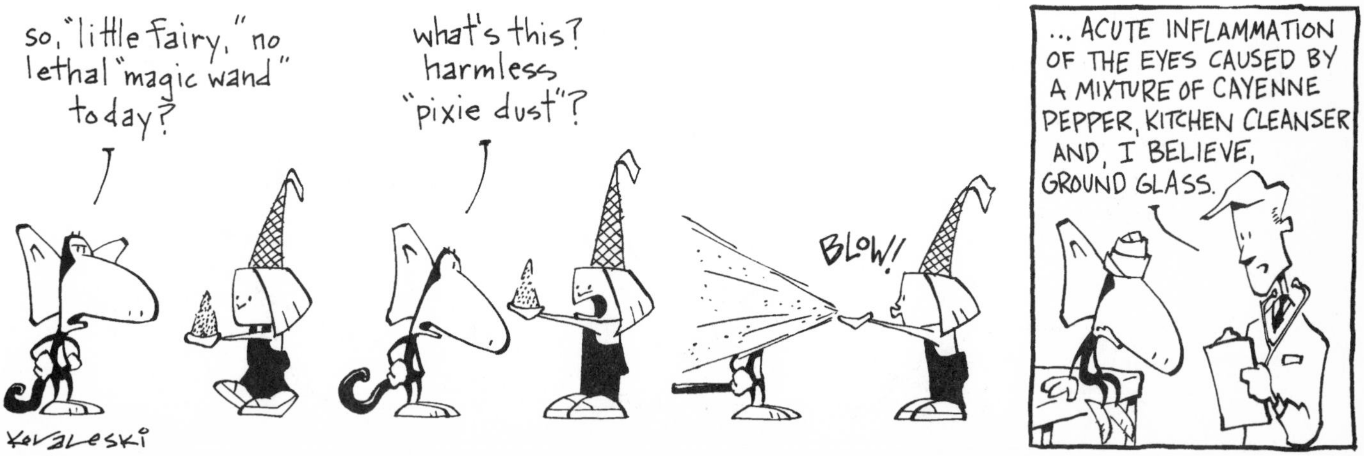
so, "little fairy," no lethal "magic wand" today?
what's this? harmless "pixie dust"?
BLOW!
...ACUTE INFLAMMATION OF THE EYES CAUSED BY A MIXTURE OF CAYENNE PEPPER, KITCHEN CLEANSER AND, I BELIEVE, GROUND GLASS.
KOVALESKI

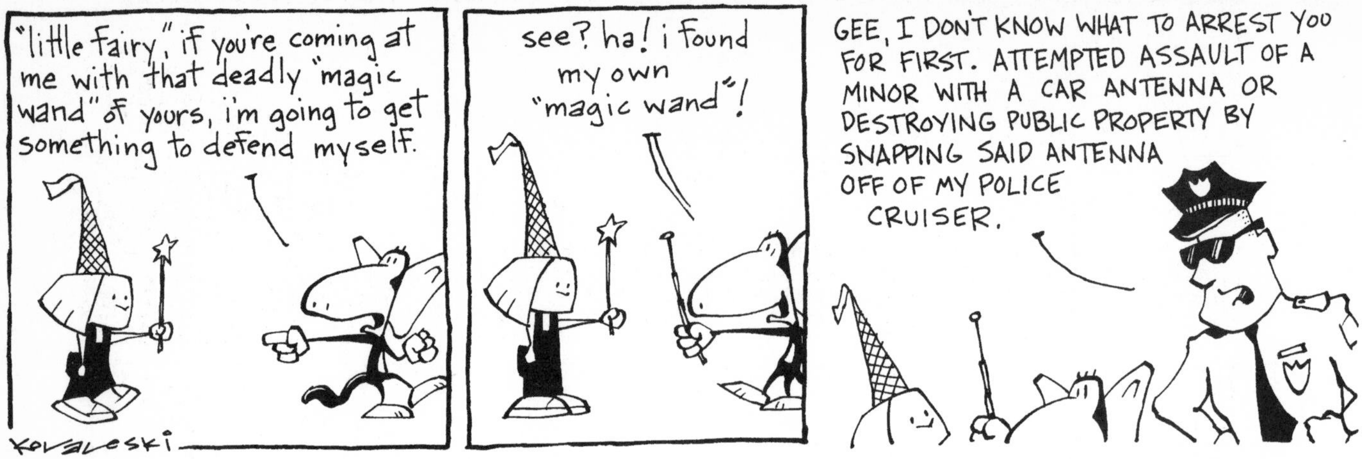
"little fairy," if you're coming at me with that deadly "magic wand" of yours, i'm going to get something to defend myself.
see? ha! i found my own "magic wand"!
GEE, I DON'T KNOW WHAT TO ARREST YOU FOR FIRST. ATTEMPTED ASSAULT OF A MINOR WITH A CAR ANTENNA OR DESTROYING PUBLIC PROPERTY BY SNAPPING SAID ANTENNA OFF OF MY POLICE CRUISER.
KOVALESKI

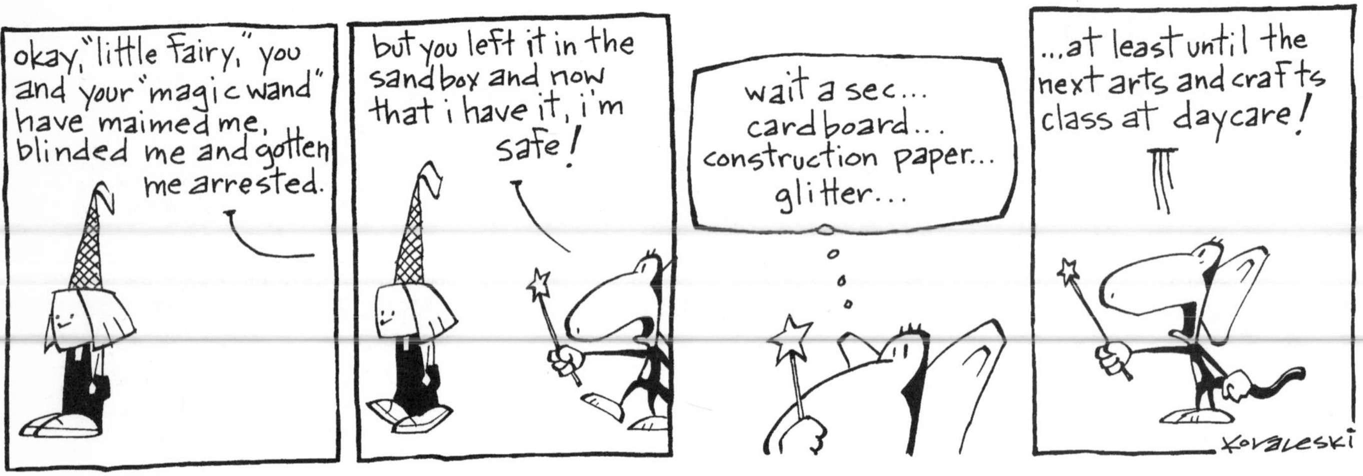
okay, "little fairy," you and your "magic wand" have maimed me, blinded me and gotten me arrested.
but you left it in the sandbox and now that i have it, i'm safe!
wait a sec... cardboard... construction paper... glitter...
...at least until the next arts and crafts class at daycare!
KOVALESKI

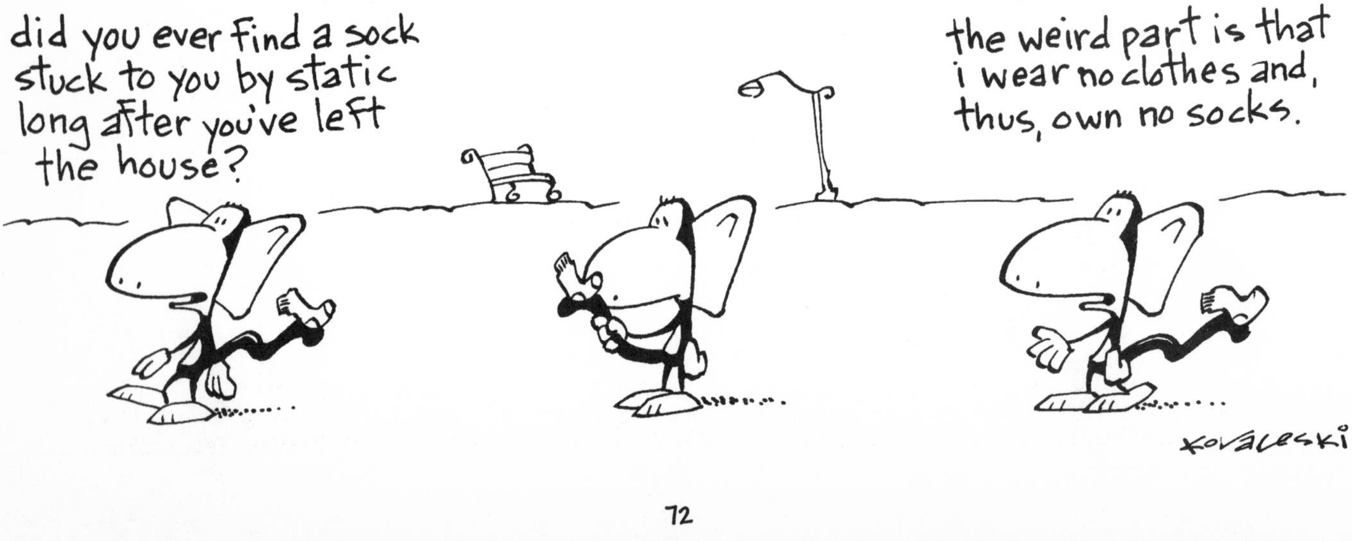
did you ever find a sock stuck to you by static long after you've left the house?
the weird part is that i wear no clothes and, thus, own no socks.
KOVALESKI

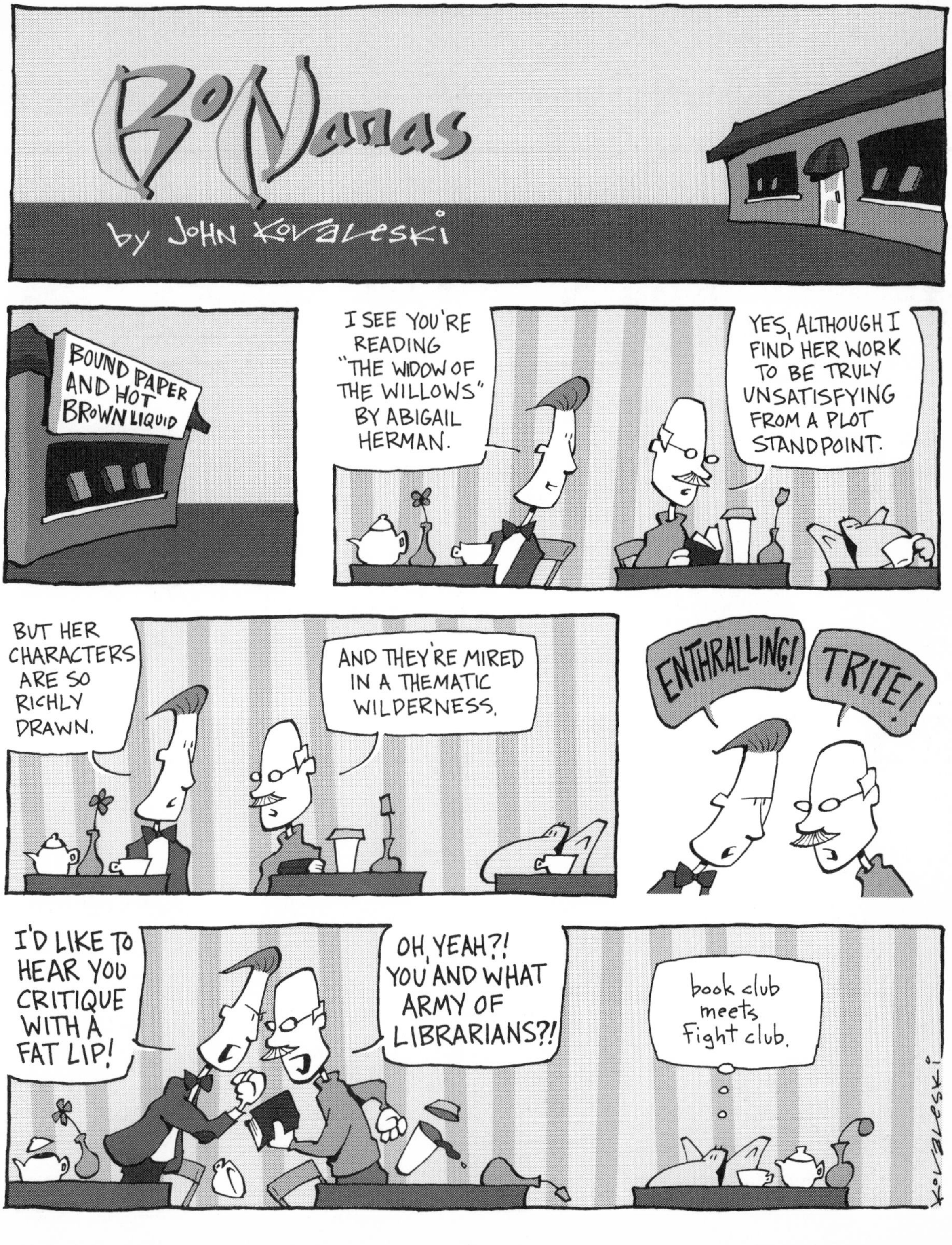
BoNanas
by JOHN KOVALESKI
BOUND PAPER AND HOT BROWN LIQUID
I SEE YOU'RE READING "THE WIDOW OF THE WILLOWS" BY ABIGAIL HERMAN.
YES, ALTHOUGH I FIND HER WORK TO BE TRULY UNSATISFYING FROM A PLOT STANDPOINT.
BUT HER CHARACTERS ARE SO RICHLY DRAWN.
AND THEY'RE MIRED IN A THEMATIC WILDERNESS.
ENTHRALLING!
TRITE!
I'D LIKE TO HEAR YOU CRITIQUE WITH A FAT LIP!
OH, YEAH?! YOU AND WHAT ARMY OF LIBRARIANS?!
book club meets fight club.
KOVALESKI

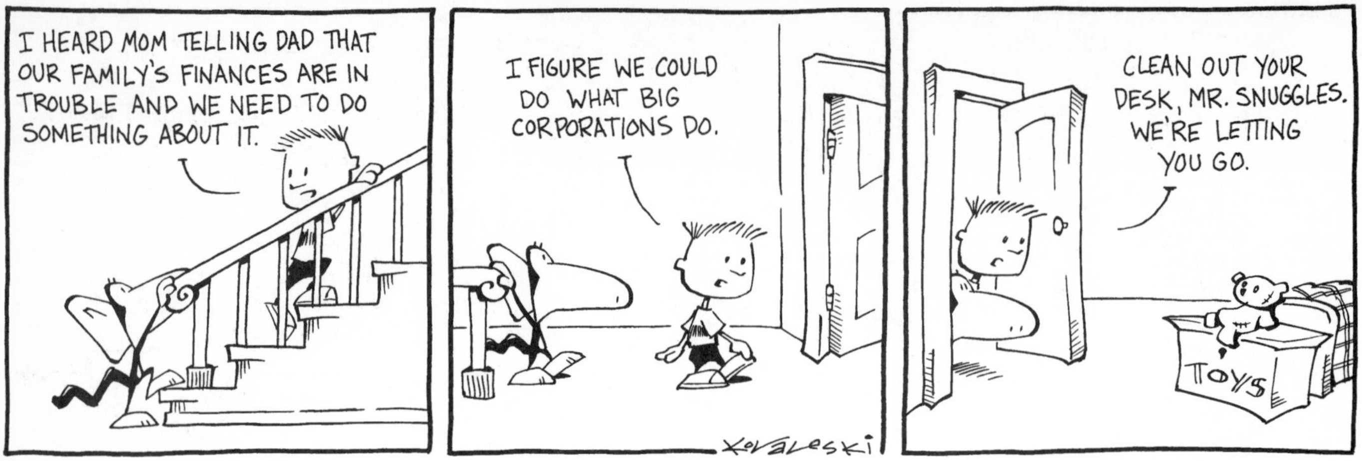
I HEARD MOM TELLING DAD THAT OUR FAMILY'S FINANCES ARE IN TROUBLE AND WE NEED TO DO SOMETHING ABOUT IT.
I FIGURE WE COULD DO WHAT BIG CORPORATIONS DO.
CLEAN OUT YOUR DESK, MR. SNUGGLES. WE'RE LETTING YOU GO.
TOYS
KOVALESKI

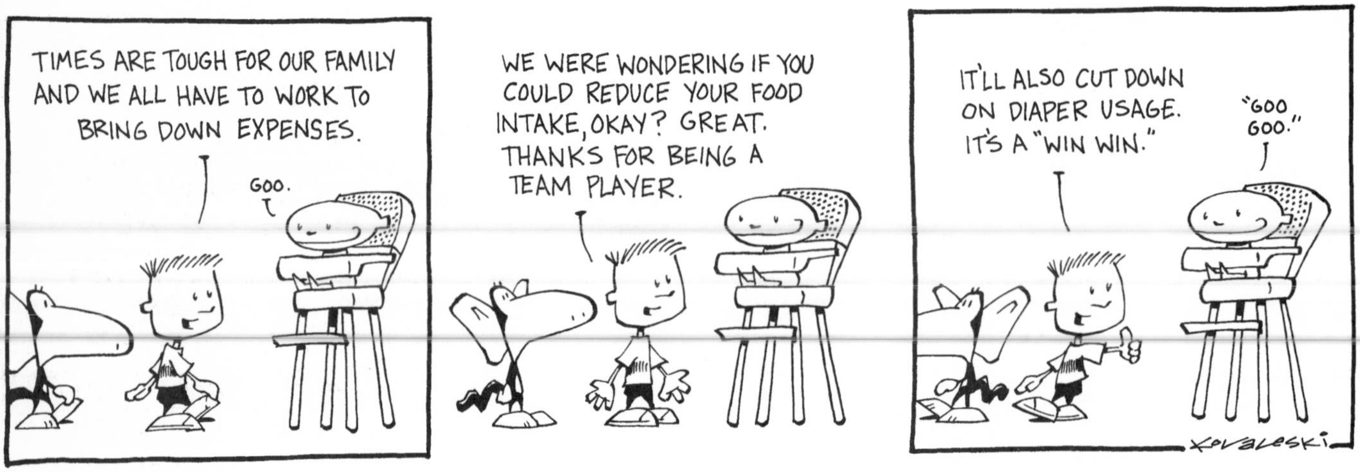
TIMES ARE TOUGH FOR OUR FAMILY AND WE ALL HAVE TO WORK TO BRING DOWN EXPENSES.
GOO.
WE WERE WONDERING IF YOU COULD REDUCE YOUR FOOD INTAKE, OKAY? GREAT. THANKS FOR BEING A TEAM PLAYER.
IT'LL ALSO CUT DOWN ON DIAPER USAGE. IT'S A "WIN WIN."
"GOO GOO."
KOVALESKI

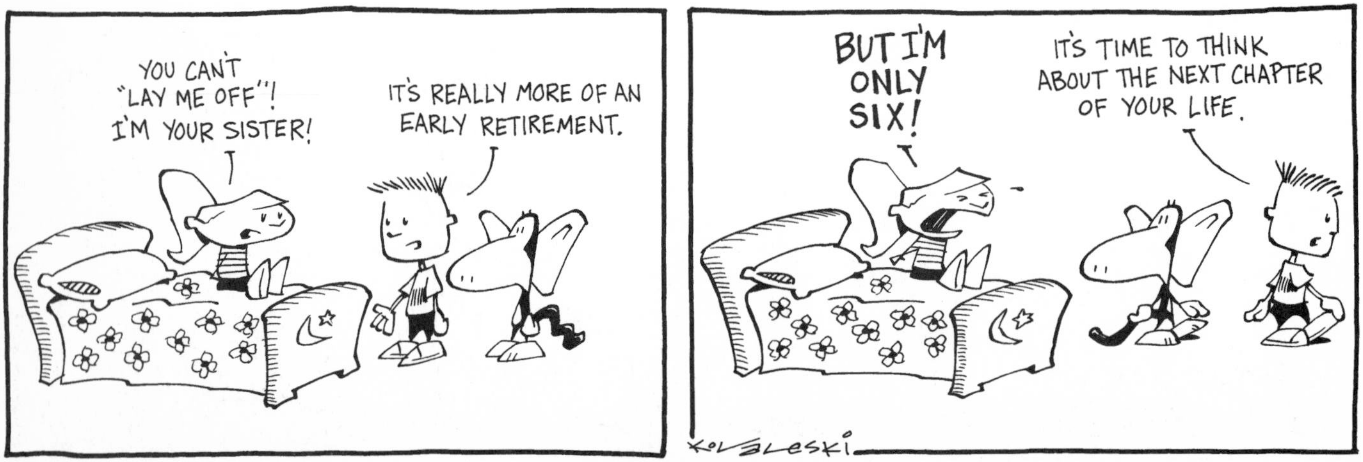
YOU CAN'T "LAY ME OFF"! I'M YOUR SISTER!
IT'S REALLY MORE OF AN EARLY RETIREMENT.
BUT I'M ONLY SIX!
IT'S TIME TO THINK ABOUT THE NEXT CHAPTER OF YOUR LIFE.
KOVALESKI

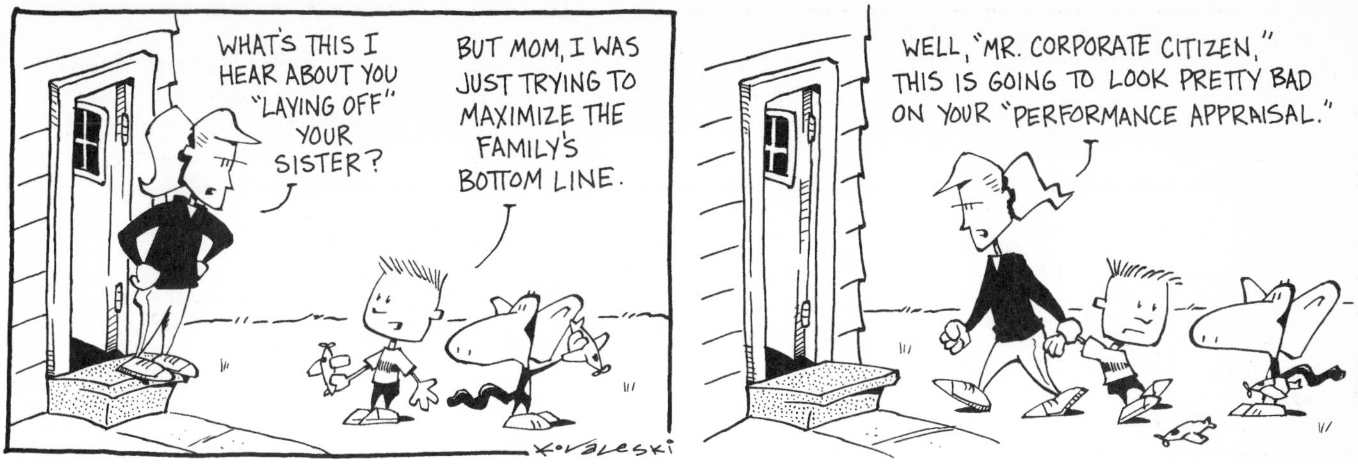
WHAT'S THIS I HEAR ABOUT YOU "LAYING OFF" YOUR SISTER?
BUT MOM, I WAS JUST TRYING TO MAXIMIZE THE FAMILY'S BOTTOM LINE.
WELL, "MR. CORPORATE CITIZEN," THIS IS GOING TO LOOK PRETTY BAD ON YOUR "PERFORMANCE APPRAISAL."
KOVALESKI

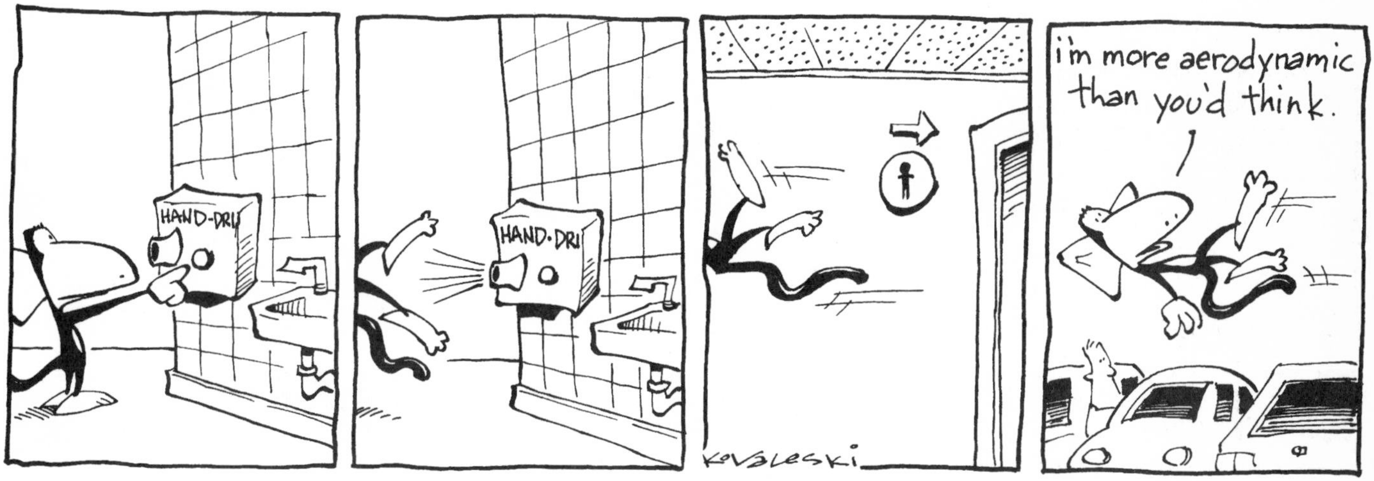
HAND-DRI
HAND·DRI
i'm more aerodynamic than you'd think.
KOVALESKI

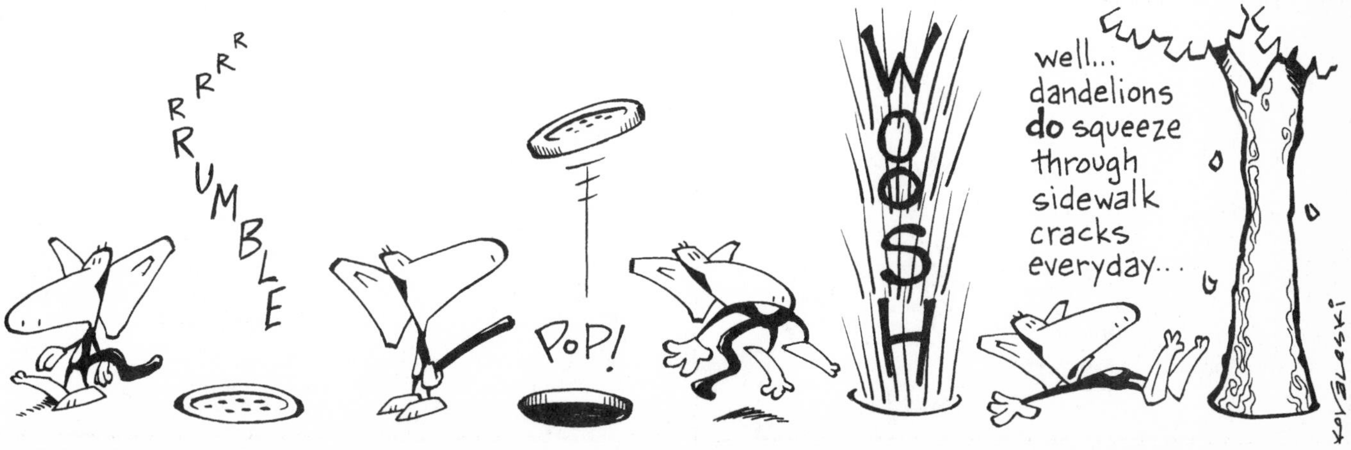
RUMBLE
RRRRR
POP!
WOOSH
well... dandelions **do** squeeze through sidewalk cracks everyday...
KOVALESKI

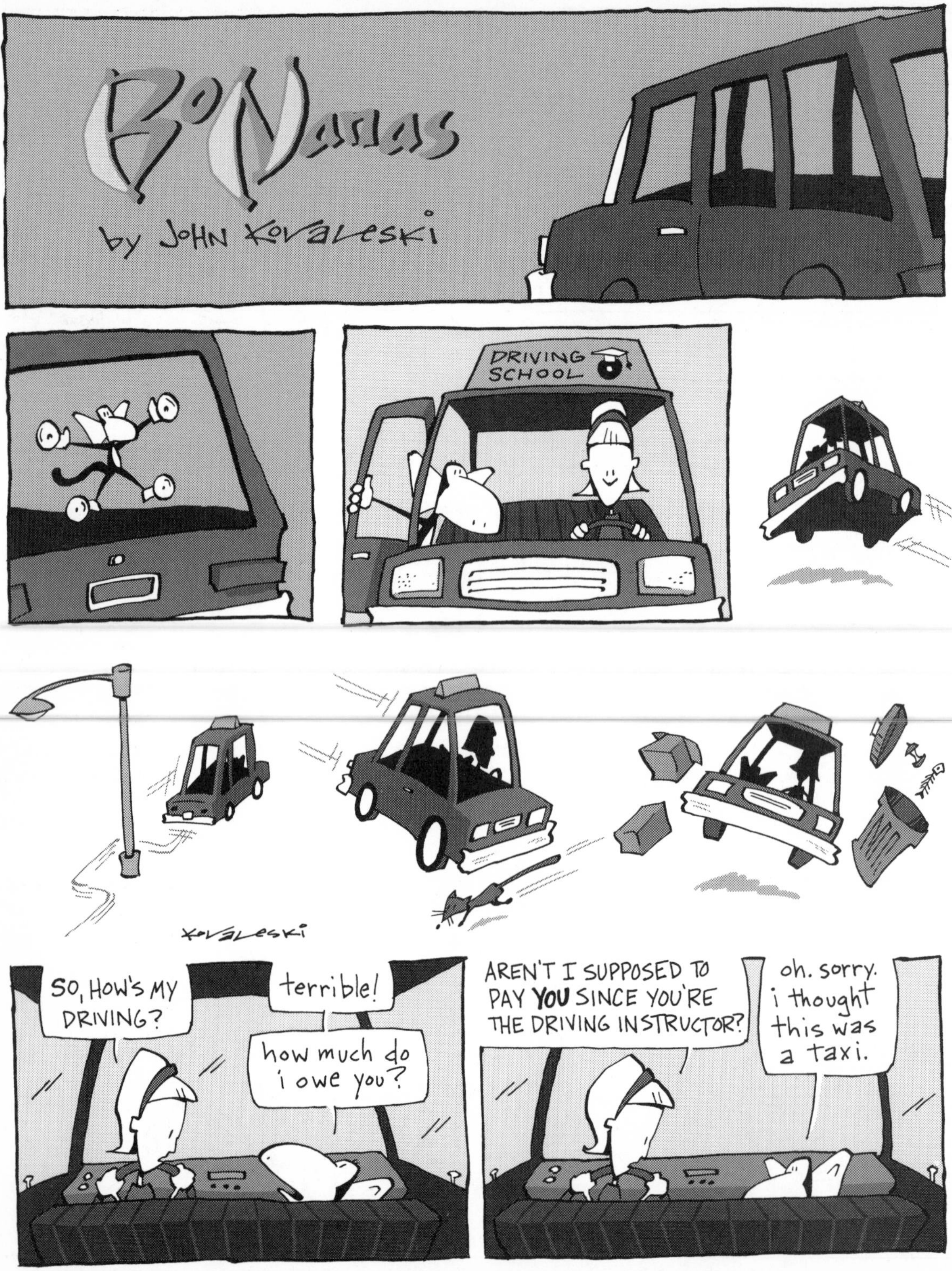
BoNanas
by JOHN KOVALESKI
DRIVING SCHOOL
KOVALESKI
SO, HOW'S MY DRIVING?
terrible!
how much do i owe you?
AREN'T I SUPPOSED TO PAY **YOU** SINCE YOU'RE THE DRIVING INSTRUCTOR?
oh. sorry. i thought this was a taxi.

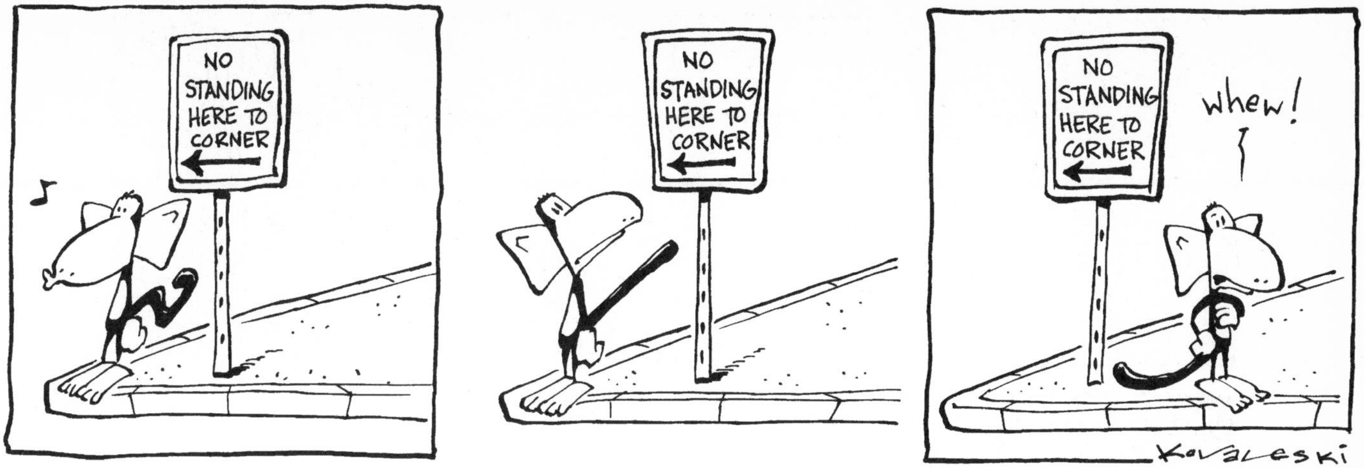
NO STANDING HERE TO CORNER
whew!
KOVALESKI

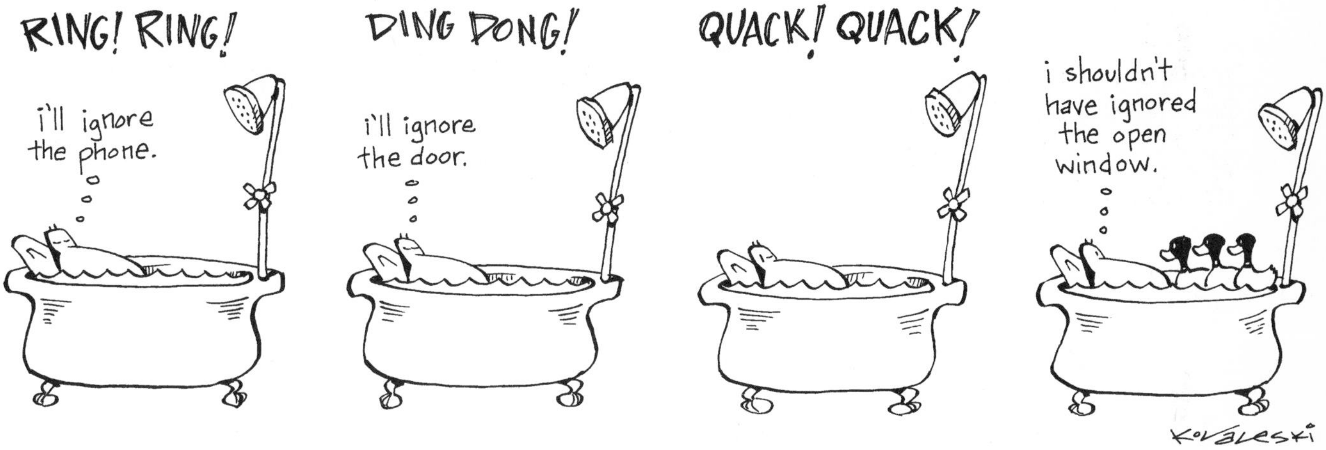
RING! RING!
i'll ignore the phone.
DING DONG!
i'll ignore the door.
QUACK! QUACK!
i shouldn't have ignored the open window.
KOVALESKI

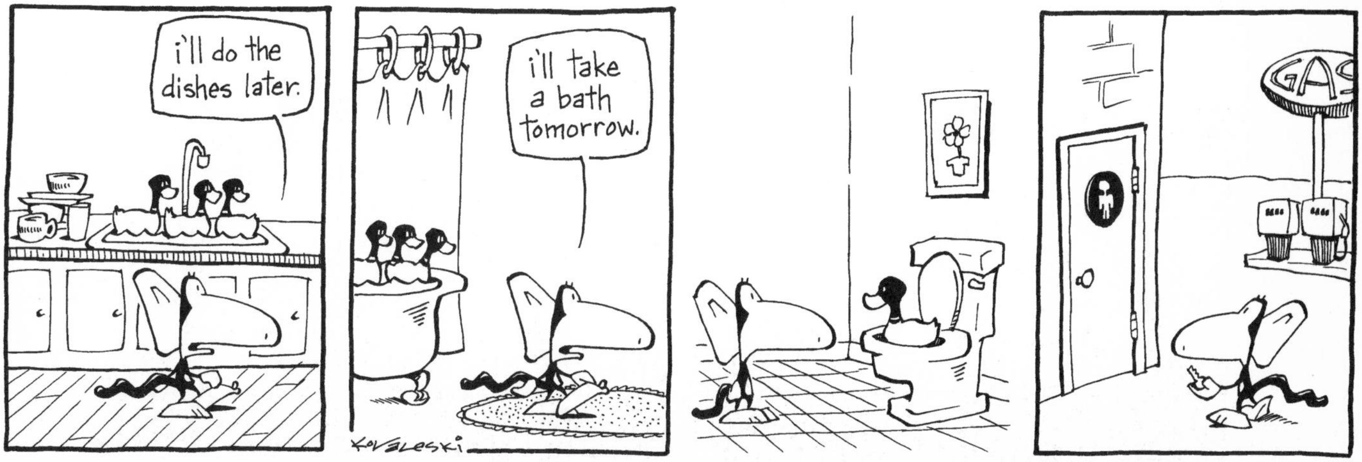
i'll do the dishes later.
i'll take a bath tomorrow.
KOVALESKI
GAS

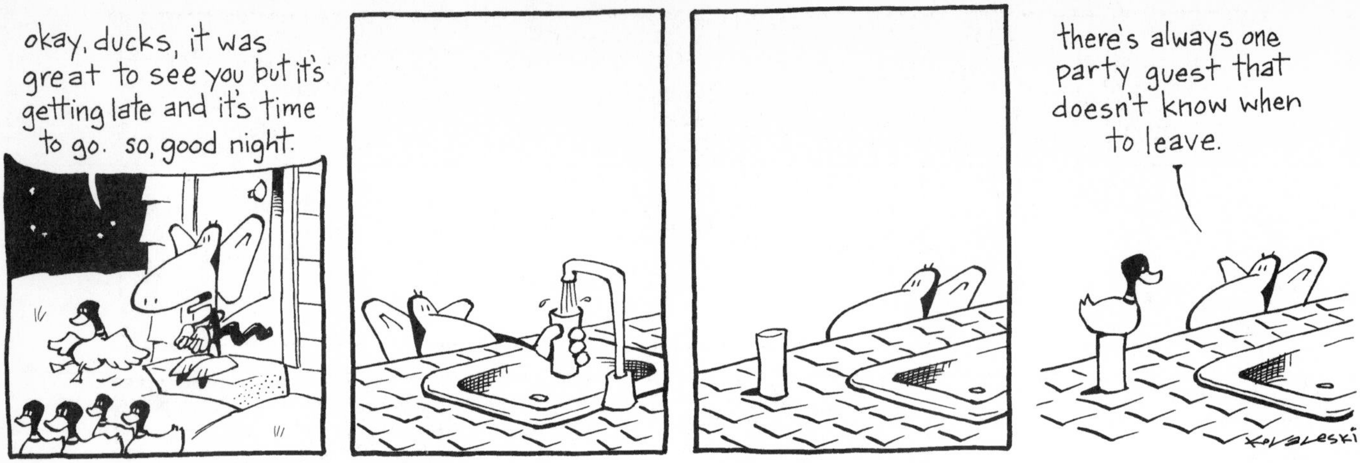
okay, ducks, it was great to see you but it's getting late and it's time to go. so, good night.
there's always one party guest that doesn't know when to leave.
KOVALESKI

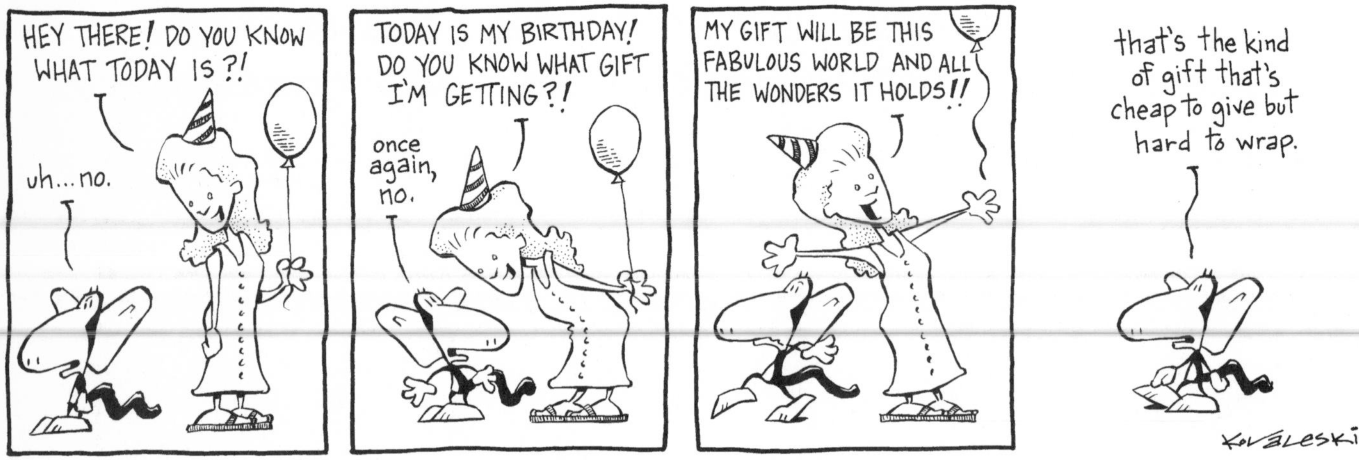
HEY THERE! DO YOU KNOW WHAT TODAY IS?!
uh...no.
TODAY IS MY BIRTHDAY! DO YOU KNOW WHAT GIFT I'M GETTING?!
once again, no.
MY GIFT WILL BE THIS FABULOUS WORLD AND ALL THE WONDERS IT HOLDS!!
that's the kind of gift that's cheap to give but hard to wrap.
KOVALESKI

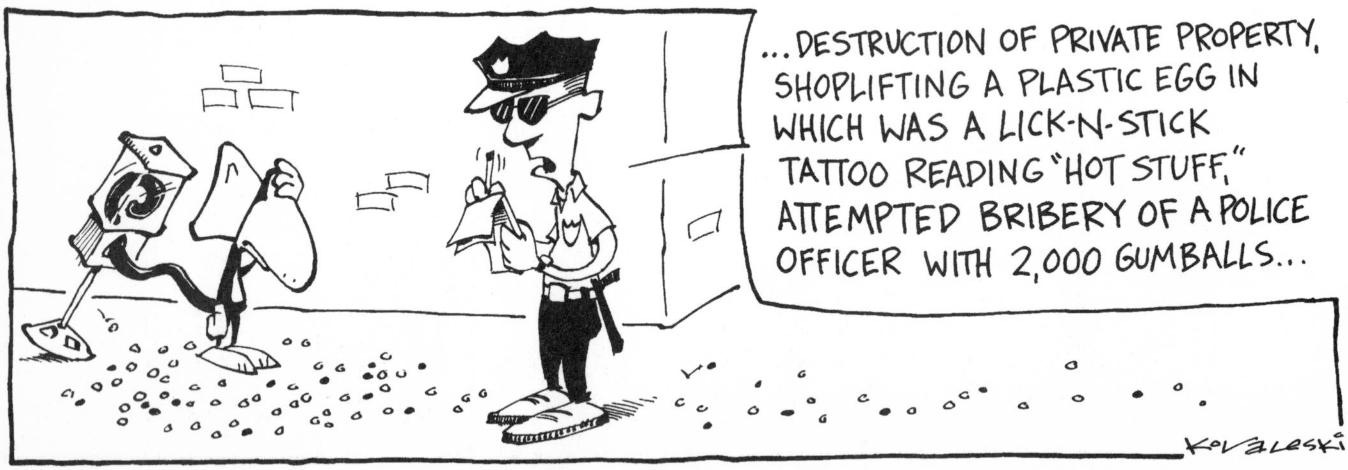
...DESTRUCTION OF PRIVATE PROPERTY, SHOPLIFTING A PLASTIC EGG IN WHICH WAS A LICK-N-STICK TATTOO READING "HOT STUFF," ATTEMPTED BRIBERY OF A POLICE OFFICER WITH 2,000 GUMBALLS...
KOVALESKI

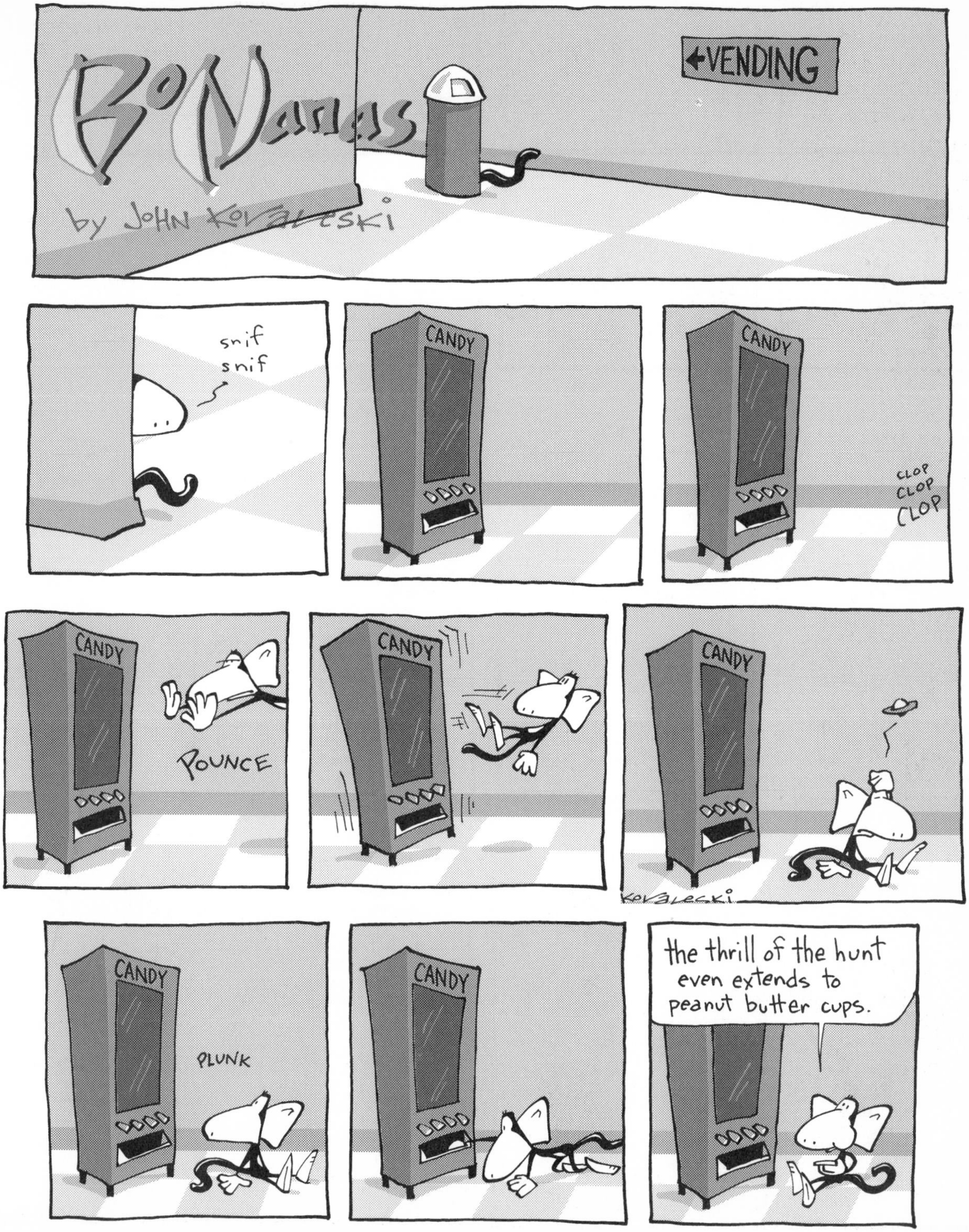
BoNanas
by JOHN KOVALESKI
VENDING
snif
snif
CANDY
CANDY
CLOP
CLOP
CLOP
CANDY
POUNCE
CANDY
CANDY
KOVALESKI
CANDY
PLUNK
CANDY
the thrill of the hunt even extends to peanut butter cups.

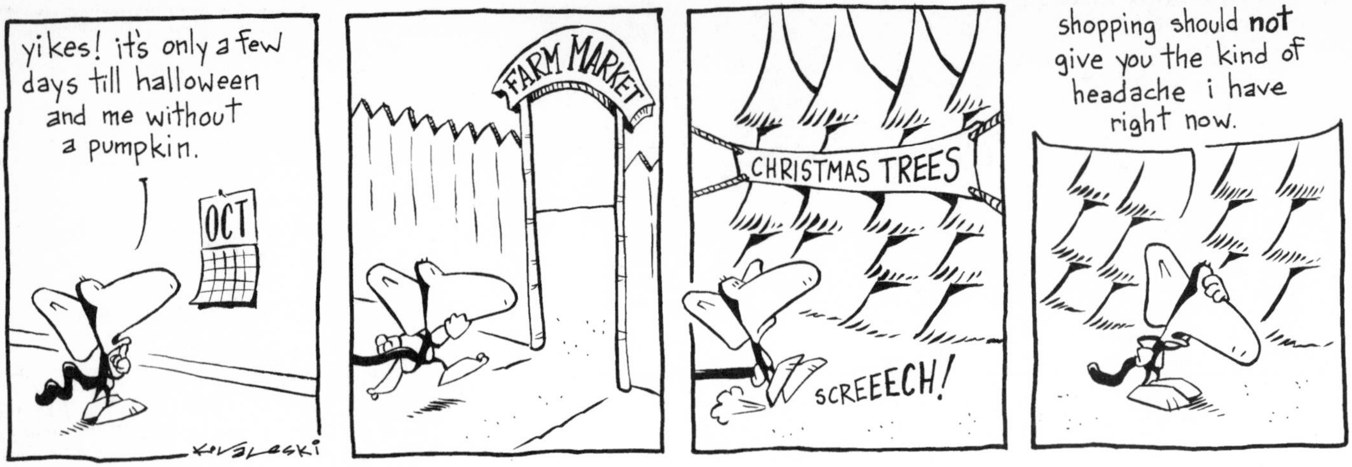
yikes! it's only a few days till halloween and me without a pumpkin.
OCT
FARM MARKET
CHRISTMAS TREES
SCREEECH!
shopping should **not** give you the kind of headache i have right now.
KOVALESKI

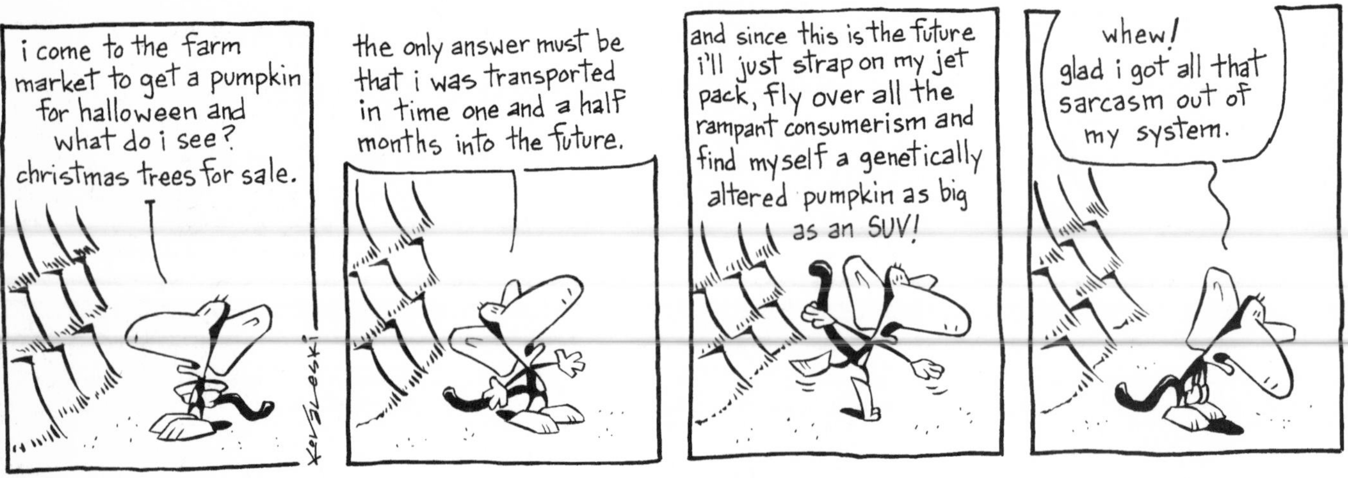
i come to the farm market to get a pumpkin for halloween and what do i see? christmas trees for sale.
the only answer must be that i was transported in time one and a half months into the future.
and since this is the future i'll just strap on my jet pack, fly over all the rampant consumerism and find myself a genetically altered pumpkin as big as an SUV!
whew! glad i got all that sarcasm out of my system.
KOVALESKI

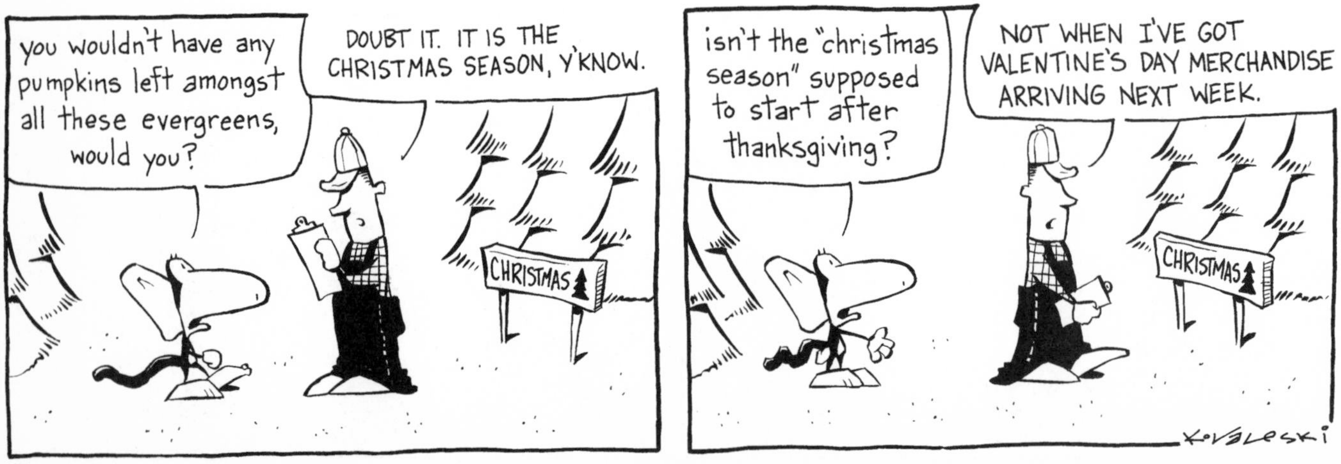
you wouldn't have any pumpkins left amongst all these evergreens, would you?
DOUBT IT. IT IS THE CHRISTMAS SEASON, Y'KNOW.
CHRISTMAS
isn't the "christmas season" supposed to start after thanksgiving?
NOT WHEN I'VE GOT VALENTINE'S DAY MERCHANDISE ARRIVING NEXT WEEK.
CHRISTMAS
KOVALESKI

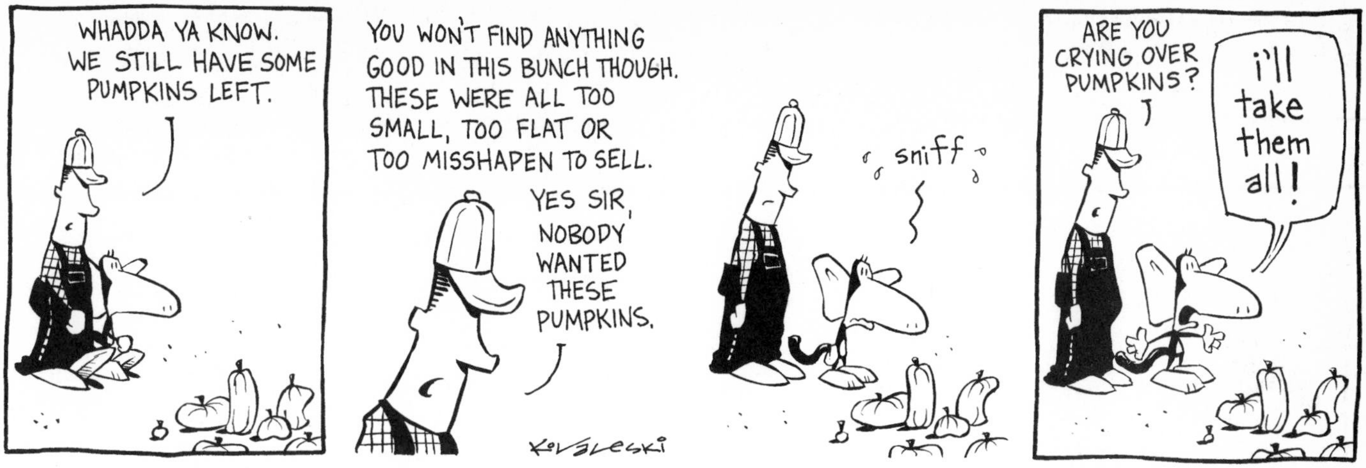
WHADDA YA KNOW. WE STILL HAVE SOME PUMPKINS LEFT.
YOU WON'T FIND ANYTHING GOOD IN THIS BUNCH THOUGH. THESE WERE ALL TOO SMALL, TOO FLAT OR TOO MISSHAPEN TO SELL.
YES SIR, NOBODY WANTED THESE PUMPKINS.
kovaleski
sniff
ARE YOU CRYING OVER PUMPKINS?
i'll take them all!

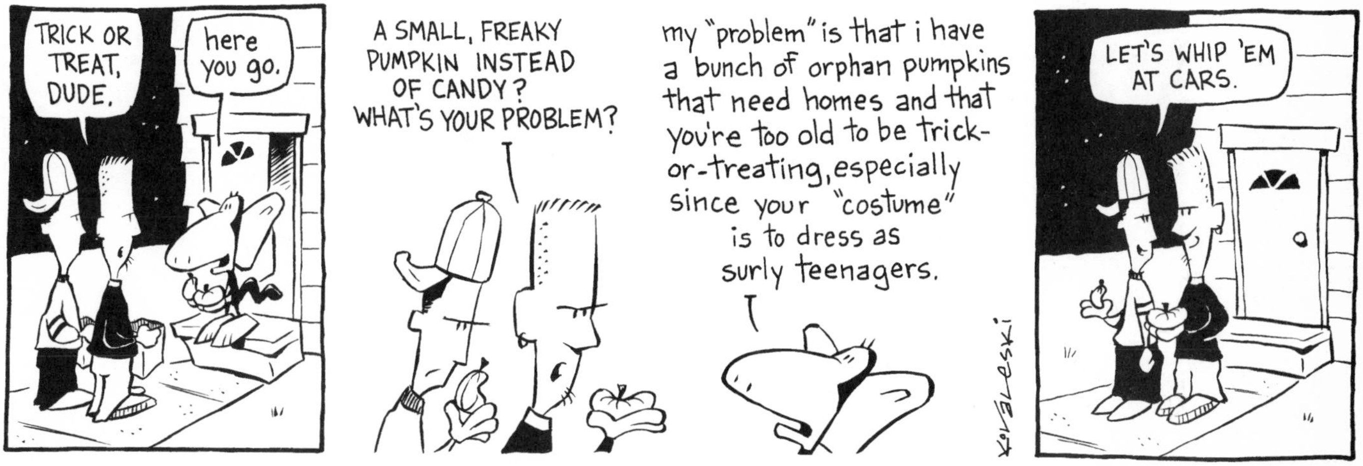
TRICK OR TREAT, DUDE.
here you go.
A SMALL, FREAKY PUMPKIN INSTEAD OF CANDY? WHAT'S YOUR PROBLEM?
my "problem" is that i have a bunch of orphan pumpkins that need homes and that you're too old to be trick-or-treating, especially since your "costume" is to dress as surly teenagers.
kovaleski
LET'S WHIP 'EM AT CARS.

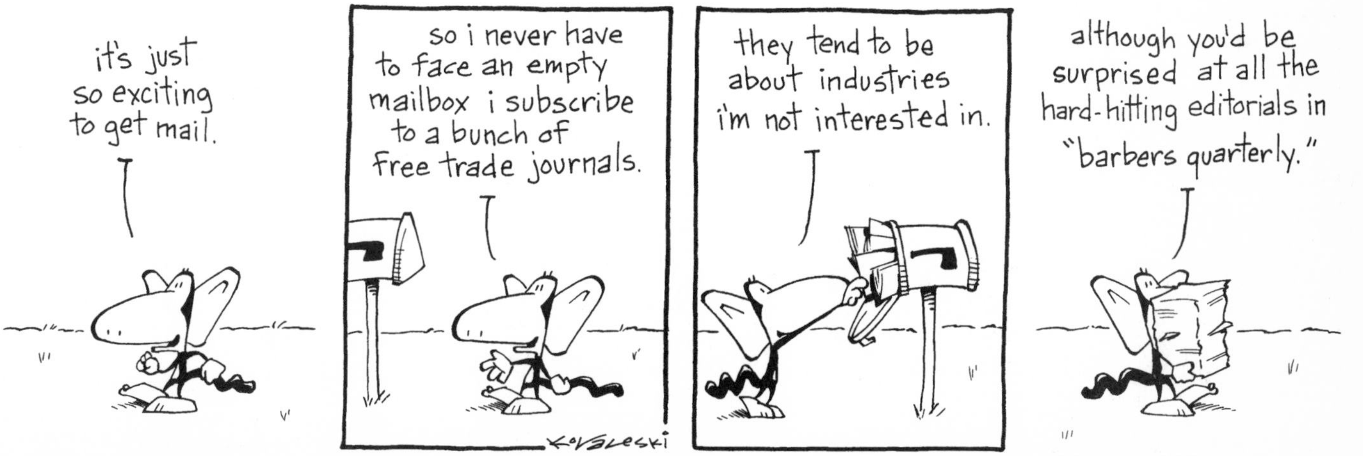
it's just so exciting to get mail.
so i never have to face an empty mailbox i subscribe to a bunch of free trade journals.
kovaleski
they tend to be about industries i'm not interested in.
although you'd be surprised at all the hard-hitting editorials in "barbers quarterly."

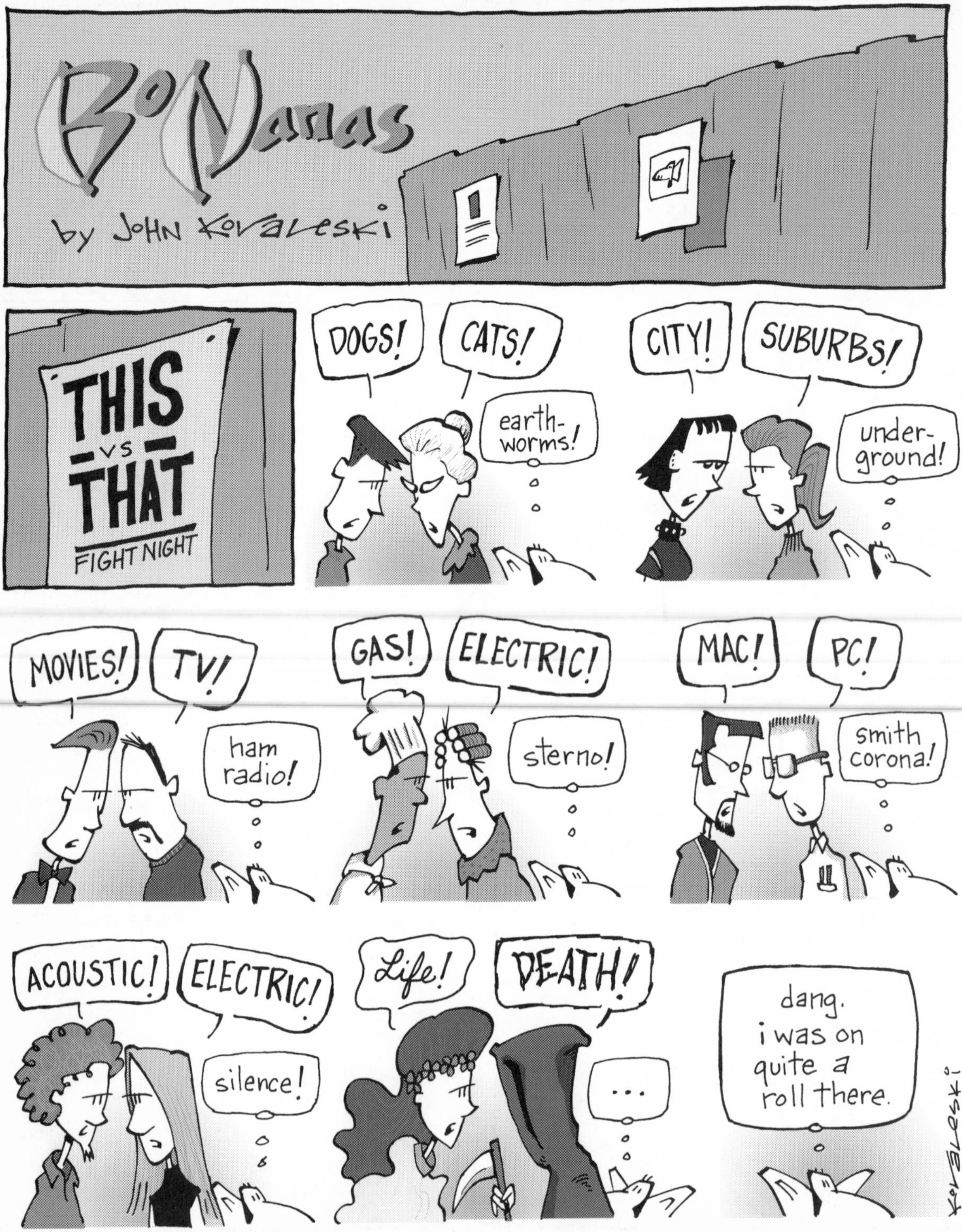
BoNanas
by JOHN KOVALESKI
THIS vs THAT
FIGHT NIGHT
DOGS!
CATS!
earth-worms!
CITY!
SUBURBS!
under-ground!
MOVIES!
TV!
ham radio!
GAS!
ELECTRIC!
sterno!
MAC!
PC!
smith corona!
ACOUSTIC!
ELECTRIC!
silence!
Life!
DEATH!
...
dang. i was on quite a roll there.
KOVALESKI

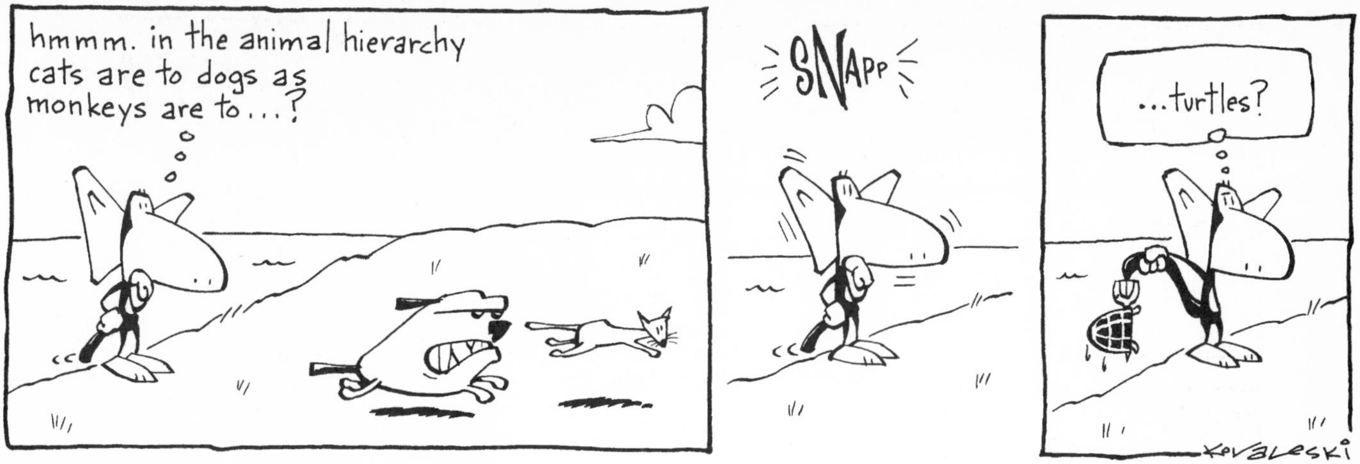
hmmm. in the animal hierarchy cats are to dogs as monkeys are to...?
SNAPP
...turtles?
kovaleski

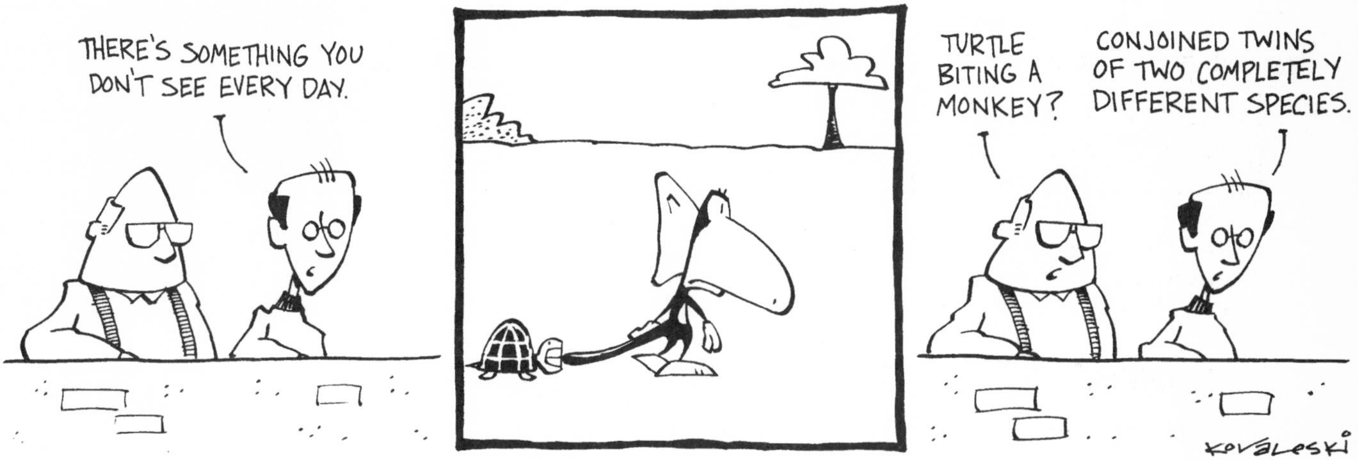
THERE'S SOMETHING YOU DON'T SEE EVERY DAY.
TURTLE BITING A MONKEY?
CONJOINED TWINS OF TWO COMPLETELY DIFFERENT SPECIES.
kovaleski

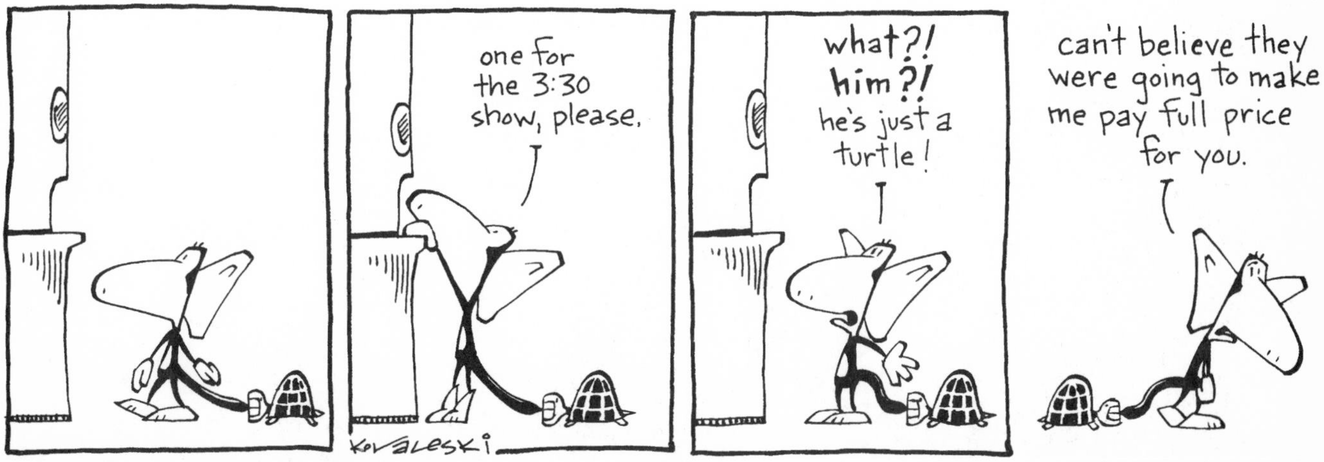
one for the 3:30 show, please.
kovaleski
what?! him?! he's just a turtle!
can't believe they were going to make me pay full price for you.

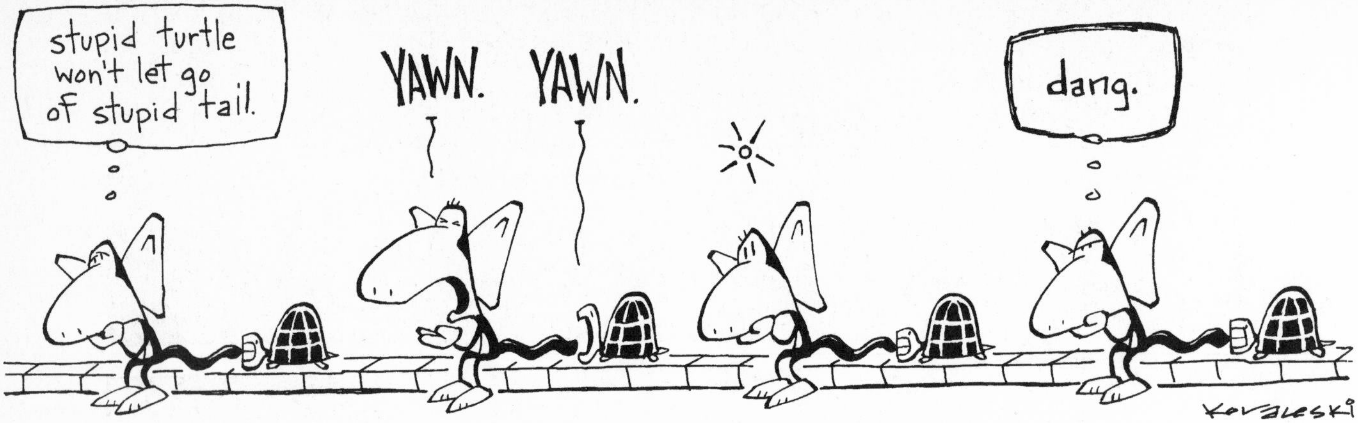
stupid turtle won't let go of stupid tail.
YAWN. YAWN.
dang.
KOVALESKI

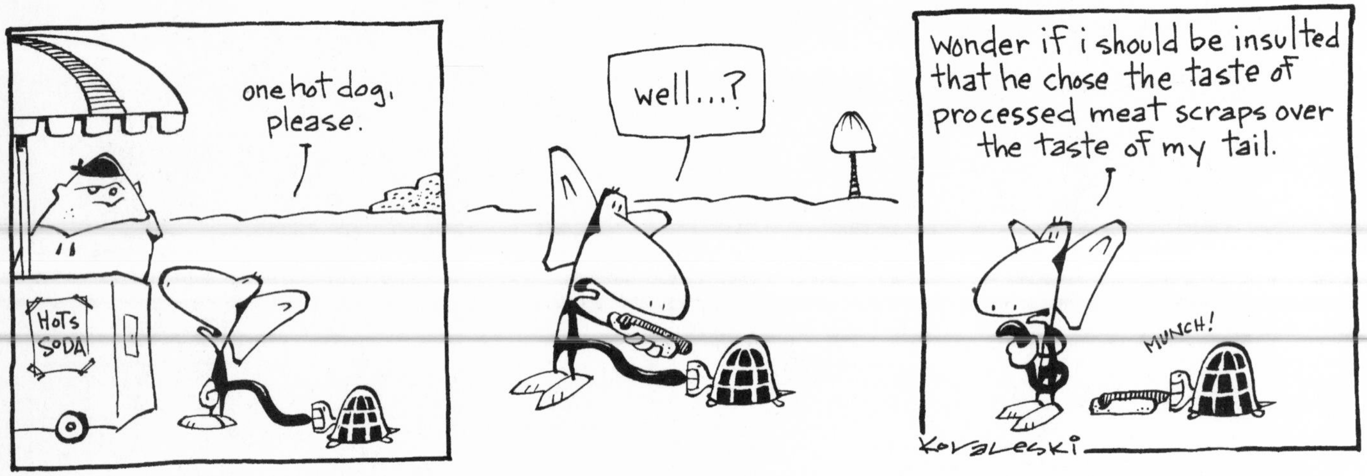
one hot dog, please.
HOTS SODA
well...?
wonder if i should be insulted that he chose the taste of processed meat scraps over the taste of my tail.
MUNCH!
KOVALESKI

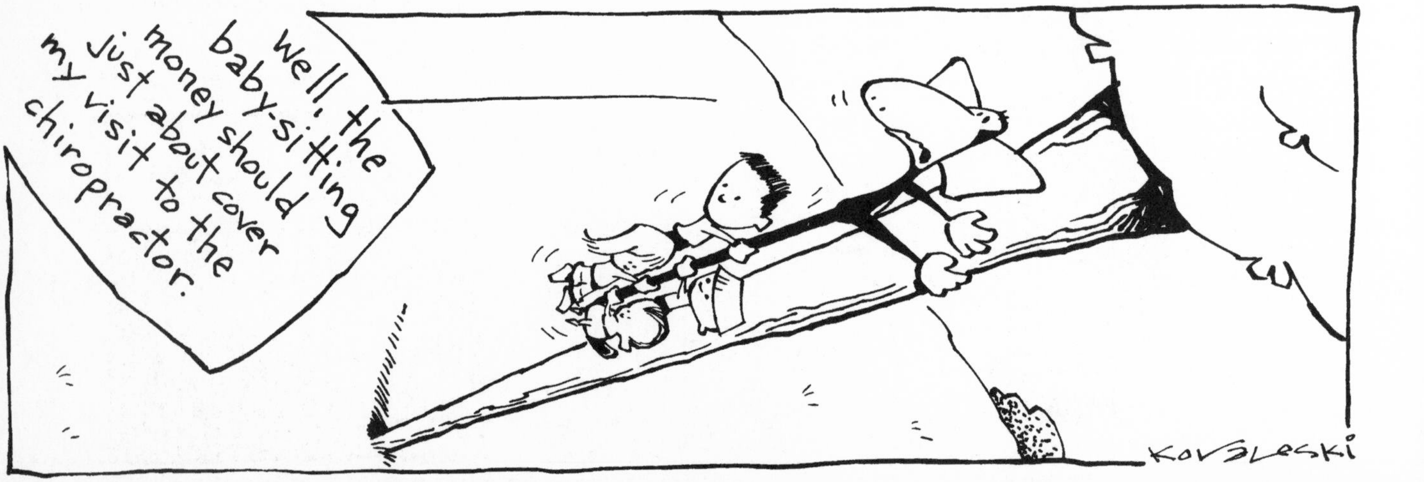
well, the baby-sitting money should just about cover my visit to the chiropractor.
KOVALESKI

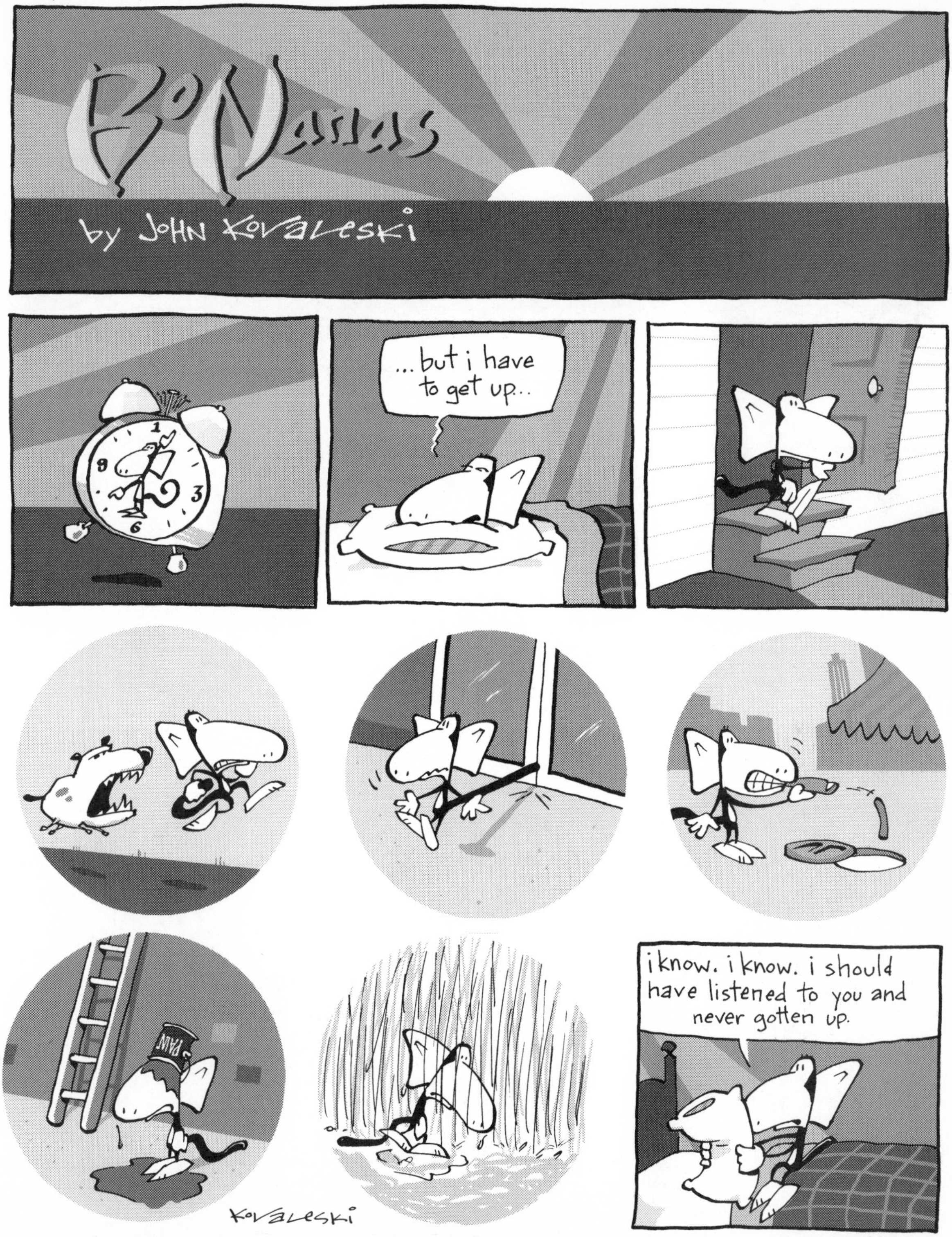
Bo Nanas
by JOHN KOVALESKI
...but i have to get up...
i know. i know. i should have listened to you and never gotten up.
KOVALESKI

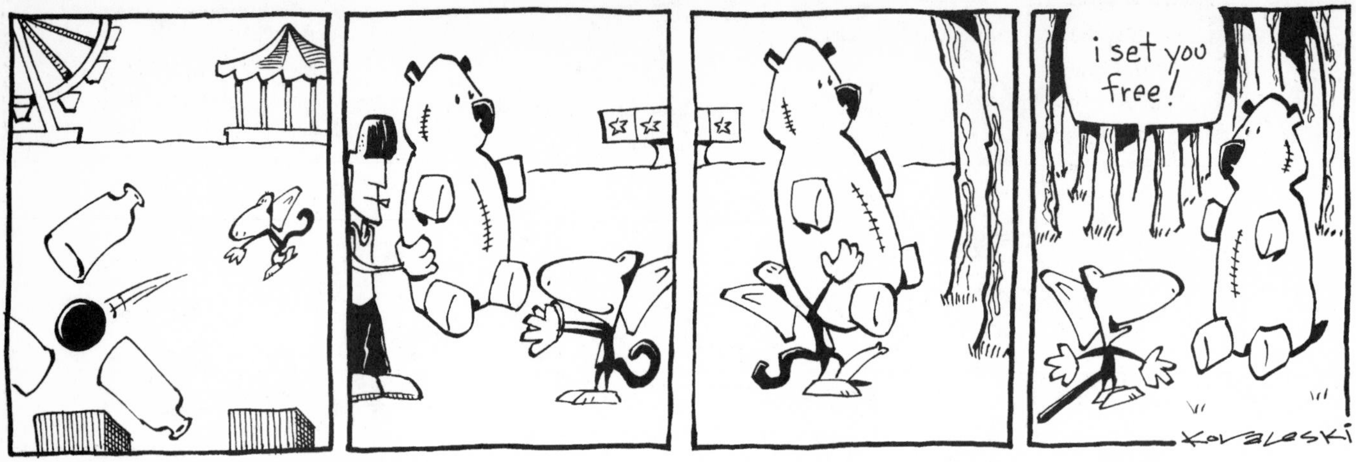
i set you free!
KOVALESKI

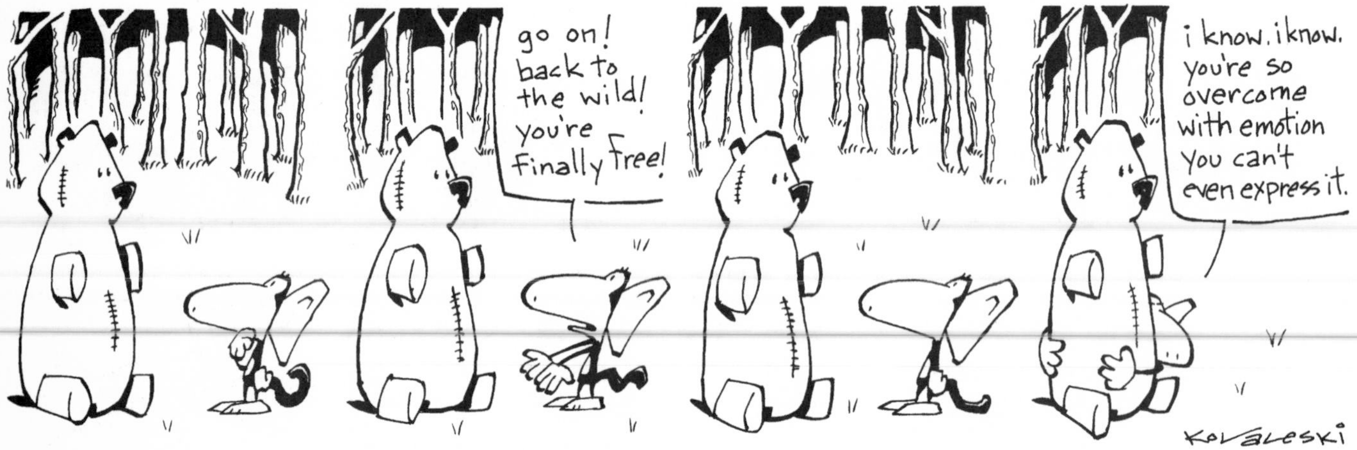
go on! back to the wild! you're finally free!
i know. i know. you're so overcome with emotion you can't even express it.
KOVALESKI

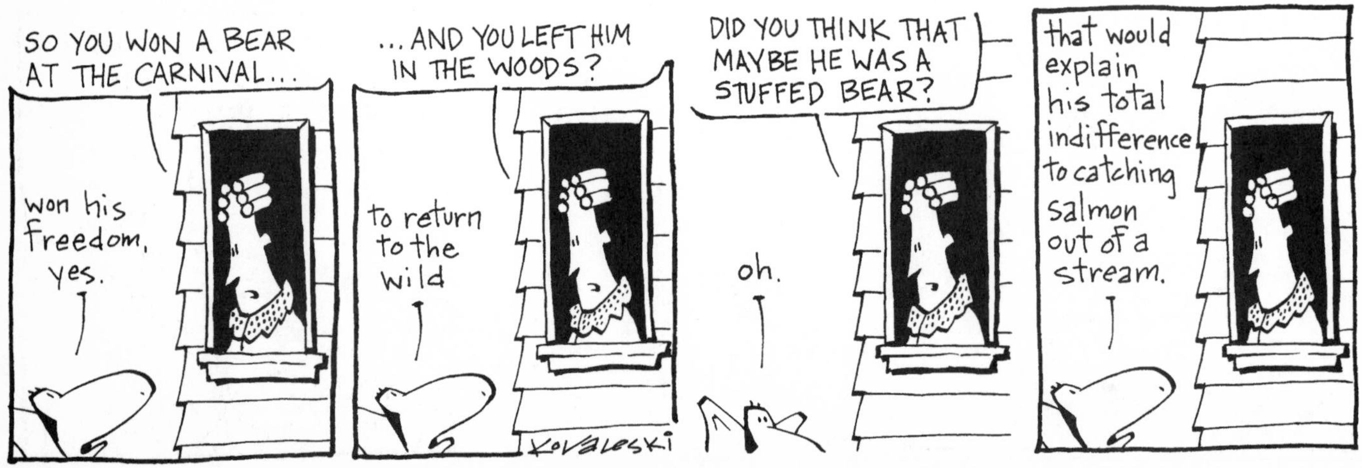
SO YOU WON A BEAR AT THE CARNIVAL...
won his freedom, yes.
...AND YOU LEFT HIM IN THE WOODS?
to return to the wild
KOVALESKI
DID YOU THINK THAT MAYBE HE WAS A STUFFED BEAR?
oh.
that would explain his total indifference to catching salmon out of a stream.

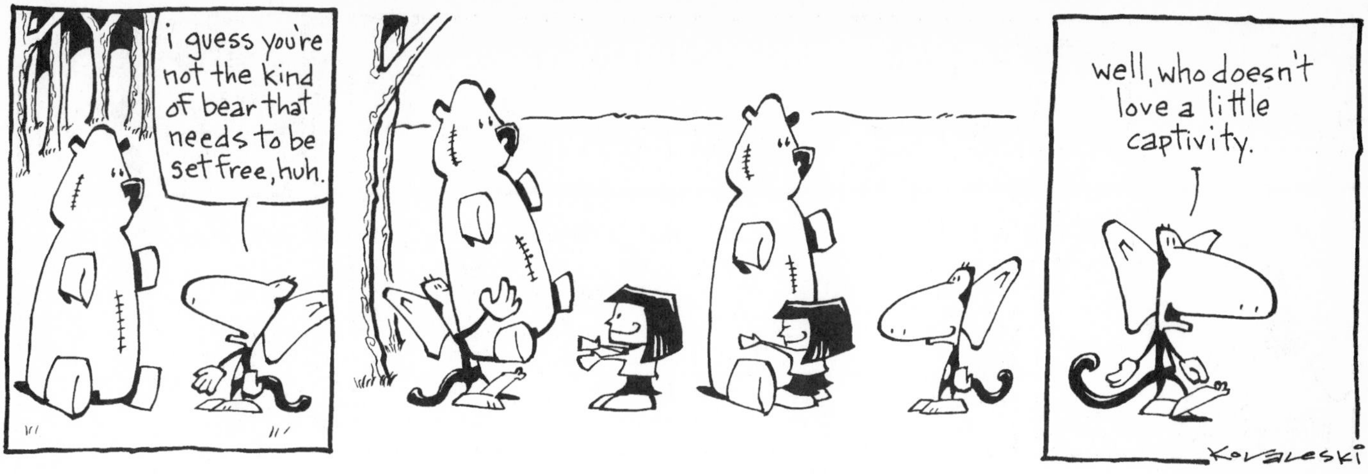
i guess you're not the kind of bear that needs to be set free, huh.
well, who doesn't love a little captivity.
Kovaleski

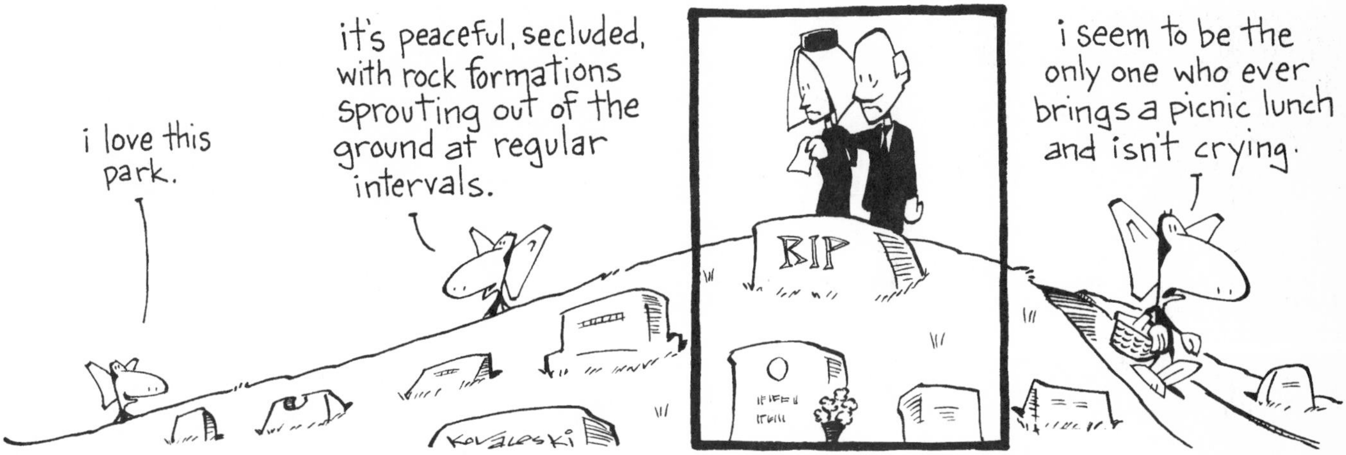
i love this park.
it's peaceful, secluded, with rock formations sprouting out of the ground at regular intervals.
RIP
i seem to be the only one who ever brings a picnic lunch and isn't crying.
Kovaleski

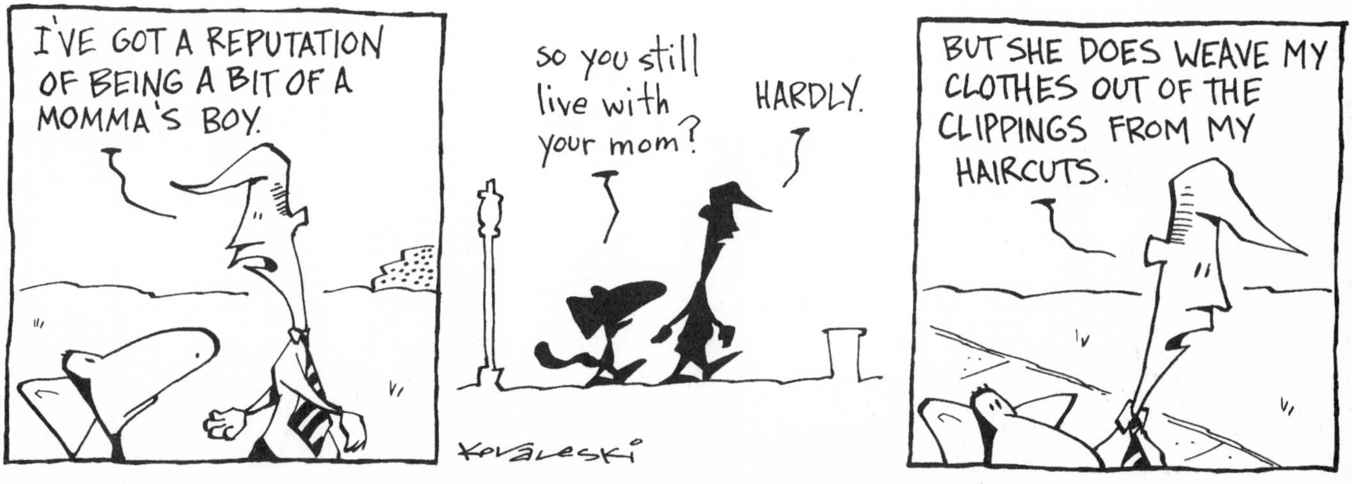
I'VE GOT A REPUTATION OF BEING A BIT OF A MOMMA'S BOY.
so you still live with your mom?
HARDLY.
BUT SHE DOES WEAVE MY CLOTHES OUT OF THE CLIPPINGS FROM MY HAIRCUTS.
Kovaleski

BoNangs
by JOHN KOVALESKI
NO HANGING HERE TO CORNER
z z Z
CLIK!
wha..?
KRASH!
KOVALESKI
AAAAAAAAAAAAAAAAAAAAAAAAAAAAAAAAAA!!
true. i do look frightful just after waking up.

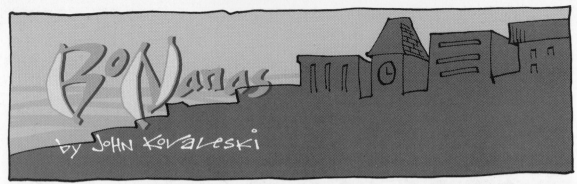

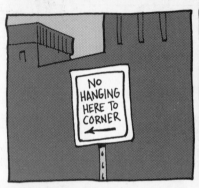

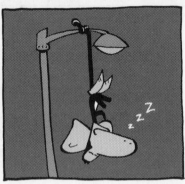

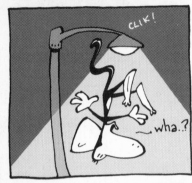

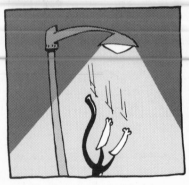

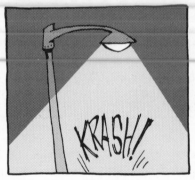

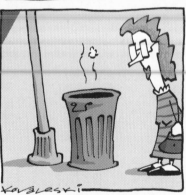

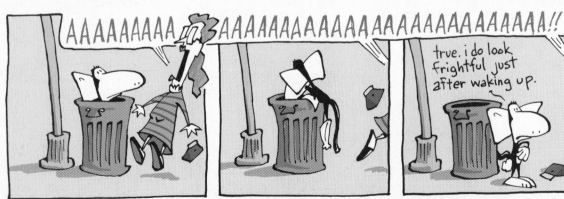

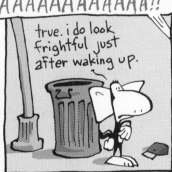

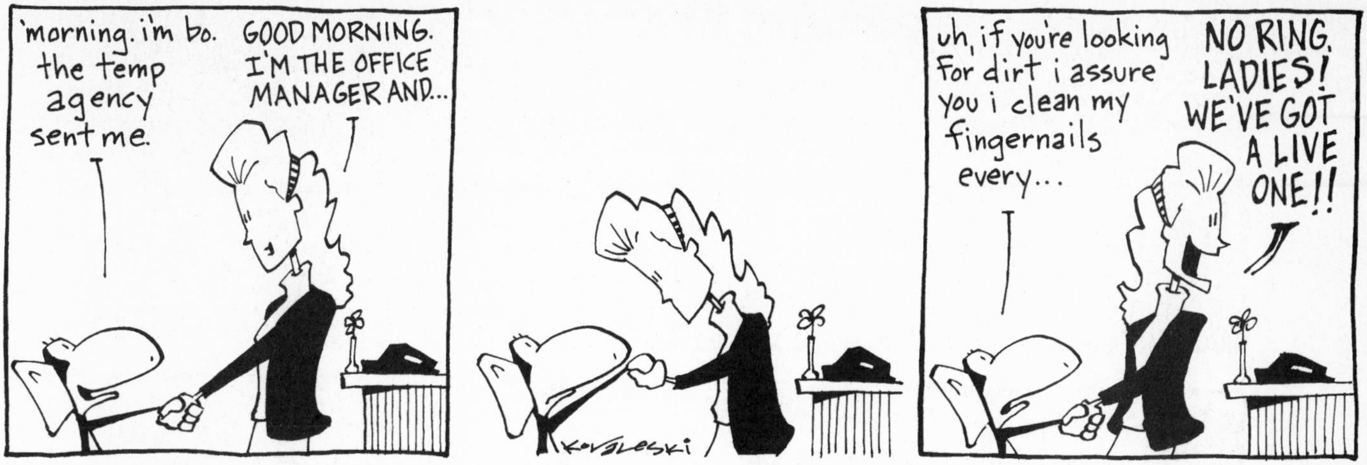
'morning. i'm bo. the temp agency sent me.
GOOD MORNING. I'M THE OFFICE MANAGER AND...
uh, if you're looking for dirt i assure you i clean my fingernails every...
NO RING, LADIES! WE'VE GOT A LIVE ONE!!

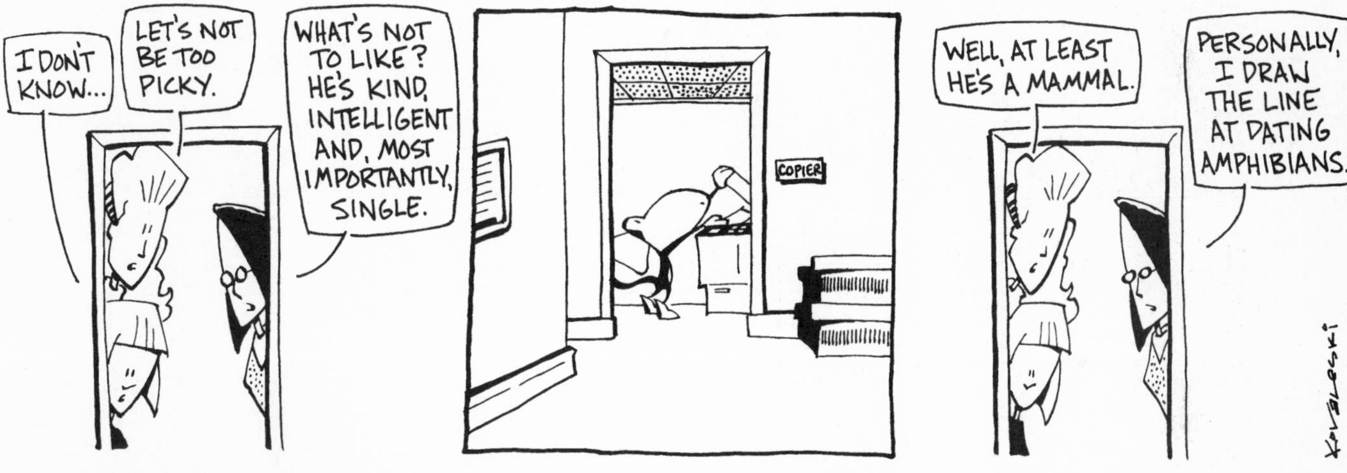
I DON'T KNOW...
LET'S NOT BE TOO PICKY.
WHAT'S NOT TO LIKE? HE'S KIND, INTELLIGENT AND, MOST IMPORTANTLY, SINGLE.
COPIER
WELL, AT LEAST HE'S A MAMMAL.
PERSONALLY, I DRAW THE LINE AT DATING AMPHIBIANS.

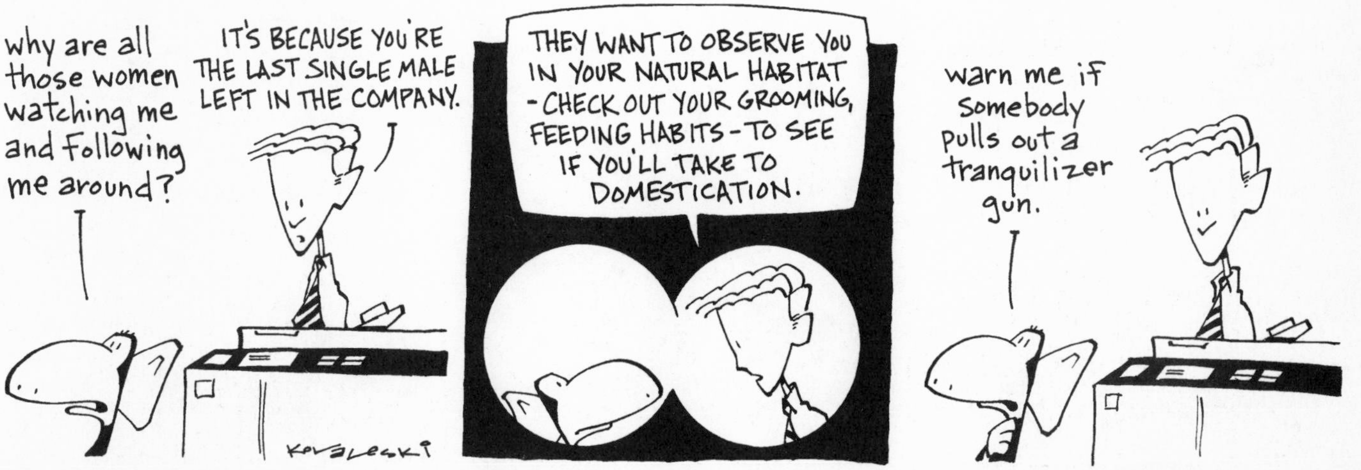
why are all those women watching me and following me around?
IT'S BECAUSE YOU'RE THE LAST SINGLE MALE LEFT IN THE COMPANY.
THEY WANT TO OBSERVE YOU IN YOUR NATURAL HABITAT - CHECK OUT YOUR GROOMING, FEEDING HABITS - TO SEE IF YOU'LL TAKE TO DOMESTICATION.
warn me if somebody pulls out a tranquilizer gun.

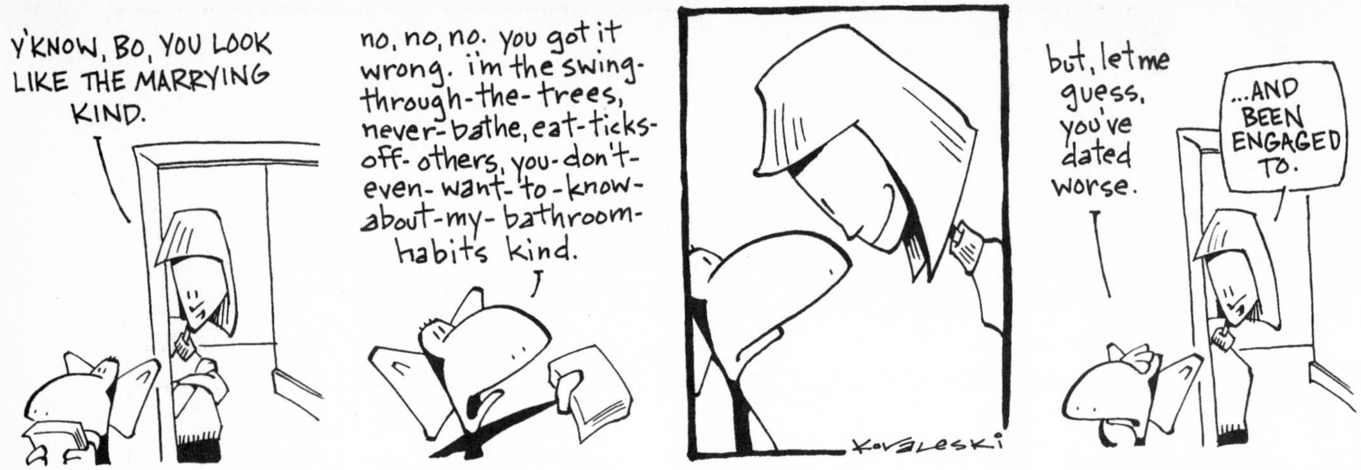
Y'KNOW, BO, YOU LOOK LIKE THE MARRYING KIND.
no, no, no. you got it wrong. i'm the swing-through-the-trees, never-bathe, eat-ticks-off-others, you-don't-even-want-to-know-about-my-bathroom-habits kind.
KOVALESKI
but, let me guess, you've dated worse.
...AND BEEN ENGAGED TO.

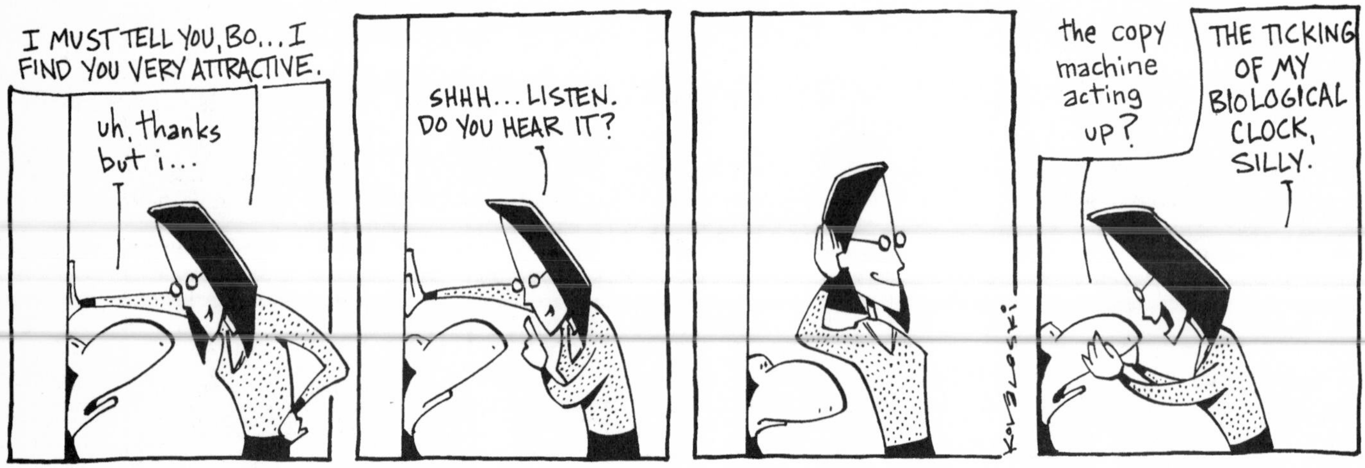
I MUST TELL YOU, BO... I FIND YOU VERY ATTRACTIVE.
uh, thanks but i...
SHHH... LISTEN. DO YOU HEAR IT?
KOVALESKI
the copy machine acting up?
THE TICKING OF MY BIOLOGICAL CLOCK, SILLY.

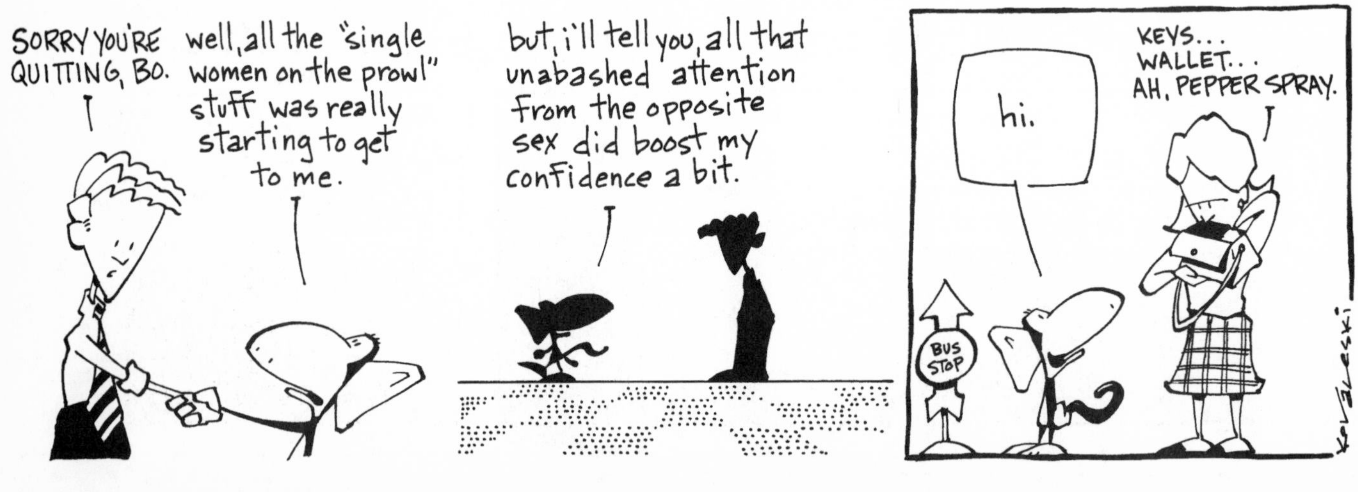
SORRY YOU'RE QUITTING, BO.
well, all the "single women on the prowl" stuff was really starting to get to me.
but, i'll tell you, all that unabashed attention from the opposite sex did boost my confidence a bit.
hi.
KEYS... WALLET... AH, PEPPER SPRAY.
BUS STOP
KOVALESKI

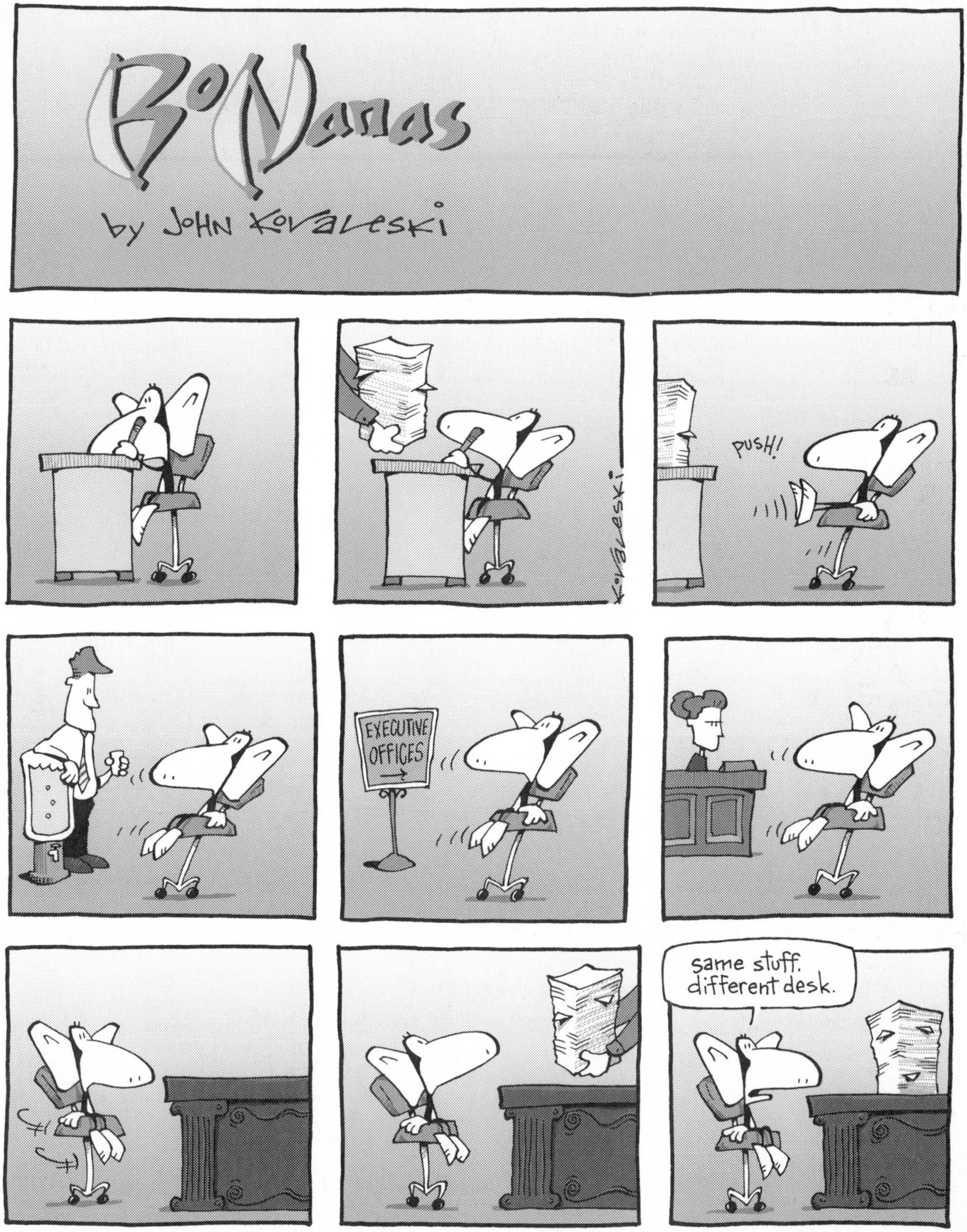

BoNanas
by JOHN KOVALESKI
KOVALESKI
PUSH!
EXECUTIVE OFFICES
same stuff. different desk.

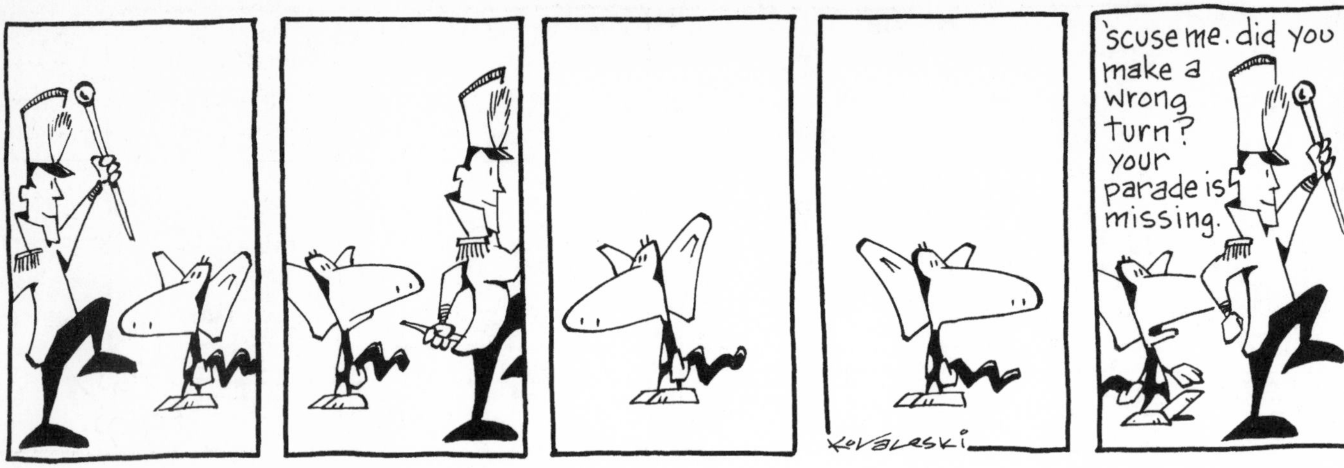
'scuse me. did you make a wrong turn? your parade is missing.
KOVALESKI

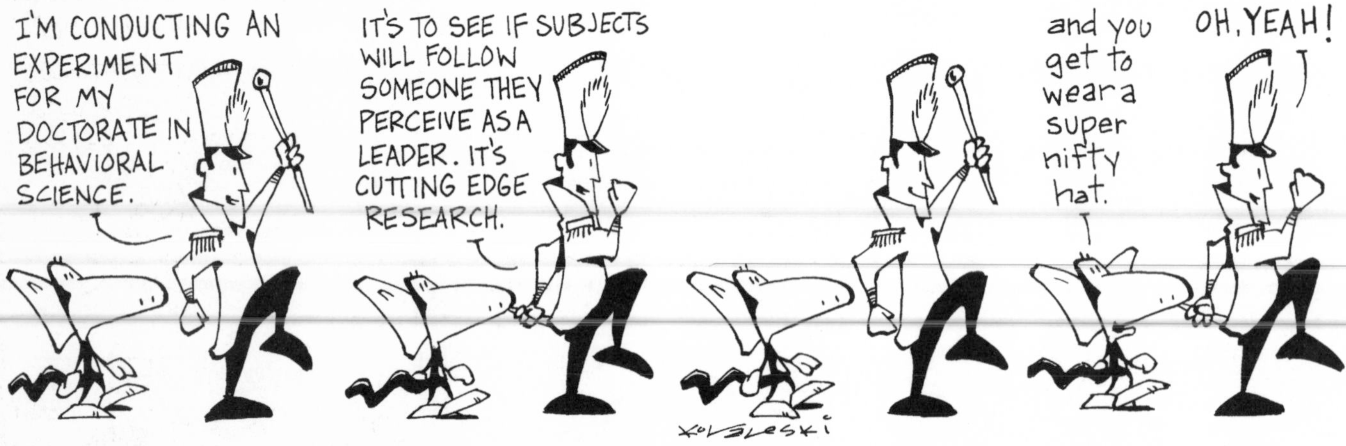
I'M CONDUCTING AN EXPERIMENT FOR MY DOCTORATE IN BEHAVIORAL SCIENCE.
IT'S TO SEE IF SUBJECTS WILL FOLLOW SOMEONE THEY PERCEIVE AS A LEADER. IT'S CUTTING EDGE RESEARCH.
and you get to wear a super nifty hat.
OH, YEAH!
KOVALESKI

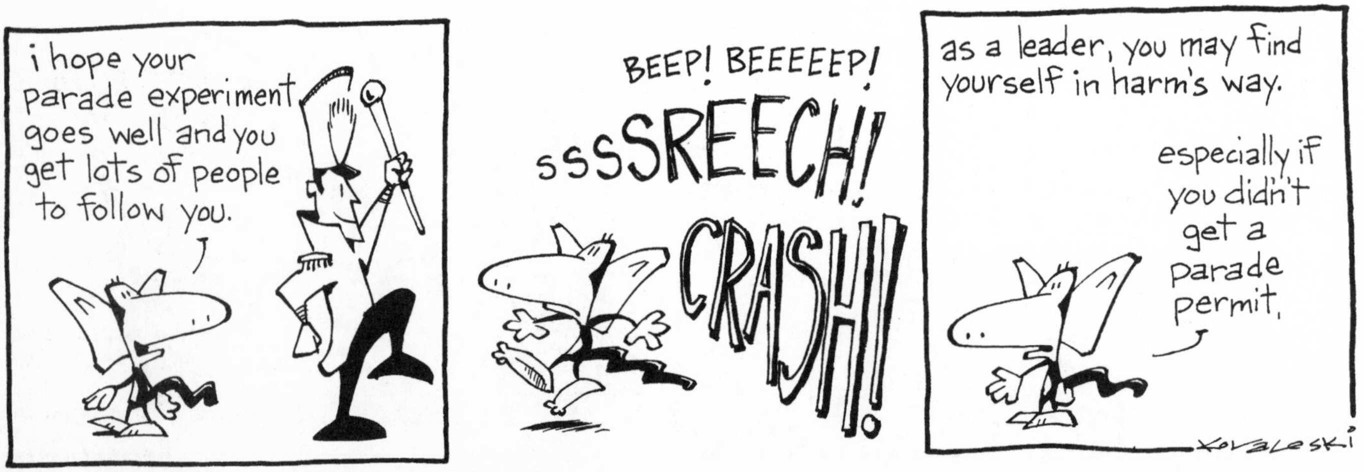
i hope your parade experiment goes well and you get lots of people to follow you.
BEEP! BEEEEEP!
sssSREECH!
CRASH!
as a leader, you may find yourself in harm's way.
especially if you didn't get a parade permit.
KOVALESKI

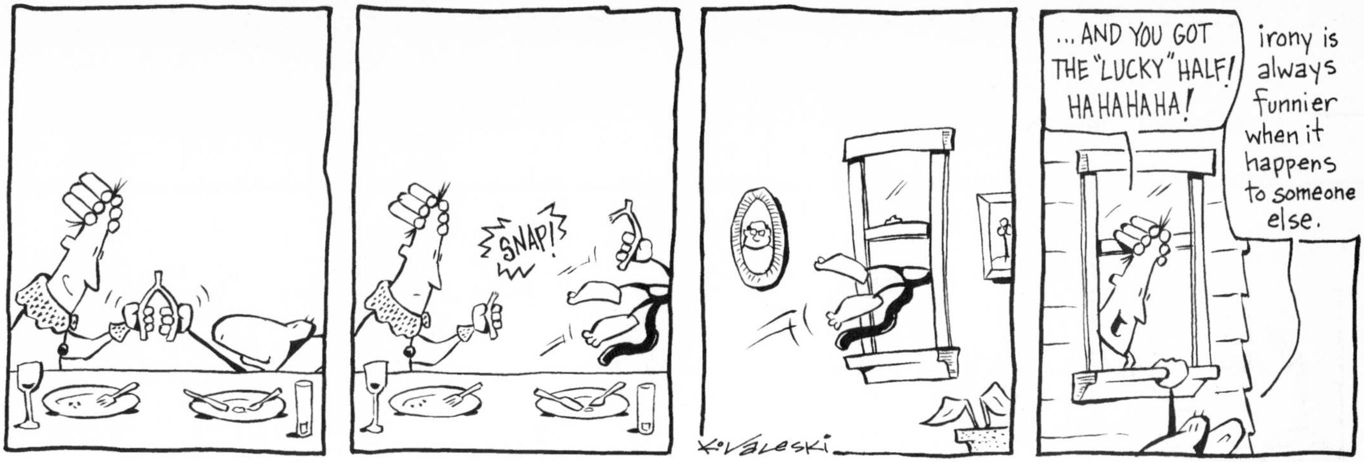
SNAP!
... AND YOU GOT THE "LUCKY" HALF! HAHAHAHA!
irony is always funnier when it happens to someone else.
KOVALESKI

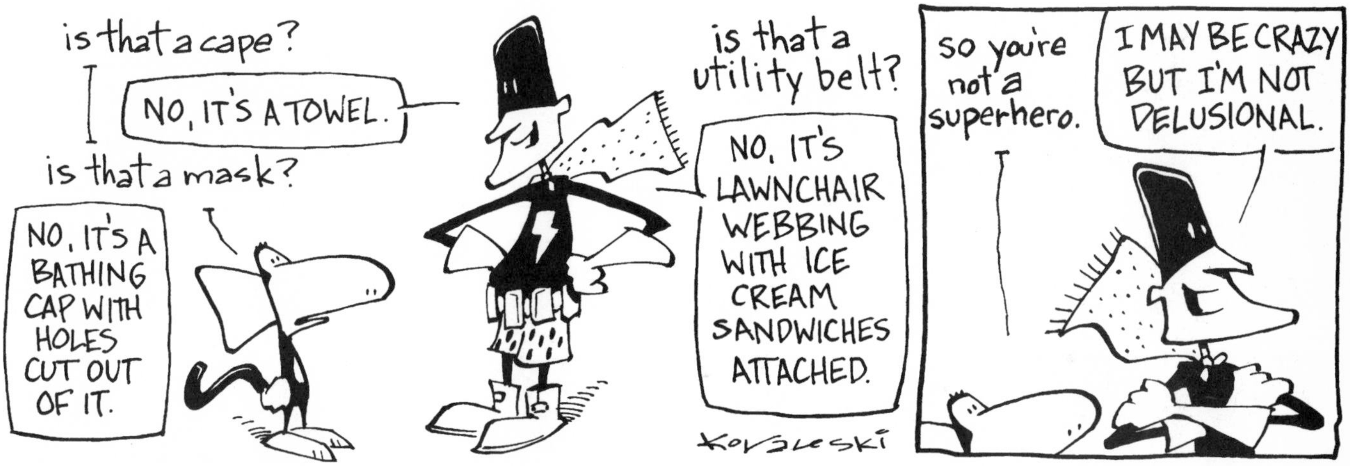
is that a cape?
NO, IT'S A TOWEL.
is that a mask?
NO, IT'S A BATHING CAP WITH HOLES CUT OUT OF IT.
is that a utility belt?
NO, IT'S LAWNCHAIR WEBBING WITH ICE CREAM SANDWICHES ATTACHED.
so you're not a superhero.
I MAY BE CRAZY BUT I'M NOT DELUSIONAL.
KOVALESKI

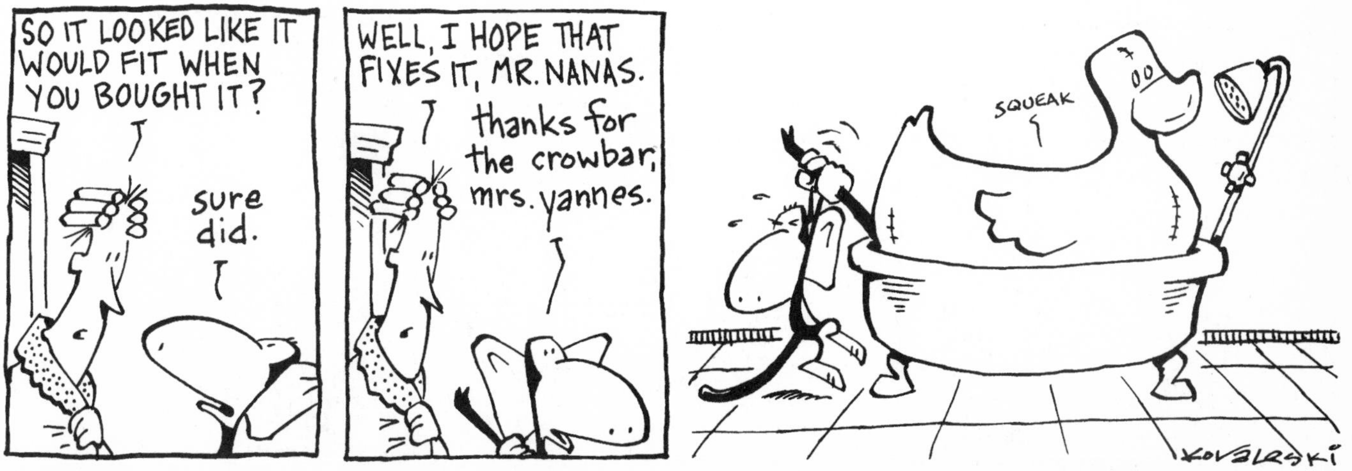
SO IT LOOKED LIKE IT WOULD FIT WHEN YOU BOUGHT IT?
sure did.
WELL, I HOPE THAT FIXES IT, MR. NANAS.
thanks for the crowbar, mrs. yannes.
SQUEAK
KOVALESKI

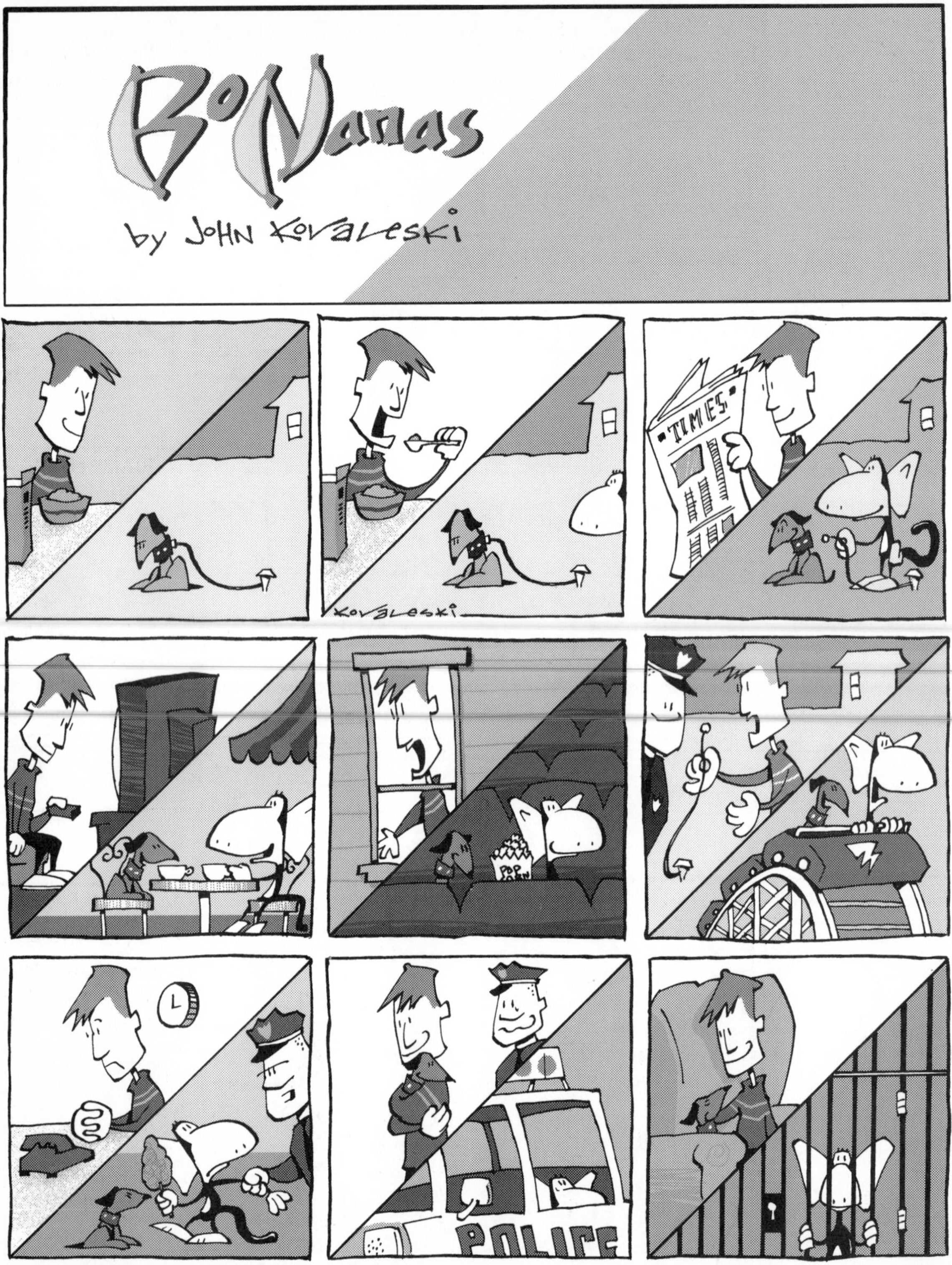

BoNanas
by JOHN KOVALESKI
KOVALESKI
TIMES
POP CORN
POLICE

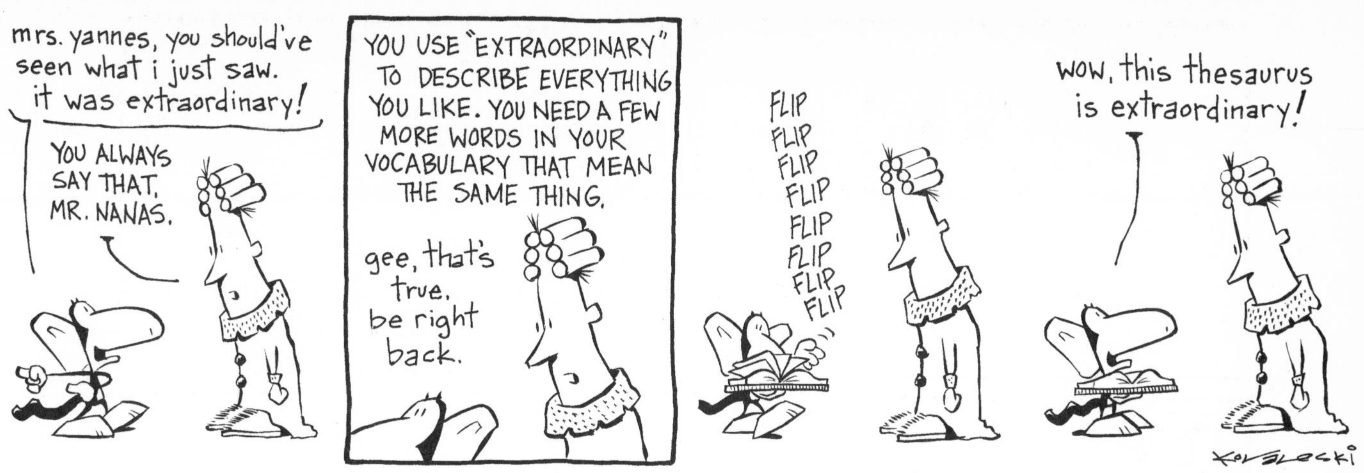
mrs. yannes, you should've seen what i just saw. it was extraordinary!
YOU ALWAYS SAY THAT, MR. NANAS.
YOU USE "EXTRAORDINARY" TO DESCRIBE EVERYTHING YOU LIKE. YOU NEED A FEW MORE WORDS IN YOUR VOCABULARY THAT MEAN THE SAME THING.
gee, that's true. be right back.
FLIP FLIP FLIP FLIP FLIP FLIP FLIP FLIP
wow, this thesaurus is extraordinary!
KOVALESKI

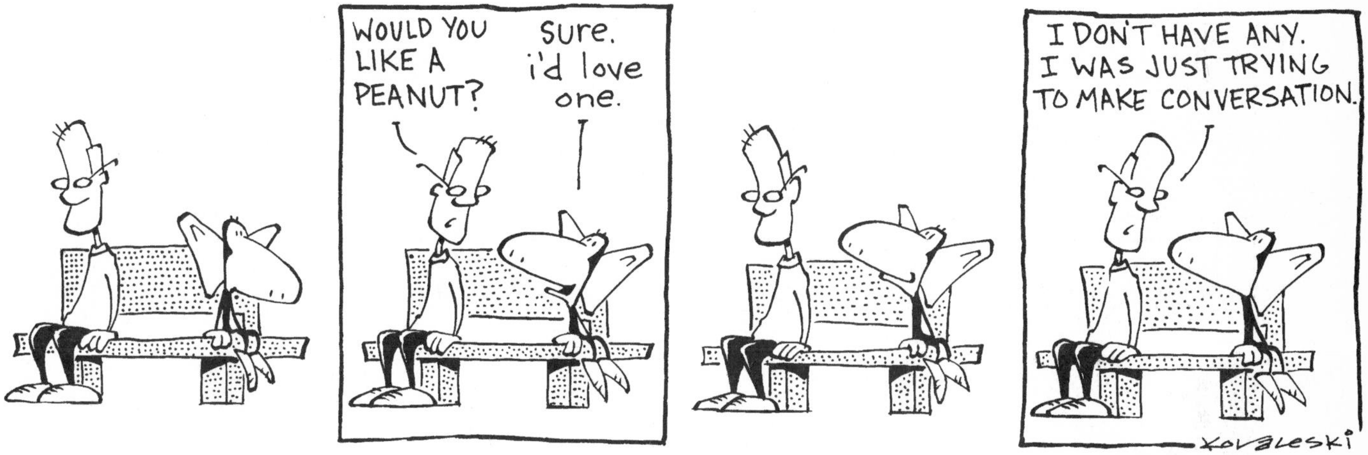
WOULD YOU LIKE A PEANUT?
sure. i'd love one.
I DON'T HAVE ANY. I WAS JUST TRYING TO MAKE CONVERSATION.
KOVALESKI

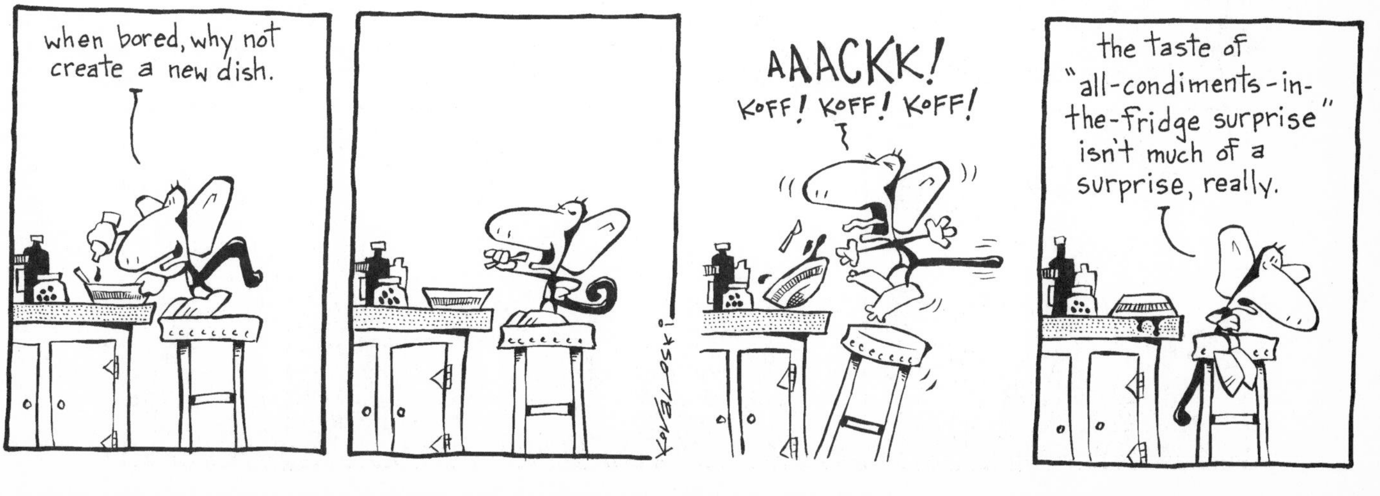
when bored, why not create a new dish.
KOVALESKI
AAACKK!
KOFF! KOFF! KOFF!
the taste of "all-condiments-in-the-fridge surprise" isn't much of a surprise, really.

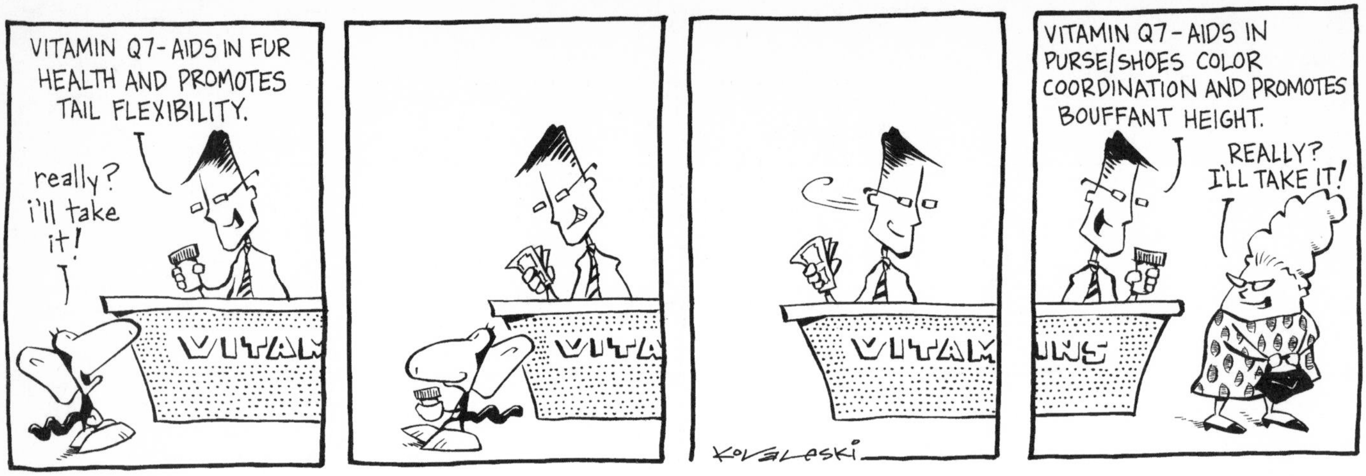
VITAMIN Q7- AIDS IN FUR HEALTH AND PROMOTES TAIL FLEXIBILITY.
really? i'll take it!
VITAMIN Q7- AIDS IN PURSE/SHOES COLOR COORDINATION AND PROMOTES BOUFFANT HEIGHT.
REALLY? I'LL TAKE IT!
KOVALESKI

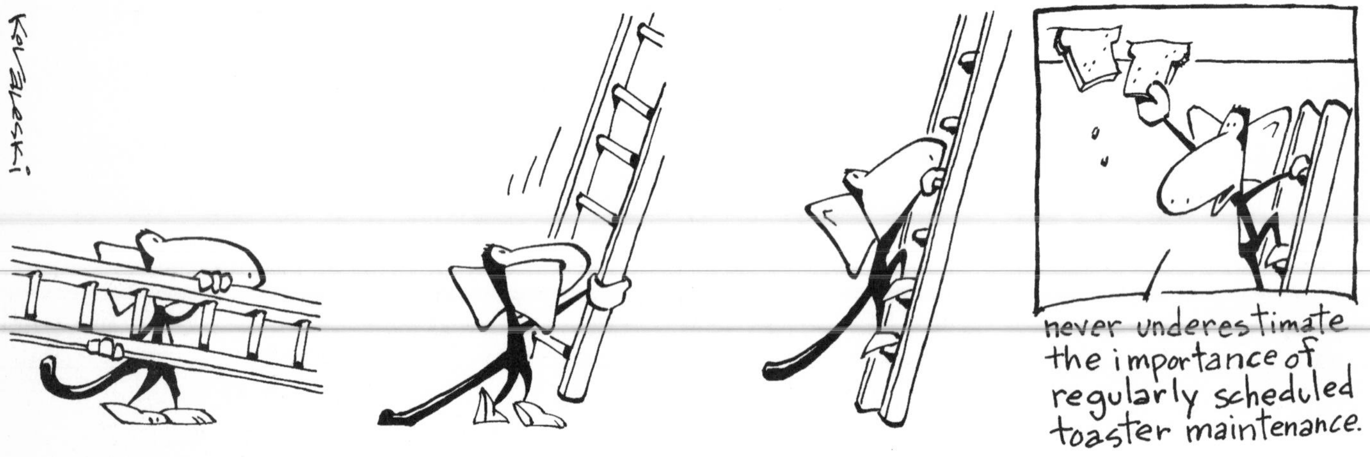
KOVALESKI
never underestimate the importance of regularly scheduled toaster maintenance.

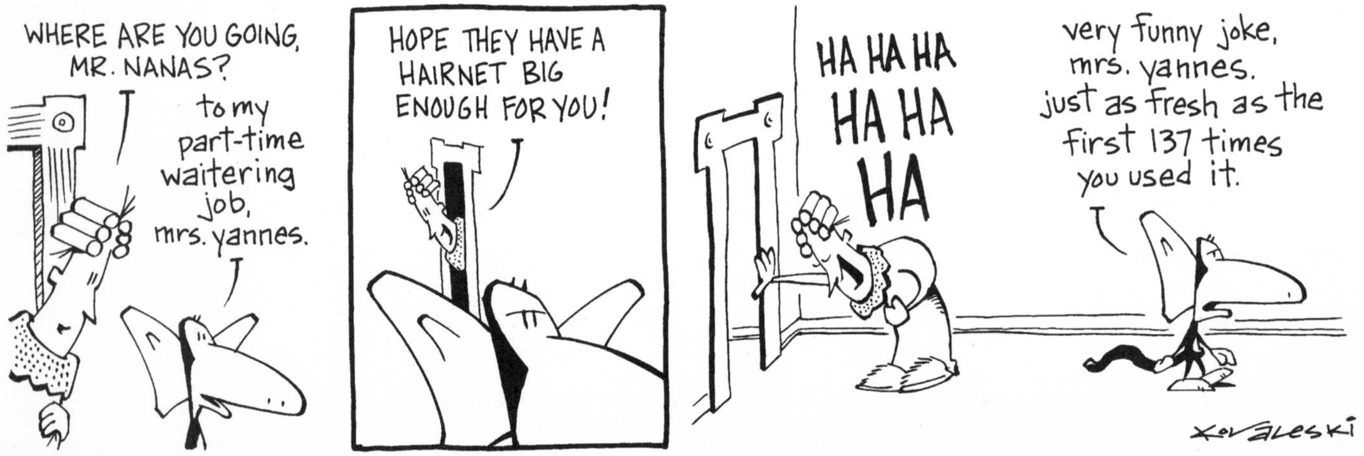
WHERE ARE YOU GOING, MR. NANAS?
to my part-time waitering job, mrs. yannes.
HOPE THEY HAVE A HAIRNET BIG ENOUGH FOR YOU!
HA HA HA HA HA HA
very funny joke, mrs. yannes. just as fresh as the first 137 times you used it.
KOVALESKI

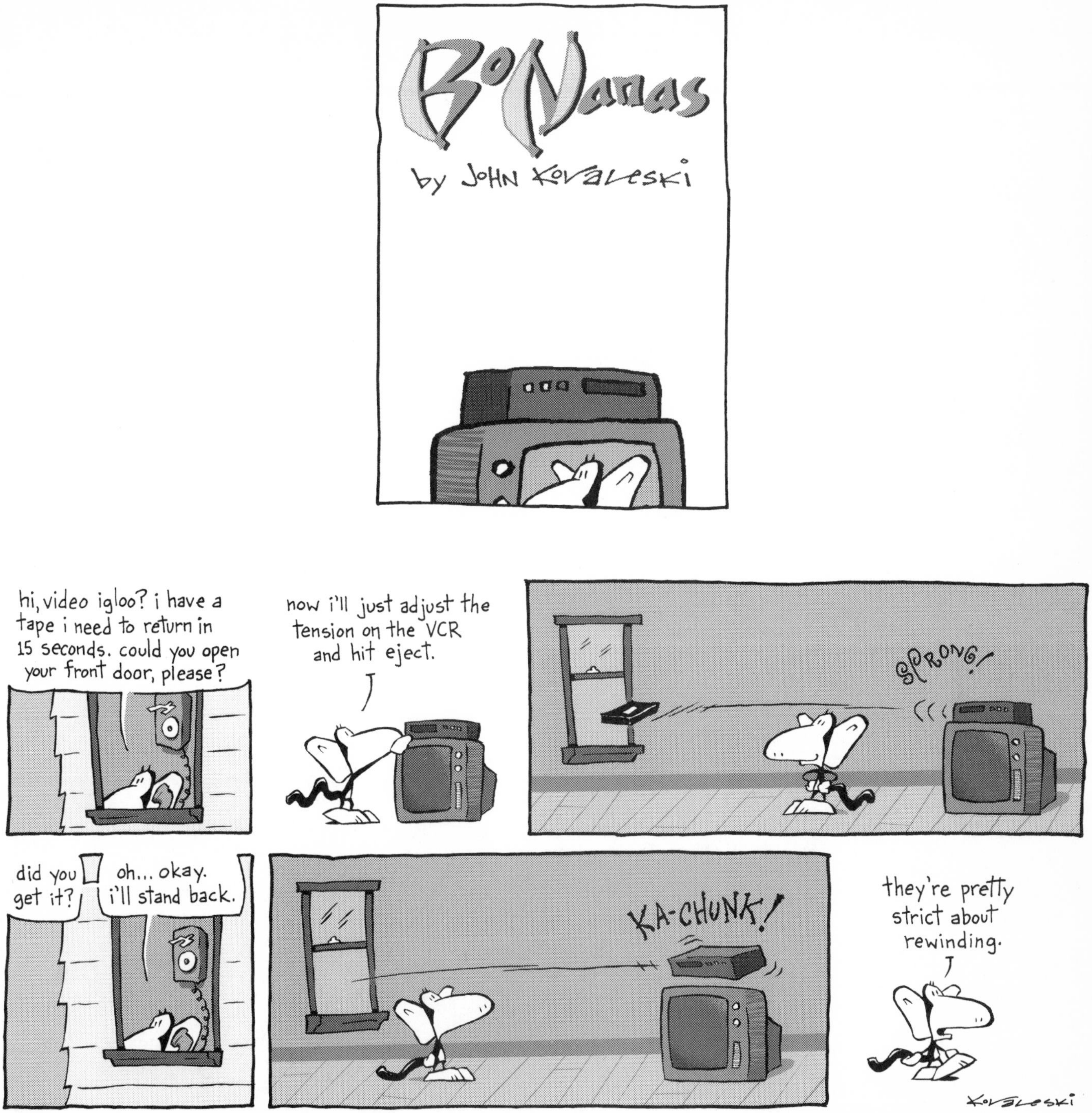
BoNanas
by JOHN KOVALESKI
hi, video igloo? i have a tape i need to return in 15 seconds. could you open your front door, please?
now i'll just adjust the tension on the VCR and hit eject.
SPRONG!
did you get it?
oh... okay. i'll stand back.
KA-CHUNK!
they're pretty strict about rewinding.
KOVALESKI

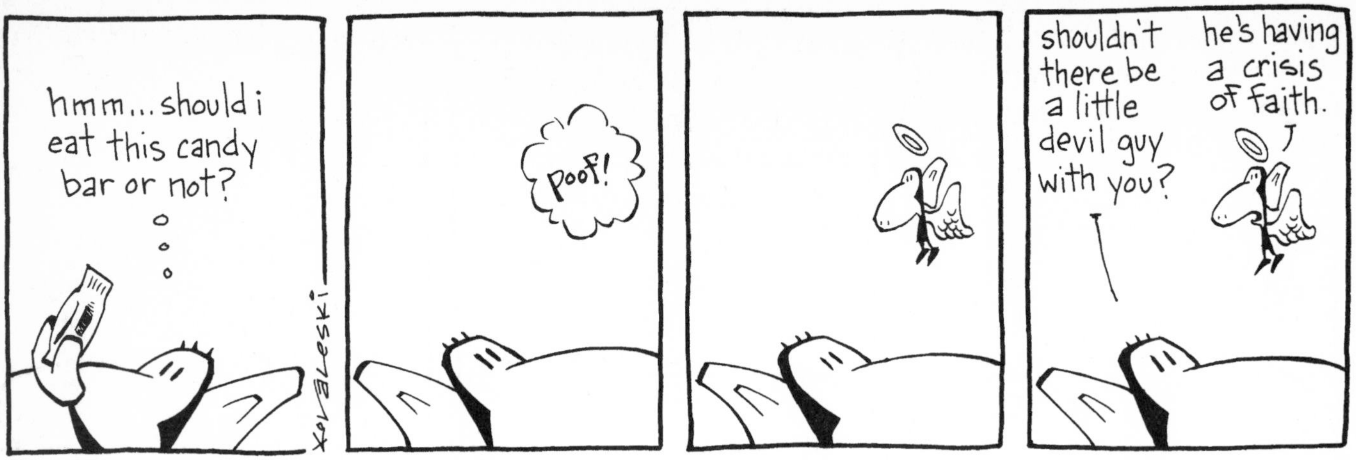
hmm... should i eat this candy bar or not?
poof!
shouldn't there be a little devil guy with you?
he's having a crisis of faith.
kovaleski

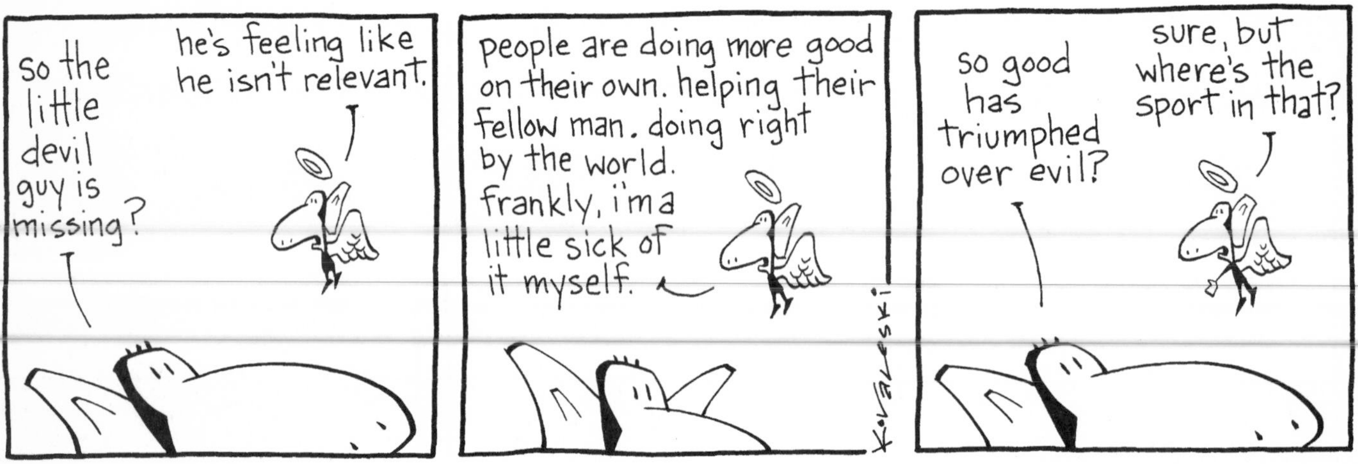
so the little devil guy is missing?
he's feeling like he isn't relevant.
people are doing more good on their own. helping their fellow man. doing right by the world. frankly, i'm a little sick of it myself.
so good has triumphed over evil?
sure, but where's the sport in that?
kovaleski

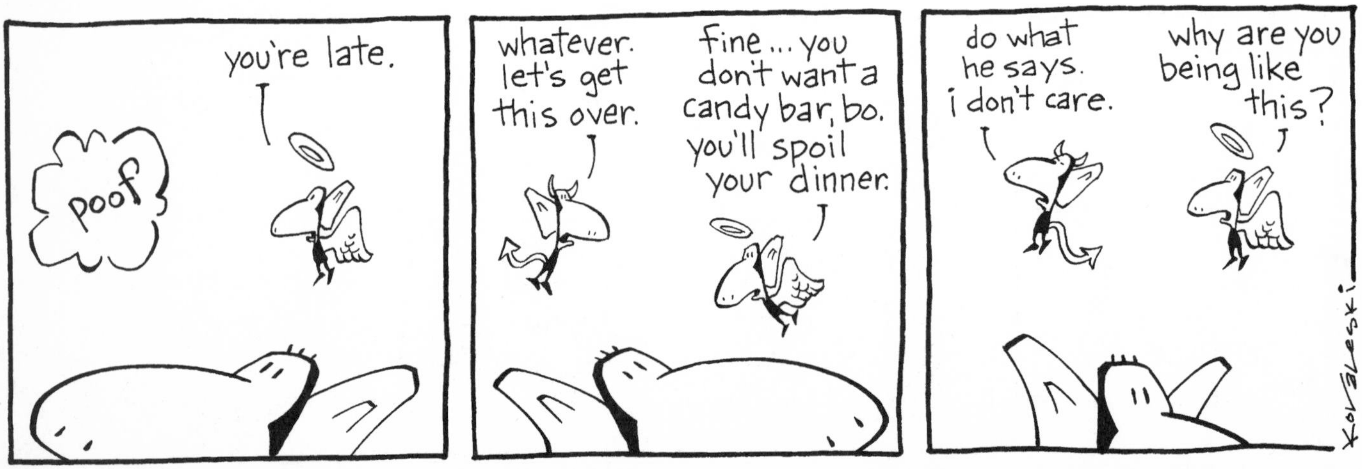
poof
you're late.
whatever. let's get this over.
fine... you don't want a candy bar, bo. you'll spoil your dinner.
do what he says. i don't care.
why are you being like this?
kovaleski

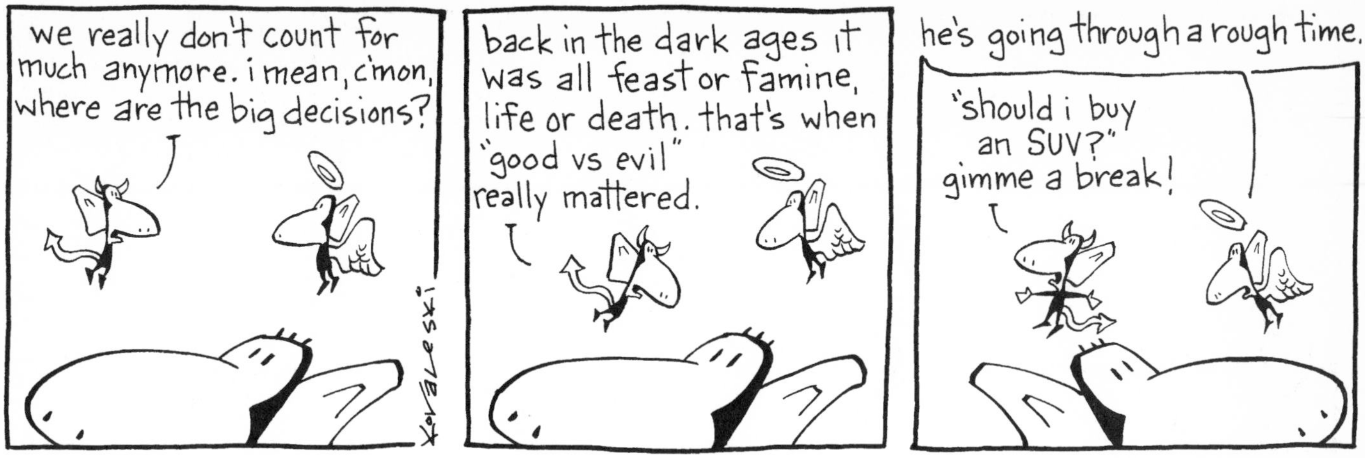
we really don't count for much anymore. i mean, c'mon, where are the big decisions?
kovaleski
back in the dark ages it was all feast or famine, life or death. that's when "good vs evil" really mattered.
he's going through a rough time.
"should i buy an SUV?" gimme a break!

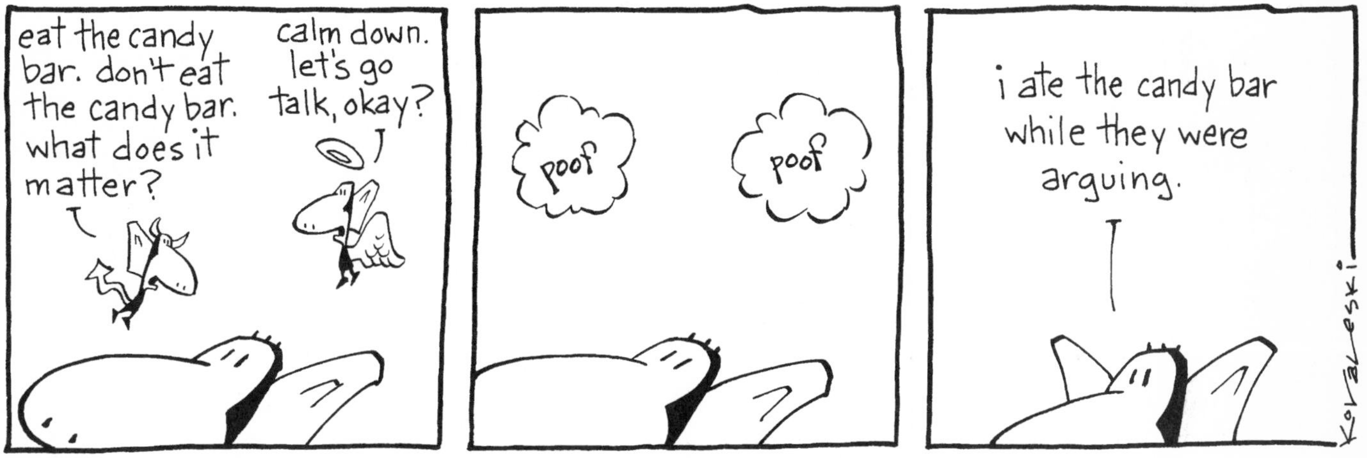
eat the candy bar. don't eat the candy bar. what does it matter?
calm down. let's go talk, okay?
poof
poof
i ate the candy bar while they were arguing.
kovaleski

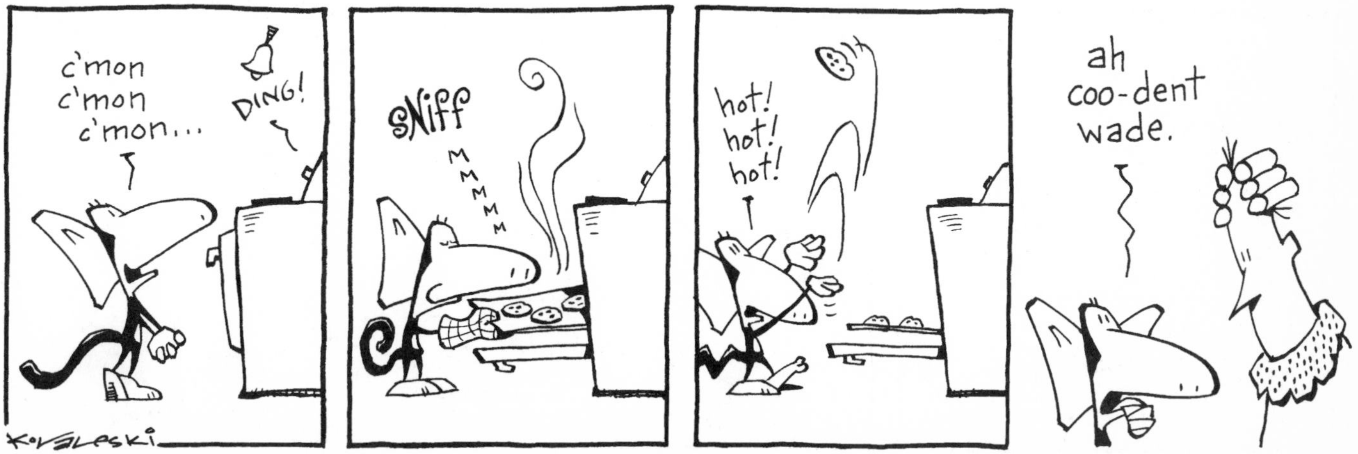
c'mon c'mon c'mon...
DING!
kovaleski
SNiff
MMMMM
hot! hot! hot!
ah coo-dent wade.

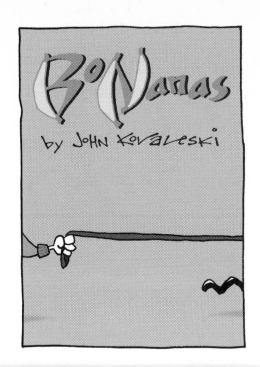

Bo'Nanas
by John Kovaleski

i'm going to put this collar on and have you lead me around the neighborhood.

people will see me — an intelligent, articulate being on a leash — and it'll make them think twice about the captivity of our animal brethren.

let's go.

OH, HE'S **SO** CUTE!

JUST AS CUTE AS COULD BE!

YOU'RE A CUTE ONE! YES, YOU ARE! **YES, YOU ARE!**

CUTIE, CUTIE, CUTE-CUTE!

WELL... YOU **ARE** CUTE.

it is my curse.

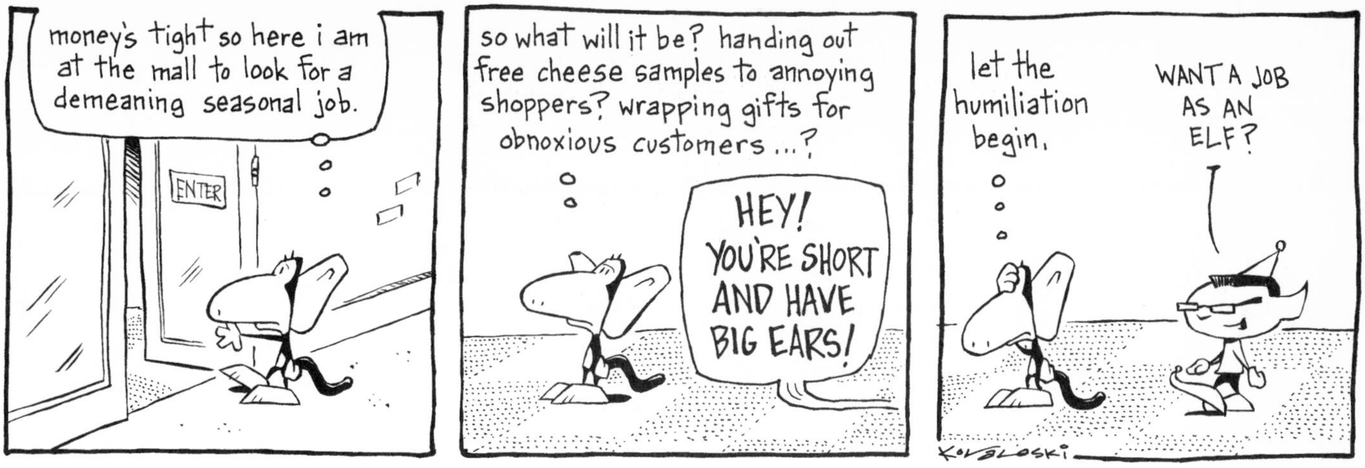
money's tight so here i am at the mall to look for a demeaning seasonal job.
ENTER
so what will it be? handing out free cheese samples to annoying shoppers? wrapping gifts for obnoxious customers ...?
HEY! YOU'RE SHORT AND HAVE BIG EARS!
let the humiliation begin.
WANT A JOB AS AN ELF?
KOVALESKI

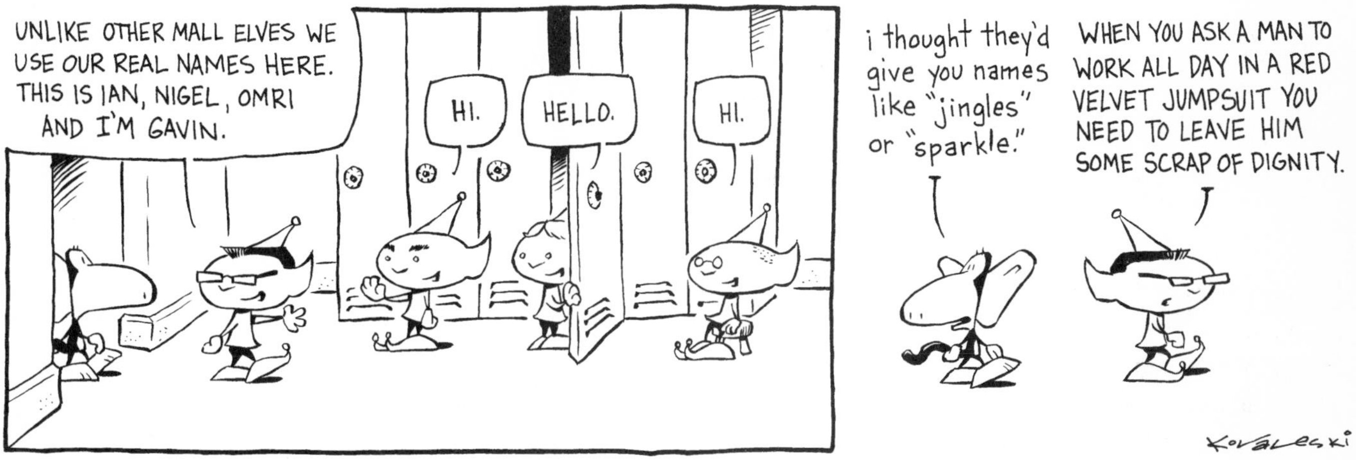
UNLIKE OTHER MALL ELVES WE USE OUR REAL NAMES HERE. THIS IS IAN, NIGEL, OMRI AND I'M GAVIN.
HI.
HELLO.
HI.
i thought they'd give you names like "jingles" or "sparkle."
WHEN YOU ASK A MAN TO WORK ALL DAY IN A RED VELVET JUMPSUIT YOU NEED TO LEAVE HIM SOME SCRAP OF DIGNITY.
KOVALESKI

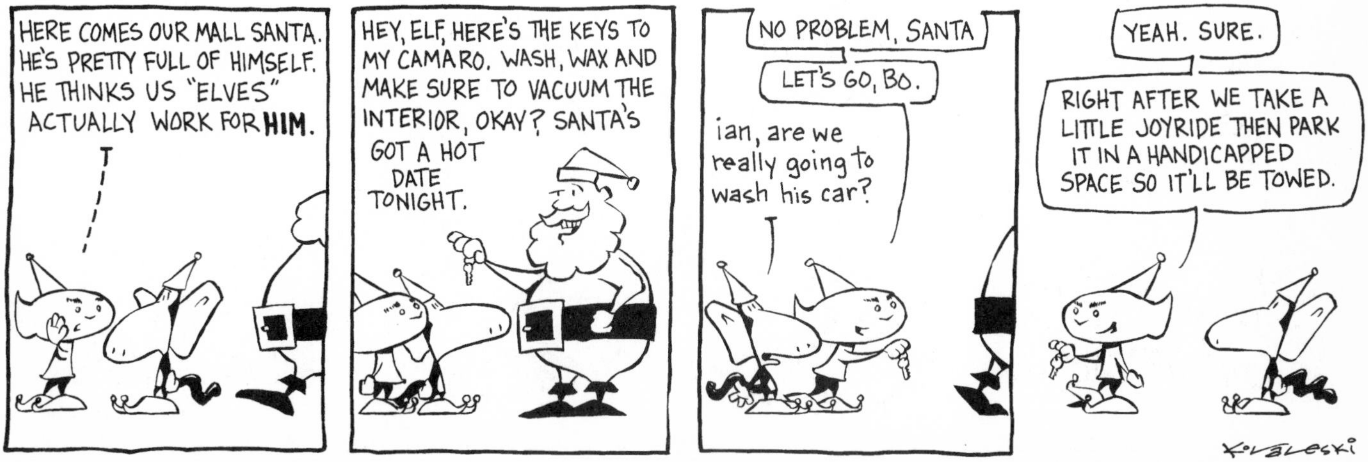
HERE COMES OUR MALL SANTA. HE'S PRETTY FULL OF HIMSELF. HE THINKS US "ELVES" ACTUALLY WORK FOR HIM.
HEY, ELF, HERE'S THE KEYS TO MY CAMARO. WASH, WAX AND MAKE SURE TO VACUUM THE INTERIOR, OKAY? SANTA'S GOT A HOT DATE TONIGHT.
NO PROBLEM, SANTA
LET'S GO, BO.
ian, are we really going to wash his car?
YEAH. SURE.
RIGHT AFTER WE TAKE A LITTLE JOYRIDE THEN PARK IT IN A HANDICAPPED SPACE SO IT'LL BE TOWED.
KOVALESKI

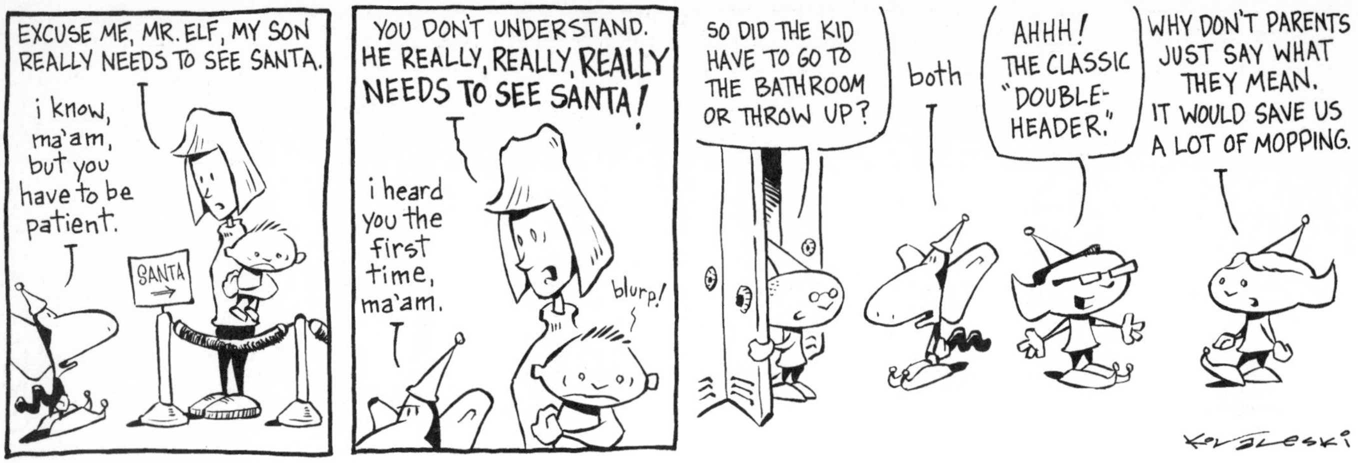
EXCUSE ME, MR. ELF, MY SON REALLY NEEDS TO SEE SANTA.
i know, ma'am, but you have to be patient.
SANTA →
YOU DON'T UNDERSTAND. HE REALLY, REALLY, REALLY NEEDS TO SEE SANTA!
i heard you the first time, ma'am.
blurp!
SO DID THE KID HAVE TO GO TO THE BATHROOM OR THROW UP?
both
AHHH! THE CLASSIC "DOUBLE-HEADER."
WHY DON'T PARENTS JUST SAY WHAT THEY MEAN. IT WOULD SAVE US A LOT OF MOPPING.
Kovaleski

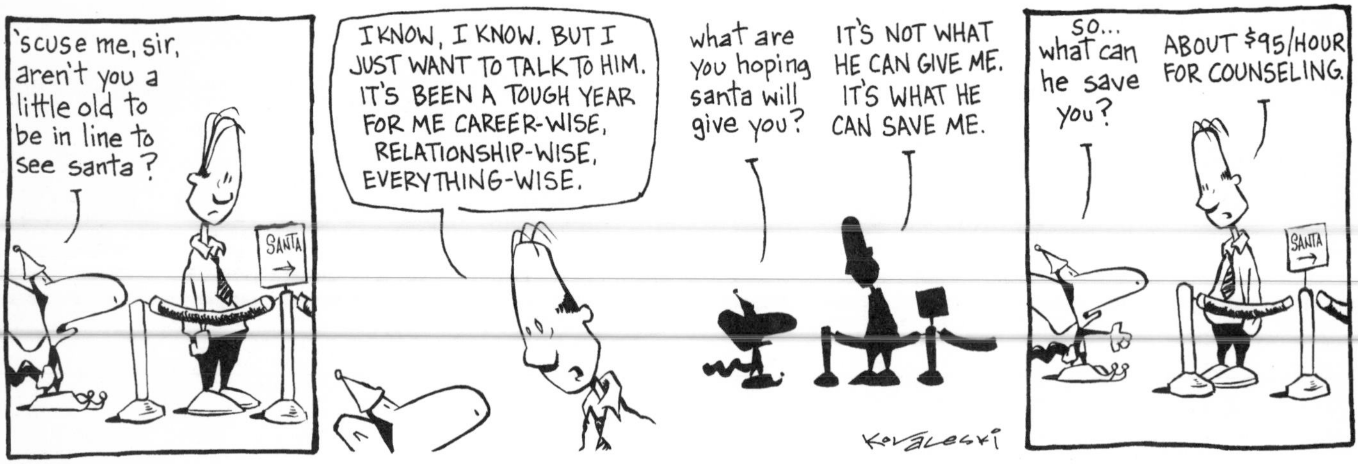
'scuse me, sir, aren't you a little old to be in line to see santa?
SANTA →
I KNOW, I KNOW. BUT I JUST WANT TO TALK TO HIM. IT'S BEEN A TOUGH YEAR FOR ME CAREER-WISE, RELATIONSHIP-WISE, EVERYTHING-WISE.
what are you hoping santa will give you?
IT'S NOT WHAT HE CAN GIVE ME. IT'S WHAT HE CAN SAVE ME.
so... what can he save you?
ABOUT $95/HOUR FOR COUNSELING.
SANTA →
Kovaleski

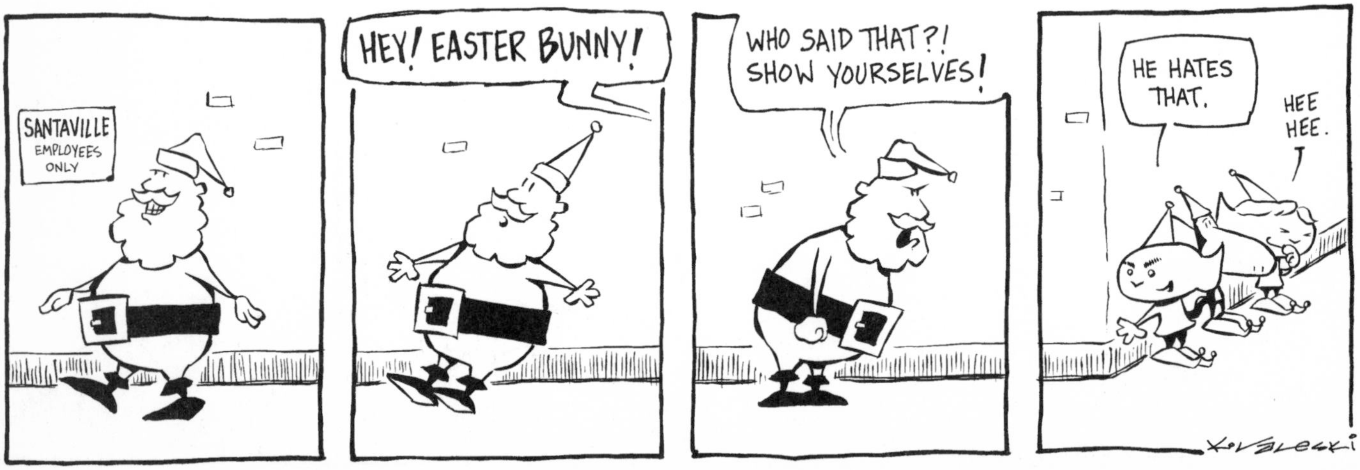
SANTAVILLE EMPLOYEES ONLY
HEY! EASTER BUNNY!
WHO SAID THAT?! SHOW YOURSELVES!
HE HATES THAT.
HEE HEE.
Kovaleski

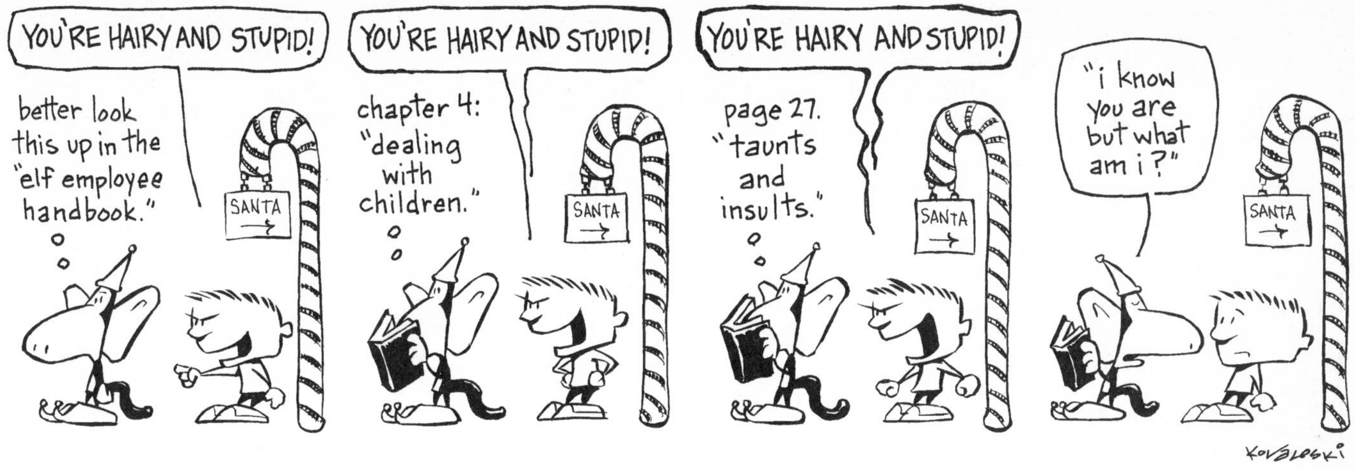
YOU'RE HAIRY AND STUPID!
better look this up in the "elf employee handbook."
SANTA
YOU'RE HAIRY AND STUPID!
chapter 4: "dealing with children."
SANTA
YOU'RE HAIRY AND STUPID!
page 27. "taunts and insults."
SANTA
"i know you are but what am i?"
SANTA
KOVALESKI

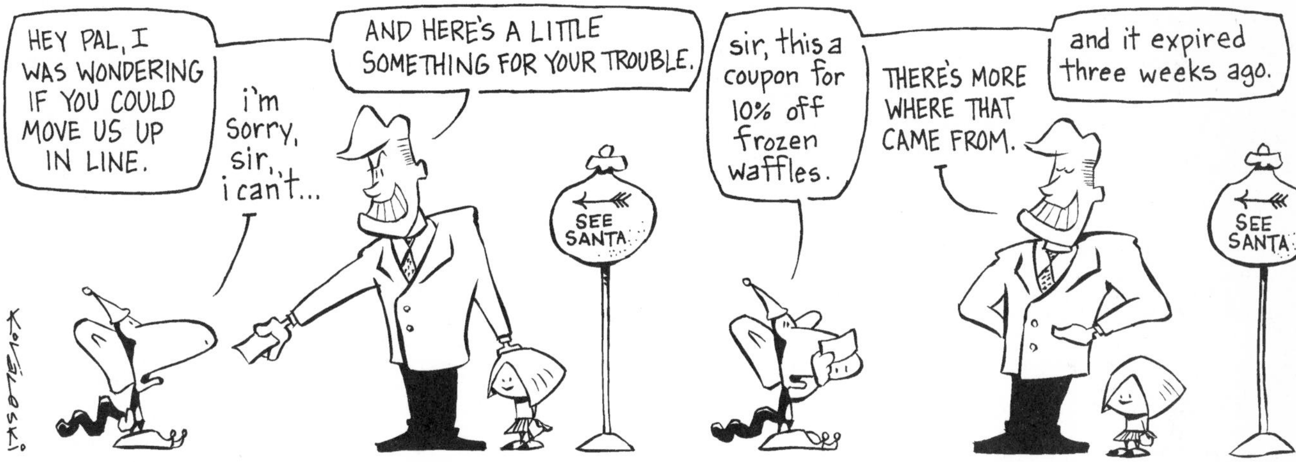
HEY PAL, I WAS WONDERING IF YOU COULD MOVE US UP IN LINE.
AND HERE'S A LITTLE SOMETHING FOR YOUR TROUBLE.
i'm sorry, sir,, i can't...
SEE SANTA
sir, this a coupon for 10% off frozen waffles.
and it expired three weeks ago.
THERE'S MORE WHERE THAT CAME FROM.
SEE SANTA
KOVALESKI

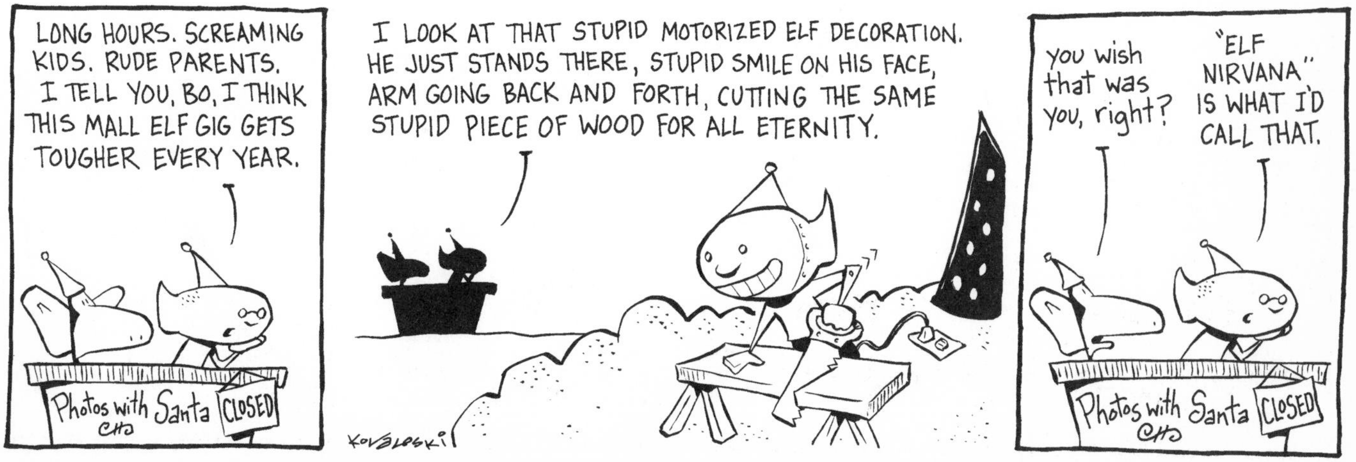
LONG HOURS. SCREAMING KIDS. RUDE PARENTS. I TELL YOU, BO, I THINK THIS MALL ELF GIG GETS TOUGHER EVERY YEAR.
Photos with Santa
CLOSED
I LOOK AT THAT STUPID MOTORIZED ELF DECORATION. HE JUST STANDS THERE, STUPID SMILE ON HIS FACE, ARM GOING BACK AND FORTH, CUTTING THE SAME STUPID PIECE OF WOOD FOR ALL ETERNITY.
KOVALESKI
you wish that was you, right?
"ELF NIRVANA" IS WHAT I'D CALL THAT.
Photos with Santa
CLOSED

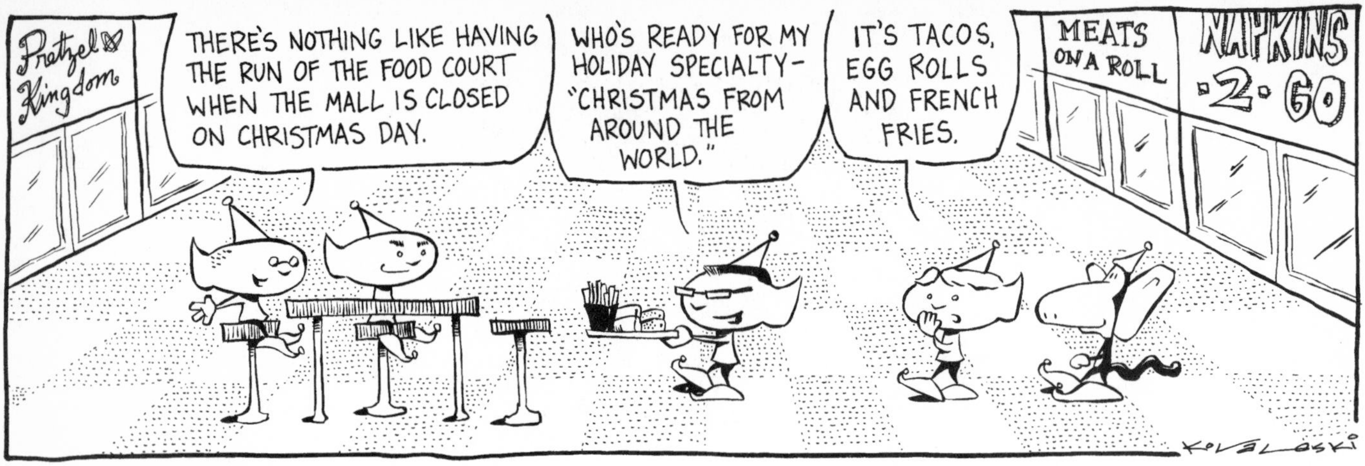
Pretzel Kingdom
THERE'S NOTHING LIKE HAVING THE RUN OF THE FOOD COURT WHEN THE MALL IS CLOSED ON CHRISTMAS DAY.
WHO'S READY FOR MY HOLIDAY SPECIALTY- "CHRISTMAS FROM AROUND THE WORLD."
IT'S TACOS, EGG ROLLS AND FRENCH FRIES.
MEATS ON A ROLL
NAPKINS 2 GO
KOVALESKI

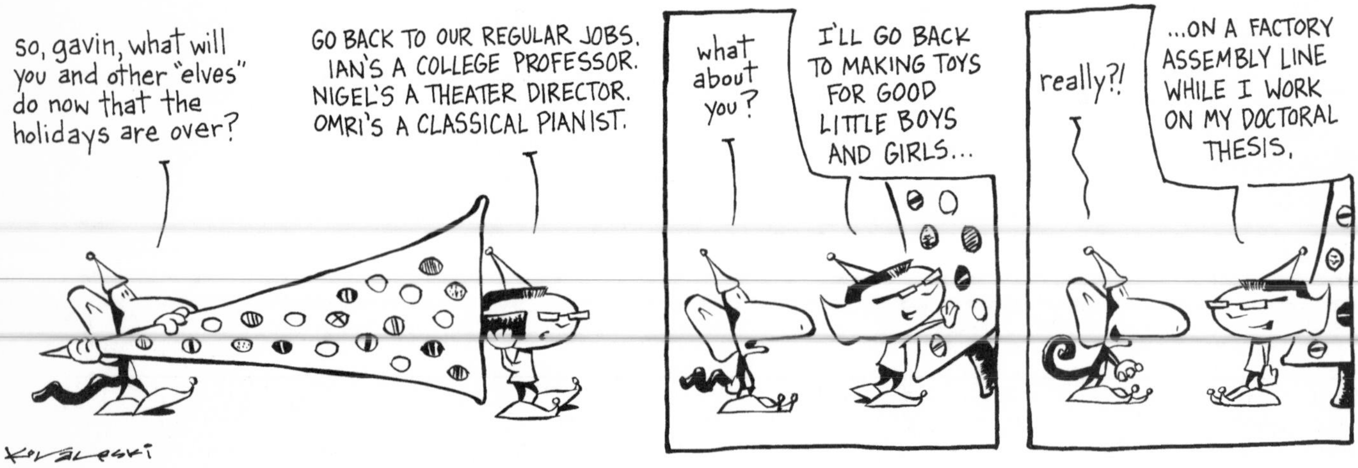
so, gavin, what will you and other "elves" do now that the holidays are over?
GO BACK TO OUR REGULAR JOBS. IAN'S A COLLEGE PROFESSOR. NIGEL'S A THEATER DIRECTOR. OMRI'S A CLASSICAL PIANIST.
what about you?
I'LL GO BACK TO MAKING TOYS FOR GOOD LITTLE BOYS AND GIRLS...
really?!
...ON A FACTORY ASSEMBLY LINE WHILE I WORK ON MY DOCTORAL THESIS.
KOVALESKI

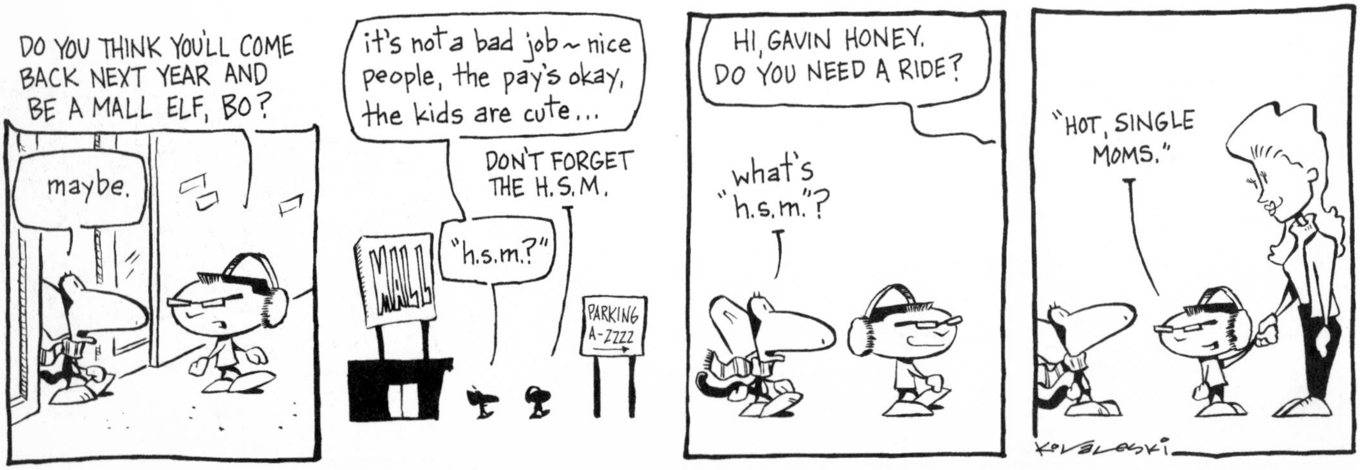
DO YOU THINK YOU'LL COME BACK NEXT YEAR AND BE A MALL ELF, BO?
maybe.
it's not a bad job ~ nice people, the pay's okay, the kids are cute...
DON'T FORGET THE H.S.M.
"h.s.m.?"
MALL
PARKING A-ZZZZ
HI, GAVIN HONEY. DO YOU NEED A RIDE?
"what's "h.s.m."?
"HOT, SINGLE MOMS."
KOVALESKI

BoNanas
by JOHN KOVALESKI

PIECE ON EARTH
SILENT KNIGHT HOLEY KNIGHT
SANTA CHAWS CHEWING TOBACCO
ON DONDER ON DANCER ON PRANCER ON SPITZEN
isn't there a petition somewhere that i could sign to stop this sort of thing?
CHRISTMAS CARDS
KOVALESKI

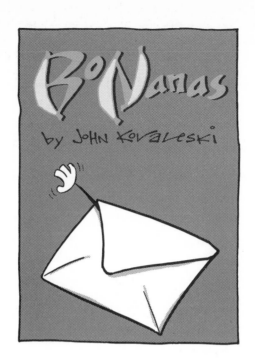

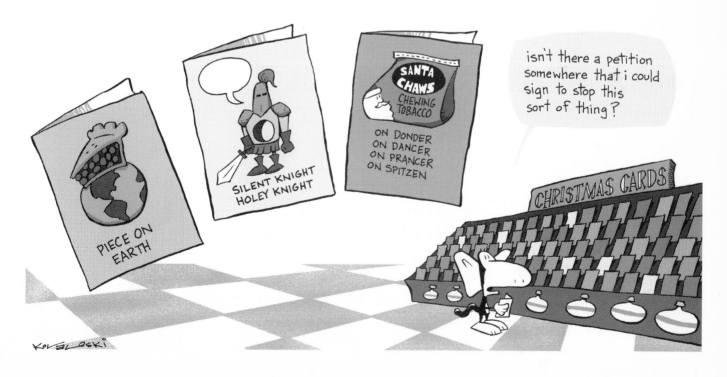

BoNanas
by JOHN KOVALESKI
FRESH

SHAKE
SHAKE
SHAKE
POP
FZZZZZZ!
WHEN DID THEY START CARBONATING SOUP?
"now with twice the caffeine of a pot of truckstop coffee."
KOVALESKI

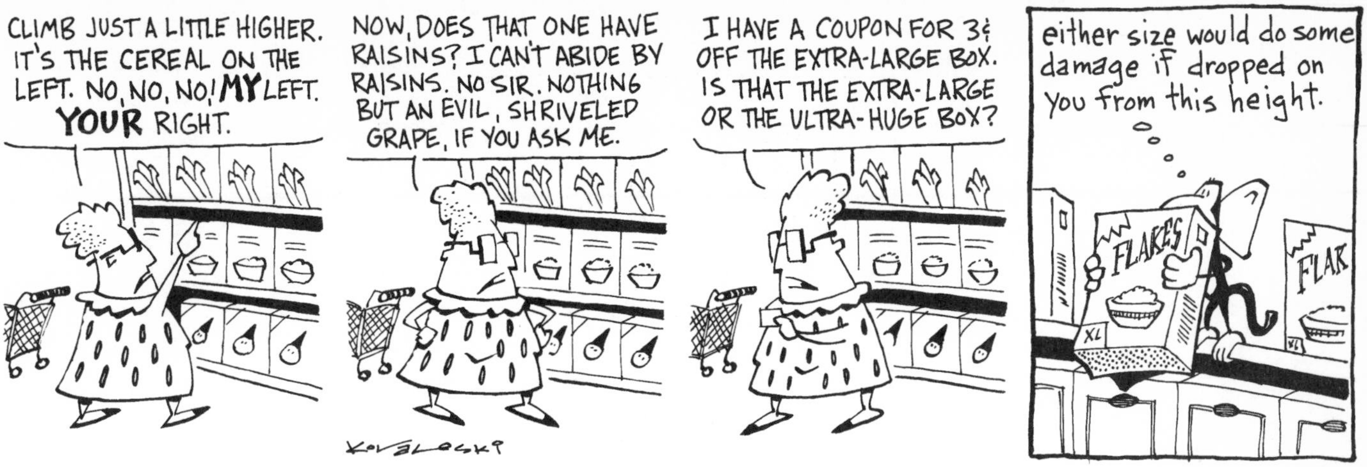
CLIMB JUST A LITTLE HIGHER. IT'S THE CEREAL ON THE LEFT. NO, NO, NO! MY LEFT. YOUR RIGHT.
NOW, DOES THAT ONE HAVE RAISINS? I CAN'T ABIDE BY RAISINS. NO SIR. NOTHING BUT AN EVIL, SHRIVELED GRAPE, IF YOU ASK ME.
KOVALESKI
I HAVE A COUPON FOR 3¢ OFF THE EXTRA-LARGE BOX. IS THAT THE EXTRA-LARGE OR THE ULTRA-HUGE BOX?
either size would do some damage if dropped on you from this height.
FLAKES
XL
FLAK

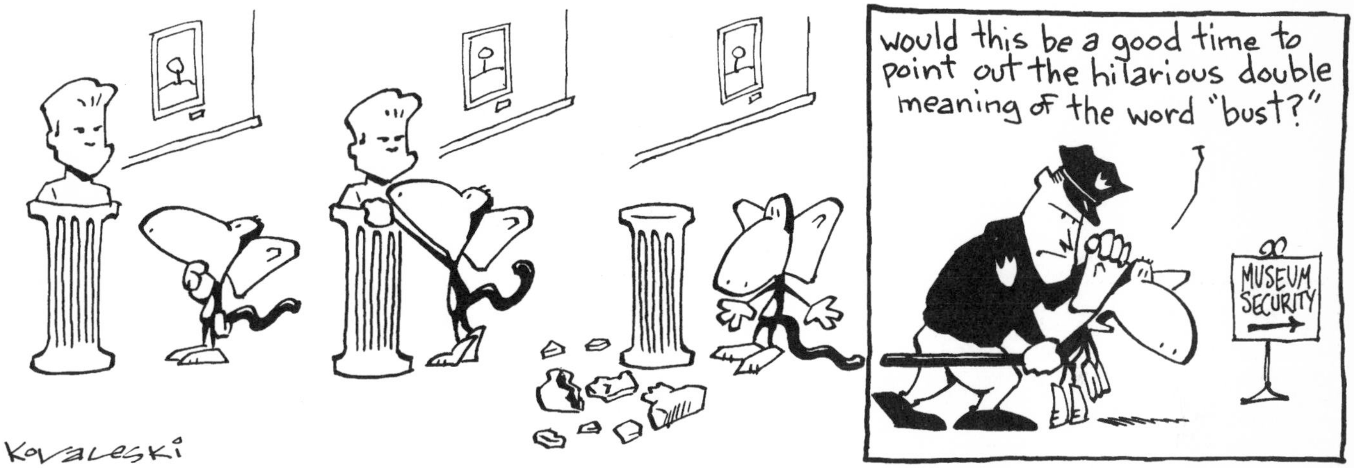
KOVALESKI
would this be a good time to point out the hilarious double meaning of the word "bust?"
MUSEUM SECURITY

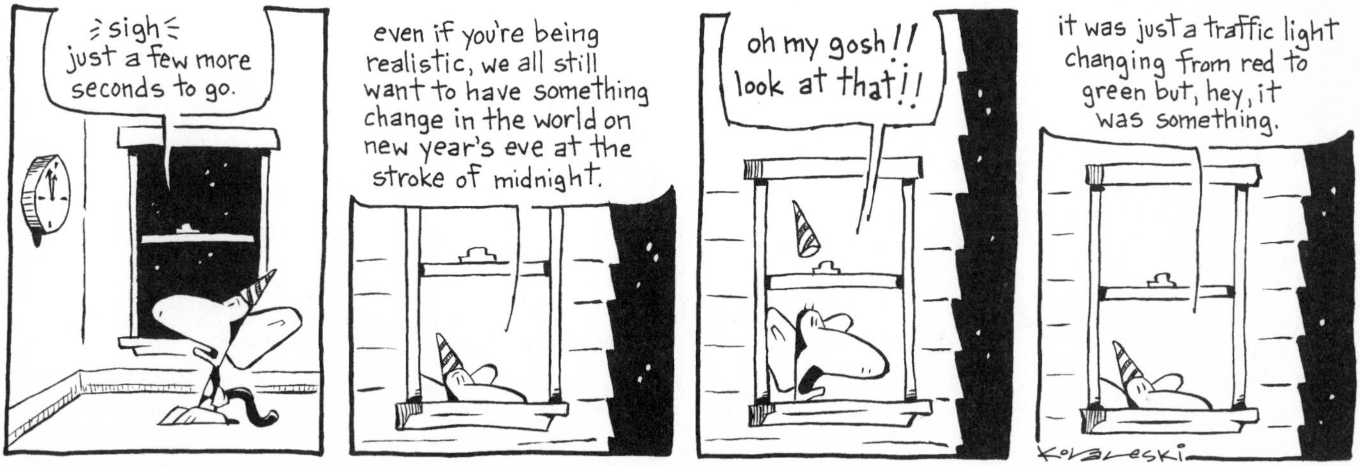
sigh
just a few more seconds to go.
even if you're being realistic, we all still want to have something change in the world on new year's eve at the stroke of midnight.
oh my gosh!! look at that!!
it was just a traffic light changing from red to green but, hey, it was something.
KOVALESKI

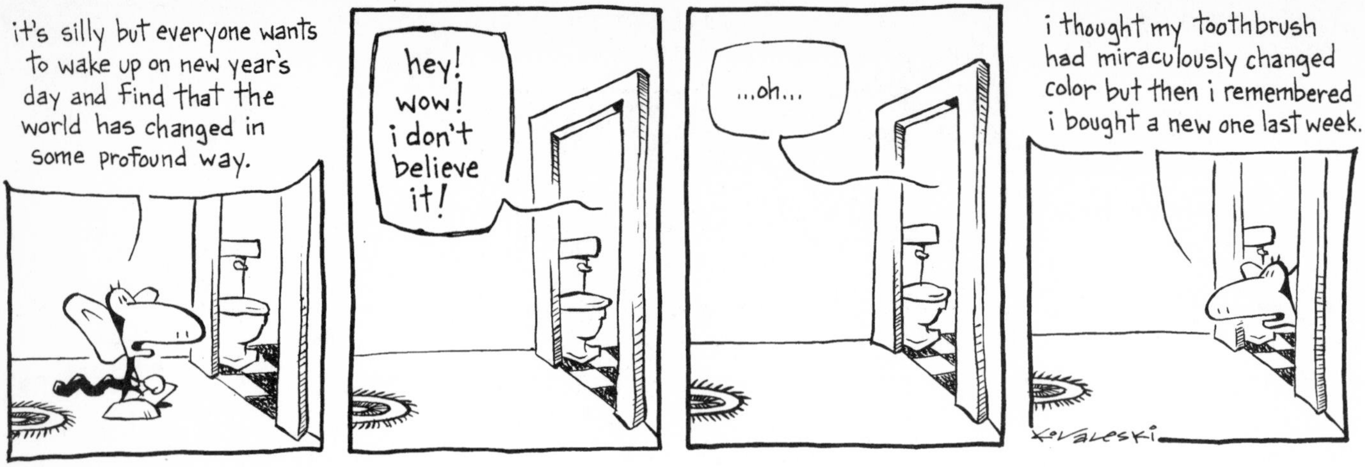
it's silly but everyone wants to wake up on new year's day and find that the world has changed in some profound way.
hey! wow! i don't believe it!
...oh...
i thought my toothbrush had miraculously changed color but then i remembered i bought a new one last week.
kovaleski

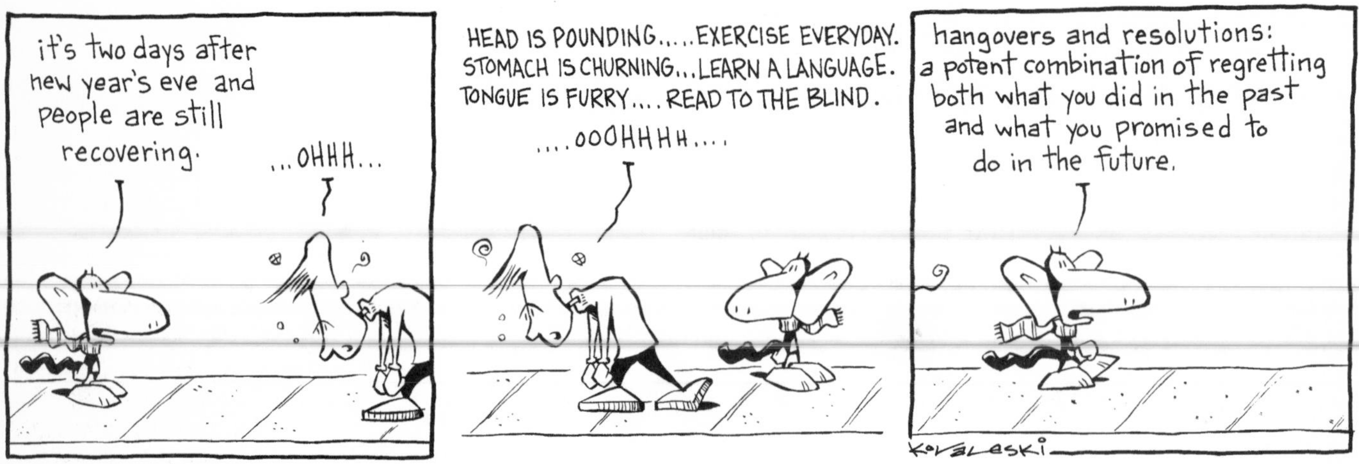
it's two days after new year's eve and people are still recovering.
...OHHH...
HEAD IS POUNDING.....EXERCISE EVERYDAY.
STOMACH IS CHURNING...LEARN A LANGUAGE.
TONGUE IS FURRY....READ TO THE BLIND.
....OOOHHHH....
hangovers and resolutions: a potent combination of regretting both what you did in the past and what you promised to do in the future.
kovaleski

A MONKEY'S GROOMING QUANDARY

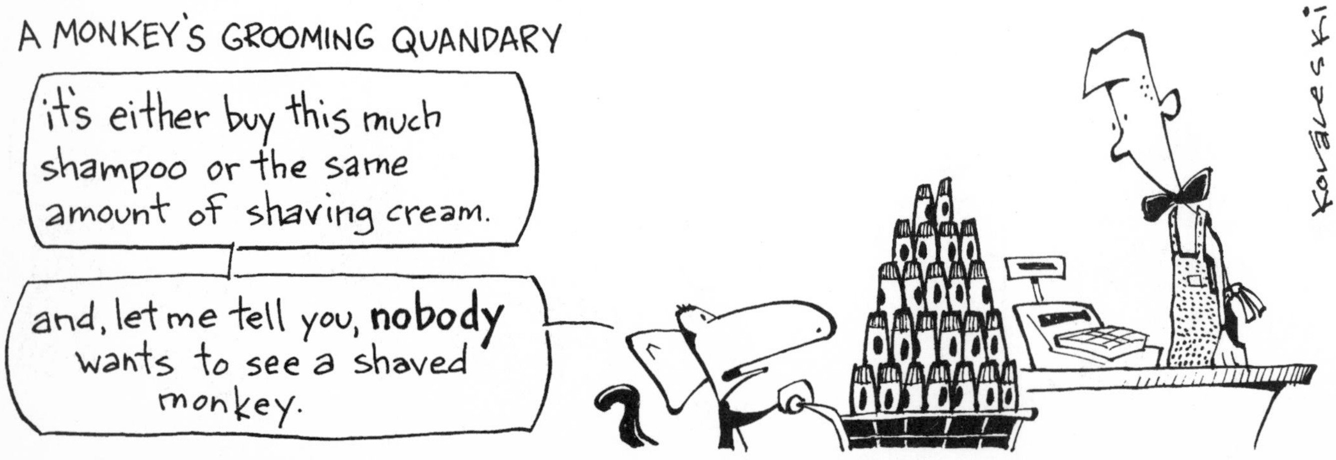
it's either buy this much shampoo or the same amount of shaving cream.
and, let me tell you, **nobody** wants to see a shaved monkey.
kovaleski

BoNeHeAdS
by JOHN KOVALESKI

a root beer, please.
WOULD YOU LIKE FRIES WITH THAT?
nope, just a root beer.
YOU COULD DUNK THEM.
pardon?
YOU COULD DUNK THE FRIES IN YOUR ROOT BEER.
that sounds awful.
HOW DO YOU KNOW? THERE HAD TO BE A FIRST PERSON WHO TRIED SCRAMBLED EGGS WITH KETCHUP OR CHICKEN WINGS WITH BLUE CHEESE DRESSING.
...i don't know...
YOU COULD BE A "TASTE PIONEER" LIKE THOSE WHO TRAVELLED ACROSS THE COUNTRY IN COVERED WAGONS.
no wonder some of those pioneers died of starvation.
KOVALESKI

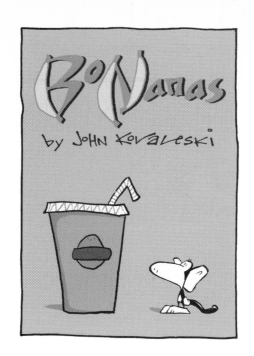

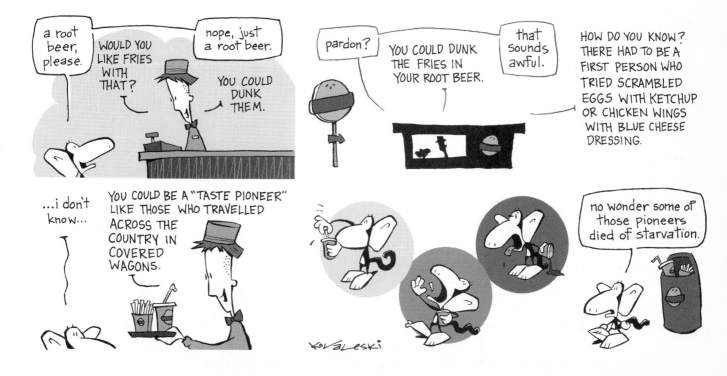

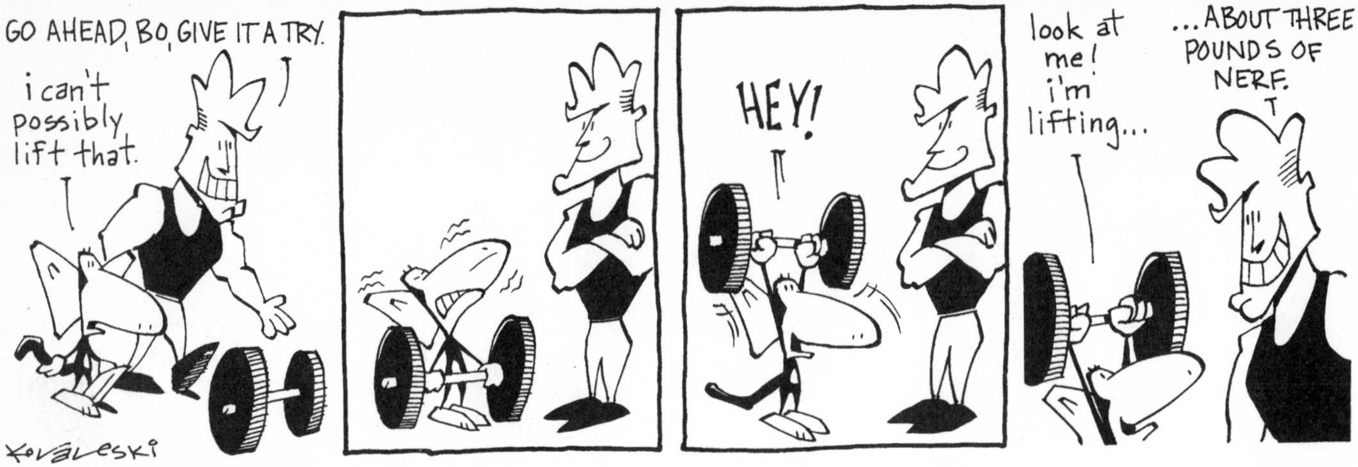
GO AHEAD, BO, GIVE IT A TRY.
i can't possibly lift that.
HEY!
look at me! i'm lifting...
...ABOUT THREE POUNDS OF NERF.
KOVALESKI

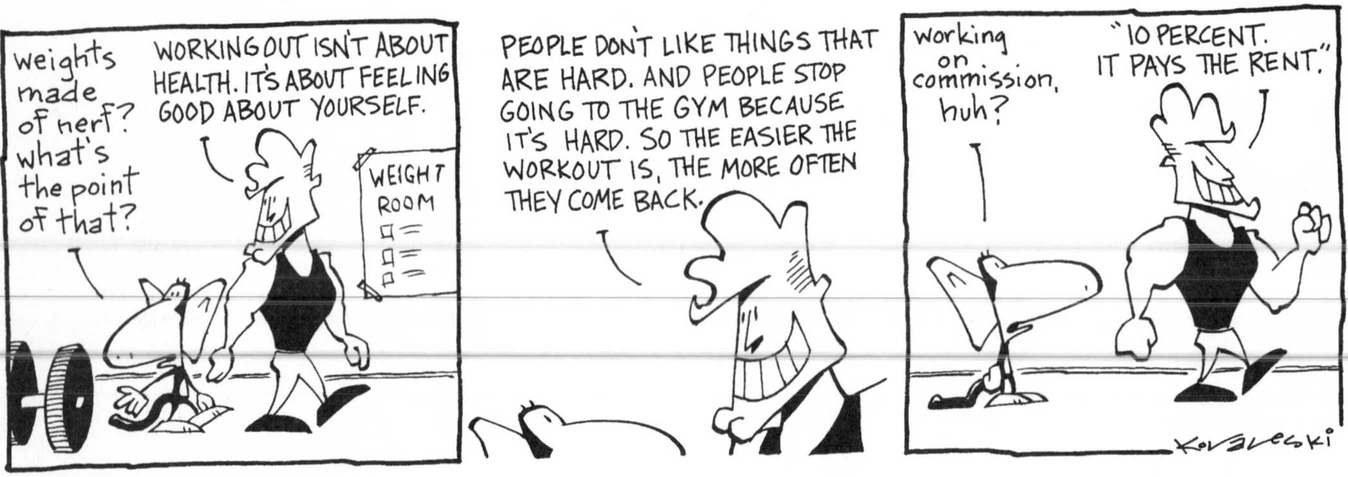
weights made of nerf? what's the point of that?
WORKING OUT ISN'T ABOUT HEALTH. IT'S ABOUT FEELING GOOD ABOUT YOURSELF.
WEIGHT ROOM
PEOPLE DON'T LIKE THINGS THAT ARE HARD. AND PEOPLE STOP GOING TO THE GYM BECAUSE IT'S HARD. SO THE EASIER THE WORKOUT IS, THE MORE OFTEN THEY COME BACK.
working on commission, huh?
"10 PERCENT. IT PAYS THE RENT."
KOVALESKI

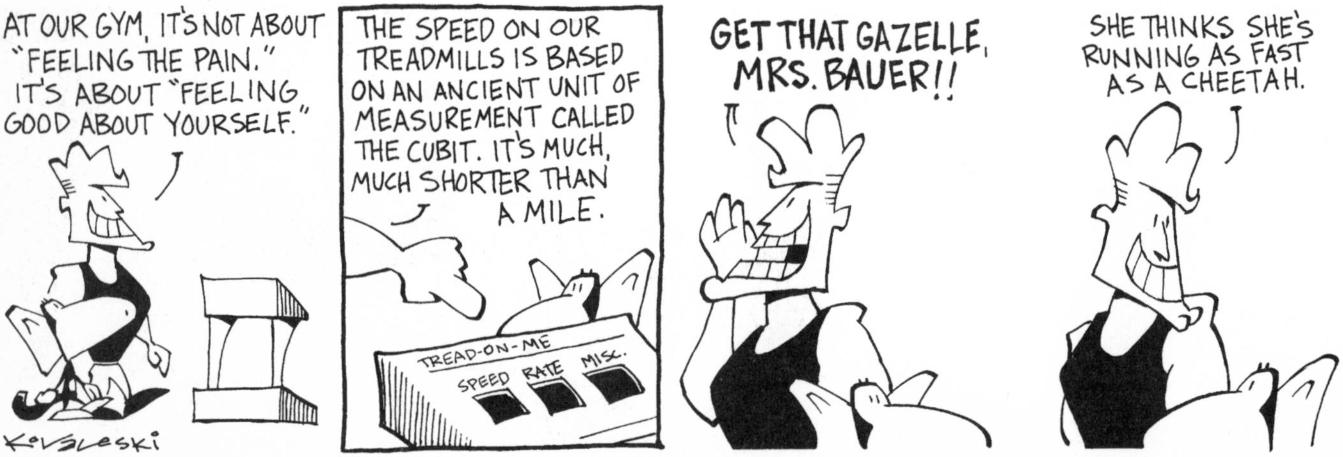
AT OUR GYM, IT'S NOT ABOUT "FEELING THE PAIN." IT'S ABOUT "FEELING GOOD ABOUT YOURSELF."
KOVALESKI
THE SPEED ON OUR TREADMILLS IS BASED ON AN ANCIENT UNIT OF MEASUREMENT CALLED THE CUBIT. IT'S MUCH, MUCH SHORTER THAN A MILE.
TREAD-ON-ME
SPEED
RATE
MISC.
GET THAT GAZELLE, MRS. BAUER!!
SHE THINKS SHE'S RUNNING AS FAST AS A CHEETAH.

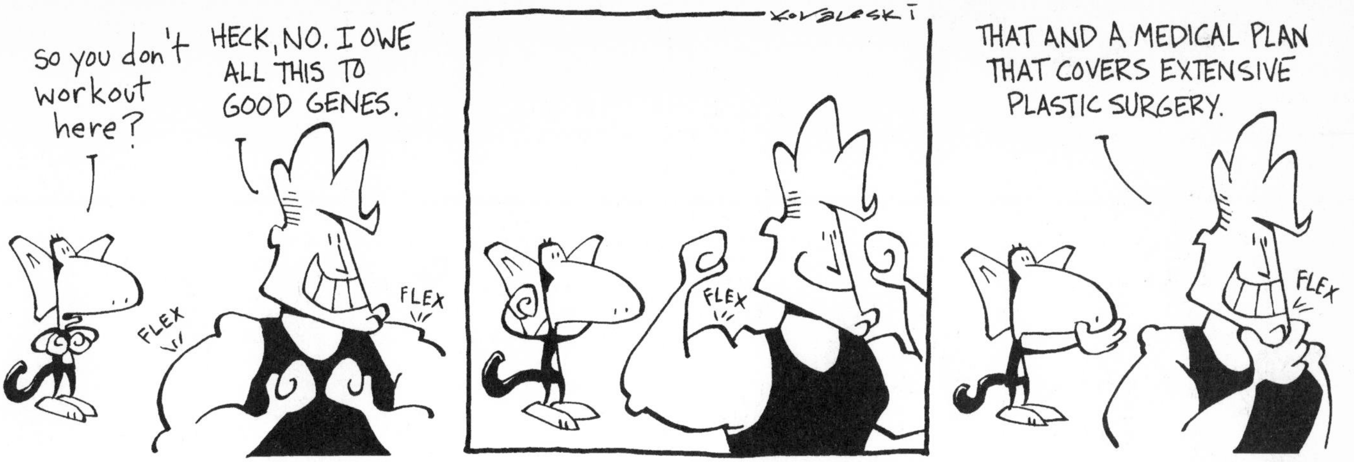
so you don't workout here?
HECK, NO. I OWE ALL THIS TO GOOD GENES.
FLEX
FLEX
FLEX
THAT AND A MEDICAL PLAN THAT COVERS EXTENSIVE PLASTIC SURGERY.
FLEX
KOVALESKI

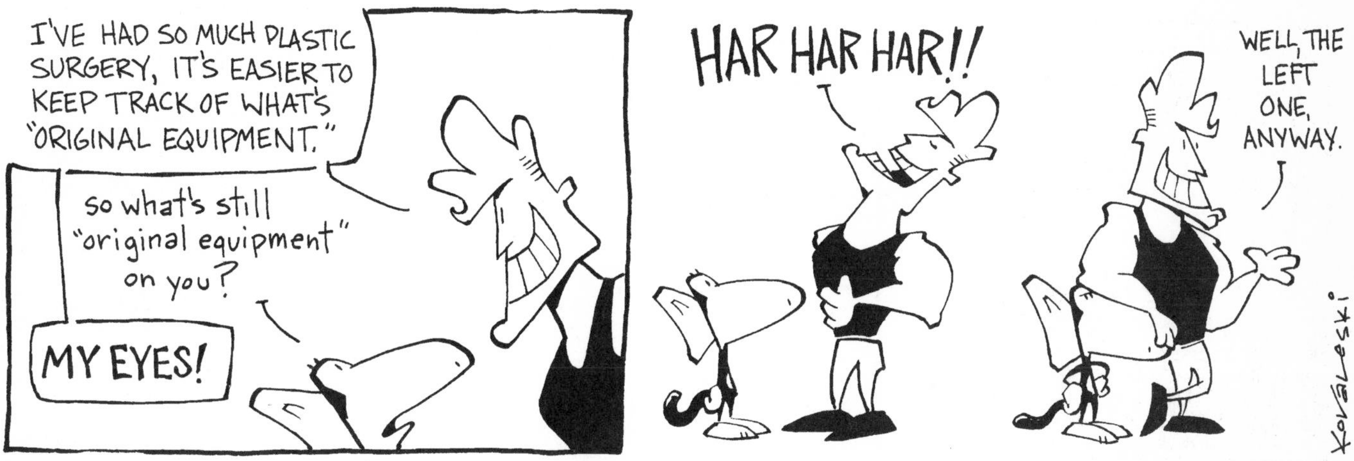
so what's still "original equipment" on you?
I'VE HAD SO MUCH PLASTIC SURGERY, IT'S EASIER TO KEEP TRACK OF WHAT'S "ORIGINAL EQUIPMENT."
MY EYES!
HAR HAR HAR!!
WELL, THE LEFT ONE, ANYWAY.
KOVALESKI

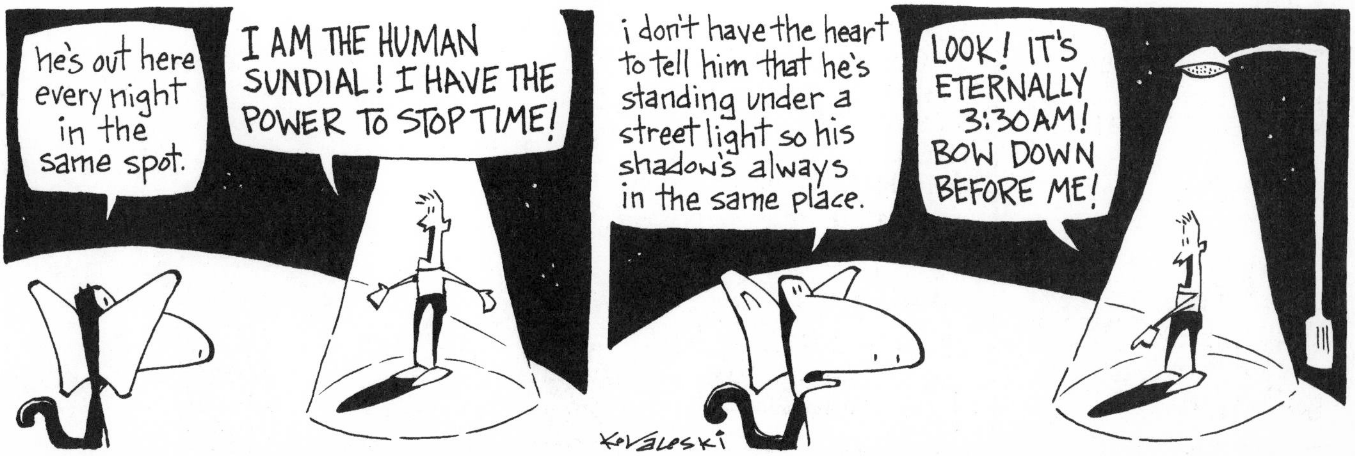
he's out here every night in the same spot.
I AM THE HUMAN SUNDIAL! I HAVE THE POWER TO STOP TIME!
i don't have the heart to tell him that he's standing under a street light so his shadow's always in the same place.
LOOK! IT'S ETERNALLY 3:30AM! BOW DOWN BEFORE ME!
KOVALESKI

BoNanas
by JOHN KOVALESKI

BUMP!
i always thought that evolution gave me big ears as a natural defense against this sort of thing.
KOVALESKI

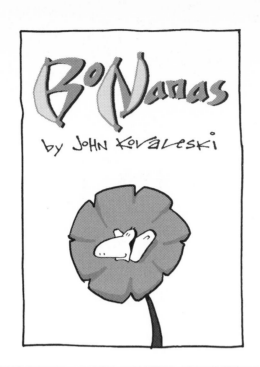

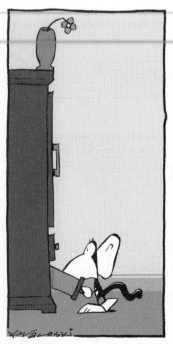

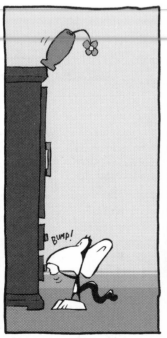

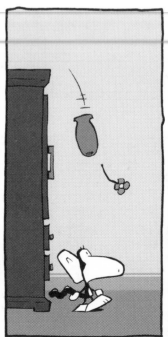

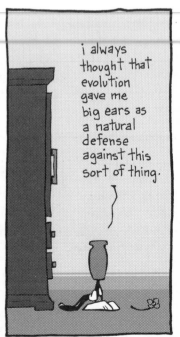

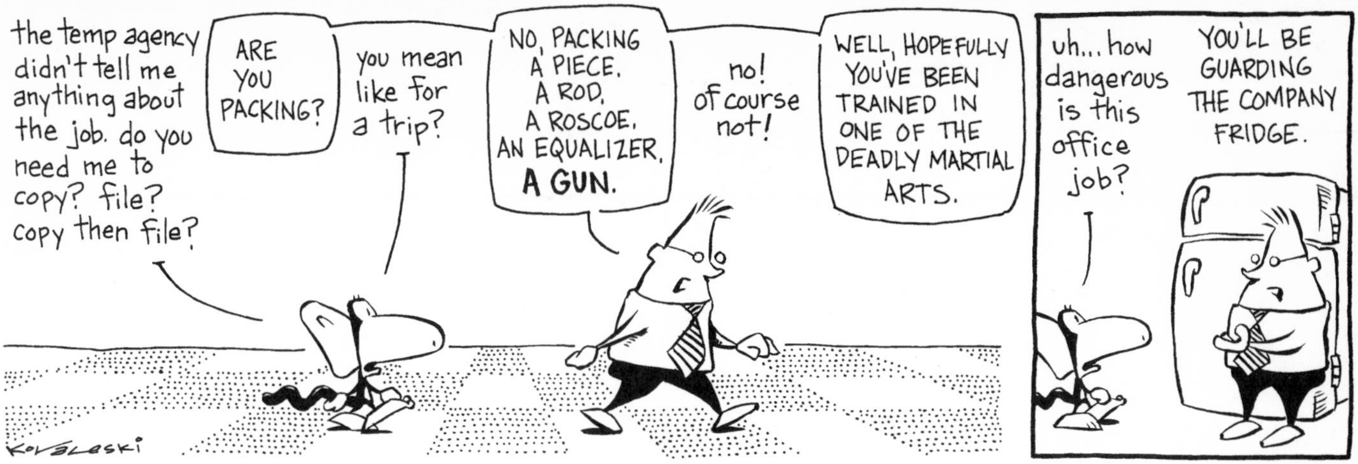
the temp agency didn't tell me anything about the job. do you need me to copy? file? copy then file?
ARE YOU PACKING?
you mean like for a trip?
NO, PACKING A PIECE. A ROD. A ROSCOE. AN EQUALIZER. **A GUN.**
no! of course not!
WELL, HOPEFULLY YOU'VE BEEN TRAINED IN ONE OF THE DEADLY MARTIAL ARTS.
uh... how dangerous is this office job?
YOU'LL BE GUARDING THE COMPANY FRIDGE.
KOVALESKI

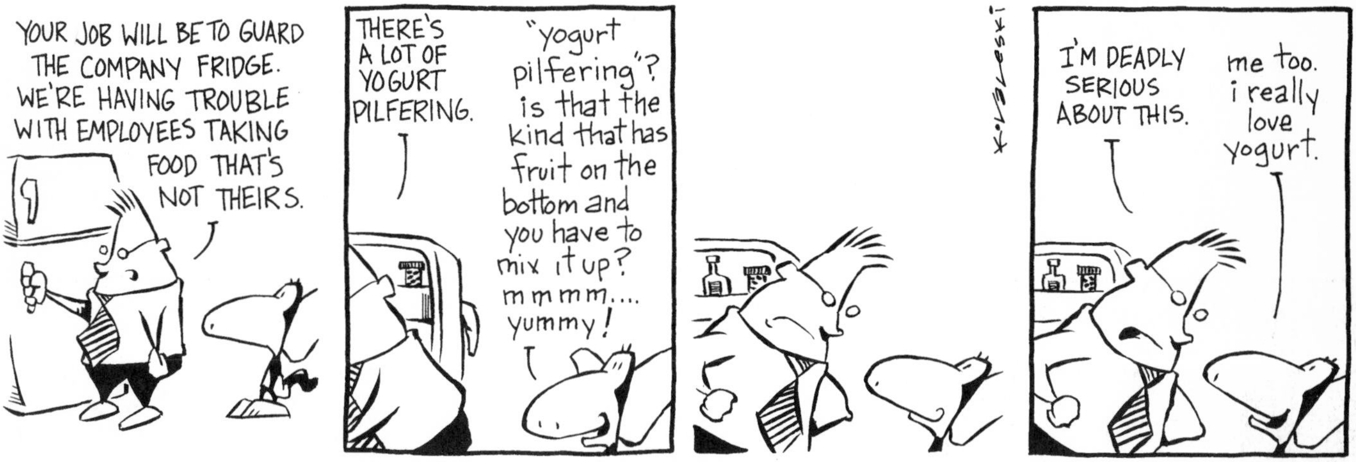
YOUR JOB WILL BE TO GUARD THE COMPANY FRIDGE. WE'RE HAVING TROUBLE WITH EMPLOYEES TAKING FOOD THAT'S NOT THEIRS.
THERE'S A LOT OF YOGURT PILFERING.
"yogurt pilfering"? is that the kind that has fruit on the bottom and you have to mix it up? mmmm.... yummy!
KOVALESKI
I'M DEADLY SERIOUS ABOUT THIS.
me too. i really love yogurt.

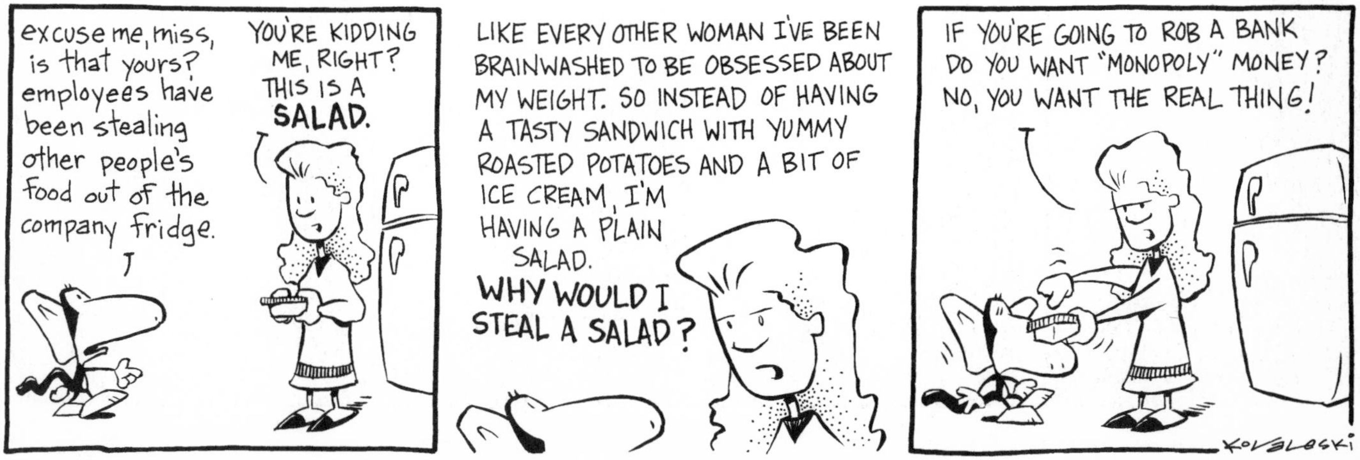
excuse me, miss, is that yours? employees have been stealing other people's food out of the company fridge.
YOU'RE KIDDING ME, RIGHT? THIS IS A **SALAD.**
LIKE EVERY OTHER WOMAN I'VE BEEN BRAINWASHED TO BE OBSESSED ABOUT MY WEIGHT. SO INSTEAD OF HAVING A TASTY SANDWICH WITH YUMMY ROASTED POTATOES AND A BIT OF ICE CREAM, I'M HAVING A PLAIN SALAD. **WHY WOULD I STEAL A SALAD?**
IF YOU'RE GOING TO ROB A BANK DO YOU WANT "MONOPOLY" MONEY? NO, YOU WANT THE REAL THING!
KOVALESKI

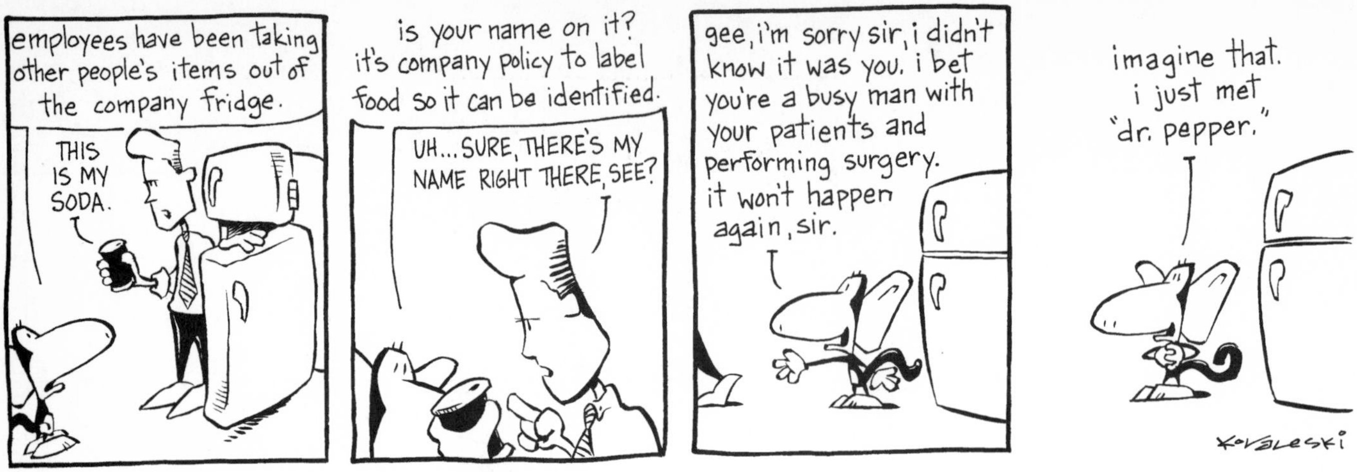
employees have been taking other people's items out of the company fridge.
THIS IS MY SODA.
is your name on it? it's company policy to label food so it can be identified.
UH... SURE, THERE'S MY NAME RIGHT THERE, SEE?
gee, i'm sorry sir, i didn't know it was you. i bet you're a busy man with your patients and performing surgery. it won't happen again, sir.
imagine that. i just met "dr. pepper."
KOVALESKI

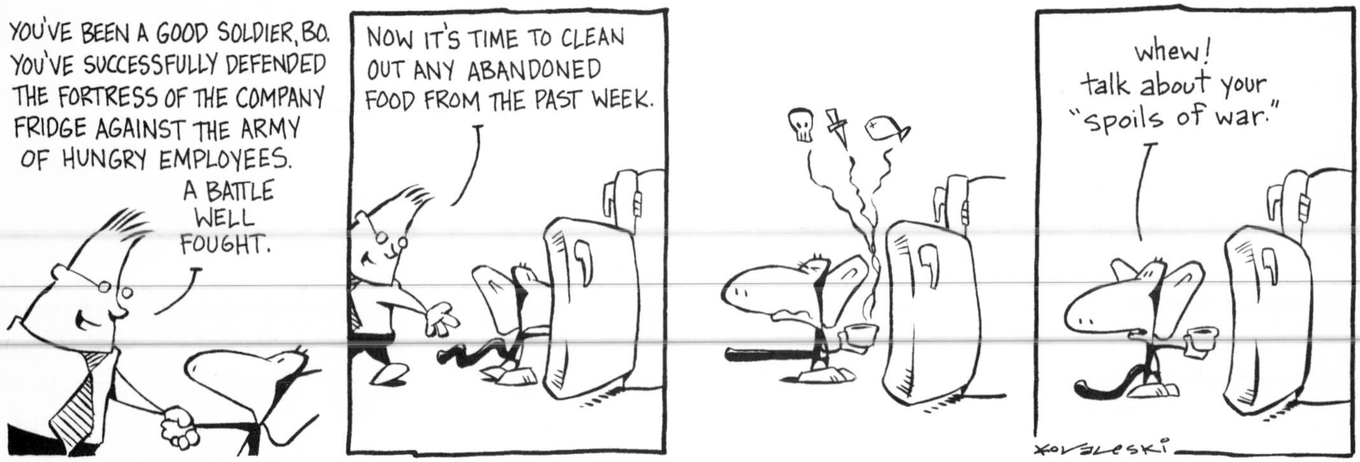
YOU'VE BEEN A GOOD SOLDIER, BO. YOU'VE SUCCESSFULLY DEFENDED THE FORTRESS OF THE COMPANY FRIDGE AGAINST THE ARMY OF HUNGRY EMPLOYEES.
A BATTLE WELL FOUGHT.
NOW IT'S TIME TO CLEAN OUT ANY ABANDONED FOOD FROM THE PAST WEEK.
whew! talk about your "spoils of war."
KOVALESKI

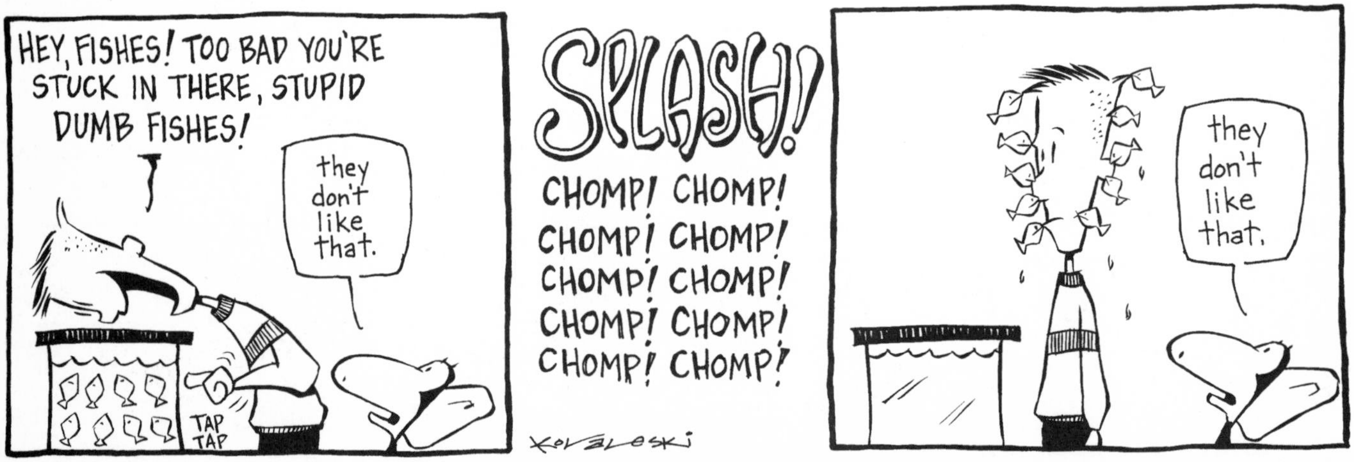
HEY, FISHES! TOO BAD YOU'RE STUCK IN THERE, STUPID DUMB FISHES!
they don't like that.
TAP TAP
SPLASH!
CHOMP! CHOMP! CHOMP! CHOMP! CHOMP! CHOMP! CHOMP! CHOMP! CHOMP! CHOMP!
they don't like that.
KOVALESKI

BoNanas
by JOHN KOVALESKI

HI!
uh...hi.
DO YOU SEE IT?
huh?
DO YOU SEE IT?
all i see is a case of hypothermia waiting to happen.
NO. NO. DO YOU SEE MY TATTOO?
you'd think i would with your lack of clothing but, no, i don't.
IT'S A FULL-BODY TATTOO OF ME!
o...kay.
IT'S KINDA SUBTLE.
i guess it would be.
i also have a tattoo. it's hard to see cuz it's black and my fur is black...
it says "born to avoid the crazy and the frostbitten."
KOVALESKI

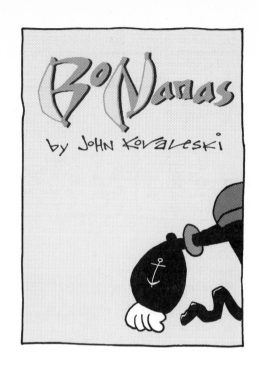

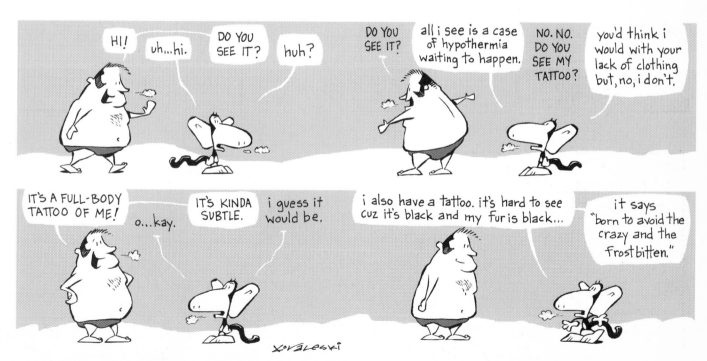

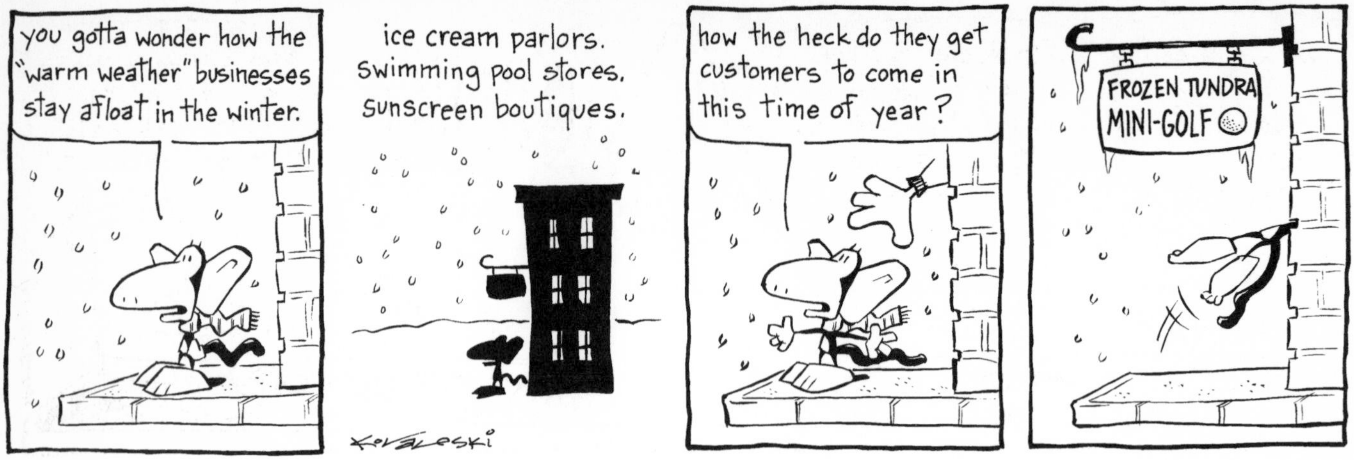

you gotta wonder how the "warm weather" businesses stay afloat in the winter.
ice cream parlors. swimming pool stores. sunscreen boutiques.
how the heck do they get customers to come in this time of year?
FROZEN TUNDRA MINI-GOLF

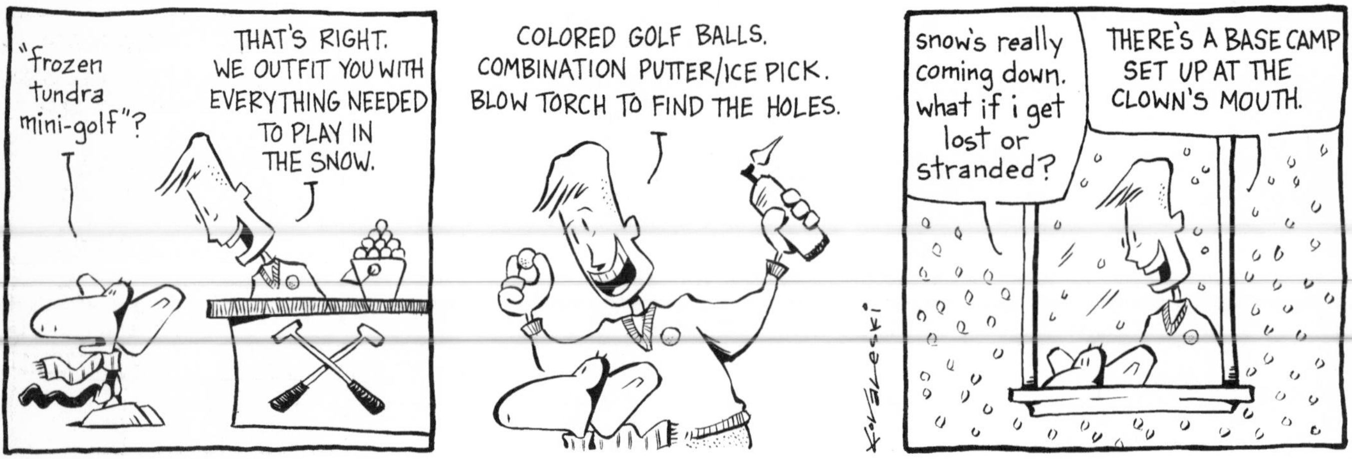

"frozen tundra mini-golf"?
THAT'S RIGHT. WE OUTFIT YOU WITH EVERYTHING NEEDED TO PLAY IN THE SNOW.
COLORED GOLF BALLS. COMBINATION PUTTER/ICE PICK. BLOW TORCH TO FIND THE HOLES.
snow's really coming down. what if i get lost or stranded?
THERE'S A BASE CAMP SET UP AT THE CLOWN'S MOUTH.

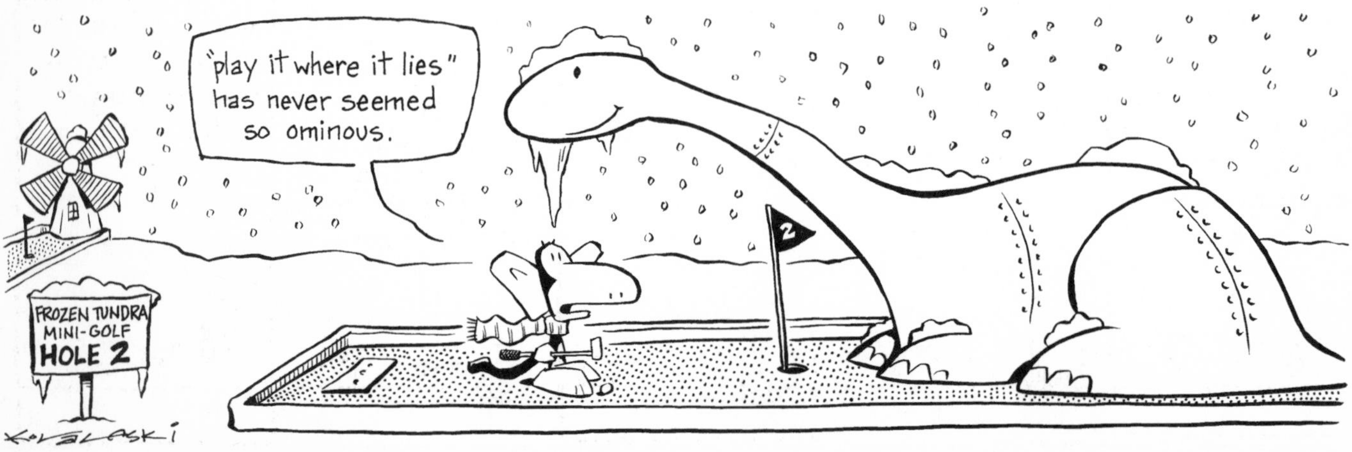

"play it where it lies" has never seemed so ominous.
FROZEN TUNDRA MINI-GOLF HOLE 2
2

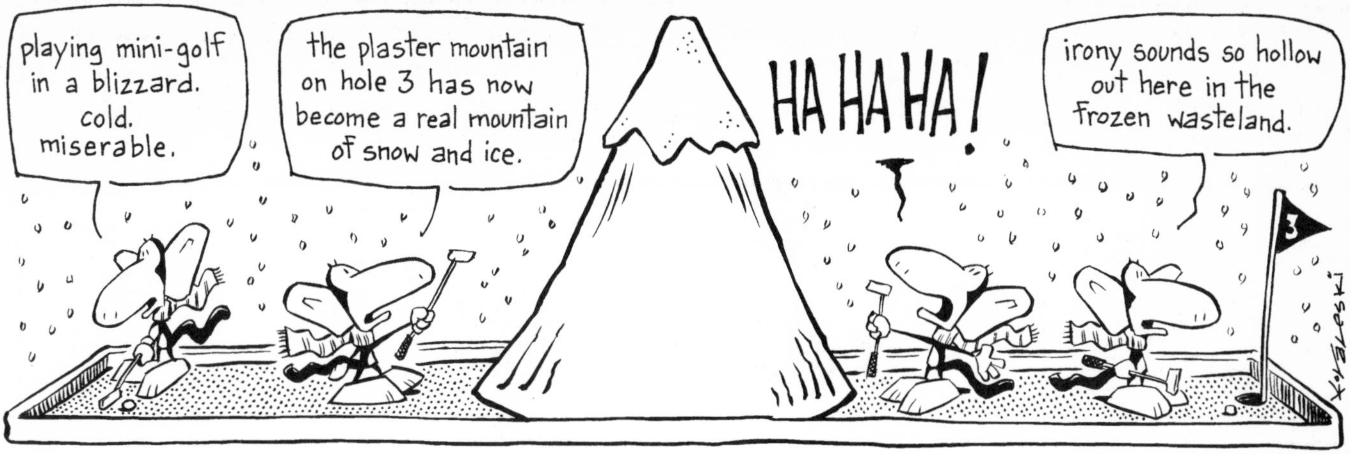
playing mini-golf in a blizzard. cold. miserable.
the plaster mountain on hole 3 has now become a real mountain of snow and ice.
HA HA HA!
irony sounds so hollow out here in the frozen wasteland.
3
KOVALESKI

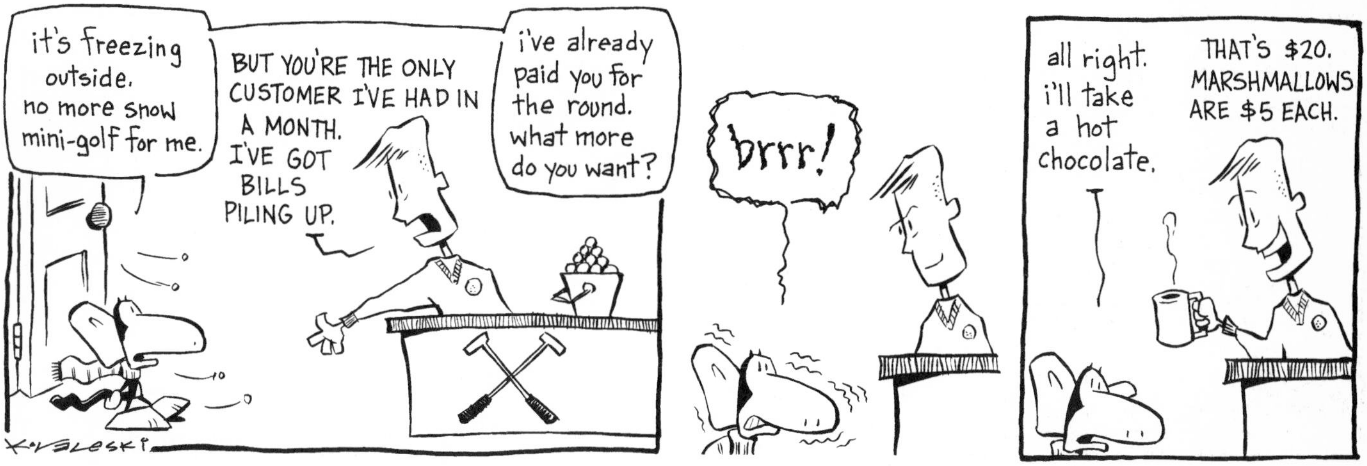
it's freezing outside. no more snow mini-golf for me.
BUT YOU'RE THE ONLY CUSTOMER I'VE HAD IN A MONTH. I'VE GOT BILLS PILING UP.
i've already paid you for the round. what more do you want?
brrr!
all right. i'll take a hot chocolate.
THAT'S $20. MARSHMALLOWS ARE $5 EACH.
KOVALESKI

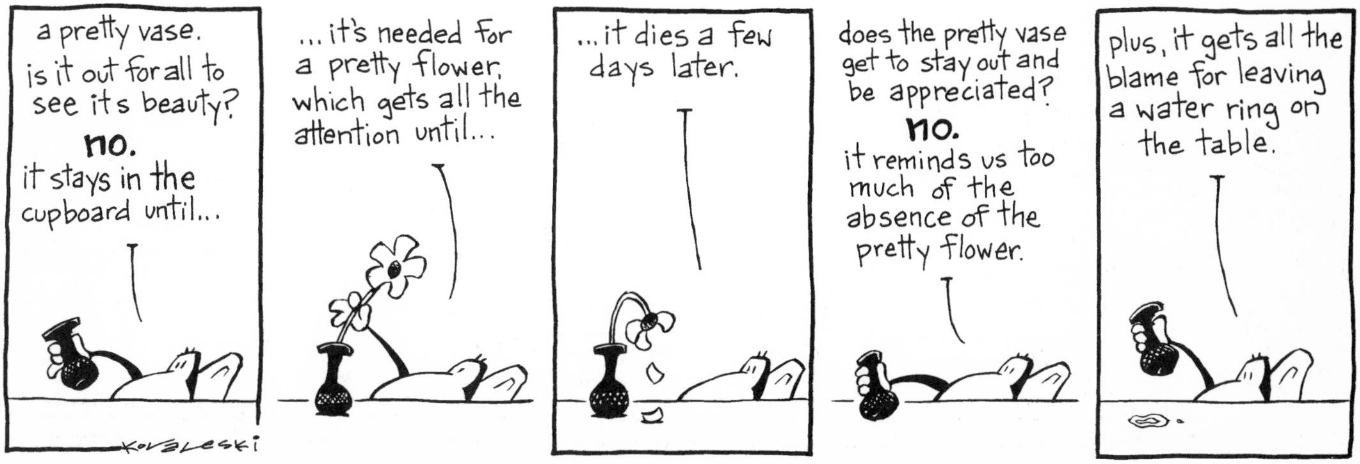
a pretty vase. is it out for all to see its beauty? no. it stays in the cupboard until...
...it's needed for a pretty flower, which gets all the attention until...
...it dies a few days later.
does the pretty vase get to stay out and be appreciated? no. it reminds us too much of the absence of the pretty flower.
plus, it gets all the blame for leaving a water ring on the table.
KOVALESKI

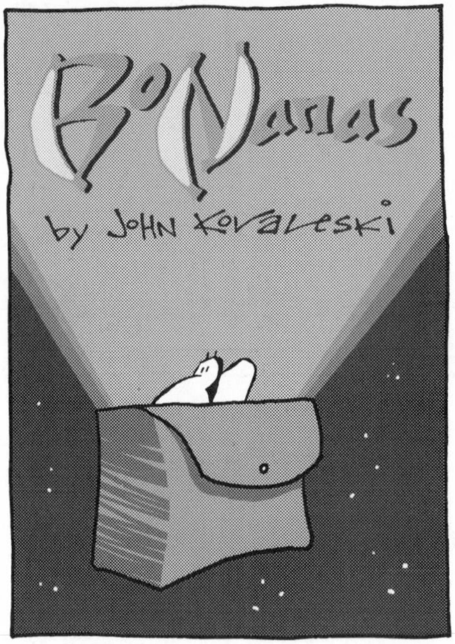

BoNanas
by JOHN KOVALESKI

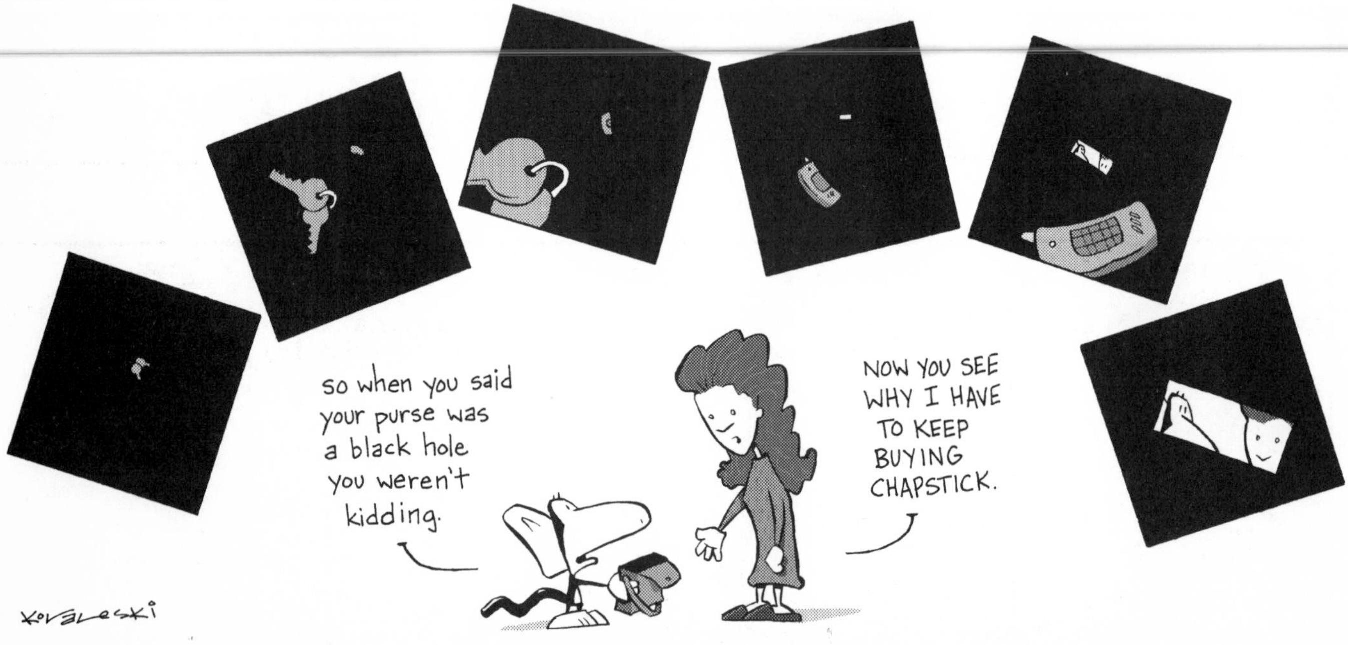

So when you said your purse was a black hole you weren't kidding.
NOW YOU SEE WHY I HAVE TO KEEP BUYING CHAPSTICK.
KOVALESKI

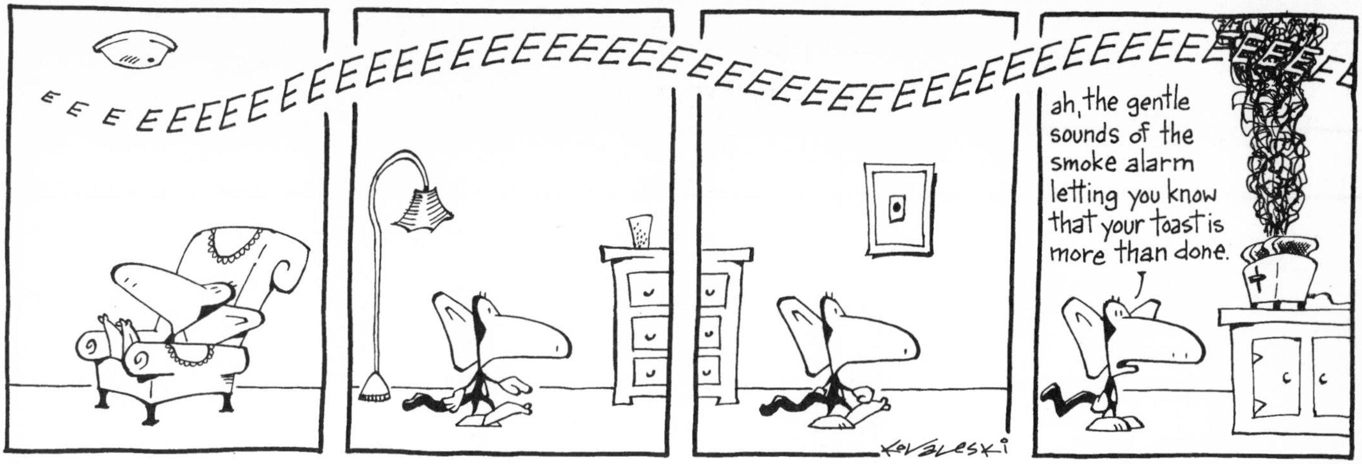
kovaleski
ah, the gentle sounds of the smoke alarm letting you know that your toast is more than done.

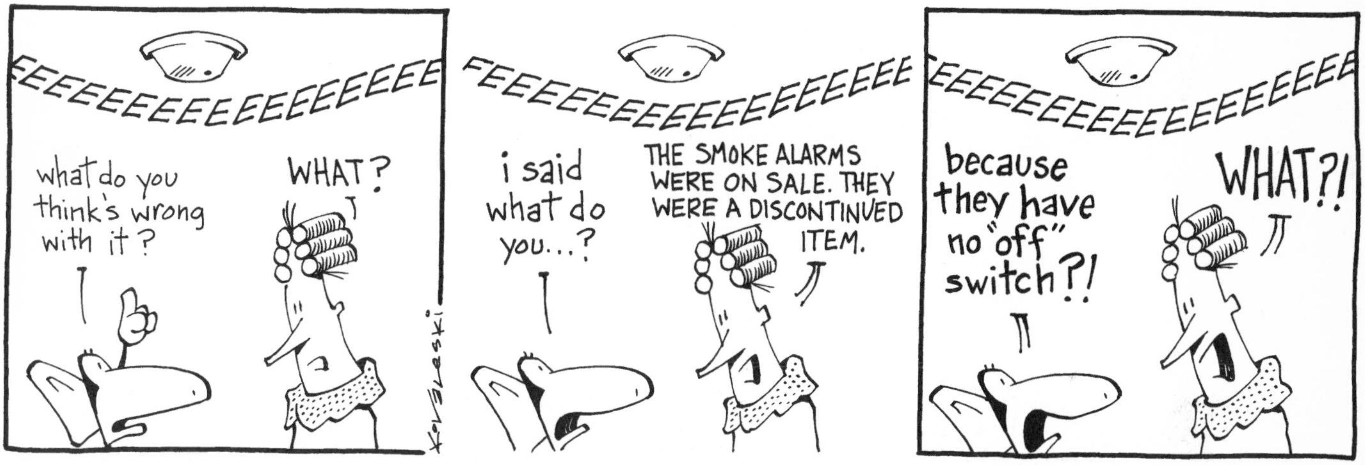
what do you think's wrong with it?
WHAT?
kovaleski
i said what do you...?
THE SMOKE ALARMS WERE ON SALE. THEY WERE A DISCONTINUED ITEM.
because they have no "off" switch?!
WHAT?!

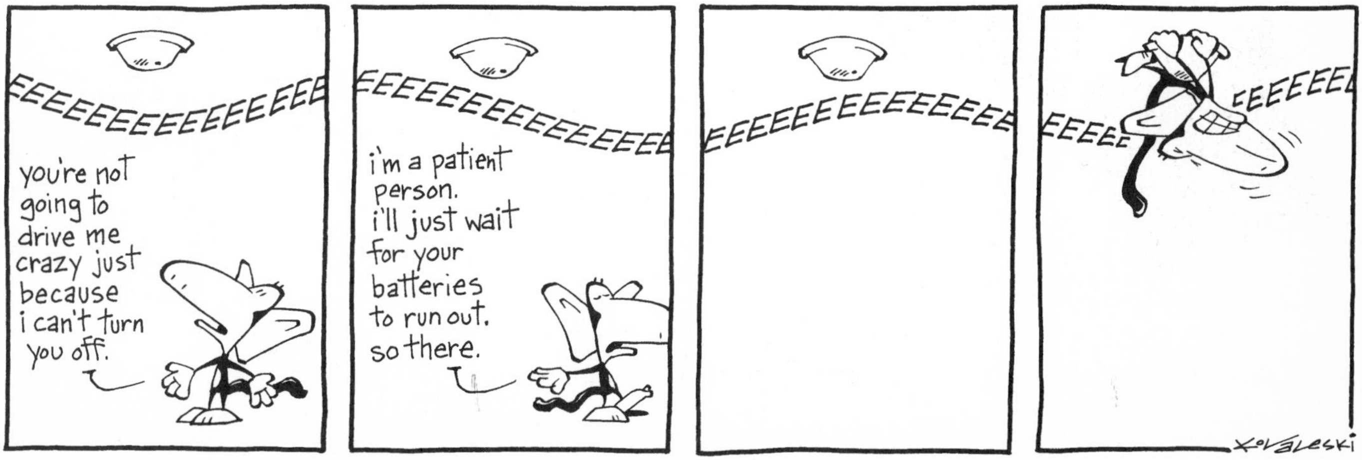
you're not going to drive me crazy just because i can't turn you off.
i'm a patient person. i'll just wait for your batteries to run out. so there.
kovaleski

EEEEEEEEEEEEEEEEEEEEEEEEEEEEEEEEEEEEEEEEEEEEEEEEEEEEEEEEEEEEEEEEEEEEEEE

hey, smoke alarm, why won't you shut off? look over there at your brother the ceiling fan.

you don't see him twirling like crazy, do you? why can't you be more like him?

with any discipline problem, first try reasoning then break out the crowbar.

Kovaleski

EEEEEEEEEE

wow. the smoke alarm has turned itself off after four straight days.

ahhhh..... the sound of silence.

...except for this ringing in my ears.

Kovaleski

i see so many crazy things every day...

...that sometimes i call it "performance art" just to make myself feel better.

Kovaleski

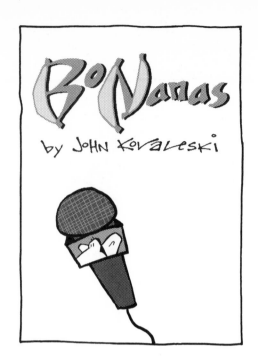

BoNanas
by John Kovaleski

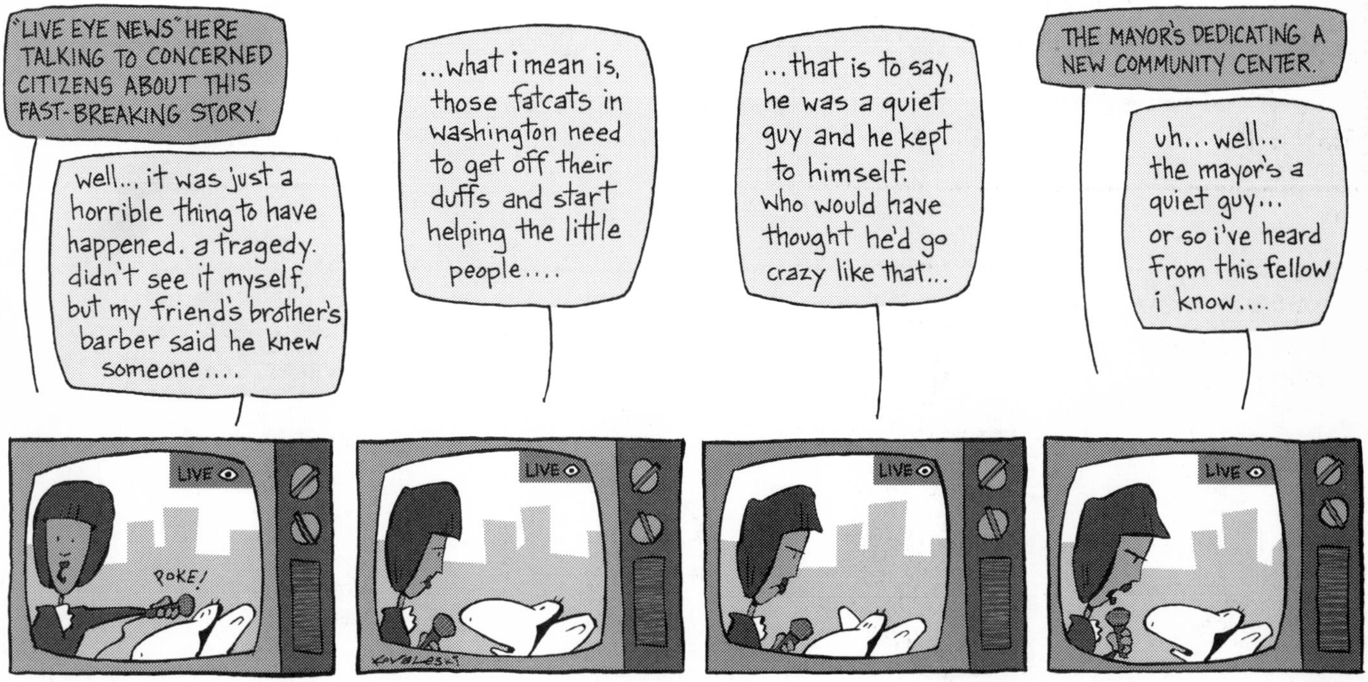

"LIVE EYE NEWS" HERE TALKING TO CONCERNED CITIZENS ABOUT THIS FAST-BREAKING STORY.
well... it was just a horrible thing to have happened. a tragedy. didn't see it myself, but my friend's brother's barber said he knew someone....
LIVE
POKE!
...what i mean is, those fatcats in washington need to get off their duffs and start helping the little people....
LIVE
KOVALESKI
...that is to say, he was a quiet guy and he kept to himself. who would have thought he'd go crazy like that...
LIVE
THE MAYOR'S DEDICATING A NEW COMMUNITY CENTER.
uh... well... the mayor's a quiet guy... or so i've heard from this fellow i know....
LIVE

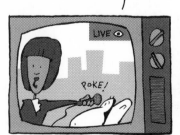

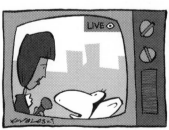

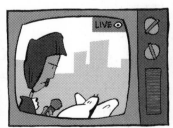

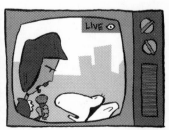

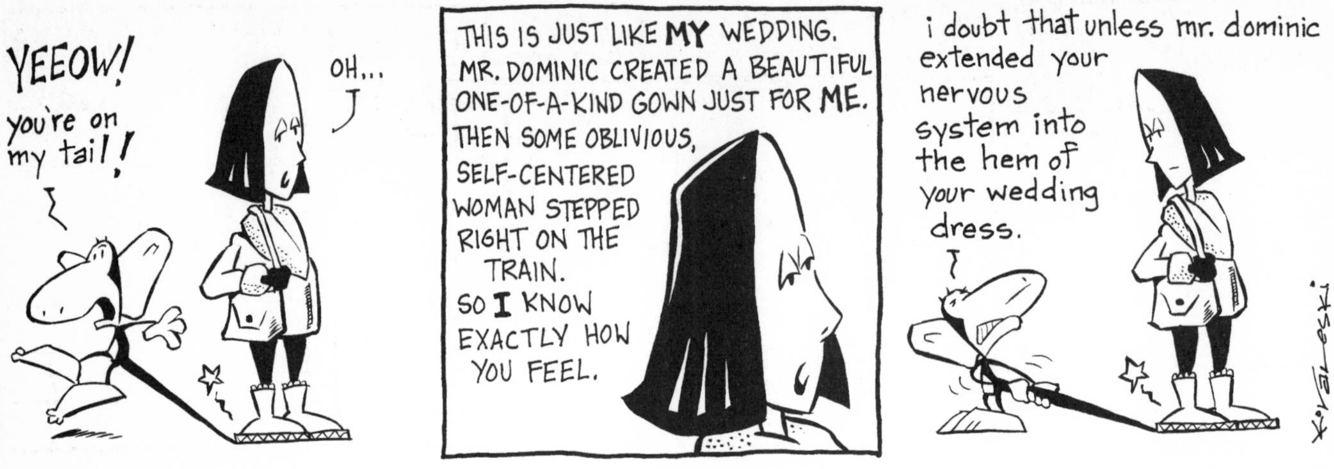
YEEOW!
you're on my tail!
OH...
THIS IS JUST LIKE MY WEDDING. MR. DOMINIC CREATED A BEAUTIFUL ONE-OF-A-KIND GOWN JUST FOR ME. THEN SOME OBLIVIOUS, SELF-CENTERED WOMAN STEPPED RIGHT ON THE TRAIN. SO I KNOW EXACTLY HOW YOU FEEL.
i doubt that unless mr. dominic extended your nervous system into the hem of your wedding dress.

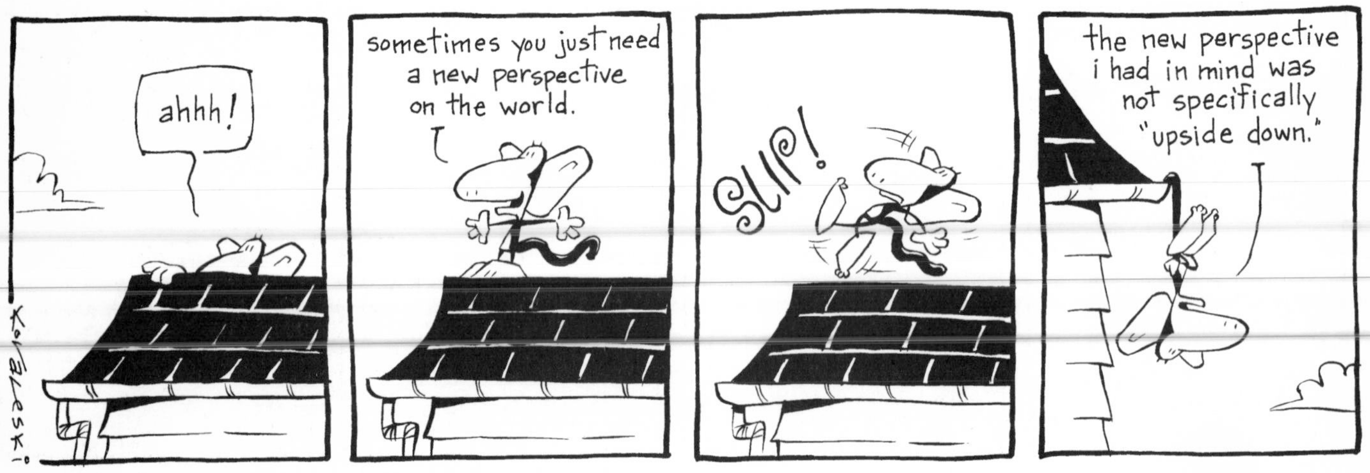
ahhh!
sometimes you just need a new perspective on the world.
SLIP!
the new perspective i had in mind was not specifically "upside down."

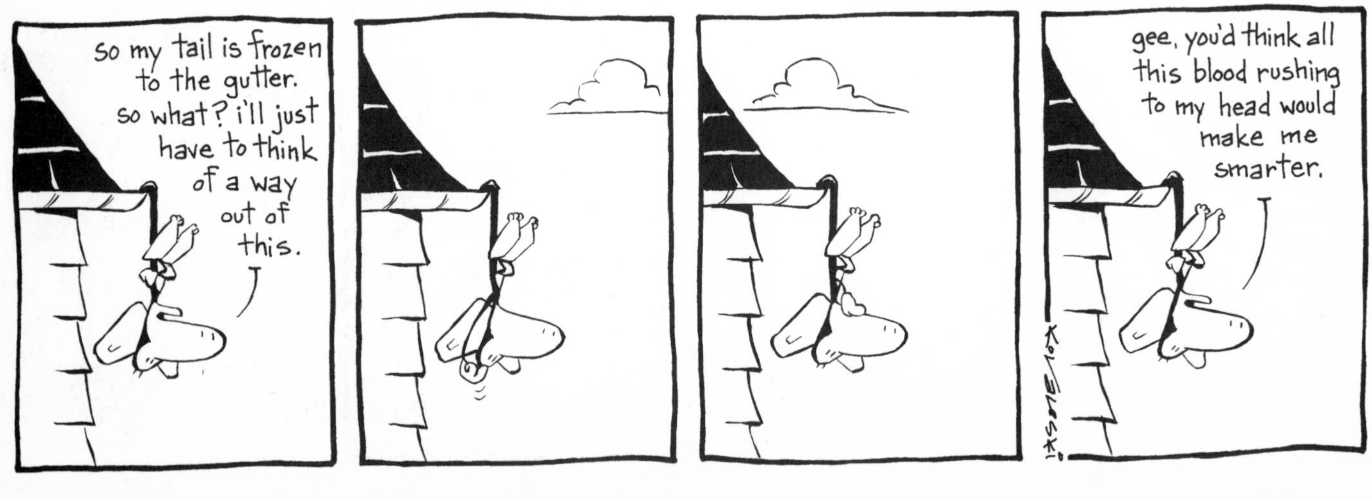
so my tail is frozen to the gutter. so what? i'll just have to think of a way out of this.
gee, you'd think all this blood rushing to my head would make me smarter.

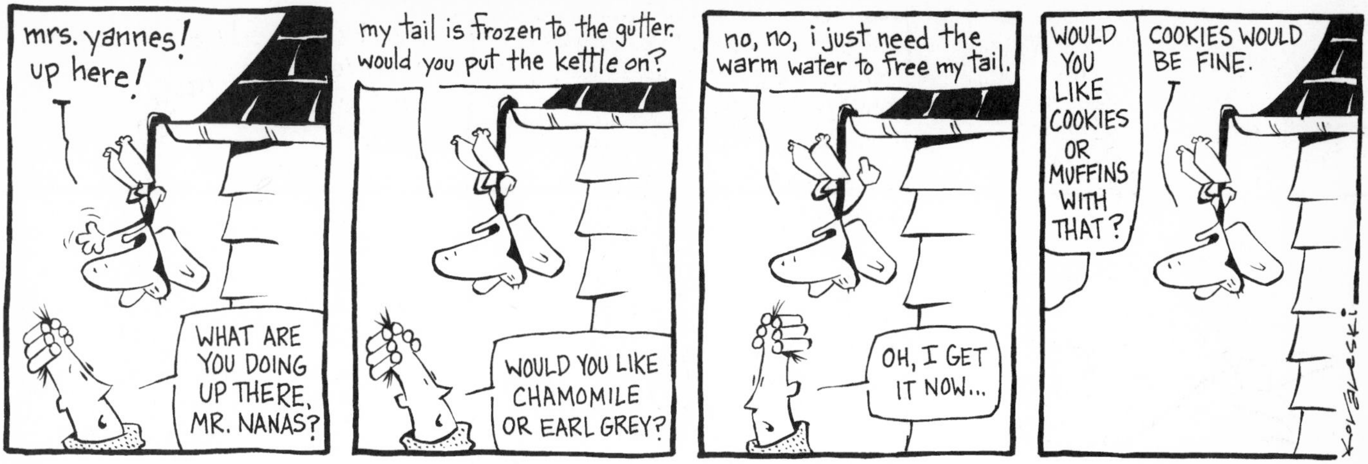
mrs. yannes! up here!
WHAT ARE YOU DOING UP THERE, MR. NANAS?
my tail is frozen to the gutter. would you put the kettle on?
WOULD YOU LIKE CHAMOMILE OR EARL GREY?
no, no, i just need the warm water to free my tail.
OH, I GET IT NOW...
WOULD YOU LIKE COOKIES OR MUFFINS WITH THAT?
COOKIES WOULD BE FINE.

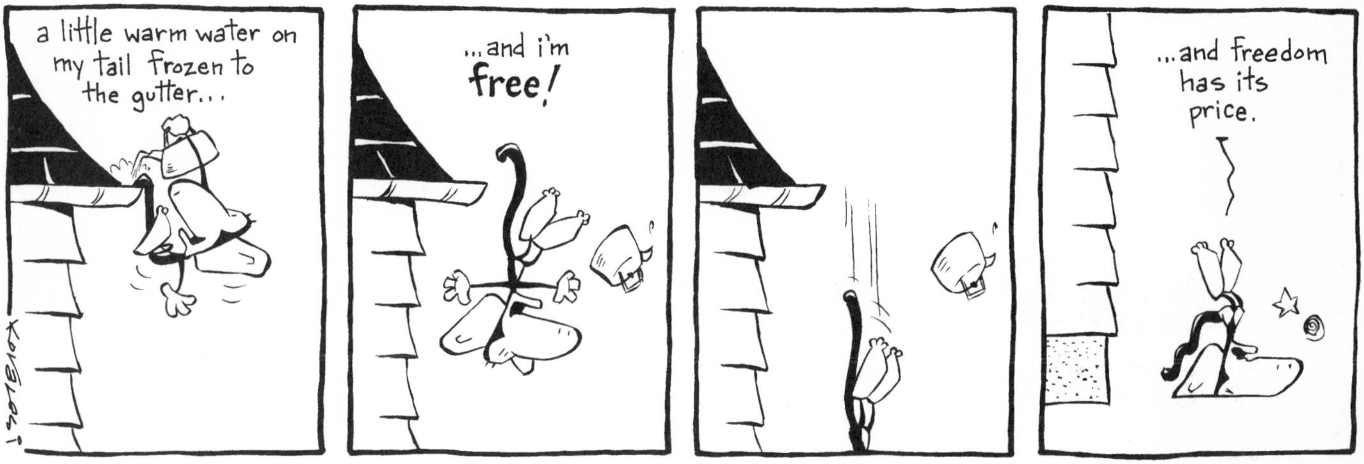
a little warm water on my tail frozen to the gutter...
...and i'm free!
...and freedom has its price.

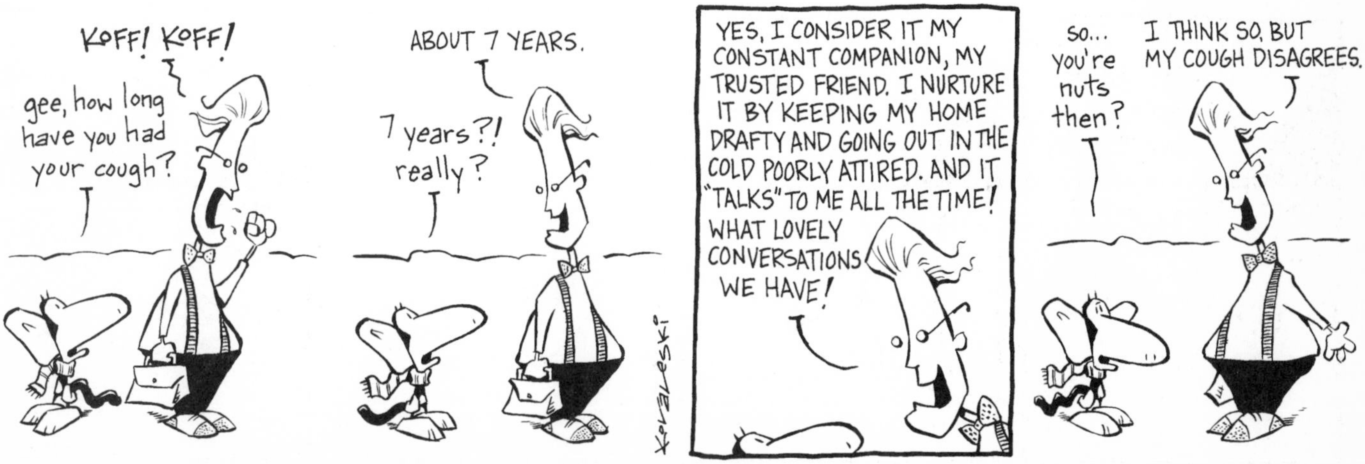
KOFF! KOFF!
gee, how long have you had your cough?
ABOUT 7 YEARS.
7 years?! really?
YES, I CONSIDER IT MY CONSTANT COMPANION, MY TRUSTED FRIEND. I NURTURE IT BY KEEPING MY HOME DRAFTY AND GOING OUT IN THE COLD POORLY ATTIRED. AND IT "TALKS" TO ME ALL THE TIME! WHAT LOVELY CONVERSATIONS WE HAVE!
So... you're nuts then?
I THINK SO, BUT MY COUGH DISAGREES.

BoNanas
by JOHN KOVALESKI

i'm snowed in.
can't travel anywhere.
what i need is a fun project like building something out of popsicle sticks.
KOVALESKI
did i mention i'm snowed in and, thus, can't go out and buy glue?

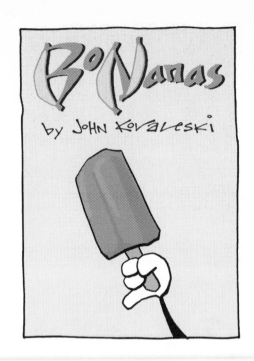

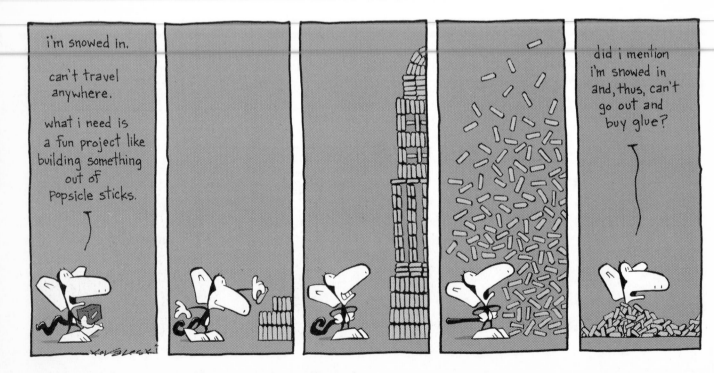

BoNanas
by JOHN KOVALESKI

never shop for groceries when you're hungry~ especially at one of those warehouse stores.
Porkee Rinds
NOW WITH 50% MORE SNOUTS
PORKRINDS?! DIDN'T I SEND YOU TO GET A RAFT OF TOILET PAPER? NOW WE'RE GOING TO HAVE TO GET A SECOND MORTGAGE.
KOVALESKI

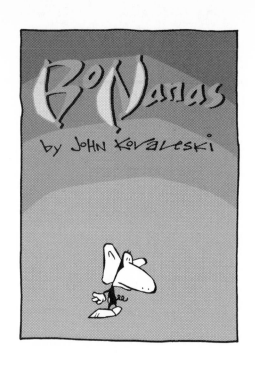

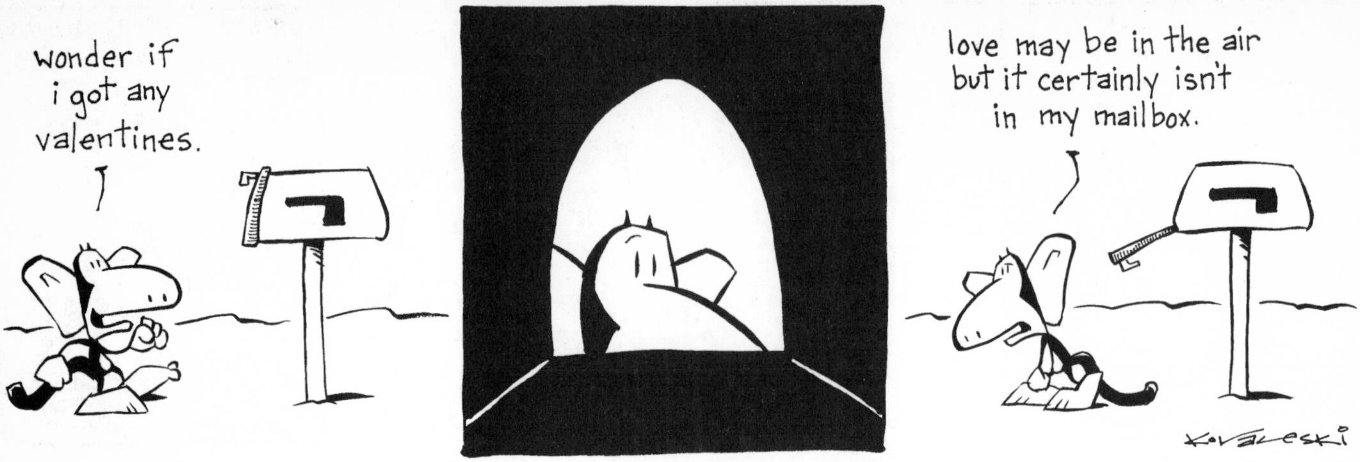
wonder if i got any valentines.
love may be in the air but it certainly isn't in my mailbox.
KOVALESKI

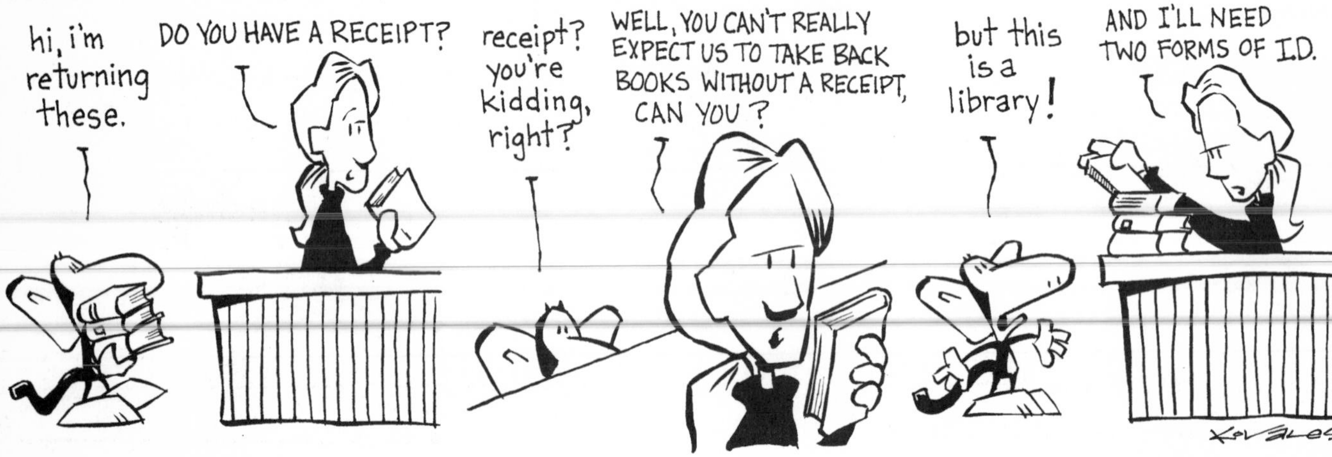
hi, i'm returning these.
DO YOU HAVE A RECEIPT?
receipt? you're kidding, right?
WELL, YOU CAN'T REALLY EXPECT US TO TAKE BACK BOOKS WITHOUT A RECEIPT, CAN YOU?
but this is a library!
AND I'LL NEED TWO FORMS OF I.D.
KOVALESKI

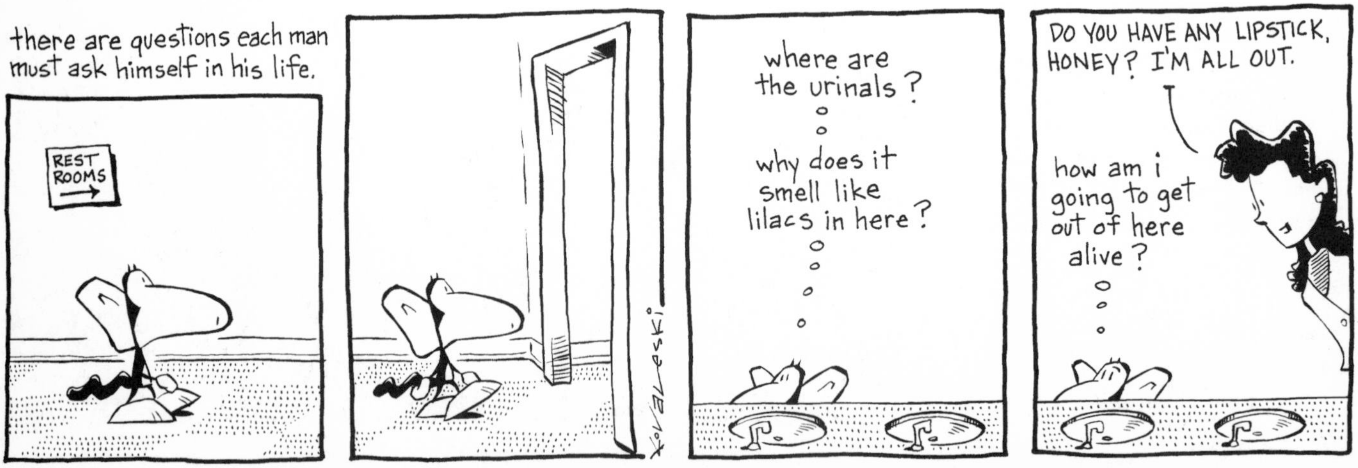
there are questions each man must ask himself in his life.
REST ROOMS
KOVALESKI
where are the urinals?
why does it smell like lilacs in here?
DO YOU HAVE ANY LIPSTICK, HONEY? I'M ALL OUT.
how am i going to get out of here alive?

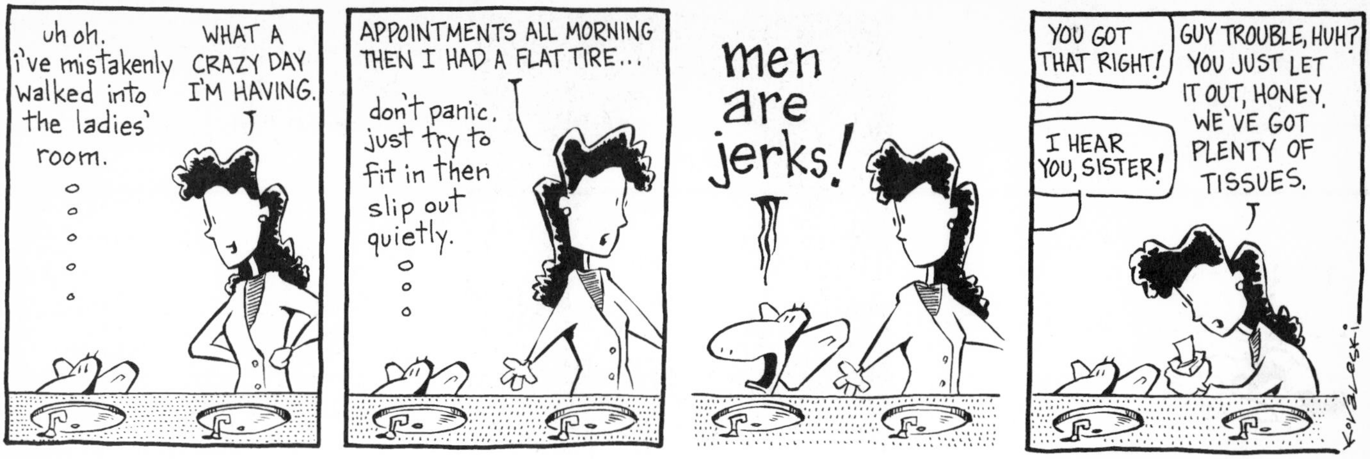
uh oh. i've mistakenly walked into the ladies' room.
WHAT A CRAZY DAY I'M HAVING.
APPOINTMENTS ALL MORNING THEN I HAD A FLAT TIRE...
don't panic. just try to fit in then slip out quietly.
men are jerks!
YOU GOT THAT RIGHT!
I HEAR YOU, SISTER!
GUY TROUBLE, HUH? YOU JUST LET IT OUT, HONEY. WE'VE GOT PLENTY OF TISSUES.
KOVALESKI

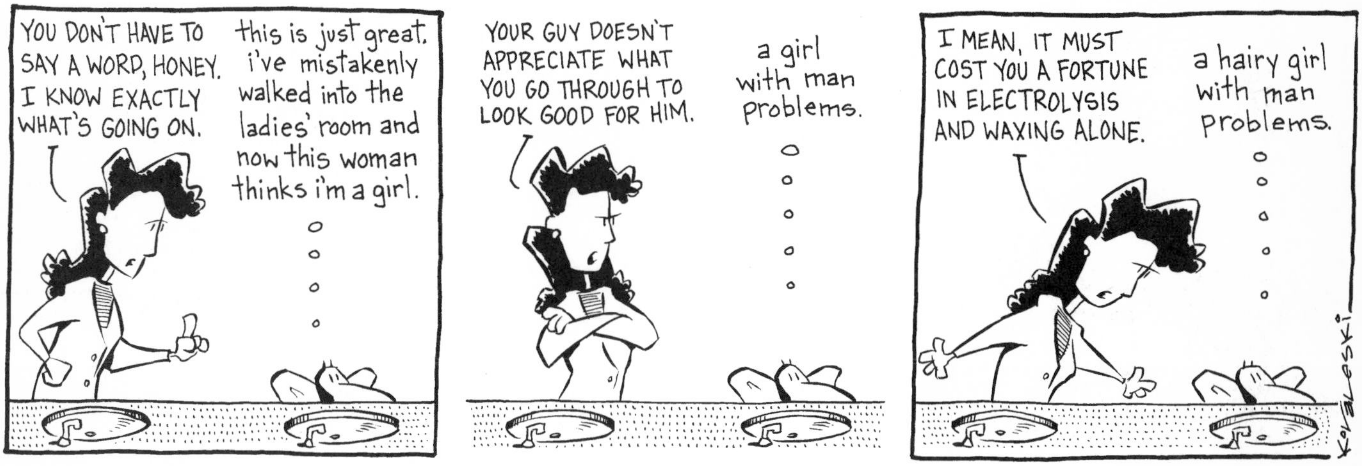
YOU DON'T HAVE TO SAY A WORD, HONEY. I KNOW EXACTLY WHAT'S GOING ON.
this is just great. i've mistakenly walked into the ladies' room and now this woman thinks i'm a girl.
YOUR GUY DOESN'T APPRECIATE WHAT YOU GO THROUGH TO LOOK GOOD FOR HIM.
a girl with man problems.
I MEAN, IT MUST COST YOU A FORTUNE IN ELECTROLYSIS AND WAXING ALONE.
a hairy girl with man problems.
KOVALESKI

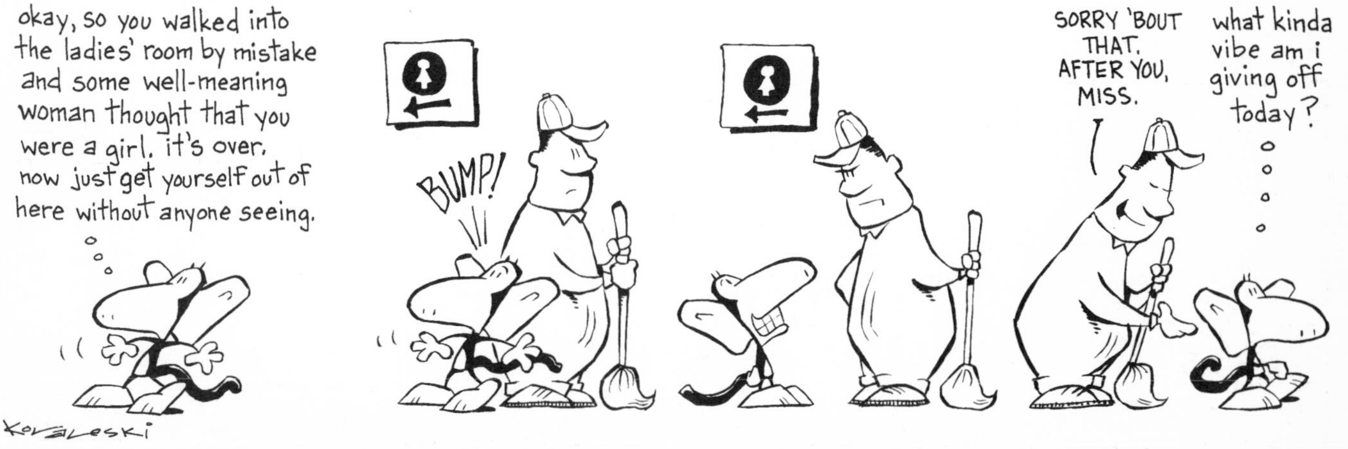
okay, so you walked into the ladies' room by mistake and some well-meaning woman thought that you were a girl. it's over. now just get yourself out of here without anyone seeing.
BUMP!
SORRY 'BOUT THAT. AFTER YOU, MISS.
what kinda vibe am i giving off today?
KOVALESKI

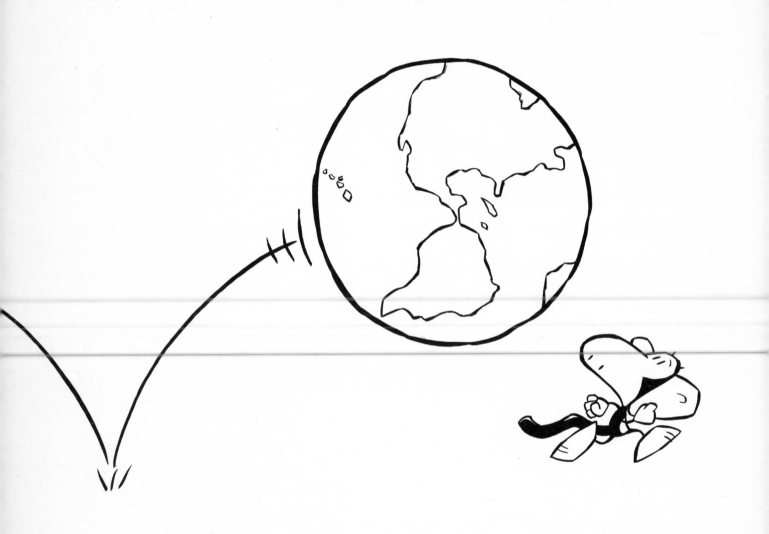